STATE FORMATION

Anthropology, Culture and Society

Series Editors:
Professor Thomas Hylland Eriksen, University of Oslo
Dr Jon P. Mitchell, University of Sussex

STATE FORMATION
Anthropological Perspectives

Edited by
CHRISTIAN KROHN-HANSEN
and KNUT G. NUSTAD

Foreword by
BRUCE KAPFERER

Pluto Press

LONDON • ANN ARBOR, MI

First published 2005 by Pluto Press
345 Archway Road, London N6 5AA
and 839 Greene Street, Ann Arbor, MI 48106

www.plutobooks.com

British Library Cataloguing in Publication Data
A catalogue record for this book is available from the British Library

ISBN 0 7453 2442 8 hardback
ISBN 0 7453 2441 X paperback

Library of Congress Cataloging-in-Publication Data
State formation: anthropological perspectives / edited by Christian Krohn-Hansen
and Knut G. Nustad.
   p. cm. — (Anthropology, culture, and society)
   Chiefly papers presented at a workshop held at the University of Oslo in
Oct. 2002.
   Includes bibliographical references.
   ISBN 0 7453 2442 8 (hardback) ISBN 0 7453 2441 X (paperback)
   1. Political anthropology. 2. State, The. 3. Politics and culture. I. Krohn-Hansen,
Christian, 1957– II. Nustad, Knut G., 1968– III. Series.
   GN492.S83 2002
   306.2—dc22

                                                          2005006706

10   9   8   7   6   5   4   3   2   1

Designed and produced for Pluto Press by
Chase Publishing Services Ltd, Fortescue, Sidmouth, EX10 9QG, England
Typeset from disk by Stanford DTP Services, Northampton, England
Printed and bound in the European Union by
Antony Rowe Ltd, Chippenham and Eastbourne, England

CONTENTS

PART III   A VIEW FROM STATE BODIES

FOREWORD

Bruce Kapferer

The question of the state has always been at the centre of political and philosophical debate but interest has intensified of late across the social sciences. This has much to do with attacks on modernism, the state being seen as the arch-culprit in the human crises, destructions and disasters that have befallen humankind throughout its history, and most of all in the more recent centuries. Political and economic developments – the fall of the Soviet Union, 9/11 and a new US militarism, the European Union and its reaction to the Treaty of Westphalia, contemporary globalisation, the further growth of corporate power, the Internet – have dramatically affected the nature of state power. How this is so is a major problem to be examined, as are the human and social consequences that follow from the redrawing of the nature of state orders and power. The importance of such inquiry cannot be overstressed. The state, at least the imagination of the state (the real or fantasised effect of the state on human existence) has likely been of major influence on the lives of human beings from the very beginnings of human history, even for those peoples who refused state forms of control and order. It has been integral within human subjectivity and part of the dynamics vital in the creation of human relations (even in contexts of the rejection of any kind of state control, as Clastres once discussed). In some approaches (particularly since the rise of modern nationalism) the state has frequently been conceived as virtually synonymous with the imaginary of society. I am suggesting that an understanding of the state is crucial to an exploration of human being, for the social sciences especially, and that it is receiving a renewed focus of interest is appropriate to its centrality. This is especially so in the current situation of what today appears to many commentators and scholars alike as major changes of an almost cosmological and ontological quality that are taking place in contemporary state orders and the surrounding political and social fields of their operation.

Of course I am talking about the state in an over-general and in a far too uniform way. The state has taken widely diverse forms throughout history and the kind of state, or modern or contemporary state, that the essays in this volume address is a recent invention, although still highly diverse in its shaping. Within that sphere too easily glossed as the West, what is discussed as the state has taken quite different forms. The highly centralised forms that grew up in Europe and frequently among its colonised outer regions are, perhaps, to be distinguished from the US form, as De Tocqueville posited. While many might contest this, I think a strong argument could be made that the currently globally dominant US form that is certainly effecting changes in state formations throughout the world has dimensions in its imaginary and in its practice quite distinct from its neighbours across the Atlantic. This was a powerful imaginative intent of its founders and in numerous aspects it was already postmodern. I suggest that the experience of the state and the way the state is subjectivised in the US are often very different from the experience and subjectivisation of the state in many other parts of the world. Such an observation is relevant to many current discussions of the state, which tend to conceive of it from within a dominant North American postmodern perspective and which, not infrequently, even if subconsciously, becomes an ideal standard against which others are measured.

But all the above does not get us very close to an understanding as to what exactly we understand by the state or the often very different formations that we might describe as involving state processes. This is one of the important contributions of the essays in this volume. Here there is a concern with the practices through which the state materially makes its appearance, whether this be through the technological construction of lines of communication (and control), the bureaucratic inscription of subjects, the presentation of official policy, the production of refugees, etc. There is a stress on the state in its diverse and differentiated aspects, a treatment of the state in its complexities of institutional manifestation, practices and experiencing rather than, as is too common, as a singular, all-embracing, totalising idea. Here there is an important shift away from the state as a transcendent imagined ideality of a Hegelian kind, which may be too disjunct from the concrete in which the state is materially realised and comes to have its embodied effects.

Recent approaches to the state have seized on the fact that it is an imagined reality, a point that is already central in Hegelian perspectives. But the very reality of the state is in the very character of its imaginary (as a spectre in human consciousness that has, as such, an effect on human action). Such an imaginary of the state is also a materiality, a force (spirit) in the constitution of persons and in the manifold arrangements and their processes of human existence. Perhaps it is of the same order as other constructed totalities such as 'society' or 'community' in the social sciences. These, for example, focus on those dimensions affecting individual action, such as identity and the institutional and relational. Notions like the state, society and community have the character of Deleuzian virtuals (yet thoroughly real) in their abstract totalisation but are simultaneously actually evident, indeed empirically evident, in the diversity of particular human practices. The state is an idea – and, as the chapters in this book indicate, an idea with numerous different histories and conceptualisations. It is not to be reduced to power (although this is the key feature of the state upon which the idea concentrates), nor to particular organisations of government or of rule (although these are the commanding centres and most material manifestations of the state). The state is these things and more, a general and diverse forming of power, authority and control, the critical force defining the political, that has sovereign claim (or is yielded such claim) to constitute the conditions of existence of those brought within its realm.

The reality of the state is to be grasped ethnographically both in its imaginary and in the concreteness of practices that have a state relation or reference. This forms the major contribution of the essays in this book. The contribution is all the more because of the focus on contemporary states, the modern state. As the editors stress, much ethnography, especially in anthropology, has until recently been focused on archaic forms, usually small in scale and concentrating on central institutions such as kings and chiefs. A strong evolutionism is present in such approaches. Many of the ethnographic studies of non-Western state systems carried the implication that they were preliminary and lower forms of modern state forms in Europe and North America. This sense is continuing and is evident in current accounts of so-called 'failed' states and their humanity-destroying excess. These do not so much critique the idea of the modern state as indicate that failed states, in Africa, for example, are merely underdeveloped possibilities of the state. Modernisation perspectives continue into postmodern conceptions of state practice, often masquerading as anti-state arguments: for instance, many of the critiques of state practice from within the situation of North America that culturally or ideologically display many of the tenets of US exceptionalism. The ethnographies presented here explore practices that reveal the distinctiveness of certain modern state formations but also the similarities that may extend across apparent difference. Dictatorships are distinct from democratic states, yet the former no less than the latter operate a dialectics of consent that is both socially constitutive and reproductive of state power. As recent events have dramatically shown, the removal of dictators or forced regime change, does not negate the socio-political dynamics that were set in place, which can transmute into heightened virulent form in the contradictory spaces occasioned by changes in the agents of state power. The state is never separate from the social world in which it operates and the ethnographies in this volume explore the intricacies of such relations.

The importance of the ethnographic position in this book is that it engages with the numerous practices in which the state is revealed and becomes inscribed in persons and their relations. It is only through such an ethnography that a thorough understanding of the modern state in its diverse formations can be grasped, as well as the complex nature of its effects on the populations it may contain. I underline the importance of an ethnography of the state as extending beyond certain kinds of philosophising, once more in the ascendant, which – while of fundamental importance – gains its insights through re-examining well-established texts or else depending on the constructions of those in dominant positions who, these days, are engaged in the control of media presentations upon which critics of state practice have sometimes become over-reliant. These ethnographic essays not only present original information but, more significantly, have the merit of transcending received wisdom or intellectual fashions. This should be the potential of anthropological ethnography, which has the advantage of the analyst being consciously and analytically located in the contexts of practice that are to be comprehended. Thus the ethnography is not necessarily illustrative of what is already well known, yet another case to add to the pile, but opens up understandings that are thoroughly dependent on analysis *in situ*. As Max Gluckman recommended for a particular anthropology that he was instrumental in promulgating, ethnography is more than producing illustrative case material but is the anthropological method whereby regnant theory can be queried and new understanding developed that is grounded in the phenomenon being examined.

The editors of this book stress the new direction that the anthropology of the state is taking one, which is acutely aware of the numerous perspectives that have opened up in related disciplines and fields of inquiry. The re-insistence on the anthropological stress on culture achieved through comparative understanding is particularly appealing. It is only through comparison that particular conceptual or theoretical approaches can be upheld, more finely honed or ultimately discarded.

The state is an artefact of culture and, in its diversities, engages assumptions and practical logics that expand from this fact. In the anthropological vision that I personally recommend it is not that state practice is meaningful, one sense of a stress on culture, but that it embeds compositional, constructional and especially orientational doxa and logics which an ethnographic approach such as those displayed here can best uncover. It is through the doxa of state practices that the state in its imaginary and materiality has effects, many of them unintended, much violence being a feature. I add here that the concentration on power, which is the stress of those who focus on the state, can overlook the fact that power, even the power of the state, can arise from practices that may have no immediate or initial link to the interests of power. A cultural perspective should be alive to this possibility. While much state power operates hegemonically, as Gramsci, Foucault and numerous others have insisted, this is a vision of state practice as always subordinating culture (however this is defined) to power. But the stronger meaning of culture in much anthropology refers to those meaningful social practices that are as much constitutive of powerful effects as themselves the effect of power. To concentrate on the cultural processes of the agents of state practice is to indicate trajectories of their effective commitments that are already directed along certain lines with particular potentialities before they may be intentionally engaged to use them in certain consciously specific ways. State practices as cultural practices have much more to them than that which would always intentionally reduce them to the interests of power. The cultural perspective in anthropology, often arraigned against essentialism or foundationalism, as in common criticisms of economism, should also be alive to the risks of reducing phenomena such as the state merely to power. Power itself is emergent or situated in a diverse field of practices of which the anthropological attention to culture is acutely aware.

This rich collection of essays opens out to new horizons of thought on the question of the state. It is a demonstration of the authority of ethnography and the challenge that such work may offer to already well-tried positions that need radical re-examination. This is so today, when the very idea of the state is being reconfigured while new formations of power, control and sovereignty are coming into more prominent being. These last certainly have state effects if not states in any conventional or traditional sense. The excellent studies here go some considerable way to laying a new foundation for a reinvigorated anthropology of the state.

PREFACE

How do we conceptualise state formations, and is it possible to study these processes ethnographically? The Department of Anthropology at the University of Oslo generously provided funds for a workshop, 'Explorations of the State: Considerations from Critical Anthropology/Ethnography', in October 2002, to discuss these questions. Our initial call for papers met with an overwhelming response, which clearly demonstrated for us that many anthropologists were grappling with these issues. The papers that were presented at the workshop indicated the breath of issues that arise when anthropologists engage with the state as an object of study. We wish to thank both presenters and participants for two days of intensely stimulating discussions.

The essays by Helga Baitenmann, Penelope Harvey, Christian Krohn-Hansen, Iver B. Neumann, Knut G. Nustad, Kristi Anne Stølen and Marit Melhuus were given as papers at the workshop. The papers by Ana M. Alonso, Clifton Crais and Cris Shore have been added. Bruce Kapferer, who participated at the workshop, was asked to write a Foreword. Clifton Crais' chapter was originally published in *American Historical Review* 108(4), 2003, and we are grateful to the American Historical Association for their permission to reprint it. Knut wishes to thank Diakonhjemmet University College, Oslo, for providing time for finalising the manuscript.

Christian Krohn-Hansen and Knut G. Nustad
Oslo, December 2004

PART I

THEORETICAL APPROACHES

1   INTRODUCTION

Christian Krohn-Hansen and Knut G. Nustad

As an object of study, the state has drifted in and out of academic focus.[1] Concern with the state as a precondition for capitalist production in the 1970s was in the 1980s replaced by a focus on forms of domination that could not be linked to a privileged place called 'the state' – as epitomised in Foucault's call for cutting off the King's head in political analyses. Much of the globalisation literature of the 1990s argued that the state was irrelevant: production, domination or resistance took place in relationships that created units either much bigger than the state, or much smaller than it. Most recently, this type of argument has been put forward by Michael Hardt and Antonio Negri (2000), who define *Empire* as a form of domination residing in values and ideas that claim universality. But at the same time, as Begoña Aretxaga (2003) and others have noted, the state form has not become extinct. On the contrary, the number of states has quadrupled since the Second World War, with the pace of new formations accelerating after the fall of the Berlin Wall and the collapse of the Soviet Union. Moreover, political activity at levels that in the 1990s were seen as undermining the importance of the state now seem to be replicating the state form. Ethnic dissidence often appears as a claim for statehood, while supranational institutions such as the European Union are mimicking the state-building processes of the European states two centuries earlier – as pointed out by Shore in this volume.

Also in the relationship between the so-called international community and poor countries, the state seems to have made a comeback. The structural adjustment programmes of the 1980s sought to protect investments by demanding a rolling back of the state – understood as public expenditure – and the creation of conditions for a free market. By contrast, the past decade has seen an increased focus on the state, with the World Bank and other institutions insisting on the importance of good governance and a rights-based approach to development – which in turn presupposes an institution that can guarantee these rights.

In all these shifts, whether the state has been treated as an important object for study or reform or as something to be minimised, the idea of the state has loomed large – either as a model for political organisation or as a negative 'other'. Philip Abrams (1988) has pointed to a similar process in Marxist writings on the state: even those theorists who viewed the state as an assembly of practices and effects, turned it into a solid object when their writings shifted from political analyses to practice. Then, the state as a concrete reality was needed as a protagonist in the struggle. Similarly, for the neoliberal reformers of the 1980s, the state functioned as a contrast to their ideal of a civil society, of private interest and the market.

It was the problematic nature of the state that inspired the workshop 'Explorations of the State: Considerations from Critical Anthropology', held in Oslo in October 2002. We invited papers that dealt with anthropology and its varying relations to the state. Two sets of concerns were especially highlighted in the workshop: first, the difficulty that anthropologists and others have had in grasping the state conceptually. The idea of what constitutes a 'state' is not only contested: usage is also flexible, dynamic and far from uniform – hence the many adjectives applied to the state, ranging from 'capitalist', 'expansionist', 'totalitarian', 'democratic', 'bureaucratic', 'socialist', to 'postcolonial', 'soft', 'patrimonial', 'collapsed' and so forth. To be able to grasp the state analytically, we need some conceptual tidying up.

Second, there is a need for empirical studies of how state formations are effected. Many authors have argued that the core of modern state formation and expansion is that centrally made state institutions refashion the worlds inhabited and thought by members of local communities on the state's territory. What these scholars have stressed is not so much the state's use of physical force as its ability to impose itself by generating a cultural revolution and a moral regulation – that is, transformations that result in profound reorganisation of how social life is lived across the national space. Others, however, insist that this 'coercive' view of state-making bears scant relation to the complex histories – the changes in power, culture and economy – that have resulted in the genesis and construction of national control in specific parts of the world. Still other writers emphasise that agents construct states by means of tactics, negotiations and exchanges – in a word, *networks*.

All this underscores the need for critical, 'grounded' ethnography – detailed, fine-grained explorations of the social relations and symbolic imaginings that produce, reproduce and transform states in different areas of the world. It is along these two lines that we offer this collection to the reader. This volume explores how anthropology can contribute to a better understanding of the field of knowledge that we call the state, and how anthropologists should set about studying the state.

WHAT IS A STATE?

Anthropology is a relative latecomer to the academic debate on the modern state, for at least two reasons. We will argue that while both these reasons help to explain the lack of focus on the state within anthropology, they also actually constitute advantages that make anthropology well equipped to study the state.

The first reason why anthropology has been slow in adopting the state as an object of study relates to the perceived nature of the state. Obviously, the state does not have an objective existence in the way that, say, a tax form has. But is it a second-order object, like a social institution such as marriage? Radcliffe-Brown answered this question with a resounding *no*. In the text that came to define political anthropology for many years, Meyer Fortes and Evans-Pritchard's *African Political Systems* ([1940] 1955), the state was specifically rejected as an object of study. In the introduction to that volume, Radcliffe-Brown explicitly argued against wasting time on the study of a fiction that existed solely as an ideological construct. The state, he wrote, is most often:

... represented as being an entity over and above the human individuals who make a society, having as one of its attributes something called 'sovereignty,' and sometimes spoken of as having a will ... or as issuing commands. The State in this sense does not exist in the phenomenal world; it is a fiction of the philosophers. What does exist is an organization, i.e. a collection of individual human beings connected by a complex system of relations.... There is no such thing as the power of the state. (Radcliffe-Brown [1940] 1955: xxiii)

This 'death by conceptualization', as Michel-Rolph Trouillot (2001) has aptly termed it, has scarcely encouraged anthropologists to engage critically with the state.

Second, anthropology created a niche for itself in political studies by studying politics in 'stateless societies'. In part, this was due to the ethnographic method as such: the state, as conceived and discussed by political scientists, appears as an object beyond the reach of anthropological methods.

We will argue that Radcliffe-Brown was partly right, but that he also did anthropology a tremendous disservice by writing off the state completely. He was correct in his insistence on not treating the state as a concrete object and on avoiding making a fetish of it. This point has been further elaborated by Abrams (1988). He follows Radcliffe-Brown in seeing the state as a form of mystification: the idea that the state exists as an objective entity, he argues, stems from a confusion of function with agency. But he disagrees with Radcliffe-Brown in the latter's call for abandoning the study of the state. What does exist, according to Abrams, is an idea of the state, the 'state' as an ideological object that obscures and masks reality. And, he holds, the reality that is masked is the disunity of the *state-system*, defined as the various government institutions. These institutions – the police, the army, prisons and so forth – constitute for Abrams a loose set of ideas and practices all seeking to establish political authority and legitimacy. They are able to achieve this, he says, because they are seen not as what they really are – an assembly of uncoordinated practices and claims – but as part of a larger whole: the state. Thus, by acting in the name of the state, these institutions take on the appearance of being part of a unified whole. The function of the state idea, then, is that it lends to these institutions a degree of coherence and legitimacy that they in reality lack. Abrams thus shifts the focus away from the state as an object, to a far more diffuse field of power relations where the state becomes an ideological object that is used by the state-system to give it legitimacy.

Abrams' intention is to focus on the effects produced as well as on who produces them. Without this latter focus, he warns, the definition of the state becomes so wide as to become meaningless. For if 'the state' is an idea that functions to legitimate domination, then a focus on the state as function would have to include all forms of domination. And since domination also occurs outside of the state-system, this leads, warns Abrams, to a conception of the state as immanent, everywhere and equal to society. But there is no reason to presuppose institutional fixities for the state-system; indeed, the conceptual anchoring of the idea of the state in a place is one of his main criticisms of Poulantzas. Abrams is thus very close to following Foucault's call for cutting off the King's head in political analyses, but instead he chooses to replace the one King with a number of smaller kings.[2]

If we follow Abrams' emphasis on functions and abandon his linking of these functions to a concrete state-system, we find ourselves approaching Foucault's notion of governmentality (1991).[3] Wanting to study how modern states can reproduce themselves without being bound to a particular location, Foucault provided an answer through the concept of governmentality. In Foucault's view, the absolutist king was limited in his power by modelling his rule on the government of the family, of the disposition of things and persons as would a head of a family. The term 'economy', he points out, originally meant the proper management of a family's resources.[4] The breakthrough came when a new entity, 'the population', was discovered as a separate reality with its own statistical laws, and 'the economy' became constructed as a separate realm of reality governed by economic laws. This made possible government through what Ian Hacking (1990) has described as the avalanche of numbers: statistics were produced about health, productivity, criminality, education, etc., which in turn enabled an unprecedented control. Foucault's perspective on this new way of ruling, his notion of governmentality, is all that Abrams warned against: a conception of the power of the state that is everywhere: in subjects, in institutions, in the knowledge that is produced. This was an important insight even if, as we argue below, the emphasis Foucault places on knowledge in contrasting the pre-modern with the modern, or the two forms of rule, sovereign power as against disciplinary power, obscures the way in which violence still reproduces the conditions of the existence of modern states.

Trouillot has recently utilised these insights to map out a programme for the anthropological study of the state (2001). He argues that state power cannot be fixed to a particular place and that therefore, a state cannot be defined as a circumscribed institution. The state is for him a 'set of practices and processes and their effects', and it is these that must be studied. Therefore, focus must be shifted to state effects, regardless of where these are produced. He defines these effects as four: first, an isolation effect, 'the production of atomized individualized subjects molded and modeled for governance as part of an undifferentiated but specific "public"'; second, an identification effect, that is 'a realignment of the atomized subjectivities along collective lines within which individuals recognize themselves as the same'; third, a legibility effect, closely related to the knowledge described above, used to classify and regulate populations; and fourth, a spatialisation effect, the 'production of boundaries and jurisdiction' (2001: 126).

Thus Trouillot seeks to avoid making a fetish of the state by instead focusing on state effects. That his approach succeeds only partly becomes clear when we examine the intellectual heritage of the effects he identifies. Bob Jessop, who coined the term 'state effects', has examined capitalist state formation (see Jessop 1990). What he, following Poulantzas (1968), terms 'atomization' and 'individuation effects' are similar to Trouillot's isolation and individuation effects. Jessop describes how these effects were produced historically with the formation of the capitalist state in Europe. Drawing on Marx, he argues that there was a complex relationship between the alienation of labour and the ideology of individual bourgeois rights. Capitalist state formation fragmented identities based on class and replaced them with the fiction of equal individuals who were all equal rights-bearing members of the nation. Therefore, in trying to create a *universal* model for the study of the modern state form, Trouillot assumes a *specific* form of state formation – the capitalist state as it evolved in Europe. However, there is no reason to assume *a priori* that a state that is differently embedded in a global history will function in the same way and produce the same effects. This must be studied empirically, and not assumed at the outset.[5]

Even Radcliffe-Brown's dismissal of the field of state studies is very close to recent insights that the state should be studied not as an institution, but as an assembly of practices and active meaning creations. And Trouillot's call for ethnographies of the processes that create state effects plays up to what is the main strength of anthropology: examining global processes by studying how these are manifest in everyday practices.

But there still remains a need for sharpening our analytical tools and research strategies. The next two sections argue for the importance of (1) viewing all state-building processes as integrated into global, historical contexts, and (2) viewing state formations as cultural processes.

HISTORY AND STATE

Statements about the state in general are too often derived from examinations of specific states. Studies of state formation must therefore be placed within a conceptual framework that enables us to grasp the world as historical global interconnectedness – as transformations of profound global structures. Different state formations constitute highly interconnected political trajectories, but these connections have created widely differing results in different parts of the world. Accounts of *the* modern state were never historically justified.

We need to get rid of a particular provincial universalism: the provincial universalism that has understood, and continues to understand, the West as if it were created in isolation from other societies, as if it were formed with no relation to large parts of the Caribbean, Latin America, Oceania, Asia and Africa. The West's self-fashioning as the self-made centre of History is an instance of what Trouillot (1995) has called the silencing of the past. We ought to see it as an effect of power relations.

Yet, the provincial universalism of the global centre continues to mobilise massive support. It draws nourishment from ideas that constantly get us tangled in polarisations of the world – into the modern enlightened (and democratic) space, and traditional (and non-democratic) areas. The contemporary world is the product of a historical, global web of interconnections. It should be understood as a set of relational processes involving the simultaneous constitution of hegemonic and subordinate modernities (Coronil 1997: 388). Let us offer an example. As two classics, Fernando Ortiz's *Cuban Counterpoint* ([1940] 1995) and Sidney Mintz's *Sweetness and Power* (1985), have so powerfully brought out, an 'old' imperial history – or a globally extended history of colonialism, plantations and slavery – gave shape to political, economic and cultural life both in the heart of the West – such as England and France – and in the Caribbean. This global history of plantations and slavery simultaneously structured forms of power and the building of states, both in the global core and in the global periphery, both 'here' and 'there'.

Examinations of a broad and deep history are important for another reason as well. Much of mainstream twentieth-century anthropology was a-historical; anthropologists ignored, neglected and froze time (Cohn 1987: 19–20, 42–9; Thomas 1996: 120). Modern states need to be understood in light of what Fernando Braudel termed the '*longue durée*', which includes at the very least relevant imperial history. This does not mean, however, that we should view postcolonial states *a priori* as solely the outcome of colonial history. As Jean-François Bayart has put it with reference to Asia and Africa:

Many political systems existed in these two continents before Western colonization: particularly in China, Korea, Japan, Vietnam, Cambodia, Siam, Afghanistan, Ethiopia, Egypt, Madagascar (and many others), and also, although it is less well known, in the Maghreb states, and, in a more subtle way, in India, where the state heritage from the Moghul period is not insignificant. When the colonialists effectively acted as a demiurge, such as by building Iraq, Syria and Jordan from the ruins of the Ottoman Empire, or by creating most of the sub-Saharan African states (with the exception of Lesotho, Swaziland, Rwanda and Burundi), they did not do so *ex nihilo*; and colonial creations were also subject to multiple acts of re-appropriation by indigenous social groups. Therefore, these states, which are reputed to be artificial, rest in reality upon their own social foundations. (Bayart 1991: 52–3)[6]

The point is that we need to work on *concrete* histories. Every modern state formation has a specific history. It is essential to acknowledge the enormous political diversity of the contemporary world and that this diversity has been historically constituted.

CULTURE AND STATE

Increasingly, scholars of diverse disciplines are realising that the production of cultural forms and meanings is what relationships of domination, politics, and forms of state-building in the contemporary world is all about (Steinmetz 1999; Hansen and Stepputat 2001; Paley 2002; Das and Poole 2004). This growing interdisciplinary recognition has helped to generate important new opportunities for anthropology and ethnography. It has created new possibilities for a discipline that, for more than a century, has sought to critically practice, reflect on and refine the comparative study of culture. Anthropologists can draw on their considerable insights into the analysis of symbolic constructs, ritual life and meanings in order to develop studies of modern forms of state-building, and several anthropologists have now begun to do this.

The current fascination with culture in state studies has had a heterogeneous set of sources of inspiration. Important works on state formation have been influenced by Gramsci's notions of class power articulated through a negotiated cultural hegemony.[7] Foucault insisted on the need to look at knowledge-practices in terms of their 'effects', both on those to whom they are addressed and in the settings in which they operate.[8] Another source of inspiration for much rethinking of the study of power and politics in the contemporary world has been Edward Said's *Orientalism* (1978), itself influenced by the work of Foucault. Said's text promoted a reinvigorated interest in the cultural history of Western imperialism. Inspired by authors like Foucault and Said, comparative literature specialists, students of religion, historians and anthropologists have in recent decades generated an impressive body of examinations of the Western imperial imagination and its effects, historical ethnographies of how representatives and builders of colonial states imagined and sought to rule colonised peoples.

Another crucial text has been *The Great Arch* (1985), Philip Corrigan's and Derek Sayer's investigation of the modern English state formation as a form of cultural revolution. *The Great Arch*, in essence a broad historical sociology, insisted that those who wish to understand modern state formations must inquire into the forms and practices of cultural life:

The repertoire of activities and institutions conventionally identified as 'the State' are cultural forms, and cultural forms, moreover, of particular centrality to bourgeois civilization.... [S]tate formation is cultural revolution; that is its supreme (if never final) achievement, and the essence of its power. (1985: 3, 218)[9]

The fascination with culture among those seeking to understand modern forms of state formation can be traced to a general intellectual movement within anthropology itself. Since the 1960s, the discipline has seen the emergence of a far-reaching and powerful interest in the analysis of symbolic forms, classification systems and structures of meaning. Clifford Geertz's *The Interpretation of Cultures*, published in 1973, was exceptionally influential.[10]

Geertz's ideas about the analysis of cultural life helped to frame and shape much later work, not only in anthropology, but also in history and other academic disciplines. In 1980, Geertz published *Negara: The Theatre State in Nineteenth-century Bali*. Here, he argued that much political analysis had been reductionist: it had ignored and silenced the importance of rituals, symbols and meanings in the construction and reconstruction of states. The rituals of the Balinese theatre state 'were what there was' (1980: 136); they were not means of representing the state or of masking its true nature – they *constituted* the state.[11]

Another important anthropological study has been Bruce Kapferer's *Legends of People, Myths of State* (1988), an unconventional comparison of two forms of modern political thinking – one expressed through Australian 'aggressively' democratic egalitarianism, and the other through the sharply hierarchical thinking of Buddhists in Sri Lanka. Kapferer examined modern political world-views 'on their own terms and in the contexts of their ideas' (1988: xii). In so doing he brought out forcefully both the enormous cultural complexity of forms of politics and state formation in the contemporary world and the way in which ideas and perspectives derived from the heart of symbolic anthropology could be used to illuminate such forms.

Michael Herzfeld's *The Social Production of Indifference: Exploring the Symbolic Roots of Western Bureaucracy* (1992) also, as the subtitle suggests, insisted on the necessity of inquiring into forms of state-building as symbolic processes. Herzfeld demonstrated that an analysis of modern national bureaucracies cannot start from the premise that they are more 'rational' than the social institutions of 'small-scale' societies. Bureaucrats, he maintained, 'work on the categories of social existence in much the same way as sorcerers are supposed to work on the hair or nail clippings of their intended victims' (1992: 62). Thus bureaucracy is at its core founded on symbolic expressions, and, as he further showed, so are people's representations of bureaucracies as impersonal and unjust.[12]

There is a difference between a Gramsci, a Geertz, a Kapferer and a Herzfeld, to be sure. The academic projects we have referred to above are diverse. But they express a common, underlying interest in their profound concern with symbolic life. They all maintain that we must study how social actors involved in the construction of power and authority – and the building of states – shape and reshape categories and meanings and understand their worlds. The contributors to this volume set out from this premise. They assume that there is a deeply cultural dimension, in the anthropological sense, to modern politics and modern state formation. As Katherine Verdery has put it, we must see political life and state-building in the contemporary world

... as something more than a technical process – of introducing democratic procedures and methods of electioneering, of forming political parties and nongovernmental organizations, and so on. The 'something more' includes meanings, feelings, the sacred, ideas of morality, the nonrational – all ingredients of 'legitimacy' or 'regime consolidation' (that dry phrase), yet far broader than what analyses employing those terms usually provide. (Verdery 1999: 25)

If we are to understand state formation, we must reinforce many of the central ideas of mainstream twentieth-century symbolic anthropology.[13] But more is needed than this. The perspectives inspired by Gramsci, Foucault and Corrigan and Sayer have the advantage of forcing the researcher to make connections between cultural forms and historically constituted systems of inequality and power. Much symbolic anthropology has had too little to say about this type of connection (see Yanagisako and Delaney 1995: ix, 16; Ortner 1999: 137–38; 158–59). We need to study state formation as cultural processes and to profoundly politicise the anthropological study of meaning. In our attempts to grasp forms of state formation, we should seek to forge links between cultural forms, institutional structures and regimes of power.

Given this, a critical question emerges. How does a state acquire its reality in everyday life? Or, put another way, how is the historical field of power relationships and cultural forms that we call the state built, rebuilt and transformed in everyday life? The chapters in this book seek in different ways to offer answers to this question. In so doing, they invite researchers to continue to work on at least five more specific problems: (1) To what extent must we understand the construction and reconstruction of states as the outcome of myriads of close 'encounters between individuals or groups and governments' (Trouillot 2001: 125)? (2) How can we examine and write about the production of the state as an entity that 'appears and acts as having a life of its own' (Aretxaga 2003: 401)? (3) How should we understand the attempts of state bodies and state representatives to generate particular sorts of citizens, particular types of subjects? (4) How do attempts to build the state articulate with gender? (5) How may we usefully think about the relationship between state formation and violence? Let us consider each of these items, and what the chapters of this volume have to say about them in turn.

CLOSE ENCOUNTERS: THE NEGOTIATION OF RULE

The formation of modern states has often been conceptualised and studied within a framework that distinguishes between 'state' and 'civil society'. Yet much recent work on state formation has questioned the validity and usefulness of this distinction (see Foucault 1980; Abrams 1988; Bayart 1991; Mitchell 1999; Alonso 1995; Nugent 1997; Trouillot 2001). This conceptual distinction was created on the basis of a specific historical experience – that of Western Europe. In Bayart's (1991: 61) words, instead of being an historic and political universal applicable to all contexts:

... this theory is nothing but 'a method of schematization belonging to one particular technology of government' (that of the West), except that (and this is the root of all the difficulties) this 'particular technology of government' was exported into non-Western countries, took root there, and penetrated their imaginary conception of politics.[14]

The basic problem, however, is not that the distinction between state and civil society expresses Eurocentrism. The problem is that the separation between society, or civil society, and the state 'does not exist in reality' (Aretxaga 2003: 398) – not anywhere, not even in the West. To reiterate: a modern state must be understood as produced by a broad and continuously shifting field of power relationships, everyday practices and formations of meaning. Instead of operating with a sharply confining and static starting point – the framework of the distinction between the state and civil society – we should begin by recognising that we need a wider and more open conception of the state. Indeed, we should even question the very assumption that the state form has an 'essence'. The modern state, writes Trouillot (2001: 126), 'has no institutional fixity on either theoretical or historical grounds'.

We need to see the construction of states as the outcome of complex sets of practices and processes. A state formation is the result of myriads of situations where social actors negotiate power and meaning. This shifts the focus of analysis to the many practices of power and the mundane and ritual forms that constitute the state. It invites the researcher to examine in detail how a particular state is produced in everyday encounters at the local level – in those contexts where the state bodies' representatives and individuals and groups interact. It is true that this makes the presence of the modern state in social life a good deal more fluid than is frequently thought. But it is precisely this fact – that the state's presence in social life *is* fluid, incoherent and messy – that makes critical, 'grounded' ethnographic work so valuable if we wish to understand state-building processes (see Harvey, this volume).

In a richly ethnographic chapter, 'Chiefs and Bureaucrats in the Making of Empire: A Drama from the Transkei, South Africa, October 1880', Clifton Crais offers a contribution to studies of the building of colonial states. His point of departure is that the state has had an uneasy position within the new cultural history of empire. He writes:

To the extent that the state has been the centre of analysis in the new cultural history of empire, it has been primarily in terms of analysing the discursive strategies of rule, the epistemologies and techniques by which Europeans ordered and understood their colonial subjects and the lands they inhabited. The emphasis has been more on strategies than on practice, more on the accumulation of knowledge than on the daily relationships of coloniser and colonised. (p. 56, this volume)

Crais is concerned with bringing the everyday state back in. There is much to be learned, he documents, from the encounters of British colonial bureaucrats and their African subjects.

His chapter focuses on the earliest moments of state formation that started with conquest itself, when the colonial state came into being. It centres on a series of interactions between a British colonial magistrate and an African chief in the late nineteenth-century Transkei. Crais examines colonial conquest as a cross-cultural encounter of a political kind. Dealing with conquest in this way, he holds, offers a means of understanding not only the nature and daily exercise of domination and resistance, but also the imbricated histories of ruler and ruled, as colonised Africans translated the European political world – a world of state institutions, discourses and practices – into indigenous concepts and practices, while European bureaucrats intentionally or inadvertently wore the political mask of the very people they were busily conquering. Crais shows how the colonial magistrate Hamilton Hope used mapping and censuses to create both a state and new kind of subjects. But Hope's actions were also read into an African understanding of the nature of power, magic and fertility – and this eventually led to his ritual murder.

In the introduction to his chapter 'State Formation through Development in Post-apartheid South Africa', Knut Nustad picks up the threads from Crais's chapter. Nustad examines the relationship between a set of state builders and a local population in contemporary South Africa. His analysis centres on encounters between a group of state agents and the impoverished and marginalised population in the Cato Manor neighbourhood of Durban. Nustad starts out with Trouillot's contention that whether an agent can be said to be a state agent depends, not on inherent characteristics, but on the effects that are produced – whether these are 'state effects' of the sort described by Trouillot, or not. Durban's Cato Manor contains the largest post-apartheid development project in the country. Nustad argues that a close look at the activities of this development project reveals that the intervention has been based on a neoliberal understanding of the role of the state, and that the development organisation had in practice set out to produce the state effects Trouillot has named and classified. But, just as for Hamilton Hope, the nineteenth-century colonial magistrate in the Transkei, the actions of state institutions and state representatives became considerably transformed and subverted by the ruled, by the people at which they were directed. A central argument of Nustad's chapter is thus that analysts must distinguish between the state effects that are intended by a collective or individual agent, and the actual effects that are produced. State formations are outcomes of encounters and forms of interaction; they have been shaped through struggles over influence, resources and meanings. Any state formation that exists in reality has been produced through constant negotiation 'on the ground'.

In Chapter 5, 'Negotiated Dictatorship: The Building of the Trujillo State in the Southwestern Dominican Republic', Christian Krohn-Hansen seeks some answers to two hotly debated questions: How should one understand the construction of an authoritarian state? What is a dictatorship? From 1930 to 1961, General Rafael Trujillo ruled the Dominican Republic. His regime proved to be one of the most long-lasting dictatorships in the history of the Caribbean and Latin America. The bulk of the existing literature on the twentieth-century Dominican Republic has emphasised almost only terror and artifice to explain this protracted rule, penning a story of an absolute despot – an all-powerful ruler. In sharp contrast to such studies, Krohn-Hansen examines 'from below' the state formation headed by Trujillo. The chapter offers a historical ethnography from one part of the country – the southwestern region. It is imperative, Krohn-Hansen maintains, to approach authoritarian histories – like other histories – on the basis of detailed investigations of power relationships, everyday practices, and meanings. Even in dictatorships, state power is far more dispersed and negotiable than is most often assumed.

In the Dominican southwest, many remember Trujillo in a surprisingly positive light. People maintain that the years under his rule brought increased civilisation through the creation and construction of the nation-state. They remember Trujillo as *the* moderniser. Their story is that, irrespective of how oppressive a form of rule is, it may still transform daily life in productive ways. The Trujillo regime not only implemented agrarian policies that benefited the country's rural masses, it also promoted a peasant-based road to state-building. In the southwestern region, rural people, or villagers and peasants, helped to bring into being and give form to the Trujillo state. They did so by means of well-tried institutions like male dominance, the extended family and patronage. Thus even heavily repressive state formations need to be examined in terms of encounters, as complex interaction at the local level.

STATE FETISHISM

From the discussion above, it should be clear that the state cannot and should not be treated as having an objective existence. Yet it is also clear that the state derives much of its power from the fact that it does appear to have an objective existence, over and above society. Still, we do not wish to echo Radcliffe-Brown's call for abandoning the study of the state. What we need to do is to study the processes that make the state *appear* as an entity. In what ways, and through what techniques, does the state appear as a real objective entity? For Marx and Weber, who both focused on capitalist state formation in Europe, this was part of a wider social transformation. The creation of the state and the dissolution of civil society into atomistic individuals was part of the same act. For Marx, what was radically new about the bourgeois state was its insistence on marking out the political and public as a distinct sphere of society, embodied in the state. This was necessary, Marx maintained, in order to construct the social force par excellence, production, as belonging to a private and individual sphere. But such analysis is still concerned with the general, and fails to indicate how this divide is actually constituted and maintained. Timothy Mitchell (1999) has demonstrated one way in which these processes might be studied. He starts by asking why it is that a state institution appears as more than the sum of its members. Taking an army as an example, he argues that the disciplining techniques analysed by Foucault – uniforms, bodily techniques such as marching, coordination and separation – help to create the appearance of a machine, something more than its individual parts. His argument is thus that we cannot separate the material form of the state from the ideological. The 'state', he argues, 'arises from techniques that enable mundane material practices to take on the appearance of an abstract, nonmaterial form'. Thus, 'any attempt to distinguish the abstract or ideal appearance of the state from its material reality, in taking for granted this distinction, will fail to understand it' (1999: 77).

This line of argument is the starting point for Penelope Harvey's contribution in this volume. In her chapter on the state in the Peruvian Andes, Harvey shows that a serious ethnographic study cannot take the state as an analytical given. If the state is seen as being more than the local, as existing as an entity over and above society, then ethnographic accounts will always be less than the state. But this conception of the state is precisely the story that the state tells about itself, and research that starts from this distinction will end up strengthening this fetishised myth. Thus, Harvey argues, studying local manifestations of the state on its own terms, as parts connected to a translocal whole, would be to partake in the fetish of the state on which state institutions depend for their power. Instead, our focus must be on how the state manifests itself, appears as material and discursive reality to local populations, and is made relevant by them. Through focusing on the different meanings attributed to a road connection between a village and the regional capital in one part of the Peruvian Andes, Harvey shows that the state appears as more than the local – as having its centre elsewhere – and, for those experiencing themselves as living on its margins, this gives rise to fears of being marginalised. Yet, at the same time, the state is experienced as translocal and part of everyday lives.

Iver Neumann's contribution in this book is closest to the perspective outlined by Mitchell. Based on his own experiences as a speech-writer for the Norwegian Ministry of Foreign Affairs, this chapter examines the processes that make the ministry appear as a coherent entity, an object, to the outside world. In the course of his work for the ministry, Neumann noted various oddities: the number of desks a simple speech had to pass through before it was accepted; the bureaucrats' lack of interest in the communicative aspect of a speech (how a speech was received by the press and the public), and the outrage engendered by an attempt of his to write a draft for the minister's annual speech that did not sum up established Norwegian foreign policy goals. Through a fascinating ethnography, the author demonstrates that all these practices are concerned with creating unity out of fragmented interests, and it is through these practices that the ministry is able to speak with one voice. Speeches are more a technology for creating unity within a state organ than a means for communicating with the public.

Neumann's material is, of course, privileged: it is rare for an anthropologist to obtain such access to the internal workings of a state body (but see Melhuus, this volume). His chapter points to one way in which the state is turned into a fetishised object: through the techniques of state actors themselves. Another way in which the state is turned into a distinctive object is through ordinary people's experiences of it.[15] Kristi Anne Stølen's chapter in this volume shows how experiences of state institutions and the crossing of an international border helped to conjure an image of the state for Guatemalan refugees. She writes of how peasants from Ixcán in Guatemala were forced to flee from government troops because they were suspected of supporting the guerrilla movement. Prior to their departure, many of the refugees experienced the state as an external force, a power that killed and persecuted them. But the concrete experience of crossing an international border and being exposed to a different kind of regime helped to relativise the experience of the state and implant a transformed idea about it in people's imaginations. While living as refugees in Mexico, the Guatemalans were exposed to an international rights discourse through the work of NGOs. This apparatus in turn helped them to use ideas about rights to negotiate their return to Guatemala. Because of this experience, the returnees were able to force the government to abide by their promises. Stølen's chapter thus demonstrates the degree to which the meaning of state-building at the local level arises out of a complex history of interactions involving (returned) refugees, NGOs and state institutions.

THE CREATION OF SUBJECTS

In the classical European literature on the state, the other side of the formation of the state as a separate domain is the creation of a new type of subject. Individuality, Marx wrote in the introduction to *Grundrisse*, presupposes the state (see Sayer 1991). Both Marx and Weber saw state formation in Europe as intimately linked to the formation of subjects. For Marx, this was part of the attempt to create the individual in the abstract, dislocated from any real social setting. It was on this abstracted individual that universal rights were conferred, including the individual's right to dispose of his or her labour power. And it was this abstracted individual who was to be transformed into a member of a new collective – the nation. Thus Weber termed the bourgeoisie the 'national citizen class'. This cultural revolution was specific to Europe. Still, what probably holds as a general abstraction is that in a process of state formation, there is an attempt to create specific subjectivities. These might not be the same everywhere, nor may the attempt succeed everywhere, but states generally seek to control a certain kind of subject, as Scott (1998) has shown. He argues that the state has to create certain abstractions and simplifications of the reality that it seeks to control. By first ordering subjects into categories, and then forcing the same subjects to correspond to these categories, a simplified and manageable version of reality is created. In this volume, the chapter by Clifton Crais demonstrates this with regard to South Africa, where colonial authorities set out to create pure, demarcated tribes as the basis for their indirect rule.

Helga Baitenmann's ethnography from Mexico demonstrates how a study of state reforms can yield insights into what kind of subjects the state seeks to create. Baitenmann shows that, in two periods more than a half century apart, state agents employed the same techniques of classification and registration to change the meaning and content of citizenship or subjecthood during two massive social engineering projects: the post-revolutionary agrarian reform created in 1915, and the neoliberal land-entitlement programme begun in 1992. In the case of the post-revolutionary agrarian reform, the censuses made official a new form of rights-bearing individual (the agrarian-rights subject), while the census undertaken as part of the land-entitlement programme was an effort to create citizens with rights to landed property regulated by the market. In both instances, state agents employing apparently neutral administrative procedures profoundly changed the content of citizenship or subjecthood in Mexico. This chapter clearly shows the extent to which state-building and the creation of citizens or subjects are part of the same process.

In another chapter, Cris Shore details the European Union's (EU's) deliberate attempts to create a new subject: the European. Shore argues that, to all intents and purposes, the EU is in the process of becoming a state. But, unlike its nineteenth-century predecessors, the EU lacks a clear population which it can claim to represent – it lacks a *demos*. Shore demonstrates that EU officials are aware of this and that they put considerable effort into creating a single European population. This is a deeply cultural process. Through such means as the creation of a European flag, a European anthem, European stamps, passports and a single currency, EU officials have consciously set out to create a new identity. Shore's chapter points out how it is necessary for the state or the state-like entity to be created, imagined and represented, in order to create and sustain the unity it will need to function. It also demonstrates the extent to which EU bureaucrats are aware of this, and how they see it as one of their most important tasks.

But the key point is that while EU political elites may celebrate the EU's nation-building strategies as part of Europe's historic march of progress, in large parts of Europe such as Britain the state-formation aspect of the EU project of European construction is assiduously denied. In this respect, the EU represents something of a theoretical anomaly: in order to establish its legitimacy and authority it must, like any state, project the illusion of its own coherence (Abrams 1988; Mitchell 1999). Yet at the same time – and for reasons linked to its absent demos and weak democratic foundations – the EU's state-like character must be denied or discursively reconfigured for fear of provoking a backlash in reaction to the loss of national sovereignty and the widening democratic deficit.

GENDERED SUBJECTS

The formation of subjects is a highly uneven process. Derek Sayer (1991) has suggested that when Marx wrote about the abstract individual as male, he was in fact doing much more than merely following the writing conventions of his days. The abstract individual, endowed with universal rights and ultimately reduced to his productive capacities, formed as an extension to the machine he worked, was indeed a man. The classical literature was interested only in these processes, and ignored the extent to which the whole system built upon the utilisation of domestic work – which was relegated to women. The creation of subjects was thus a highly gendered process, but its gender bias was neglected and silenced by early theoreticians.[16] Feminist anthropologists have been at the forefront in denaturalising the gender divide. They began by creating studies based on the insight that gender inequality and gender hierarchy, in the words of Sylvia Yanagisako and Carol Delaney (1995: ix–x), 'come already embedded in symbolic systems as well as elaborated through contextualized, material practices'.[17]

The gendering of the subjects created by processes of state formation is apparent in many contributions in this volume. As Ana Alonso insists in her chapter, the processes of modern state formation cannot be fully grasped unless they are understood as gendered. This is apparent in Helga Baitenmann's analysis. The post-revolutionary agrarian reform in Mexico did not seek only to redistribute land; it also created a new form of rights-bearing subject: the agrarian-rights subject. Aimed at redistributing land to those who worked it, but did not own sufficient land to support themselves and their families, the new law sought to create family-based entities. This concept incorporated a highly gendered notion of the new form of state subjects. Only family heads, responsible for providing for a family, would become the new rights-bearing subjects. These family heads were male as long as there was a man in the family. Pre-revolutionary laws were still in operation that subjected women and children to the control of the *pater familias*. Women could only become rights-bearing subjects 'in default of a male spouse'. Baitenmann's chapter thus clearly demonstrates Sayer's (1991) point that not all people are included in a state formation's creation of new subjects, but that categories of people who are excluded from these new definitions also are profoundly affected by it.

In a different context, Marit Melhuus's chapter demonstrates convincingly how the anthropology of law can enrich studies of modern state-building as a gendered process. The chapter focuses on the legislative process of creating a law to regulate assisted conception in Norway. Here, the 'creation of subjects' takes on a literal meaning as the law is concerned with regulating the creation of persons. The justifications for regulating assisted conception provide insights into how Norwegian state officials perceive the person; and they reveal how a person is assumed to be linked into a network of relations that together constitute a society. The law in question is restrictive: egg donations are banned and anonymous sperm donations regulated, with reference to the child's right to know about its biological parents. The politicians and bureaucrats that Melhuus interviewed see it as fundamental to a person's identity that its relation to its biological parents is known. Every child has a right to a mother and a father, some interviewees maintained. Melhuus shows the interplay of two incommensurable discourses: one, the scientific, seeing the embryo as an assembly of cells that can be used in medical research; the other, that of the lawmakers, to whom the embryo is an abstract individual with a right to know its identity. The gendered aspect of this latter conception is demonstrated in what this fundamental identity is held to relate to: biological parenthood. The heterosexual family emerges as a precondition, both for a person's ability to gain an identity and for contemporary Norwegian state formation. Both Baitenmann's and Melhuus's contributions thus demonstrate, through ethnographic studies, that state formation and the creation of subjects are gendered processes.

VIOLENCE AND STATE FORMATION

Walter Benjamin long ago indicated that testimonies of civilisation are simultaneously testimonies of barbarism (1969: 256). Today's world continues to see and experience state massacres, state terror and state torture. From the Tiananmen Square protests in Beijing of 1989 to the Abu Ghraib US military prison west of Baghdad in the post-Hussein era, the building and rebuilding of states is inseparable from the deployment of state violence.

Writing on the semantics of political violence in late twentieth-century Venezuela, Fernando Coronil and Julie Skurski have correctly maintained that 'a myth central to modernity, whose paternity can be traced to Hegel and Foucault (1979), contends that as heirs to the Enlightenment, modern states establish their authority by embodying not divine will or force but reason' (1991: 332). According to this myth, the state's use of 'naked' violence in order to produce and reproduce the conditions of its existence is primarily a key characteristic of the pre-modern stage. Having finally 'domesticated the bloody theater of violence of the ancient régime', the modern state, for its part, 'replaces publicly inflicted punishment with a myriad of disciplinary procedures that permeate the body politic and engender the modern soul' (Coronil and Skurski 1991: 332).

Like Coronil and Skurski, we reject this mode of thinking about the relationship between state formations and violence. We reject it for three reasons: first, this perspective is permeated by ethnocentrism; second, it divides history into fixed, progressive stages; and, third, it silences the violence that is wielded by modern states.[18]

Ana Alonso's discussion in this volume rests upon these ideas. She deeply questions the validity of Foucault's distinction between pre-modern, sovereign power and modern, disciplinary power, and argues that his emphasis on the rationality of modern power is too tidy. In Alonso's view, Foucault's dichotomy obscures too much of what should really attract our attention – not least after the terrorist attacks of 9/11. Foucault's distinction, she contends, is in practice blind to the violence through which modern states reproduce the conditions of their existence. And it prevents us from fully recognising that the roots of contemporary forms of power and politics – both in the global centre and in the global periphery, both 'here' and 'there'– lie in colonialism and imperialism.

Alonso views the construction of a state as order-making. The order-making of modern states is anchored in a politics of territory, typically undertaken in the name of fighting chaos. 'But', as Zygmunt Bauman has observed, 'there would be no chaos were there no ordering intention already in place' (2002: 287, cited in Alonso, this volume). The ordering intention is therefore the birthplace of chaos.[19] The historically and socially constructed struggle against chaos (or terrorism, or barbarism, or impurity) makes it not only possible but also indeed necessary to view the deployment of force and violence as a legitimate part of the fight. In her discussion, Alonso draws a connection between two different historical situations – that which resulted in the making of colonial frontier warriors in northern Mexico in the eighteenth and nineteenth centuries, and that which has shaped today's agents of the US border patrol in the US–Mexico border area. Both situations, she holds, should be understood as spaces where the boundaries between property and wilderness, between the civility of settled life and the animality of transhumance, between the juridical order of the polity and the ferocity of the state of nature, between citizens and bandits, are maintained by violence. Ironically, she sums up, when wielded by the state, the very violence which is said to characterise the savages, illegals and terrorists, provides the occasion and technology for producing an ordered, civilised regime.

The part played by violence in the formation of states must be understood in terms of historical trajectories, social and cultural worlds, and clashes between forms of agency, interests and rationalities. The forms of modern state violence may vary considerably from one society to another, in part as a product of how governments and state institutions seek to divert, fight and control what they view as threats and dangers. State violence is inseparable from the wider historical, political, social and cultural configuration of which it forms a part (Mintz 1985; Farmer 2004), and here Guatemala offers an example. Stølen's chapter tells of a late twentieth-century Guatemala shaped and haunted by nightmarish violence. This violence cannot be separated from the other forms of social violence that marked this country during the same period. We cannot understand it in isolation from twentieth-century Guatemala's appalling forms of political, economic and social polarisation, which were shaped by colonialism and imperialism.

Political violence is used and contested in the idiom of a social formation's specific history. This applies also to modern state violence. Such violence is shaped by each society's myths of authority and identity, by each society's cultural formations (Taussig 1987; Feldman 1991; Daniel 1996; Das 1996; Krohn-Hansen 1997; Aretxaga 2000; Hansen 2001; Crais, this volume).

This may in turn produce prolonged spirals of violence. In some parts of the world, those considered as the state (government representatives, military personnel, policemen, tax collectors, and so on) and their enemies (viewed as bandits, guerrillas or terrorists) are shaped and reshaped in daily life as powerful myths or fantasies through what Aretxaga has aptly described as a 'mirroring paranoid dynamic' (2003: 402). In these contexts, life becomes permeated by distrust and fear. The state formation is a structure that constructs reality as an infinite story of mirror images and violent interactions.

ANTHROPOLOGY AND THE STATE

As recently as 1994, Carole Nagengast could claim in an *Annual Review of Anthropology* essay that 'Recent debate in other social sciences about the nature of the state ... and analyses that interrogate the state as ethnographic subject are not as commonplace in anthropology, although that is changing slowly' (1994: 116).

This lack of focus on the modern state form has weakened our discipline. It continues to undermine anthropologists' capacity to deal satisfactorily with important forms of power and politics in the contemporary world. In sharp contrast to this tradition, we have insisted that states have a powerful presence in the lives of most people. The relevance of the state in many, perhaps most, parts of the world is not declining. Therefore, we must continue to ask: how can we usefully conceptualise and examine the state form? Anthropologists must strengthen their ways of dealing with the state in order to be able to improve the anthropology of politics. Today's world is marked by a series of battles that centre on definitions of states, nations and peoples. There are dozens of ethnic conflicts taking place, largely within the borders of diverse nation-states. The desire for self-determination and statehood continues to be profound in many areas, despite – or perhaps owing to – the fact that citizens in several countries are legally electrocuted, shot or stoned to death by their states for what are claimed to be political, moral, economic or violent crimes.

A strengthened anthropology of the state will necessarily contribute to the comparative study of cultural life as well. Much of the huge literature in anthropology on symbolic forms and ritual practices is marked by a lack: the uses of symbols and rituals are analysed in isolation from the wider political and historical context. A different starting point is required: we need to forge connections between examinations of cultural forms and studies of state formation. This will also help us better understand symbolic activities and meaning creations. Shamanistic and other religious practices; the production of origin narratives; uses of descent stories; kinship and marriage; eating and dressing rituals; naming activities; identification practices; uses of language – in today's world, these and other symbolic processes are typically woven together with forms of state-building (for examples, see Kanitkar 1994; Carsten 1995; Cohn 1996; Thomas and Humphrey 1996; Scott 1998: 53–83; Lund 2001).

As the chapters in this volume demonstrate, the anthropology of the state remains solidly rooted in examinations of everyday life. The analyses of forms of state formation are created by means of an important tool – ethnography. They remain tied to studies of politics and culture as embedded in practices, in specific forms of agency. And it is here that we can recognise how anthropology can contribute to the study of state formations and the way in which states affect us all.

NOTES

1. We would like to thank Helga Baitenmann, Marit Melhuus and Cris Shore for their helpful comments.
2. Abrams develops this argument in his critique of Nicolas Poulantzas. He argues that Poulantzas' functional conception of the state is problematic because 'large parts of the process of cohesion ... are not performed within commonsensically "political" structures at all but are diffused ubiquitously throughout the social system ...' (1988: 73). The problem with this focus on functions, according to Abrams, is that it loses sight of the actors who actually uphold the state idea: 'the move is towards an abstract understanding of the state which is so structurally unspecific as to seem either to make the conception of the state redundant, or to substitute it for the conception of society' (1988: 74).
3. Since Poulantzas was heavily influenced by Foucault, and Abrams develops his argument in dialogue with Poulantzas, this similarity is not surprising.
4. The word 'economy' derives from the old Greek language – from the two words '*oikos*' (house) and '*nomos*' (management). Jane Austen used the term in this sense when she referred to a housewife as a 'good economist' (Keith Hart, personal communication).
5. This objection pertains more to Trouillot's conceptualisation of state effects as these are set out in his 2001 article than to his other written works. In his case study from Haiti (1990) Trouillot is at pains to avoid universalised definitions of concepts such as 'state' and 'nation'. He writes:

    The problem with concepts of the nation that emphasise a specific cultural feature ... is not their emphasis on culture-history as such but the search for a cultural feature that would repeat itself *mutatis mutandis* in each and every situation. In other words, 'nation' has no fixed cultural content – and that is what makes its cross-cultural conceptualization a difficult one. (1990: 24)

    In his more theoretical *Global Transformations* (2003), he argues for an anthropology that places the phenomena under study in their political, historical and global context – an argument similar to the one made here. Moreover, the idea about state effects can be a useful starting point for examining specific historical state formations, even if the universality of the concept is questionable for the reasons given here (see Nustad, this volume).
6. For some instructive studies, see Tambiah (1977); Geertz (1980); Apter (1992); Stoller (1995); Crais (this volume).
7. See Gramsci ([1929–1935] 1971). For two instructive discussions of the notion of hegemony, see Scott (1985: 304–50) and Roseberry (1994). For a fine empirical study of state formation influenced by Gramscian ideas, see Trouillot's work on Haiti (Trouillot 1990).
8. See Foucault (1979, 1980, 1991). For works on forms of governance inspired by critical readings of Foucault's ideas, see Mitchell (1988), Miller and Rose (1990), Thomas (1990), Malkki (1995), Gupta (1995, 2001), Shore and Wright (1997); Dean (2001); Ferguson and Gupta (2002); Alonso (this volume).
9. *The Great Arch* helped to give shape to Gilbert Joseph's and Daniel Nugent's important edited collection, *Everyday Forms of State Formation: Revolution and the Negotiation of Rule in Modern Mexico* (1994). This work has already become a classic in the new literature on state formation as historically constituted cultural processes (see, for example, Baitenmann in this volume). For empirical works from, respectively, Peru and the Dominican Republic that seek to challenge a certain Eurocentric confinement conveyed even through the work of Corrigan and Sayer, see Nugent (1997) and Krohn-Hansen (this volume).

10. Also highly influential were works by Claude Lévi-Strauss, Victor Turner, David Schneider, Edmund Leach and Mary Douglas, who helped to define the growing general anthropological interest in the study of symbols, rituals and meanings.

11. For a more recent work, see Geertz (2004).

12. For a couple of other pioneering attempts to use insights derived from the core of the anthropology of symbolic forms and practices, shaped since the 1960s, in order to understand aspects of state formations, see Handelman (1990) and Delaney (1995).

13. Anthropologists often associate 'symbolic anthropology' with a late twentieth-century American school led by Clifford Geertz and perhaps Marshall Sahlins. We do not intend to be as specific as that. In this chapter, we are not interested in how to separate symbolic from cultural or even social anthropology. By 'mainstream twentieth-century symbolic anthropology' we refer to an anthropology largely focused on studies of ideas about kinship and locality, rituals, classification systems and meanings.

14. Bayart quotes Michel Foucault, *Résumé des Cours, 1970–1982* (1989: 113).

15. Michael Taussig has suggested that an important part of creating the state as a fetish is accomplished by the 'mysterious, mystifying, convoluting, plain scary, mythical, and arcane cultural properties and power of violence to the point where violence is very much an end in itself – a sign, as Benjamin put it, of the existence of the gods' (Taussig 1992: 116).

16. George L. Mosse (1985) has shown that the middle-class revolution in Europe was as much a moral as an economic revolution. Sexual morals and the regulation of behaviour were used to set the bourgeoisie apart from both the lower classes and from the aristocracy. Later, with the consolidation of modern states and the growth of nationalism, sexual morals came to constitute an important means by which to create constants in an abruptly changing world.

17. For important examples, see Rosaldo and Lamphere (1974); Ortner and Whitehead (1981); Strathern (1988); and Yanagisako and Delaney (1995).

18. Max Weber recognised that state violence is a part of modernity. He formulated the viewpoint that the modern state and violence are clearly linked. His influential definition of the modern state – that it has a monopoly on the legitimate use of violence within a specified territory – is based not on what the state does, but on its means, which is violence (Weber 1970: 77–78).

19. For related perspectives, see Douglas (1966), Ricoeur (1967), Girard (1977), Kapferer (1988), Malkki (1995) and Scott (1998).

REFERENCES

Abrams, P., 1988. 'Notes on the Difficulty of Studying the State', *Journal of Historical Sociology*, 1(1): 58–89.

Alonso, A.M., 1995. *Thread of Blood*. Tucson, AZ: University of Arizona Press.

Apter, A., 1992. *Black Critics and Kings*. Chicago, IL, and London: University of Chicago Press.

Aretxaga, B., 2000. 'A Fictional Reality: Paramilitary Death Squads and the Construction of State Terror in Spain', pp. 47–69 in J.A. Sluka, ed., *Death Squad: The Anthropology of State Terror*. Philadelphia, PA: University of Pennsylvania Press.

Aretxaga, B., 2003. 'Maddening States', *Annual Review of Anthropology*, 32: 393–410.

Bauman, Z., 2002. 'The Fate of Humanity in the Post-Trinitarian World', *Journal of Human Rights*, 1(3): 283–303.

Bayart, J.-F., 1991. 'Finishing with the Idea of the Third World: The Concept of the Political Trajectory', pp. 51–71 in J. Manor, ed., *Rethinking Third World Politics*. London and New York: Longman.

Benjamin, W., 1969. *Illuminations*. New York: Schocken Books.

Carsten, J., 1995. 'The Politics of Forgetting: Migration, Kinship and Memory on the Periphery of the Southeast Asian State', *Journal of the Royal Anthropological Institute (Incorporating Man)*, 1(2): 317–35.

Cohn, B.S., 1987. *An Anthropologist among the Historians and Other Essays*. Oxford: Oxford University Press.

Cohn, B., 1996. *Colonialism and Its Forms of Knowledge*. Princeton, NJ: Princeton University Press.

Coronil, F., 1997. *The Magical State: Nature, Money, and Modernity in Venezuela*. Chicago, IL, and London: University of Chicago Press.

Coronil, F. and J. Skurski, 1991. 'Dismembering and Remembering the Nation: The Semantics of Political Violence in Venezuela', *Comparative Studies in Society and History*, 33(2): 289–337.

Corrigan, P. and D. Sayer, 1985. *The Great Arch: English State Formation as Cultural Revolution*. Oxford: Basil Blackwell.

Daniel, E.V., 1996. *Charred Lullabies*. Princeton, NJ: Princeton University Press.

Das, V., 1996. 'Sexual Violence, Discursive Formations and the State', *Economic and Political Weekly*, 31: 2411–25.

Das, V. and D. Poole (eds), 2004. *Anthropology in the Margins of the State*. Santa Fe, NM: School of American Research Press.

Dean, M., 2001. ' "Demonic Societies": Liberalism, Biopolitics, and Sovereignty', pp. 41–64 in T.B. Hansen and F. Stepputat, eds, *States of Imagination*. Durham, NC, and London: Duke University Press.

Delaney, C., 1995. 'Father State, Motherland, and the Birth of Modern Turkey', pp. 177–99 in S. Yanagisako and C. Delaney, eds, *Naturalizing Power*. New York and London: Routledge.

Douglas, M. 1966. *Purity and Danger*. London and New York: Routledge/Ark Paperbacks.

Farmer, P., 2004. 'An Anthropology of Structural Violence', *Current Anthropology*, 45(3): 305–25.

Feldman, A., 1991. *Formations of Violence*. Chicago, IL, and London: University of Chicago Press.

Ferguson, J. and A. Gupta, 2002. 'Spatializing States: Toward an Ethnography of Neo-Liberal Governmentality', *American Ethnologist*, 29(4): 981–1002.

Fortes, M. and E.E. Evans-Pritchard, eds, [1940] 1955. *African Political Systems*. London: Oxford University Press.

Foucault, M., 1979. *Discipline and Punish*. New York: Vintage Books.

Foucault, M., 1980. *Power/Knowledge*, ed. Colin Gordon. New York: Pantheon Books.

Foucault, M., 1989. *Résumé des Cours, 1970–1982*. Paris: Julliard.

Foucault, M., 1991. 'Governmentality', pp. 87–104 in G. Burchell, C. Gordon and P. Miller eds, *The Foucault Effect: Studies in Governmentality*. Chicago, IL, and London: University of Chicago Press.

Geertz, C., 1973. *The Interpretation of Cultures*. New York: Basic Books.

Geertz, C., 1980. *Negara: The Theatre State in Nineteenth-Century Bali*. Princeton, NJ: Princeton University Press.

Geertz, C., 2004. 'What Is a State If It Is Not a Sovereign? Reflections on Politics in Complicated Places', *Current Anthropology*, 45(5): 577–93.

Girard, R., 1977. *Violence and the Sacred*. Baltimore, MD: Johns Hopkins University Press.

Gramsci, A. [1929–1935] 1971. *Selections from the Prison Notebooks*, ed. and trans. by Q. Hoare and G. Nowell-Smith. New York: International Publishers.

Gupta, A., 1995. 'Blurred Boundaries: The Discourse of Corruption, the Culture of Politics, and the Imagined State', *American Ethnologist*, 22(2): 375–402.

Gupta, A., 2001. 'Governing Population: The Integrated Child Development Services Program in India', pp. 65–96 in T.B. Hansen and F. Stepputat, eds, *States of Imagination*. Durham, NC, and London: Duke University Press.

Hacking, I., 1990. *The Taming of Chance*. Cambridge: Cambridge University Press.

Handelman, D., 1990. *Models and Mirrors*. Cambridge: Cambridge University Press.

Hansen, T.B., 2001. *Wages of Violence: Naming and Identity in Postcolonial Bombay*. Princeton, NJ: Princeton University Press.

Hansen, T.B. and F. Stepputat, eds, 2001. *States of Imagination*. Durham, NC, and London: Duke University Press.

Hardt, M. and A. Negri, 2000. *Empire*. Cambridge, MA: Harvard University Press.

Herzfeld, M. 1992. *The Social Production of Indifference: Exploring the Symbolic Roots of Western Bureaucracy*. Chicago, IL: University of Chicago Press.

Jessop, B. 1990. *State Theory: Putting the Capitalist State in its Place*. Cambridge: Polity Press.

Joseph, G.M. and D. Nugent, eds, 1994. *Everyday Forms of State Formation*. Durham, NC, and London: Duke University Press.

Kanitkar, H., 1994. ' "Real True Boys": Moulding the Cadets of Imperialism', pp. 184–96 in A. Cornwall and N. Lindisfarne, eds, *Dislocating Masculinity*. London and New York: Routledge.

Kapferer, B., 1988. *Legends of People, Myths of State*. Washington, DC, and London: Smithsonian Institution Press.

Krohn-Hansen, C., 1997. 'The Construction of Dominican State Power and Symbolisms of Violence', *Ethnos*, 62(3–4): 49–78.

Lund, S., 2001. 'Bequeathing and Quest: Processing Personal Identification Papers in Bureaucratic Spaces (Cuzco, Peru)', *Social Anthropology*, 9(1): 3–24.

Malkki, L.H., 1995. *Purity and Exile*. Chicago, IL: University of Chicago Press.

Miller, P. and N. Rose, 1990. 'Governing Economic Life', *Economy and Society*, 19(1): 1–31.

Mintz, S.W., 1985. *Sweetness and Power: The Place of Sugar in Modern History*. Harmondsworth: Penguin Books.

Mitchell, T., 1988. *Colonizing Egypt*. Cambridge: Cambridge University Press.

Mitchell, T., 1999. 'Society, Economy, and the State Effect', pp. 76–97 in G. Steinmetz, ed., *State/Culture: State-formation after the Cultural Turn*. Ithaca, NY, and London: Cornell University Press.

Mosse, G.L., 1985. *Nationalism and Sexuality*. Madison, WI: University of Wisconsin Press.

Nagengast, C., 1994. 'Violence, Terror, and the Crisis of the State', *Annual Review of Anthropology*, 23: 109–36.

Nugent, D., 1997. *Modernity at the Edge of Empire: State, Individual, and Nation in the Northern Peruvian Andes, 1885–1935*. Stanford, CA: Stanford University Press.

Ortiz, F. [1940] 1995. *Cuban Counterpoint: Tobacco and Sugar*. Durham, NC, and London: Duke University Press.

Ortner, S., 1999. 'Thick Resistance: Death and the Cultural Construction of Agency in Himalayan Montaineering', pp. 136–63 in S. Ortner, ed., *The Fate of 'Culture'*. Berkeley, CA: University of California Press.

Ortner, S. and H. Whitehead, eds, 1981. *Sexual Meanings*. Cambridge: Cambridge University Press.

Paley, J., 2002. 'Toward an Anthropology of Democracy', *Annual Review of Anthropology*, 31: 469–96.

Poulantzas, N., 1968. *Political Power and Social Classes*. London: New Left Books.

Radcliffe-Brown, A.R., [1940] 1955. 'Preface', in M. Fortes and E.E. Evans-Pritchard, eds, *African Political Systems*. London: Oxford University Press.

Ricoeur, P., 1967. *The Symbolism of Evil*. New York and London: Harper & Row.

Rosaldo, M. and L. Lamphere, eds, 1974. *Women, Culture and Society*. Stanford, CA: Stanford University Press.

Roseberry, W., 1994. 'Hegemony and the Language of Contention', pp. 355–66 in G.M. Joseph and D. Nugent, eds, *Everyday Forms of State Formation*. Durham, NC, and London: Duke University Press.

Said, E., 1978. *Orientalism*. New York: Pantheon Books.

Sayer, D., 1991. *Capitalism and Modernity: An Excursus on Marx and Weber*. London: Routledge.

Scott, J., 1985. *Weapons of the Weak: Everyday Forms of Peasant Resistance*. New Haven, CT, and London: Yale University Press.

Scott, J.C., 1998. *Seeing Like a State: How Certain Schemes to Improve the Human Condition Have Failed*. New Haven, CT, and London: Yale University Press.

Shore, C. and S. Wright, eds, 1997. *Anthropology of Policy: Critical Perspectives on Governance and Power*. London: Routledge.

Steinmetz, G., ed., 1999. *State/Culture: State-formation after the Cultural Turn*. Ithaca, NY, and London: Cornell University Press.

Stoller, P., 1995. *Embodying Colonial Memories*. New York and London: Routledge.

Strathern, M., 1988. *The Gender of the Gift*. Berkeley, CA: University of California Press.

Tambiah, S.J., 1977. 'The Galactic Polity: The Structure of Traditional Kingdoms in Southeast Asia', pp. 69–97 in S. Freed, ed., *Anthropology and the Climate of Opinion*. New York: New York Academy of Sciences.

Taussig, M., 1987. *Shamanism, Colonialism, and the Wild Man: A Study in Terror and Healing*. Chicago, IL, and London: University of Chicago Press.

Taussig, M., 1992. *The Nervous System*. London: Routledge.

Thomas, N., 1990. 'Sanitation and Seeing: The Creation of State Power in Early Colonial Fiji', *Comparative Studies in Society and History*, 32(1): 149–70.

Thomas, N., 1996. *Out of Time: History and Evolution in Anthropological Discourse*, 2nd edn. Ann Arbor, MI: University of Michigan Press.

Thomas, N. and C. Humphrey, eds, 1996. *Shamanism, History, and the State*. Ann Arbor, MI: University of Michigan Press.

Trouillot, M.-R., 1990. *Haiti: State against Nation: The Origins and Legacy of Duvalierism*. New York: Monthly Review Press.

Trouillot, M.-R., 1995. *Silencing the Past: Power and the Production of History*. Boston, MA: Beacon Press.

Trouillot, M.-R., 2001. 'The Anthropology of the State in the Age of Globalization', *Current Anthropology*, 42(1): 125–38.

Trouillot, M.-R., 2003. *Global Transformations: Anthropology and the Modern World*. New York: Palgrave Macmillan.

Verdery, K., 1999. *The Politics of Dead Bodies*. New York: Columbia University Press.

Weber, M., 1970. *From Max Weber: Essays in Sociology*, ed. H.H. Gerth and C. Wright Mills. London: Oxford University Press.

Yanagisako, S. and C. Delaney, eds, 1995. *Naturalizing Power*. New York and London: Routledge.

2 SOVEREIGNTY, THE SPATIAL POLITICS OF SECURITY, AND GENDER: LOOKING NORTH AND SOUTH FROM THE US–MEXICO BORDER

Ana M. Alonso

During the 1990s, scholars argued that 'deterritorialisation', the detachment of social and cultural processes from specific places, was both a condition and an effect of globalisation (e.g. Tomlinson 1999).[1] Meanwhile, Foucault and his followers 'cut off the King's head' declaring that 'sovereignty' was an inadequate concept for capturing the productive, dispersed and decentred character of power in modern societies (Foucault 1984: 63–65). The conjunction of these (and other) theoretical currents led scholars to announce that the territorial state was now 'irrelevant' (Krohn-Hansen and Nustad, Introduction). A decade later, these theoretical moves seem premature. Projects of state sovereignty and of place-based identification such as nationalism have not gone away, and new strategies of reterritorialisation and border enforcement have emerged in tension with the deterritorialising effects of increasingly complex global networks, flows and interconnections.

In the field of international relations, neorealist orthodoxy defines 'sovereignty' as a natural attribute of the state, a product of state monopoly of violence within a territory (Thomson 1994: 11–14). In this chapter I argue that sovereignty is not an attribute but rather an ongoing and variable project of states which is more or less realised in practice. Rather than taking sovereignty for granted, anthropologists should draw on ethnographic and historical methods in order to analyse projects of state sovereignty in everyday-life practices such as warfare, political performances, forms of surveillance and knowledge production, and spatial politics. How are such practices linked to the formation of subjects? What are the tensions between state projects of sovereignty and the challenges posed to them? Here, I share some reflections on how 'sovereignty' might be understood in the current historical moment, retracing the route of my own thinking and acknowledging some of my guides.

SOVEREIGN POWER AND DISCIPLINARY POWER

For Foucault, pre-modern, sovereign power is associated with the territorial state and operates through signification, spectacle and interdiction, whereas

27

modern, disciplinary power is associated with the state of the population and works off-stage by transforming the life of the body itself, remoulding 'formless clay' (Foucault 1979: 135–37). He argues that sovereignty is necessarily centred on 'law and prohibition', on repression (Foucault 1984: 63), rather than on the productive forms of capillary power which characterise political modernity. Throughout Foucault's work one notices an inconsistent stance on the relation between juridico-institutional forms of power, centred in the state, and disciplinary power, dispersed throughout the social body. In some of his writings Foucault declares that the state is 'superstructural' to capillary forms of modern power (1984: 64) while in others he makes the state central to the government of the body and of the population.

In 'The Subject and Power', Foucault states that the objective of his work has been to 'create a history of the different modes by which, in our culture, human beings are made subjects' (1982: 208). These modes of subjectification include 'dividing practices' which endow subjects with distinct identities through classificatory processes based on knowledge. Commonly objectified in social space, these distinctions are the basis for techniques of domination which control, contain and discipline categories of persons such as 'vagabonds' and 'criminals' (Foucault 1979). State power combines such 'individualisation techniques' with 'totalising procedures' (Foucault 1982: 213) as evinced in bio-power, which has two poles, the species and the human body (1984: 262–63). Bio-power, Foucault argues, replaces the sovereign's right to 'take life, or let live' by 'a power to foster life or to disallow it' (1984: 261) centred on the health and welfare of the population.

Foucault's work has made a key contribution to the development of a notion of politics that includes everyday life and that does not assume that the workings of power in society are necessarily unified. But more recently, Foucault's blind spots, such as his failure to link modern power to colonialism or to incorporate gender and race in his analysis of bio-power (e.g. Stoler 1995), as well as the opposition he draws between pre-modern, sovereign power and modern, disciplinary power, have been the object of deserved criticism (Agamben 1998; Alonso 2005; Hansen and Stepputat 2005). Recent perspectives on state formation, exemplified by the chapters in this volume, put into question Foucault's opposition between state power as repressive and capillary power as productive (Foucault 1984: 63–67).

In the Introduction to their edited volume, *Sovereign Bodies* (2005), Hansen and Stepputat argue that scholars need to reconsider the place of sovereign power in the contemporary, post-11 September world. *Pace* Foucault, territorialised constructions of sovereignty as indivisible, transcendent and self-referring 'still remain the hard kernel of modern states', especially in periods of crisis (Hansen and Stepputat 2005). Centripetal processes put into motion by projects of sovereignty exist in tension with centrifugal forces which challenge state efforts to selectively legitimise or criminalise uses of violence within its national territory as well as internationally (Alonso 1995). State control over violence is not only 'multidimensional but highly variable. Whether the state exerts control, direct control, or monopolistic control over the use, means, or principal means of violence is an empirical question' (Thomson 1994: 9).

One of the main arguments I make in this chapter is that the state can respond to centrifugal and deterritorialising forces, which include but are not limited to globalisation processes, by affirming sovereign power, developing techniques to recentralise authority and institutionalising forms of reterritorialisation. The Bush administration's response to 11 September 2001 is a case in point.

The decentred organisation but international scale of *jihad* has put into question the state-based monopoly of transnational warfare as well as organic notions of sovereignty which presume that if one cuts off the head of the King, one kills the body. Nevertheless, the Bush administration has been unable to respond to these new conditions of violence with anything other than the old vision of a world organised into violence-monopolising sovereign states: this is one assumption behind the logic of making the attack on Iraq, a nation-state, a cornerstone of the 'war on terrorism', despite the lack of evidence linking Hussein's administration to al-Qaida.

The 'war on terrorism' has had unanticipated reterritorialising effects. A spatial politics of security whose roots lie in colonialism and imperialism but whose idiom is that of the care of the population is being reworked. In addition, the US is reaffirming its sovereignty on a number of levels of scale, from the international to the national to the regional.

All states are sovereign but some are more sovereign than others. While conducting the 'war on terrorism', the Bush administration has declared the US exempt from selected international norms and national laws. From a Latin American perspective, the 'new' unilateralism and imperialism is not so new, recalling the nineteenth- and twentieth-century North American rhetoric of 'Manifest Destiny' and the 'Monroe Doctrine', invoked to justify the annexation of half of Mexico's territory, multiple invasions of Latin American nations, as well as the Platt Amendment, which made Cuba a US Protectorate and Guantanamo a US naval base. The mission of Uncle Sam, the 'world policeman' who can invade other nations in the name of human rights, democratic 'nation building' and the global free market, has been extended from the Western hemisphere to the whole world.

In this socio-historical context, Foucault's relegation of the territorial state to the 'pre-modern' sidelines a lot of key issues. His emphasis on the rationality of modern power is too tidy. Moreover, after the rollback of the welfare state, Foucault's notion of biopower needs updating.

By contrast, the work of the Italian political philosopher, Giorgio Agamben, particularly his book, *Homo Sacer: Sovereign Power and Bare Life*, has generated great interest. Written in 1995, *Homo Sacer* develops a political philosophy which seems uncannily prescient in the aftermath of 11 September. Agamben's point of departure is a critique of Foucault's relegation of sovereign power, the territorial state, the juridico-legal order and the public spectacle of power to the archaic. The analysis of power over death and power over life, of subjectification technologies and the state, cannot be separated, Agamben argues, because 'the inclusion of bare life in the political realm constitutes the original – if concealed – nucleus of sovereign power' (1998: 6) in Western political culture since the Greeks. Rather than discard the juridico-institutional model of power, Agamben suggests that scholars should identify its points of intersection with the bio-political model (1998: 6), a challenge I take up in this chapter.

READING AGAMBEN

Agamben's logic has a paradoxical structure which he claims characterises that which he is analysing. First he lays out concepts as if they were contraries. Then he discusses how each concept presupposes and includes the other. Hence, he typically concludes, the distinction between these concepts is actually blurred. In order to convey this point visually, he repeatedly invokes the topological figure of the Moebius strip.

Agamben takes Carl Schmidt's definition of sovereignty as his point of departure: 'Sovereign is he who decides on the state of exception' (1998: 11). Sovereign power has a paradoxical structure (1998: 11). The juridical can only be defined in relation to the non-juridical, that is, to 'mere violence in the form of the state of nature' (1998: 20). Since the juridical order grants the sovereign the power of proclaiming a 'state of exception' from its own norms, then the sovereign both stands outside and is included within this order. Two surfaces turn into one: the 'state of exception' is marked by the same violence that the *polis* projects onto the state of nature. This foundational logic, Agamben notes, characterises the canon of Western political philosophy (1998: 35).

Aristotle's definition of the polis, according to Agamben, rests on an opposition between *zoe* (natural life) and the *bios politicus*, the political life proper to men. This foundational logic of the *polis* is paradoxical: 'an inclusive exclusion ... of zoe in the polis almost as if politics were the place in which life had to transform itself into good life and in which what had to be politicised were always already bare life' (1998: 7). Once located at the margins of the political order, natural life increasingly comes to be 'a principal object of the projections and calculations of State power' and hence 'to coincide more and more with the political realm' so that 'exclusion and inclusion, outside and inside, bios and zoe, right and fact, enter into a zone of irreducible indistinction' (1998: 9).

Scholars rarely try to capture how they read in what they write. As I read Agamben, I transpose his concepts and arguments to historical and ethnographic contexts which have since become supplements to his text in my memory, introducing commas, periods, ellipses and question marks. As a Latina (born in Cuba) living on the US–Mexico border, I look north to the US and south to Mexico and Latin America as I read. I annotate my discussion of the paradoxes of *Homo Sacer* with examples drawn from the US–Mexico border, in the past and the present, as well as from Mexico and elsewhere in Latin America. My use of examples follows a different logic from that of traditional area studies and is in keeping with newer, more inclusive definitions of 'America' that link rather than separate north and south (Brady 2000).

Geographically, the US–Mexico border area consists of the 960,000 square miles comprised by the ten border States in the US and Mexico (Lorey 1999: 8). Before 1848, when it was conquered by the US, this area was Mexico's northern frontier and, prior to Mexican independence in 1821, it was New Spain's. In the eighteenth and nineteenth centuries, this northern frontier was a zone of exception in which law was selectively suspended and in which distinctions between civilised and savage, law and violence, reason and instinct, fact and value, inside and outside, property and desert, settled life and transhumance, had to be constantly reaffirmed because they were continuously blurred. The Spanish colonial and later, the Mexican national state, encouraged colonists to regard the northern frontier as a desert wilderness, empty space waiting to be conquered and made part of the royal, and subsequently national, patrimony. As I discuss in *Thread of Blood* (1995), the state gave non-Indian settlers, known as *gente de razón* ('people having the capacity for reason') property rights to land on which they were instructed to set up 'civilised' outposts, zones of law, property and settlement in the midst of the wilderness (Nugent 1993; Alonso 1995). In return, they had to defend these outposts from Apache raids.

Agamben's definition of *homo sacer* – that is a 'man who may be killed and yet not sacrificed' (1998: 8) – illuminates the political dynamics of colonisation of native peoples who were considered 'bare life' because they did not conform to colonists' notions of what it meant to be 'civilised'. Colonists located the northern frontier's inhabitants, in particular the transhumant Apache who resisted colonisation, outside the realm of the polity and its juridical order. The Apache became figured as homo sacer, Hobbes' man who 'is a wolf to other men', located in a 'zone of indistinction between the human and the animal', between order and chaos (Agamben 1998: 106).

Because the Apache lived from a mixture of hunting, gathering and raiding, they existed outside the borders of what colonists considered political order, in a state of nature that purportedly required civilisation. As Jennifer Jo Thompson stresses, 'the Apache truly were *homines sacri* in Agamben's sense: they could be killed but not sacrificed, and those who took the lives of the Apache were not considered guilty of murder' (personal communication).

Zygmunt Bauman notes that 'Order-making tends to be ... undertaken in the name of fighting the chaos. But there would be no chaos were there no ordering intention already in place.... Chaos is born as a non-value, an exception. Ordering ... is its birthplace' (2002: 287). The state's territorialisation of politics on the northern frontier supposed a regime of property which had key consequences for social ordering. 'Property, space and corporeal violence', Blomley points out, 'are closely entangled' (2003: 122). Colonists thought the transhumant Apaches lacked any notion of property and hence were the bearers of chaos. They defined the Apache as thieves and their territories as virgin space to be conquered. Indeed, in 1740 one priest wrote, 'The Apache who harass these lands are extremely ferocious by condition, bloodthirsty by nature, barbarians in their way of life, of an indomitable temperament; they are a great rabble of thieves who live like wild beasts in the countryside' (cited in Alonso 1995: 57). Held to be deficient in reason due to their natural condition, they were seen as 'indomitable' incarnations of the violence of masculinity in its natural state. This allegedly explained their resistance to incorporation into the bios politicus, the good life of men.

In order to be able to fight the Apache, frontier settlers rejected conventional tactics of warfare and learned to fight like their enemies, some of the world's most formidable guerrillas. Not only did this include the development of a discipline of the body, but also a bodily rhetoric of honour, aimed at provoking respect and fear in the opponent. Through a reciprocal mirroring of practices of warfare, Apache and colonists learned to mutilate the bodies of the dead; indeed, it was the Spanish who began taking enemy ears as trophies. Mexican fighters returned to their communities bearing Apache testicles and scalps as emblems of their sovereign manhood well into the second half of the nineteenth century.

ORDERING INTENTIONS, SPACE AND SOVEREIGNTY

Agamben sees the concentration camp rather than the prison or the clinic as the locus of banishment of contemporary homines sacri, the exemplary site of the bio-politics of modern sovereign power. His theory is applicable to current 'zones of exception', including sites of offshore penality such as Camp X-Ray at Guantanamo, Cuba.[2] Invoking a Second World War decision regarding the rights of German prisoners of war, the US District of Columbia Court of Appeals stated that it could not 'assert habeas corpus jurisdiction at the behest of an alien held at a military base leased from another nation … outside the sovereignty of the US',[3] in its decision of 11 March 2003. Paradoxically, de jure sovereignty was denied so that de facto sovereignty in its most naked form – the state of exception – could be affirmed. This decision was subsequently overruled by the Supreme Court of the US on 28 June 2004; significantly, legal reasoning hinged on the meaning of 'sovereignty', with the Supreme Court asserting that even though Guantanamo is leased from Cuba, the US has complete jurisdiction and control there.[4]

Ironically, Cuba was an offshore site of penality for New Spain in the 1770s. Apaches taken captive on New Spain's frontier were shipped out in chains to be subjected to the redemptive power of forced labour on plantations or in the homes of the rich (Alonso 1995: 37). Though Agamben hints at it, he does not develop the argument that the concentration camp has colonial antecedents. Yet, as Bauman suggests, the concentration camp had a colonial genealogy:

When somewhat later the technique of summary exclusion from the human race, developed during the conquest of distant lands, was to ricochet on Europe, Aimé Cesaire pointed out ... that what the Christian bourgeois ... could not really forgive Hitler was not the crime of genocide as such (by then it was an acknowledged, legitimate method of dealing with the vexing presence of undersirables), but the crime of having applied to Europe the colonialist actions meant till now to be borne by the Arabs, the coolies of India, Negroes and other aborigines of distant lands [such as the native Americans]. (2002: 289–90; my interpolation)

Indeed, under Spanish colonial rule, indigenous Americans were relocated to settlements called *reducciones* where, through the application of a number of disciplines and technologies of the self, they might be 'reduced' to a semblance of 'civilised life', subjected to the sovereign power of missionaries who exploited their labour, reformed their bodies, raped women and sometimes men, destroyed their sacred places and objects, while inducting them into the Christian community. There the boundary between power over death and power over life became blurred. These reducciones and the camps subsequently set up for Apaches 'at peace' in northern New Spain at the end of the eighteenth century, were the inspiration for the US Indian Reservation – a place where ethnoracialised homines sacri, those who were included in exclusionary terms, could be visibly located.[5]

The genealogy of forms of reterritorialisation evident on the US–Mexico border today lies in these earlier frontier colonialisms. This history puts into question Agamben's assertion that 'if today there is no longer any one clear figure of the sacred man, it is perhaps because we are all virtually homines sacri' (1998: 115). For the Department of Homeland Security,[6] created by the Bush administration in the wake of 11 September, the figures of the Mexican 'illegal', the 'smuggler' and the 'terrorist' (but not that of the law-abiding Anglo citizen) are today's homines sacri, embodiments of the violence 'natural' to men as well as of thievery, illegality and menace. There may no longer be one figure of homo sacer (if indeed, there was ever only one) but that does not mean that all subjects are positioned in the same ways.

Two moments in time, like two surfaces, can seem to turn into one. The Apache Wars ended in 1886. In 2004, low-intensity warfare continues to mark the 2000-mile long US–Mexico border, formed 'during 1845–1853 by conquest, [which] destroyed the rules and power of Mexicano U.S. citizens' (Heyman 1994: 53).

Popular Anglo-American stereotypes of the border today echo those of the past, stressing once again the area's character as a zone of indistinction, filled with homines sacri:

Often U.S. citizens, even those who live in the border region, perceive the area in terms of undocumented migration, drug trafficking, and decaying cities. Some feel they have lost control of 'their' border. One observer summarizes the popular images as follows: 'The border is drowning in the filth of a putrescent Rio Grande aglow with toxic wastes; it is terminally ill with the rampant pox of poverty ... swarms of huddling illegals poise nightly to pour northward across the border to overwhelm American social services and steal jobs from honest workers while free-loading on the largesse of hard-pressed American taxpayers.' (Lorey 1999: 5)

These ideas underlie the thinking of border reinforcers like John Dougherty, author of *Illegals: The Imminent Threat Posed by Our Unsecured US–Mexico Border* (2004). In a recent post to a Navy Seals website, Dougherty wrote, 'Anyone who assumes the Wild West faded into the sunset a hundred years ago hasn't spent much time along the border. Then again, that's probably a good thing, you might live longer.'[7]

Ironically, when deployed by the sovereign state, the very violence which is held to characterise the barbarians and illegals 'provides the occasion and method for founding a property regime' (Blomley 2003: 126). This can be clearly seen in the reterritorialising, 'gatekeeping' operations of the Department of Homeland Security as well as in the increase of gated communities in the border area. These reterritorialisations are centred on a concern with state care for the population's 'security'.

SPATIAL POLITICS IN 'FORTRESS AMERICA':[8]
GATING THE BORDER AND GATING COMMUNITIES

In the US, new forms of governance predicated on security are joining, and to some extent recentring, those based on health in the wake of the rollback of the welfare state, the increase of immigration from periphery to core, and the threat of militant Islamic fundamentalism. Security and sovereignty are tightly interrelated:

Sovereignty is defended by the use of security resources – military might and political power.... Without a working social system, or social order, security could not be maintained, so on top of the defense of sovereignty, the social order must also be secured. (Bislev 2004: 282)

That personal security and the integrity of the social order are outcomes of the successful defence of sovereignty has been one of the more insistent messages of the Bush administration. From the neo-Republican perspective, 'security receives a new meaning.... Security is not only the physical protection of a regime and its associated social order, but also a political function.... Without the state to ensure basic security,' so the story goes, 'there would be no [Western] civilization' (Bislev 2004: 283; my interpolation). In this sense, the bio- and spatial politics of security, like the bio-power of health, is 'a power to foster life or to disallow it', cast in the idiom of 'care of the population'; Foucault's distinction between sovereignty and disciplinary power fades into indistinction.

A tension between a politics of sovereignty, predicated on the security of territorial boundaries, on the one hand, and a neoliberal notion of the economy and free trade that fosters deterritorialisation on the other, characterises US policy and is especially evident in the US–Mexico border area. Hobbes and Agamben are uncannily relevant not just to the politics of securing the northern frontier in the eighteenth and nineteenth centuries, but also to understanding the forms of reterritorialisation that have emerged on Mexico's 2000-mile border with the US today.

Scholars have long recognised the regional particularity of the US–Mexico border area, a zone marked by cultural paradoxes and social contradictions, where complex cultural and economic flows cross the sharp social boundaries among unequal ethnic and class groups. Located on the periphery of two nations, the border is at once shaped by concerns with state sovereignty and by transnational as well as intraregional flows of people, labour, commodities, resources, environmental pollutants, music, art, cultural meanings; some of these transborder flows are legalised while others are criminalised by the US or Mexico or both nations.

Recent scholarship has questioned Anzaldúa's (1987) influential notion of the border as a space of cultural hybridity where ambiguity is tolerated (Huspek 2001; Ortiz 2001; Alonso 2004). The particularities of this area are not only the product of the cultural border crossings highlighted by Anzaldúa but also, of reterritorialisations of borders between and within Mexico and the US, along lines of class, gender, ethnicity, race and nationality. 'This constant challenging and reinforcing of boundaries', Ortiz observes, 'generates the contradictory perception of the border region at once as a linking area and a dividing zone under increasingly militarized intervention' (2001: 101). Likewise, Heyman stresses the importance of defining the border not only in relation to interculturality but also, with reference to 'the massive state apparatuses of the boundary, and especially the overt and hidden force of the U.S. state' (1994: 51).

New procedures are being developed by the US state to monitor human and commodity flows across the border. The model of Operation Gatekeeper, launched in the San Diego/Tijuana area a decade ago, 'to restore integrity and safety' to that part of the border, has since been extended to other 'vulnerable' areas such as Arizona, the most important site of entry by 'illegals' into the US today.[9] On 15 March 2004, the Department of Homeland Security (DHS) launched a multi-agency operation, the Arizona Border Control initiative (ABC),[10] which has perpetuated the militarisation of the border which began in the 1990s (Huspek 2001). According to DHS, the goal of ABC is to 'strengthen the rule of law in the Sonoran Desert' and to 'secure the Southwest border' by 'detecting, disrupting and deterring all cross-border illicit smuggling and trafficking – including people, money, drugs, weapons and other contraband'. Officials have expressed a fear that smugglers may also be bringing in additional contraband – that is, terrorists. The DHS has dedicated more permanent as well as temporary personnel to ABC's 'targeted, intelligence based operations', including new intelligence and surveillance technologies such as unmanned drones, underground sensors, infrared scopes, distributed computing and IDENT, an automated fingerprinting system and database.

That Mexican immigrants are 'trespassers' who pose threats to state and private property is a conception shared by white American border vigilantes and officers of the Immigration and Naturalization Service (INS) and Border Patrol:

Immigrants are said to routinely trudge across privately owned property. Some are purported to have pilfered food and water, and others to have killed household pets. The Border Patrol has blamed immigrants for the increase in wildfires across the borderlands, claiming the fires result from immigrants' careless tending of makeshift campfires. (Huspek 2001: 36)

Though ABC claims to be strengthening the rule of law, in practice it has been tacitly tolerating the illegal activities of white American border vigilantes who are now even accosting Mexican-American citizens. In a recent incident, a rancher from Douglas, Arizona, 'known for armed patrols of his property and roundups of illegal border crossers', warned Mexican-American citizens off state lands, claiming they were 'private property'.[11]

How effective the new and very expensive strategies of border control are in achieving their stated goals remains debatable (Huspek 2001). What is undeniable is that these strategies are increasing surveillance over Mexicans and Mexican-Americans, putting into play forms of subjectification based on new intelligence technologies which divide and classify, individualise and totalise, normalise and criminalise people living in and crossing the border area. Heyman shows that 'criminalization at the border is not only a new technology and policy gone awry, but also ... a modern enterprise of creating and tracking a marked population' classified as 'criminal aliens' (1999: 43). As Huspek notes:

The imagery of illegal immigrants has been implanted in the public consciousness in ways that instil fear, anger and resentment among U.S. citizens. They are said to be disposed toward criminal activity, intent on taking much-needed jobs from citizen workers, or inclined to bilk the coffers of the state's social welfare system. Thus, they and the coyotes who aid them are said to be a threatening force that must be stopped. (2001: 57)

This fear and resentment underlies recent ballot initiatives, such as Arizona's Proposition 200, passed by voters in November 2004, and intended to make proof of citizenship a requirement for voting and receiving public benefits.

Since the 1990s, the criminalisation of 'illegals' has been conflated with the criminalisation of 'smugglers' (Huspek 2001: 57); after 11 September 2001, both of these categories have been metonymically linked to that of the 'terrorist', resulting in a more threatening stigmatisation of Mexicans at the border.[12] As someone who was mistaken for a Mexican terrorist and held at gunpoint by an American border guard while crossing at Columbus,

New Mexico some years ago, I realise how easily anyone who does not look like a white American can be so classified.

The spatial politics of security on the border is not only a state effect. Private sector sites include the gated community as well as shopping malls or office complexes which are loci of dividing, normalising and disciplinary practices which secure the normative social order. Gated communities, particularly prevalent in Arizona[13] as well as in other border states such as Texas and California (Plaut and Plaut 2004), have been linked to spatial segregation along lines of class, ethnicity and race in the literature. According to Low, a social imaginary which views the city as a 'fortress' figures the gated community as a secure space where '"people like us" are defended from "criminals" – strangers of lower socioeconomic class, often people of colour' (Low 2003). In San Antonio, Texas, for example, Low found that youth in gated communities feared Mexican day-labourers whom they considered to be armed and dangerous.[14]

Metro Tucson, where I live, is clearly segregated by class as well as by ethnicity and race. South Tucson is mostly Mexican with a sprinkling of working-class Anglos. Gated communities located in Tucson's exclusive Foothills district to the north are almost exclusively white, spaces where propertied consumers live while poor people of colour, many of them immigrants, enter and leave as 'guest workers' who do the menial maintenance. Their comings and goings are no doubt monitored by video surveillance.

The video surveillance characteristic of these more exclusive gated communities and increasingly, of semi-public and public sites, ranging from churches to nursing homes to shopping malls to streets, 'changes the ways in which power is exercised, modifies emotional experiences in urban space and affects the ways in which "reality" is conceptualised' (Koskela 2000: 243). Electronic surveillance, geographer Koskela argues (somewhat against the grain of current orthodoxy), induces an experience of space as 'a container in which social interaction takes place', replacing informal social control mechanisms and making space 'more defended' or 'defensible' (2000: 243).

There is an ongoing exchange of knowledge between state and private sector regarding technologies of security. In private as well as in public areas, the imagery of spatial containment which gives space an inside and an outside as well as a set of proper contents is reinforced in ways that are vital to the politics of sovereignty. 'Sovereignty is unthinkable without an "outside"; it is inconceivable in any form but a localised entity' (Bauman 2002: 288). The surveillance technologies used to create home spaces of class, ethnic and racial privilege by the private sector are used by the US state to create the homeland, to control access to national territory and to track the unwanted activity of undesirables inside its borders.

Living on the US–Mexico border it has become hard for me not to think of the US as a gated nation, putatively contained and protected by the state. Like the gated community, the border is the site of dividing, normalising and disciplinary practices, which situate the white and propertied very differently from the non-white and property-less in relation to 'Western civilization' as well as to 'the rule of law' which ensures the 'civility' of society.

But the layers of fortification of the security regime do not end there: they are replicated on a larger scale in the national missile defence system and on a smaller scale in SUV's or in the increasingly fortified ideal of a normative masculinity organised around the capacity for violence. The upper bodies of the ever-popular GI Joe action figures began to 'bulk up' in the 1980s in response to national anxieties about 'inadequate masculinity' in the wake of the North American defeat in Vietnam (Ehrenreich 2002); they have become steadily bulkier. Athletes taking steroids to increase muscle mass are beginning to look like action figures. Even the image of President George Bush that is presented to the public by Republican spin doctors (not to mention that of California governor, Arnold Schwarzenegger) emulates this ideal of a powerfully muscled, 'hot' masculine body.[15] Indeed KB toys now sells a 12-inch George W. Bush 'Elite Force Aviator' action figure.[16] Contemporary agents of the US Border Patrol and other enforcement agencies in the border area today also have fortified bodies. In addition to being armed, they are trained to develop an aggressive stance and a swaggering walk, and asked to grow large moustaches to mask facial expressiveness (Thomas 2004). These agents, like the colonial frontier warriors I discussed earlier, have been subjected to training in a masculinity predicated on the capacity for violence, to an embodied semiotics which gives meaning to, even as it transforms the forces of, the body.

Some of these technologies of homeland, community and personal security that interweave knowledge, space and power are relatively unobtrusive – the visibility of public video cameras is downplayed so as to preclude the Orwellian experience of 'Big Brother is watching'.

In the past buildings representing power and authority were imposing and showy, often built on high, clearly visible sites, and their entrances were emphasised. By contrast, in contemporary architecture, power is hidden and unnoticeable and authority is represented not through its visibility but rather through its invisibility. (Koskela 2000: 249)

This invisibility is echoed by the secrecy that is integral to the security regime. A sign of the state of exception, secrecy is both an effect and a condition of sovereignty.

The security regime's efficacy in limiting risk and threat is debatable: fire engines have difficultly getting into gated communities; operations on the border do not seem to have significantly diminished the flow of illegal immigrants; the invasion of Iraq has made the world a more dangerous place. In this sense it is important to distinguish between the imagery of spatial containment and its objectification: on the border, distinctions such as inside/outside are continually rendered indistinct in practice only to be reaffirmed as binaries yet again.

The security regime has succeeded in exacerbating what Michael Moore calls 'a culture of fear' that cannot be palliated merely by a rationality of risk but is increasingly being eased by the ritualisations of faith. Many of the technologies and performances of security seem to be located in a zone of indistinction between reason and faith. How else can we account for the rush to buy gas masks, the exhaustion of duct tape and plastic sheeting supplies in much of the country after citizens were given instructions for making dwellings more impenetrable containers by the DHS, whose system of colour-coded levels of threat only induces more fear and confusion. The compulsion to gather information is no longer simply dictated by instrumental rationality but also by the obsessiveness of ritualisation; a significant portion of the overwhelming amount of data collected by the multitude of surveillance and tracking technologies simply remains uninterpreted.

The border is being remade into the frontier. Beyond the fortresses of 'civility' lie the spaces of stereotypical frontier chaos, proper to homines sacri. This understanding of the border as a frontier – as contested space where US sovereignty is challenged and must be defended – is becoming more and more generalised, a topic of discussion on numerous patriotic and vigilante websites.

'HOMO SACER' AND 'SELF/OTHER': GENDERING SOVEREIGNTY

The concept of homo sacer developed by Agamben, is a useful corrective to the anthropological notion of 'the Other'. Much writing on power and inequality has been constrained by an opposition of 'Self' and 'Other', where the 'Other' is above all a category for those considered to be 'culturally different' from the so called Western self. Yet the reduction of the Apache was primarily a political project, as is the deportation of Mexican illegals today; hypostasised difference seems to be not only an issue of culture but also one of power. By putting the stress on the political character of the sovereign ban that locates some categories of persons outside the polis, rather than on reified cultural difference, the concept of homo sacer captures that which 'the Other' sidelines.

Though Agamben is writing primarily about the development of the state in the West, the concepts of homo sacer and the sovereign can be mapped onto relations between different categories of persons, institutions, spatialisations and so on. At first glance, homo sacer appears to be the opposite of the sovereign. According to Agamben, 'the sovereign and homo sacer represent two symmetrical figures that have the same structure and are correlative: the sovereign is the one with respect to whom all men are potentially homo sacer and homo sacer is the one with respect to whom all men act as sovereigns' (1998: 84) These categories require each other and, hence, are defined through an internal relation which makes neither prior to the other. This generates a paradox: the sovereign can become the 'wolf-man', the protector, the tyrant (1998: 108).

Agamben's discussion of the relation between the sovereign and homo sacer recalls the feminist understanding of Self and Other first formulated by Simone de Beauvoir in her gendered rereading of Hegel's dialectic between Master and Slave. For de Beauvoir, Self and Other are not predefined terms but rather products of their very relationship. Throughout Western history, de Beauvoir argues, 'Woman' has been deemed to be 'Man's Other', the object via which 'Man' can construct himself as a sovereign subject. Within patriarchal ideology, Woman has been represented as immanence, as animality, as body, as zoe and Man as transcendence, as humanity, as mind, as he who is capable of political life, actively shaping rather than merely reproducing zoe. What does this imply for Agamben's theory? How have normative forms of gender and sexuality been central to the construction of sovereign power?

Agamben notes that 'In the classical world ... simple natural life is excluded from the polis in the strict sense, and remains confined – as merely reproductive life – to the sphere of the *oikos*, "home"'(1998: 2). Gatens has argued that 'the body politic men give birth to assumes both the appropriation and the disavowal of woman's ability to reproduce life' (1996: 55). One of the blind spots in Agamben's work is that he does not recognise that the natural life which is the precondition for the polis is not only represented by homo sacer, the embodiment of outlaw masculinity, but also by Woman. The opposition between oikos and polis is gendered.

'The political significance of the problem of sex is due to the fact that sex is located at the point of intersection of the body and the control of the population' (Foucault 1984: 67). 'Bare life' is not only identified with violence as Agamben insists, but also with sexuality and reproduction. Many nations have distinguished between men's and women's relationships to life and hence to the perpetuation of the imagined community. Men's role in the reproduction of the polity has frequently been linked to their willingness to die and their capacity to kill for the nation. By contrast, women's generative capacities, rights and roles have been regulated by nation states so as to produce suitably socialised citizens and workers.

The regulation of sexuality and reproduction continues to be a central concern of sovereign power in Fortress America. To paraphrase Bislev's remarks, quoted earlier in this chapter, security is a political function of the state which entails not only the protection of a regime but also of its associated social order. Putting the house and homeland 'in order' has placed a premium on 'moral values' which affirm the normativity of heterosexual, reproductive sexuality. State interventions are placing new restrictions on the everyday sexual and reproductive lives of women and challenging their control over their own bodies. A recent *Newsweek* column warns: 'Not since Margaret Sanger's crusade to legalise birth control in the 1920s has family planning come under such assault.' Pharmacists are exercising the right conferred on them by the profession's code of ethics to refuse to fill birth control prescriptions if it is against their moral beliefs.[17] By the end of 2004, Bush is expected to have signed the 'Hyde-Weldon Abortion Non-

Discrimination Act' into law. This would allow insurance companies to opt out of covering abortion services, and doctors and hospitals to refuse to provide such services.[18] Significantly, as Joanna Stone notes, figurations of the 'undocumented woman' differ from those of the 'undocumented man': if the Mexican man is the 'outlaw', the Mexican woman is the pregnant ethnoracial Other, crossing the border in order to have an alien baby on US soil (Stone, personal communication).

The politics of sovereignty and security frequently stigmatise homosexuals. For example, in Cuba, the figure of the '*pajaro*' or feminised male homosexual is regarded as the epitome of the counter-revolutionary; such men were made scapegoats during the Mariel boatlift, blamed for the whole debacle and subjected to collective 'acts of repudiation'. *Patria o muerte! Venceremos!*, 'The Homeland or Death! We will prevail!' (my translation). This familiar Cuban rallying cry, coined by Fidel in 1960, indicates that what is exalted in the figure of the heroic *Revolucionario* is the capacity to kill and die in the name of the nation. The stigma associated with the figure of the pajaro is linked to his purportedly diminished virility, and hence his lessened capacity to kill or die. If the pajaro lacks killing power, the lesbian lacks what allegedly defines the feminine, those supposedly 'natural' instincts to serve as mates and mothers to men.

Gayness more than lesbianism has been problematised in the US military; gay men are figured as 'pansies' who might threaten the homosocial but heterosexual masculinity of the American ideal of the soldier and diminish his lethal capacity. Opposition to gay marriage has become a national issue.

Significantly, Agamben cites the Marquis de Sade's statement, 'there is no man ... who does not want to be a despot when he has an erection' (1998: 135) in order to argue for the primacy of sexuality, and hence bio-power, in modernity. But he fails to note that de Sade's statement locates men and women rather differently. Men as subjects are encouraged to identify with sovereign power, with Leviathan, which for Hobbes is:

... a commonwealth, or state ... which is but an artificial man; though of greater stature and strength than the natural, for whose protection and defence it was intended; and in which the sovereignty is an artificial soul, giving life and motion to the whole body. (Hobbes 2004: xxxviii:)

Sovereign power is constructed *against* outlaw masculinities. But it is constituted *through* domesticated femininity and the objectification of women. While outlaw men are naturalised, outlaw women, including lesbians and all those who refuse motherhood, are deemed to be 'unnatural'. Paradoxically, forms of domesticated or reproductive femininity that have been deemed to be 'natural' are located in the oikos, that zone of indistinction within the political community.

Performances of sovereign power are endlessly reiterated because phallic masculinity itself is a fragile achievement, one ultimately dependent on the representation of femininity as 'lack' and of women as objects. A brief comparison of the politics of masculinity in the Trujillo era (1930–61) in the Dominican Republic and under the Bush administration in the US will illustrate this dimension of the gendered politics of sovereign power.

Historian Robin Derby writes that in the era of the military dictator, Rafael Trujillo, 'public space was a hall of mirrors all of which reflected Trujillo in one of his many costumes: Trujillo the statesman in jacket and tie, the caudillo on horseback, or the army general in full military brass with his distinctive Napoleonic chapeau' (2003: 5). But why did Trujillo make an exhibition of himself? How did a dictator who relied on the torture and imprisonment of those who opposed him make 'many marginal rural and urban poor feel proud to be Dominicans' (Derby 2003)?

Krohn-Hansen (this volume) points out that many peasants in the rural community he studies saw Trujillo as a moderniser who brought civilisation, development and integration into the nation-state to the countryside. He notes also that dictators like Trujillo present themselves as all-powerful, as the source and embodiment of the state. Trujillo's political success can partly be attributed to the style of rule which he personified, a 'populist style based upon vernacular images of masculinity' (Derby 2003: 3). Today, Trujillo has come to be regarded in the Dominican Republic as the embodiment of a now-dominant figuration of masculinity, the 'Dominican *tíguere*' or tiger (Krohn-Hansen 1996: 132, n. 30), developed by working-class urban men during his dictatorship.[19]

Trujillo's slogan, 'My best friends are the men of work' was not simply 'propaganda' according to Krohn-Hansen (this volume). In mirroring vernacular idioms and images of masculinity, Trujillo made it possible for lower-class, non-white, urban and rural men to identify with him; they could become tígueres too. This identification enabled them to become bearers of the sovereignty of the national political community. Like the King and Leviathan, Trujillo came to have at least two bodies – a 'natural body' and an 'artificial' or 'political body'. Trujillo constructed his 'political body' through the reciprocal mirroring of masculinity which linked him to men of the popular classes.

Personifications of gendered power have been an integral part of the modernity of Latin American states, and are not usefully viewed as vestiges of a 'traditional' past. Indeed, they are an important part of staging sovereignty in the contemporary US, where media discussions of Bush's 'neo-macho' personification of the Texas cowboy are legion (e.g. Baard 2004; Lutz 2002; Brooks 2003; Goldstein 2003a, 2003b). By wearing jeans set off by a large belt buckle, cowboy boots that show signs of wear and a white Stetson hat, and adopting a Clint Eastwood squint and swaggering Texas walk, Bush embodies the image of the Western cowboy:

He guns his rhetoric with frontier lingo, saying that he'll 'ride herd' over ornery Middle Eastern governments and 'smoke out' enemies in wild mountain passes. He brands Saddam Hussein's an 'outlaw regime' and took the vanquished dictator's gun as a trophy. As for Osama bin Laden, Bush declared 'I want justice. And there's an old poster out West, I recall, that says, "Wanted: Dead or Alive"'. (Baard 2004)

Media commentators note that, in the eyes of most Americans, Bush is empowered by the cowboy image, since the myth of the frontier has played a key part in 'rough and ready' American nationalism since Teddy Roosevelt. Ironically, the genealogy of the Western cowboy goes back to the Mexican frontier *vaquero*. Much cowboy lingo in fact consists of loan words and phrases taken from Spanish; but this is not widely acknowledged.

The persona of the cowboy is split into two, signified by the wearing of a white versus black hat. The black-hatted cowboy (whose downward-tilted hat hoods his eyes) is an outlaw, a force of chaos and barbarity on the frontier. The white-hatted cowboy (whose hat is tilted neither too far up nor too far down) is a hero, a force of order and civilisation. In popular lore and Hollywood movies, the white-hatted cowboy sometimes has to become like the black-hatted cowboy in order to win the gun battle, but he is always on the side of justice (which is not necessarily that of the law). Bush, who always wears a white hat at just the right angle, is widely viewed by Americans as the Western cowboy, a strong and resolute man of action who has the will and the 'balls' to defeat terrorists, but who is civilised enough to watch his manners around the ladies, and law-abiding enough to build political and social order where only the chaos of the state of nature reigns.[20]

Widely perceived as a 'regular guy', Bush mirrors vernacular idioms of masculinity making it possible for white men – some of whom are resentful in the wake of feminism, while others feel disempowered by uncertain economic circumstances – to identify with him and his power. By doing so, they too become bearers of national sovereignty, white-hatted cowboys who will win the 'war on terrorism' (as cowboys always do) (see Lutz 2002).

Significantly, media commentators have begun to call the Republicans the 'Daddy party', which 'represents patriarchal values of strength and order', and Democrats the 'Mommy party' (Goldstein 2003b). The contest between Bush and Kerry was dubbed the 'testosterone election' and success in the debates, according to the media, would hinge on whom the audience considered 'the most macho man'. As Joanna Stone (2004) argues, in the debates, masculinity was enacted somewhat differently by each candidate. The contest came down to the relative value of different masculine styles in a post-11 September world: the rough and ready cowboy, America's Everyman, versus the formal statesman of the East Coast establishment who 'knows better'. In the end, the cowboy was more reassuring to a fearful nation than the statesman; moreover, if conservative interests supported Bush's policies, working-class white men supported Bush because they could identify with him and hence feel personally empowered.

Stagings of masculine power have been a component in the systematic use of violence against enemies, a part of the 'state of exception'. Indeed, violence itself is sexualised and gendered. That the genitals are privileged sites of torture has now been reiterated to the world through the photographs of American abuse of Iraqi prisoners. Significantly, contemporary visual technologies have made the space of punishment once again a space of spectacle in which sexual humiliation, rape and the threat of castration are deployed to reduce persons to mere lack.

A recent report by the national Immigrant and Refugee Rights network states that 'Heightened military and law enforcement along the U.S.–Mexico border have escalated human rights abuses of migrants and people of color in the Southwest' (Cho 2001). For women this has meant sexual molestation and rape; Falcon (2001) discusses a number of cases of this in which the perpetrators were INS or Border Patrol officers. Though most of the victims were women, some were men. The same gendered and sexualised dynamics of sovereign power are evident in the iconography of the 'war on terror'. A flyer circulating in New York in November 2001 depicted Osama bin Laden being sodomised by the World Trade Center with the caption, 'You like skyscrapers, bitch?' (Ehrenreich 2002).

HISTORICISING SOVEREIGNTY: COLONIAL AND POSTCOLONIAL PROJECTS

Like the other contributors to this volume, I stress that anthropologists must historicise sovereignty rather than make it a part of the ontology of the state as Agamben does. State sovereignty is a contested, and not always successful, political project (Alonso 1995), rather than a modern manifestation of an a-historical foundational logic. Indeed, Hansen and Stepputat (2005) enjoin us to question 'the obviousness of the link between sovereignty and the state' and to pay attention to how this link is actually produced in different societies.

Forms of colonial sovereignty, Hansen and Stepputat note, had decisive implications for postcolonial state formation. 'The formation of national identity is, in part, a meditation on the meanings and significance of land as property' (Blomley 2003: 122). Lands inhabited by transhumant indigenous groups on New Spain's northern frontier were considered virgin and were recast as 'royal patrimony'. After Mexican independence, as Elizabeth Ferry argues, lands, resources and objects previously categorised as royal patrimony became redefined as 'national patrimony': the state became the custodian of the territory and heritage which now defined the nation (Ferry 2005).

After the revolution of 1910–20, lands that were not legally titled continued to be categorised as national patrimony. This conflation of polis and property underlay the legal basis for the formation of the *ejido* system, the cornerstone of the post-revolutionary agrarian reform, in which land rights were to be vested in rural communities which would give usufruct rights to male heads of families. Revolutionary ideologists saw the ejido as the modern expression of ancient indigenous forms of land tenure such as the Aztec *calpullis*. They approved of the Spanish colonial paternalism which had given Indians usufruct but not property rights to land, since indigenous people supposedly lacked the reason requisite for buying and selling (Nugent and Alonso 1994). Indeed, as Baitenmann writes in her chapter in this volume, 'the agrarian reform was intended to be a school or training ground' for those whom agrarian engineers considered to be 'unproductive Indians'. Indians, then, continued to be situated on the internal frontiers of the nation, where they were pronounced to be in need of the integration and development that would be encouraged by the agrarian reform and its civilising practices. These civilising practices fostered stable families. Agrarian reform, as Baitenmann demonstrates, was a deeply gendered process which empowered adult men, custodians of the family patrimony, rather than adult women, who could only become heads of family when there was no living male spouse.

Hansen and Stepputat point to an important difference between metropolitan and colonial forms of sovereignty:

Colonial forms of sovereignty were always more fragmented and complex, less concerned with legitimizing their own presence and more excessively violent than their European forms. This difference was intimately tied to pragmatic reliance on local, indigenous forms of rule, to distinctions between Christian and non-Christian subjects, and to notions of white racial superiority. As importantly, European states never aimed at governing the colonial territories with the same uniformity and intensity as was applied to their own populations. The emphasis was less on forging consent and the creation of a nation-people and more on securing obedience through performances of sovereign power. (Hansen and Stepputat 2005: 4)

As a result, postcolonial states 'became marked by multiple, overlapping layered and contending forms of sovereignty', which plunged many of them into chronic warfare and crisis.

Postcolonial states in Latin America have been more liable to crises than metropolitan states. Their differential responses to North American imperialism on the one hand, and to their colonial legacies on the other, are two factors shaping the forms of sovereignty they have institutionalised. As I argue in Alonso (2005), state formation in post-revolutionary Mexico had to contend with the imperial designs of the United States, with the colonial legacy of ethnoracial inequality, and with the multiple sovereign bodies that characterised a country that had just been through a decade of social revolution (1910–20). In contrast to Guatemala and Peru, two other countries with large indigenous populations which did not undergo successful popular revolutions, Mexico developed a distinct and much more stable form of popular sovereignty.

According to the Mexican Constitution of 1917, Article 39, 'National sovereignty resides essentially and originally in *el pueblo*. All public power originates in the people and is instituted for their benefit' (my translation). But in a country which was not yet a nation, who were the people to become?

For the architects of post-revolutionary nationalism, the sovereign popular subject was to be the *mestizo*, conceived as the ideal blend of the Spanish and Indian. On the one hand, this mythohistory of *mestizaje* emerged as a challenge to North American imperial ambitions, which rested on a notion of Mexicans as a 'mongrel race', purportedly incapable of governing themselves. Mestizo nationalism and pan-Americanism envisioned a Mexico

and a Latin America that would play a significant role in world history and
be something other than 'the backyard' of the United States. On the other
hand, the revolution had made the disjunction between state and people
only too clear. Lacking a monopoly of force, the new state, in the name of
the sovereign pueblo, tried to claim a monopoly on the authority to create
social order out of revolutionary chaos and violence. Contending sovereign
bodies were to be unified into one nation, creating a homogeneous citizenry
out of a divided multitude. State power was legitimated by reference to the
need for a neutral arbitrator to rein in contending sovereignties and keep
the differences among the people from exploding into revolution once again;
only the state had the ability to transcend social divisions and represent the
indivisible will of the imagined national mestizo community. The figure of the
mestizo represented the transformation of heterogeneity into homogeneity,
the bridge between the past and the future, the common origin point for the
nation. The Indian element in the mestizo was to ground the nation's claim
to territory, providing a continuity of blood, and rooting the nation's history
in that of ancient, pre-colonial civilisations, whose art and mythology were
praised as expressions of national spirit. By contrast, the European element
was to guarantee the nation's future through its purportedly greater capacity
for enlightened scientific knowledge (Alonso 2004).

Though mestizo nationalism has been deservedly criticised for valuing
the Indian and Spanish components of the mix in unequal terms, we need
to recognise that in its time and place it was a relatively progressive project.
Indigenous people in Mexico have been subject to political marginalisation
and structural inequality, as well as state violence. But their situation has
been immeasurably better than that of the Maya in Guatemala (see Stølen,
this volume), where the elite continues to believe that Indians need to be
fully conquered in order for the nation to develop, a belief that has fuelled the
intensity and scale of violence against the Maya (Alonso 1994). It has also
been better than that of the indigenous people of Peru, whose misery made
a deep impression on me when I lived in Lima as a child.

Can 'modern discourses of popular or democratic sovereignty be anything
other than a barely disguised form of absolutism'? (Hunt and Wickham
1994: 61). Agamben's political ontology enjoins us to answer this question
in the negative. But, if approached from a historical rather than ontological
perspective, this question requires a different, more nuanced and perhaps more
paradoxical answer: 'Yes and no'. The Mexican vision of popular sovereignty,
codified in the Constitution of 1917, aimed to ground itself more in the power
over life than in the power over death. Mexican governments have abrogated
the ideal order of national politics that these laws set up. Nevertheless, as
Krohn-Hansen argues in his chapter, there are significant differences in state
formation among countries in the South. Whereas the state of exception has
become the norm in Guatemala and Peru, it is not the norm in Mexico. Law
and absolutism cannot be seen naively as mere opposites, but neither can
one be reduced to the other. 'Law is not a unitary phenomenon', as Hunt

and Wickham stress; instead it is 'a complex of practices, discourses and institutions' (1994: 39).

CONCLUSION

State projects of sovereignty are also projects of subjectification which entail dividing practices, forms of classification and totalising procedures. In this chapter, I show how the territorial politics of sovereignty at the US–Mexico border totalises the imagined community of 'Americans' and individualises subjects through a binary logic of classification which situates persons as 'citizens' or 'illegals', 'property owners' or 'trespassers', 'people like us' versus 'criminals', 'smugglers', 'terrorists' or even 'invaders', the homines sacri identified with uses of violence not legitimated by the state. This logic contrasts the mothers of Americans with the Mexican bearers of alien babies who unfairly consume public benefits. Stigmatised versus normalised categories of persons are racialised in different ways according to their degree of 'brownness' or 'whiteness', signified not only by phenotypical markers but also by signs of class and lifestyle. I stress that this politics has colonial roots and show how subjectification, violence and property have been interlinked in the conquest of the northern frontier and in the militarisation of today's border area.

Rather than discard the juridico-institutional model of power, Agamben suggests that scholars might identify its points of intersection with the biopolitical model (1998: 6). I have tried to bring out some points of intersection in the examples I have used, showing how categories of subjectification such as 'gente de razon' or 'barbáros', 'illegals' and 'citizens' are predicated on a juridical and territorial logic, as well as in my analysis of the spatial politics of security.

In 'Fortress America', governance is increasingly organised around security as a form of state care of the population and the individual. Significantly, there has been an accompanying shift in bio-politics. Health emerges as salient state concern when tied to national security, as exemplified by government support for the development of an anthrax vaccine or for research into bioterrorism. Increased state regulation of sexuality is part of securing the social order. Notions of sovereign space as a defended container (tacitly female) are echoed by images of the fortified body as a container for the sovereign self (tacitly male). Such images of the body are especially visible in the neo-macho norm or in medical discourse, which figures many corporeal processes through military metaphors.

New technologies of surveillance and intelligence can be viewed as supplements which extend and reinforce the body's defensive and offensive capacites. Visual surveillance supplements the limitations of the eye in increasingly ambitious ways; a secret plan to set up a new $9.5 billion 'spy satellite system' that would take photographs during daylight hours and in clear weather was uncovered by the *New York Times* (Jehl 2004). These new forms of 'the gaze' continue to be gendered and sexualised as evinced in the rise of 'video voyeurism', in which the men who monitor the images focus on attractive women and engage in a form of virtual stalking (Koskela 2000).

Overall, as the boundary between 'police' and 'politics' becomes more indistinct, 'the *police* ... becomes *politics*, and the care of life coincides with the fight against the enemy' (Agamben 1998: 147). Foucault's distinction between a sovereign power which inscribes the surfaces of the body, and a disciplinary power which transforms its forces, is not useful in understanding these changes in bio-power.

Foucault draws a contrast between the ideal figure of the soldier in the early seventeenth century, a figure marked by a 'bodily rhetoric of honour', with that of the soldier in the late eighteenth century, 'something that can be made out of a formless clay' into a killing machine (Foucault 1979: 135–36). He argues that the historical transition from pre-modern sovereign power to modern disciplinary power entailed a change in the scale, modality and goal of control over the body: 'the object of the control ... was no longer ... the language of the body, but the economy, the efficiency of movements, their internal organisation, constraint bears upon the forces rather than upon the signs' (1979: 137). The examples I have used put into question such a distinction and the concept of the body that underlies it.

In *The Second Sex*, de Beauvoir affirms that the body is not 'a thing but a situation ... the instrument of our grasp upon the world' (1974: 38). Reading somewhat against the grain of de Beauvoir's text, I interpret this as implying that the active capacities of bodies are always already caught up in history, social relations and semiosis. Matter and signification are conjoined in ways that transcend Cartesian dualism.

However, the shortcomings of Foucault's work by no means make him irrelevant. There is a productive tension between Agamben's unitary vision of power and Foucault's stress on its dispersal. Agamben's homogenising assertion that 'today we are all homo sacer' is countered by Foucault's demonstration that subjectification is a product of dividing, classifying and normalising practices which situate categories of persons in relation to power in rather different ways.

Agamben provides a useful if partial critique of Foucault's opposition between sovereign and disciplinary power. What Agamben does not point out, however, is that the inclusionary exclusion of zoe in bios politicus has been a deeply gendered and sexualised process. The opposition of oikos and polis is part of this process, as is the political and economic marginalisation of women, and of men who are outlaws due to their 'illegal status', ethnicity, race, sexual orientation or class position.

The twentieth century's state-centred, global order of violence is being undermined in the new millennium by 'rogue' forms of violence which, though organised into flexible, decentred networks, have demonstrated their international reach. Territorial forms of political sovereignty are in tension with supra- and sub-national processes of economic integration and cultural flows which promote gobalisation on the one hand, and regionalism on the other. Yet these tensions have not made the territorial state irrelevant; instead they have engendered processes of reterritorialisation and subjectification. Arguably, the more fragile a state's hold on power, the more insistently it stages its 'artificial body', what we might call its sovereign 'mask' (cf. Abrams 1988).

NOTES

1. This chapter is based on a plenary lecture presented at the Society for Cultural Anthropology 2004 Spring Conference, Portland, Oregon; thanks to Bruce Grant and Lisa Rofel for the invitation. I thank Christian Krohn-Hansen, Knut Nustad, David Killick, Jennifer Jo Thompson, Joanna Stone, Hannes Gerhardt, Andrea Sturzen and Leesa Lana for their helpful comments on the text.
2. However, it should not be applied uncritically to refugee camps, since, as Stølen demonstrates in her chapter in this volume, camps can be sites of political learning and mobilisation for refugees.
3. US DC Court of Appeals, AL Odah Khaled A.F. v USA. District of Columbia Circuit Court decision no. 02-5252, 11 March 2003; http://caselaw.lp.findlaw.com/scripts/getcase.pl?navby=case&court=dc&no=02-5251, accessed 4 December 2004.
4. President Bush contends that he has the sole authority to designate a person as an 'enemy combatant' whether or not he/she is a US citizen (as in the case of José Padilla) and in this sense declares a 'state of exception' to citizens' constitutional rights (Elsea 2004).
5. The paradoxical status of Indian reservations, as J.J. Thompson notes, is a telling example of a 'state of exception' within the US border:

   > Indian Tribes possess a nation-within-a-nation status. They are recognized as sovereign nations, with autonomy for self-government (except in cases were rights were negotiated away in treaties); however, Congress continues to possess the overriding power to limit tribal sovereignty as it sees fit. For example, Public Law 280, passed in 1953, established the right for several states to criminal and legal jurisdiction on Indian Reservations, because it was argued that tribes did not have the resources to fully fulfill criminal and legal responsibilities. (personal communication; see AIPC, 2002)

6. http://www.whitehouse.gov/homeland/, accessed 12 December 2004.
7. As posted on a Navy Seals site, http://www.navyseals.com/community/articles/article.cfm?id=2904, accessed 12 December 2004.
8. 'Fortress America' was first used as the title on a 1986 Milton-Bradley board game which:

   > ... depicts an alternate near future in which all of the world attacks and invades the continental United States. From the west arrive hordes of Asian foes; from the south arrives a union of South American countries through Mexico, and from the east lands legions of Soviets who have taken over all of Europe. America besieged has to rely on the remaining ground and air forces left in the country along with partisan uprisings to defend mom's apple pie. (http://www.boardgamegeek.com/game/99, accessed 8 December 2004)

   It has since become the title of a number of books concerned with either US national politics or gated communities, as well as of a new computer game.
9. US Department of Justice, INS Fact Sheet, 'Operation Gatekeeper: New Resources, Enhanced Results', http://uscis.gov/graphics/publicaffairs/factsheets/opgatefs.htm, accessed 10 December 2004.

10. 'New Approach to Border Security Shows Results in just Six Months', Office of the Press Secretary, Department of Homeland Security, 21 September 2004; http://www.dhs.gov/dhspublic/display?content=3358, accessed 4 December 2004.

11. *The Arizona Daily Star*, Tucson Region section, 30 November 2004.

12. For example, 'primeval patriot' posted an online news article on the danger of terrorists crossing into the US through the SW border on 14 November 2004; http://209.157.64.200/focus/f-news/1279916/posts, accessed 10 December 2004.

13. By 1999, 12 per cent of the population of Metro Phoenix or 320,000 persons were living in 641 gated communities according to a study by K. Frantz (see Webster et al. 2002).

14. There is some debate in the literature on the relationship between ethnic and racial segregation and gated communities. Plaut and Plaut (2004) point out that the 2001 American Housing Survey results suggest that minorities also live in gated communities; however this survey had no information as to whether gated communities were internally integrated along racial lines. See also Kirby (2003); http://216.239.57.104/search?q=cache:Fgp1SP5AB2MJ:www.hicsocial.org/Social2003Proceedings/Andrew%2520Kirby.pdf+andrew+kirby+arizona+state+university+&hl=en, accessed December 2004.

15. George Bush's self-presentation as a 'neo-macho' has been a topic of extensive media coverage and commentary. For example, the *Village Voice* (Goldstein 2003a) published a detailed analysis of how the aviator suit he wore when landing on an aircraft carrier while visiting American troops assigned to Iraq in May 2003, enhanced both his masculinity and his 'hotness', literally demonstrating that he has 'balls'.

16. http://www.kbtoys.com/genProduct.html/PID/2431939/ctid/17?_ts=y&ls=toys&_e=41b78&_v=41B786EA7hgCaA9AC66148C0&_ts=y, accessed 8 December 2004.

17. Eleanor Clift, 'At Risk', *Newsweek On Line*; http://www.msnbc.msn.com/id/6645204/site/newsweek/, accessed 5 December 2004.

18. Jill McGivering, 'Abortion Battle Rages On in US', BBC News Online, http://news.bbc.co.uk/2/hi/americas/4067103.stm, accessed 5 December 2004.

19. The *tiguere* is a type, Krohn-Hansen writes, who is a 'survivor in his environment', 'both astute and socially intelligent; both courageous and smart; both cunning and convincing' (1996: 109). Not surprisingly, the power of the tíguere is morally ambiguous (1996: 115–16). Indeed, the Dominican national and masculine ideal can be interpreted as a figuration of the paradoxical relation of sovereign and wolf man.

20. Websites which portray Bush as the white-hatted cowboy include: 'My Heroes Have Always Been Cowboys', http://www.catsprn.com/cowboys.htm, accessed 10 December 2004; see Lutz (2002).

REFERENCES

Abrams, P., 1988. 'Notes on the Difficulty of Studying the State', *Journal of Historical Sociology*, 1(1): 58–89.

Agamben, G., 1998. *Homo Sacer.* Stanford, CA: Stanford University Press.

AIPC (American Indian Policy Center), 2002. *American Indian Tribal Sovereignty Primer*, http://www.airpi.org/pubs/indinsov.html, accessed 9 December 2004.

Alonso, A.M., 1995. *Thread of Blood: Colonialism, Revolution and Gender on Mexico's Northern Frontier.* Tucson, AZ: University of Arizona Press.

Alonso, A.M., 2004. 'Conforming Disconformity: "*Mestizaje*," Hybridity and the Aesthetics of Mexican Nationalism', *Cultural Anthropology*, 19(4): 459–90.

Alonso, A.M., 2005. 'Territorializing the Nation and Integrating the Indian: "*Mestizaje*" in Mexican Official Discourses and Public Culture', in T.B. Hansen and F. Stepputat, eds, *Sovereign Bodies*. Princeton, NJ: Princeton University Press.

Anzaldúa, G., 1987. *Borderlands/La Frontera*. San Francisco, CA: Spinsters/Aunt Lutte.

Baard, E., 2004. 'George W. Bush Ain't No Cowboy', *The Village Voice*, 28 September, http://www.villagevoice.com/issues/0439/baard.php, accessed 12 December 2004.

Bauman, Z., 2002. 'The Fate of Humanity in the Post-Trinitarian World', *Journal of Human Rights*, 1(3): 283–303.

Bislev, S., 2004. 'Globalization, State Transformation, and Public Security', *International Political Science Review*, 25(3): 281–96.

Blomley, N., 2003. 'Law, Property, and the Geography of Violence: The Frontier, the Survey, and the Grid', *Annals of the Association of American Geographers*, 93(1): 121–41.

Brady, M.P., 2000. 'Scaling the West Differently', *Western American Literature*, 35(1): 97–104.

Brooks, R., 2003. 'The Character Myth', *The Nation*, 29 December.

Cho, E., ed., 2001. *From the Borderline to the Colorline: A Report on Anti-Immigrant Racism in the United States*. Oakland, CA: National Network for Immigrant and Refugee Rights. Executive summary at http://www.nnirr.org/projects/border_color.html, accessed 12 December 2004.

de Beauvoir, S., 1974 [1952]. *The Second Sex*. New York: Vintage Books.

Derby, R., 2003. 'The Dictator's Seduction: The Moral Economy of Domination During the Trujillo Regime in the Dominican Republic', paper presented at the American Association for Anthropology Annual Meetings, Chicago, IL.

Dougherty, J.E., 2004. *Illegals: The Imminent Threat Posed by Our Unsecured US–Mexico Border*. Nashville, TN: Thomas Nelson.

Ehrenreich, N., 2002. 'Masculinity and American Militarism', *Tikkun*, Nov./Dec., http://www.tikkun.org/magazine/index.cfm/action/tikkun/issue/tik0211/article/021113d.html, accessed 6 December 2004.

Elsea, J.K., 2004. 'Detention of American Citizens as Enemy Combatants', *CRS Report for Congress*, http://wttpww.fas.org/irp/crs/RL31724.pdf, accessed 9 December 2004.

Falcon, S., 2001. 'Rape as a Weapon of War: Advancing Human Rights for Women at the US–Mexico Border', *Social Justice*, 28(2): 31–51.

Ferry, E., 2005. *Not Ours Alone: Patrimony, Value and Collectivity in Contemporary Mexico*. New York: Columbia University Press.

Foucault, M., 1979. *Discipline and Punish*. New York: Vintage Books.

Foucault, M., 1982. 'The Subject and Power', in H. Dreyfus and P. Rabinow, eds, *Michel Foucault: Beyond Structuralism and Hermeneutics*. Chicago, IL: University of Chicago Press.

Foucault, M., 1984. *The Foucault Reader*. New York: Pantheon Books.

Gatens, M.,1996. *Imaginary Bodies*. New York: Routledge.

Goldstein, R., 2003a. 'Bush's Basket: Why the President Had to Show His Balls', *The Village Voice*, 21–27 May.

Goldstein, R., 2003b. 'Neo-Macho Man: Pop Culture and Post-9/11 Politics', *The Nation*, 6 March.

Hansen, T.B. and F. Stepputat, 2005. *Sovereign Bodies*. Princeton, NJ: Princeton University Press.

Heyman, J.McC., 1994. 'The Mexico–United States Border in Anthropology: A Critique and Reformulation', *Journal of Political Ecology*, 1: 43–66.

Heyman, J.McC., 1999. 'United States Surveillance over Mexican Lives at the Border: Snapshots of an Emerging Regime', *Human Organization* 58(4): 430–38.

Hobbes, T., 2004, *Leviathan*. New York: Barnes and Noble Books.

Hunt, A.I. and G. Wickham, 1994. *Foucault and the Law*. London: Pluto Press.

Huspek, M., 2001. 'Production of State, Capital, and Citizenry: The Case of Operation Gatekeeper', *Social Justice*, 28(2): 51–69.

Jehl, D., 2004. 'New Spy Plan Said to Involve Sattelite System', *New York Times*, 12 December.

Kirby, A., 2003. 'Community and Environment in a Desert Metropolis', http:// 216.239.57.104/search?q=cache:Fgp1SP5AB2MJ:www.hicsocial.org/Social2003 Proceedings/Andrew%2520Kirby.pdf+andrew+kirby+arizona+state+university+&h l=en, accessed 27 April 2005.

Koskela, H., 2000. '"The Gaze Without Eyes": Video-Surveillance and the Changing Nature of Urban Space', *Progress in Human Geography*, 24(2): 243–65.

Krohn-Hansen, C., 1996. 'Masculinity and the Political among Dominicans: "The Dominican Tiger"', in M. Melhuus and Kristi Anne Stølen, eds, *Machos, Mistresses and Madonnas*. London and New York: Verso.

Lorey, D.E., 1999. *The US–Mexico Border in the Twentieth Century*. Wilmington, DE: SR Books.

Low, S.M., 2003. *Behind the Gates: Life, Security and the Pursuit of Happiness in Fortress America*. New York: Routledge.

Lutz, W., 2002. 'The Cowboy in Us All', *The Tocquevillian Magazine*, 30 November.

Nugent, D., 1993. *Spent Cartridges of Revolution: An Anthropological History of Namiquipa, Chihuahua*. Chicago, IL: University of Chicago Press.

Nugent, D. and A.M. Alonso,1994. 'Multiple Selective Traditions in Agrarian Reform and Agrarian Struggle: Popular Culture and State Formation in the Ejido of Namiquipa, Chihuahua', in G. Joseph and D. Nugent, eds, *Everyday Forms of State Formation*. Durham, NC: Duke University Press.

Ortiz, Victor, 2001. 'The Unbearable Ambiguity of the Border', *Social Justice* 28(2): 96–113.

Plaut, P.O. and S. Plaut, 2004. 'The Demand for "Gatedness"', unpublished paper, http://216.239.57.104/search?q=cache:mH-WWrfWE1AJ:www.ceu.hu/econ/ economic/gatedness.pdf+gatedness&hl=en, accessed 3 January 2005.

Stoler, A.L., 1995. *Race and the Education of Desire*. Durham, NC: Duke University Press.

Stone, J., 2004. 'Conceptions of the Masculine: Bush vs. Kerry 2004', unpublished paper.

Thomas, T., 2004. 'The Threatened Sovereign: Strategies of Difference and Imperialism in the War on Drugs at the US–Mexico Border', paper presented at the Society for Cultural Anthropology 2004 Spring Conference, Portland, Oregon.

Thomson, J.E., 1994. *Mercenaries, Pirates, and Sovereigns*. Princeton, NJ: Princeton University Press.

Tomlinson, J., 1999. *Globalization and Culture*. Chicago, IL: University of Chicago Press (in conjunction with Polity Press).

Webster, C., G. Glasze and K. Frantz, 2002. 'Guest Editorial', *Environment and Planning B: Planning and Design*, 29(3): 315–20.

PART II

A VIEW FROM COMMUNITIES

3   CHIEFS AND BUREAUCRATS IN THE MAKING OF EMPIRE: A DRAMA FROM THE TRANSKEI, SOUTH AFRICA, OCTOBER 1880

Clifton Crais

Scholars are beginning to develop a new history of the state that brings to the study of power and politics the rich offerings of cultural studies.[1] This development in part reflects a commitment to rethinking contemporary topics such as authoritarianism, civil society, ethnic conflict and political instability. It also marks an attempt to extend the now considerable body of recent work on the cultural history of nineteenth-century imperialism produced over the past two decades.[2] Comparative literature specialists, many encouraged by new historicist approaches, have produced numerous studies on the imperial imagination, particularly on European representations of non-European peoples. Inspired by the work of Edward Said (1978) and other postcolonial critics, they have historicised seemingly static categories such as race and have provided important historical depth to issues ranging from sexuality to the social sciences. This rich literature has advanced more than simply our understanding of colonial history. Studies of Mughals and missionaries, of explorers and entrepreneurs, have reshaped metropolitan studies, including the character of imperial expansion itself. One recent study, for example, has explored how the missionary experience in Africa created an 'imperial culture' within England, in which a domestic middle-class 'missionary spirit' racialised the English poor and working classes (Thorne 1999; cf. Cannadine 2001).

What unites these diverse studies is a common fascination with culture, the ways people produced meaning and understood their world in diverse settings typically characterised by highly unequal relationships. These studies form part of a broader historiographical trend shaped by scholars such as Clifford Geertz (1973) and more generally by history's discovery of anthropology. This concern with culture has shaped recent work on the making of the colonial order itself, that is, on the local structures of dominance within the vast areas that came under European control in the nineteenth century. As Nicholas Dirks put it, 'culture was what colonialism was all about' (1992: 3). The historical anthropologist Anne Stoler (2002), for example, has argued for the importance of studying the constitution of colonial categories, for bringing anthropology's classic concern with culture to the study of the colonial past. In this and in other similar works scholars have centred their research on identity, power and knowledge, discourse, sexuality, race, ideology, religion, even clothing – colonial culture read as so many texts amenable to anthropological and new historicist perspectives.

The state specifically, and politics more generally, has had an uneasy position within the new cultural history of empire. Jean Comaroff and John Comaroff (1997: 16), for example, have argued that the new literature proves 'that colonization was everywhere more than merely a process of political economy – or one vested primarily in the colonial state'. Less glamorous are the studies of institutions, the lives of bureaucrats, or analyses of the causes of empire exemplified some three decades ago by Robinson and Gallagher's monumental *Africa and the Victorians: The Official Mind of Imperialism* (1961). To the extent that the state has been the centre of analysis in the new cultural history of empire, it has been primarily in terms of analysing the discursive strategies of rule, the epistemologies and techniques by which Europeans ordered and understood their colonial subjects and the lands they inhabited. The emphasis has been more on strategies than on practice, more on the accumulation of knowledge than on the daily relationships of coloniser and colonised.[3] Particularly where the emphasis on missionaries is strongest, the state enters later, after the colonisation of consciousness, after the damage has been done, to regulate a world reshaped in the name of empire and modernity.[4] Yet as Fred Cooper and Anne Stoler (1997) have cautioned, understanding the 'working of the colonial state' remains centrally important to comprehending the rise and fall of European colonialism.

This chapter is concerned with bringing the state back in without leaving culture out, much as a new generation of scholars has revitalised the study of state formation and political culture in twentieth-century Latin America.[5] The chapter focuses primarily on the earliest moments of state formation that began with conquest itself, as the state, as it were, came into being. The challenge, as Corrigan has put it generally, is to focus 'not [on] who rules but [on] how rule is accomplished' (1994: xvii). Looking at state formation this way offers a way of bridging recent anthropologically-oriented history concerned with culture with an older politically centred literature committed to understanding precisely how it was that Europeans extended control over such vast areas of the world so quickly and ruled with relatively few people. I am especially interested in exploring colonial conquest as quintessentially a cross-cultural encounter of a political kind. Conquest as cross-cultural encounter highlights how state formation consists of 'a *claim* that in its very name attempts to give unity, coherence, structure, and intentionality to what are in practice frequently disunited, fragmented attempts at domination' (Sayer 1994: 371). There is, I suggest, much to be learned from the encounters of bureaucrats, whose charge was to create a new political order, and their sometimes recalcitrant colonial subjects who were trying to make sense of their occupation by outsiders.

At first glance this may seem unsurprising, especially along the edge of empire where European claims to rule could be very weak indeed. Scholars of early European expansion in the period before the administrative revolution of the late eighteenth and early nineteenth centuries have long been attuned to the often bewildering complexity of cross-cultural encounters. Richard White (1991: 50) has written of the necessity of people having to 'arrive at some common conception of suitable ways of acting', as he has suggested, a 'middle ground'. Studies of Africa in the nineteenth century, however, usually have emphasised the differences separating European administrators from their African charges. Scholarship produced during the era of decolonisation inclined to see colonialism in terms of foreign imposition, the monolithic intrusion of Europe into other parts of the world. With few exceptions the trend has continued. The recent literature concerned with culture not surprisingly gravitated towards individuals like early missionaries whose exciting lives and rich texts offered the possibility of complex readings of early colonialism. In contrast, the lives of bureaucrats, beyond mere conveyors of policy, seemed relatively wearisome. There has been a tendency to foreclose analysis of the creation of nineteenth-century colonial rule, including moments of violence, as a 'dialogue of cultures' (Todorov 1982) and the emergence of African understandings of a political world in which they became the subjects of a colonial state. Colonial conquest and rule, it is suggested here, were just as much cross-cultural encounters as were the interactions of Africans with European missionaries and traders. For conquest involved peoples with often radically different conceptions and practices coming together and struggling to make sense of what was happening to themselves and to others. Seen this way, resistance is thus not simply oppositional but, rather, represents part of a historic conversation Africans had about power, authority and legitimacy, a conversation that engaged with colonialism but significantly extended beyond it.

The chapter centres on a drama of power and politics in the nineteenth-century Transkei, South Africa, played out in the relationship between a colonial magistrate and an African chief, the representatives of two different polities. The last quarter of the century saw rapid British expansion in South Africa and, indeed, across the continent. International rivalries partly motivated British expansion in the Transkei. The discovery of diamonds in Griqualand West in 1865, and the granting of responsible rule to the Cape Colony in 1872, however, created an environment for more spirited expansion. Most of the Transkei came under colonial rule in the space of about ten years. In 1868, the British High Commissioner annexed near-by Basutoland, which was taken over by the Cape three years later, only to be returned to British control. Widespread resistance began in the late 1870s and had engulfed much of the Transkei and Basutoland by 1880, largely because of the introduction of the magistrate system and the attempt to disarm Africans under the infamous 1878 Peace Preservation Act. To the north-east tensions erupted in the Anglo-Zulu War of 1879 where the British suffered one of their worst defeats anywhere in the nineteenth century in the Battle of Isandlwana. On the subcontinent the pace of imperial expansion and consolidation quickened after the discovery of gold in the 1880s, ending in one of the great wars of the age of empire, the 1899–1902 South African War.

Bureaucrats played a central role in imperial expansion into the Transkei. In 1862 the Department of Native Affairs (NAD) – at the time probably the most sophisticated bureaucracy within the Cape government – was created to manage conquered African territories. With responsible government granted in 1872, the NAD emerged as a far more powerful bureaucratic agency.[6] In the 1870s the department sent its employees into the Transkei to establish treaties, survey land and proclaim British control. This move into the region entailed more than simply the presence of weapons and the proverbial Gatling gun. Bureaucrats brought with them papers, pens, forms, stamps, rules, legislation, law books and, especially, telegraphs, into unconquered lands. While colonial control remained tenuous, the material presence of the state became unmistakable; the instrumental power of the state might not be hegemonic, but its material artefacts were everywhere.[7]

The relationship between African chiefs and colonial officials represented a principal feature of the emerging political order of colonialism. These sorts of cross-cultural encounters between officials and chiefs took place across the continent, shaping in powerful ways the colonial order within an expanding British Empire in Africa. Officials arrived with new forms of power and communication, and of course entirely new institutions and procedures such as trials and jails. Their mission was to establish areas of control, if need be to 'pacify' their new subjects, and to create orderly systems of administration among 'barbarous' peoples. Africans, and especially chiefs, had their own ideas. They pursued avenues of self-strengthening, an African 'race for power' often in direct conflict with European intentions and aspirations.[8] The situation on the ground, as it were, could be considerably 'messy', blurring what might appear at first sight to be so many clear differences and distinctions. As we shall see, for example, Africans perceived officials using a political grammar that connected authority and legitimacy with magic and agricultural fertility. Bureaucracy could become positively bewitching.

THE DEATH OF HOPE

'Go on I will follow,' the Mpondomise paramount chief Mhlontlo told the British magistrate, Hamilton Hope, in early days of October, 1880. And 'Where you die I will die.' In the north, war had broken out in Basutoland. A punishing drought had brought widespread crop failure. Nearby the chief's wife lay ill, slowly perishing from a long disease. Mhlontlo had been busily organising his warriors as the moon reached its fullness and showered the land with shadows and then began to wane. Ritual specialists ministered magic to make the warriors strong, to protect them in battle, to vanquish their enemies. Hope expected the ritually strengthened warriors to be British allies in the colonial war against rebel Basotho. The white magistrate also had been preparing himself: dashing off letters and telegraphs to colleagues and superiors; forging alliances with African chiefs; amassing a considerable arsenal of modern weapons; and asserting in ways both banal and ritualised the political supremacy of the British Empire.[9]

Hope remained somewhat apprehensive of his dealings with the paramount chief. The magistrate had been warned that he 'was plunging blindfold into a trap laid for me' by the Mpondomise paramount chief. 'I shall be rather amused,' Hope wrote, if the chief, 'true to his reputation disappoints everybody's expectations; if he does not I shall no doubt have convincing proof that everybody is right. My own opinion,' he concluded, aware both of the moment's drama and contingency, 'is that as in a game of cards, having led my King of Trumps if anybody in the game holds the Ace I lose the trick, if not my King wins.'[10]

On 20 October 1880 Hamilton Hope departed from his offices for Mhlontlo's location and the seat of the Mpondomise paramountcy at Sulenkama. The day before Hope had written that 'I meet Umhlonhlo and his Impi [warriors] tomorrow at Sulenkama, and take as many as I can with me from here [sic]; but though I go without hesitation, it is as well to provide for contingencies.' 'I go strengthened', he continued, 'by the feeling that I am doing right, and that the Almighty will guide me.... I have done my utmost to steer a straight and proper course in these matters, and if I fail, and have been deceived, I shall have shown that I backed my opinion.'[11]

Hope took with him three white officials, four African policemen and a Khoikhoi servant. The nine men proceeded on horseback and on two scotch carts along the wagon road that stretched north to Natal and south to Umtata, the colonial capital of the Transkei. Just over 5 kilometres out from the magistracy the men turned left, onto the narrow path that led north into foothills and to Mhlontlo's residence. The men, carts and horses lumbered up a broken and uneven path. Rain further complicated their journey. By now the drought was finally coming to an end, replaced not by light rains but by furious downpours that turned rivulets into rushing streams and made the track the men were travelling slippery and unstable. They stopped and made camp for the night. Rain was not the only complication hindering their progress. For the men brought with them 51 Snyder rifles, 7,000 cartridges, percussion caps and gunpowder, in addition to a substantial provision of food. This was a not inconsiderable supply of weaponry. All told, the men were transporting more than 1,000 lbs of weapons and supplies. A far larger quantity of weapons was in transit to the magistracy and arrived there by early Saturday morning.[12] Mhlontlo had requested the arms in return for agreeing to fight as allies of the British against the Basotho rebels in what became known as the Gun War of 1880–81. In return Mhlontlo assured Hope that he would assemble his warriors at Sulenkama, where chief and magistrate, ruler and subject, would gather in preparation for war.

Hope arrived in Sulenkama on the morning of 21 October. He anxiously wanted to press north to Matatiele. He was, after all, a conqueror in the great age of British imperial expansion in South Africa and around the world.[13] Not to press immediately to battle was for Hope to acquiesce with barbarism.

But delays ensued. Hope suspected treachery. Were the warnings correct? Mhlontlo assured Hope that his army would collect on Friday. On Thursday evening the chief dined with the magistrate and spent the night sleeping under the scotch cart filled with ammunition.[14]

By Friday morning only some 400 men in arms had arrived. Hope 'addressed a few words to them', explaining his intention and his desire 'to make as much haste as possible'. The chief intervened. '[A]ll his men were not present,' he told the magistrate. Mhlontlo suggested, and Hope agreed, reluctantly, to wait until the following day, Saturday, 23 October. On Friday evening the chief again dined with Hope, along with his brother and four other men. Chief and magistrate 'had a long conversation'. Hope again explained to Mhlontlo the urgency of departing from Sulenkama on Saturday to make war on the rebel Basotho.

Saturday morning the number of armed men had nearly doubled. The rains had stopped. The army, including the 'principal men of the various clans', formed a 'great curve a short distance' from Hope's encampment.[15] Warriors continued arriving during the day. In the early afternoon Mhlontlo 'came to Mr. Hope and sat down in the Marquee with us all, and after partaking of a friendly glass of Brandy and water, asked us all to go up to the "Umguyo"' ritual celebrations that fused agricultural fertility and chiefship and 'where he said it would be decided upon what number of men would be enrolled' to fight in the colonial war.[16]

Hope saw the event as affirming the political supremacy and power of the magistrate, another moment when Africans recognised the power and legitimacy of the British Empire. This was not the first but the second time the magistrate had attended, indeed had participated in, the ritual ceremony. To garner so many warriors would unequivocally demonstrate the magistrate's mastery over a chief who had too long resisted acknowledging the fact of colonial subjugation. The chief asked the magistrate to address the warriors, many of whom were then performing a war dance. Hope agreed. The men – chief, magistrate, Hope's clerk and two other white men – entered the great curve. Hope and another official 'seated' themselves 'upon the rug' of Hope's favourite horse. Another man stood behind them, while the last was 'a short distance away watching the men as they danced and sang their war songs', the warriors with weapons in hand pretending to stab their victims.[17]

Suddenly a great piercing whistle followed by a loud shout rang through the air. Everyone 'stood still'.[18] 'Pondomise there is no word from me,' Chief Mhlontlo told his people, 'the words you will hear [are] from your Magistrate.' 'We are Government people in the true sense of the word,' the chief continued. 'Government is our rock and shade.' If Hope found these words comforting, what the chief now said mystified the magistrate, reversing in his mind the very semantic logic of the chief's declaration. 'I am going to inform Sunduza [Davis, one of the white men],' Mhlontlo declared, 'the words which *I wish* Mr. Hope to say.'[19]

The chief led Davis away from the magistrate, out of the great curve of assembled men. Some 30 feet from where Hope and the other whites sat the chief stopped and turned around. He pointed to Hamilton Hope, and cried out 'You Pondomise! There are your chiefs!'[20]

Six men, all ritual specialists, rushed upon Hope and the two other white men. Mhlangeni, who also served as one of the chief's councillors, 'seized' the magistrate by his long white beard and, 'so drawing upwards his head, stabbed him in the breast'. Within minutes all three men were dead. The remaining white, Davis, survived; Mhlontlo saved him because Davis's father and now his brother served as missionary to the Mpondomise.[21] Mhlontlo, Davis reported, 'was fighting only against the Government'.[22] 'The English government', Mhlontlo said:

... has either entirely changed from what it was doing a few years ago, or it must be ignorant of what its Magistrates are doing. We are harshly treated. We came under the Government in order to gain peace and quietude, instead of which we have been in a continual state of unrest from the treatment we have received. Faith has been broken with us over and over again.... Our cattle are to be branded; our arms are to be taken away; and after that our children are to be seized and carried across the water.

'I shall not be taken alive,' Mhlontlo ended, 'a man can only die once.'[23]

The chief later refused requests by Davis and his brother to bury the mutilated bodies. They were to remain there as fallen enemies, as carrion for birds and scavenging animals, their bones scattered to the winds; 'the bodies must be eaten by birds, or their medicines would not act'.[24] Mandondo, one of the chief's ritual specialists, mutilated the body 'for war purposes'.[25] Hope's long beard was cut off, and his clothes stripped. Mhlangeni wore Hope's trousers and donned his long white beard. He subsequently led attacks on colonial troops.[26] A few years later he was arrested but miraculously managed to escape from the Kokstad jail. Another ritual specialist took the magistrate's coat. On 24 October this man led an attack on the Maclear magistracy, where a colonial official shot him dead. He was wearing the great bull's coat.[27]

The day of Hope's death Mhlontlo organised an escort to bring Davis back to the magistracy. There he packed his bags and fled to a near-by mission station. The telegraph wire had been cut, a few poles destroyed, the telegraph stolen; rebels would destroy most of the telegraph wires that webbed themselves across the Transkei. Mhlontlo had confiscated the munitions that had arrived the day of Hope's murder: 265 Snyder rifles and 15,750 rounds of ammunition. By 29 October 1880 the magistrate's offices and jail had been destroyed by fire.

Before the destruction of the buildings Chief Mhlontlo briefly occupied the magistracy. He sat in Hope's 'great chair', before the law of the man and empire that had ruled over him. The 'great table from the house of trials [court-room]' lay before the chief. On it sat 'that great book, the book of causes [criminal record book]'. A man 'turned over the leaves of the book and read aloud from it: "So-and-so charged with the crime of so-and-so; found guilty; sentenced to so-and-so".'

And then there would arise a great shout, and the armed warriors would rush upon the book and stab it with their spears, the while they shouted the death shout.... the warriors exulted and laughed aloud and made mock of the Government, who, they said, was now dead.[28]

THE CULTURE OF CONQUEST

Scholars have tended to distinguish the violence of conquest from the 'cultural technologies of rule' (Dirks 2001: 9). Maps, censuses and other statistical operations, the accumulation of ethnographic information, and so on, typically follow the crude force of foreign intervention. What is striking about nineteenth-century colonial conquest in the Transkei, however, is precisely how central these technologies were to conquest itself – and to African resistance to imperial expansion. Mapping, censuses, telegraphy and so on represented a crucial part of conquest. Africans were as much conquered by bureaucrats as by soldiers, by procedures as much as by bullets, by institutions, techniques and Enlightenment rationality as by Snyder-Enfield rifles and the proverbial Gatling gun. Culture was from the beginning an essential feature of colonial state formation, not something the state later 'discovered' in formulating its policies of segregation and apartheid. The 'science of government' was an integral feature of conquest and state formation, much like the magistrate in J.M. Coetzee's luminous novel, *Waiting for the Barbarians* (1980: 23), who has accumulated 'shelves and shelves of paper ... the records of decades of humdrum administration'. For the most part, violence took place after magistrates had subjected new regions to the technologies of the modern state. The relative absence of initial large-scale violence meant that the principal encounters Africans had were with bureaucrats charged with creating a colonial state.

Certainly military force remained a possibility. Bureaucrats, however, preferred conquering with paper, forms, censuses and law books. The extension of rule initially entailed the application of what Foucault described as the new 'science of government' (Foucault 1991: 99). Officials were instructed to render Africans and the landscape they inhabited cognisable to law and to regular administration. As Hamilton Hope put it in 1879, his job was 'To take cognizance of everything that goes on.'[29] Officials such as Hope typically rendered Africa cognisable through the application of political technologies such as censuses, surveying and mapping, the application of law and detailed descriptions of social life.[30] With the mapping of space came the counting and classification of bodies; the two were closely associated (Patriarca 1996: 50). A preoccupation of the state, its 'classificatory logic' (Appadurai 1993: 315), drawing lines and counting people were among the first duties of new resident magistrates. As with maps, over the course of the late nineteenth and twentieth centuries censuses became more accurate and more detailed. To count was to know. To do both entailed the creation of fixed categories. As magistrates drew maps they also collected statistical data so that they could then 'fix' colonial subjects on a spatial grid.

The most stereotyped of images was that of tribal society. Map and census were important instruments in the creation of a model of African society upon which officials could act. Maps and numbers, space and numeracy, made possible the creation of colonial categories that could be fixed spatially, thus allowing for a state-sponsored territorialisation of culture. The ethnographic diagram of chiefly genealogies and the maps of native reserves represent the two end-points of the fixing of culture in space; in one sense the latter circumscribed the former. Power and control lay at the centre of both. The genealogy is precisely a schematic representation, indeed an instrument, of power and jurisdiction premised on a putative 'common characteristic or interest'.[31] This location of culture in space comprised an intrinsic feature of conquest and early colonial rule, of rendering Africans 'cognisable', for example through sedentarisation and by attempting to create ethnically pure districts. Early state formation entailed bureaucratic attempts to organise space on the basis of homogeneous tribal designations demarcated by administrative boundaries; indeed early colonial officials forcibly removed Africans designated as belonging to a different 'tribe'.

Imperial expansion in the Transkei colonial rule generally proceeded in two waves. The first wave, depending on the areas roughly in the period between the 1850s and the 1870s, entailed a series of political agreements in which African rulers nominally accepted British rule. In so doing the British expected them to end political conflicts, glossed in the archive as 'tribal wars'. Until the late 1870s the British were not always clear how they intended to rule these new possessions. In some respects early rule in areas like Thembuland and further to the east was similar to protectorates. Few in number and their control nominal, resident magistrates ruled 'principally through their own Chiefs and in accordance with Kaffir laws and customs, when not opposed to justice or humanity'.[32] Chiefs thus retained much of their power. In many areas chiefs in effect appropriated the first magistrates as part of their attempts to consolidate and extend their power. Generally in this early period, magistrates evinced 'an unwillingness to measure' their 'power and authority with that of the Chief' under them.[33]

Conquest proceeded mainly through a series of agreements between chiefs and officials. Again, violence typically took place after, not before, colonial rule had been extended over a given area. Chiefs initially agreed to have their people 'placed ... under the protection' of the Cape government. Chiefs saw these agreements as so many alliances and, importantly, not recognition of colonial status. Indeed, technically Africans were not colonial subjects, even if 'the colonial government had been exercising de facto jurisdiction'.[34] And magistrates, including the Chief Magistrate, the head NAD official in the Transkei, 'had no legal status independently of the will of the Chiefs'.[35] This muddled situation changed towards the end of the 1870s, when bureaucrats received instructions from their superiors to definitively reduce the power of chiefs and, in their place, to create an orderly system centred on resident magistrates who would no longer have to act on the sufferance of African rulers.[36]

In 1878 Hamilton Hope became the third magistrate appointed to the Mpondomise. As with other magistrates, Hope spent much of his time gathering statistical data, demarcating boundaries, collecting information on African custom and, of course, extending the British rule of law.[37] In the early 1870s, following a period of political expansion and contraction, Mhlontlo and a number of other chiefs in the East Griqualand area had accepted British suzerainty. Hut tax first became payable in 1875. In a long report written at the end of 1877, the second magistrate confidently asserted that 'Magistrates now occupy the *position* formerly held by the Chiefs.'[38] The official exaggerated; the situation was far more complex. Mhlontlo was not so compliant; indeed he remained very much committed to expanding his authority. In an 1878 witchcraft case Mhlontlo had confiscated the property of one of his subjects. The magistrate had intervened, fining the chief fifteen head of cattle. While 'he has not refused to pay the demand', Mhlontlo 'greatly embarrassed me by his passive opposition and non-compliance'.[39] In other respects the chief seemed cooperative; officials often had difficulty understanding why a chief might appear pliant in one instance and intractable in another. The chief, for example, 'personally afforded' the magistrate's 'clerk every assistance in making' a census of his people 'as accurate as possible, and in which he evidently took considerable interest'.[40] In this and in other instances the chief was attempting to use the British in such a way as to enlarge his political domains, even as colonial officials were concluding that the chief was submitting to their control.

Hope previously had served in nearby southern Basutoland, where he ruled as the first magistrate over Chief Moorosi. There Hope did his duty as a bureaucrat, deploying the political technologies of the modern state and, if necessary, flogging his subjects. Hope earned the dubious 'reputation for being cruel and vindictive' (Atmore 1970). The next magistrate inherited a discontented people who rebelled shortly after his arrival, and then again in the Gun War of 1880.[41]

Hope's reputation surely would have been known to Mhlontlo. His arrival among the Mpondomise created some considerable concern. It also offered an opportunity to roll back some of the previous magistrate's efforts to erode chiefly rule. In late August 1878 Mhlontlo called a meeting with the new magistrate. This itself was important. Colonial rituals of subordination usually entailed a new magistrate first calling a meeting of his subjects. Equally importantly, Mhlontlo attended the meeting, instead of sending his chief councillors and ritual specialists.

The Mpondomise leaders wasted no time. 'We are here today about the letter sent by Government appointing you as our Magistrate,' said Tyali, one of the Mpondomise leaders. 'We have not come for anything else.' Next the recently appointed headman Zenzo raised the central issue of the jurisdiction of chiefs and headmen.

We thank Government.... Our first complaint we made to the first Magistrate [Orpen] who said your ground is your inheritance. Well I don't see the ground today. Again, I was once a chief, but when Government came I had to give up my chieftainship. I was a chief under Umhlonhlo I am now no longer able to get any fines.[42]

Others continued in much the same vein. When another headman criticised Shaw's rule, Hope chastised him. He was not deterred: 'We want all cases to be taken first to Umhlonhlo.' Then Noranga added: 'Why do you stop us when we talk about Shaw? He ruled us wrong – he beat us with the "cats" without the word from the Chief.'

Hope was unimpressed:

Some of you have spoken very well, but you are all making one mistake – it is this: That although you admit you are under the Government you seem to expect Government to come down to your level and adopt your customs and let you dictate to the Magistrate ...

You want me always to consult Umhlonhlo – who is the leader – but I will not when it is necessary.... So long as he behaves well and is willing to assist me, I will consult him ... [but] he and the other headmen may act as arbitrators in civil cases, but not must use force to carry out their decisions, and every man may appeal to me before he complies with the judgements of chiefs and headmen – but you must not expect me to send cases to the Chief.

The magistrate ended by saying 'that the Government is first and the chief second'.[43]

Finally Mhlontlo spoke:

I asked Mr. Shaw to show me the first letters from Government, those that refer to our being taken over so that we could discuss them, but he declined to go into old matters.... We want you in the presence of the Minister to take those first letters and read them to us so that we can understand the law. The letters are still here, let them be read – they are not dead.

Hope ended the meeting:

You were only trying a new horse, to see if you could tease him, and whether he was likely to buck if you were not careful – each [speaker] has had a little ride on him to try, and now that you have seen what sort of horse you have got, I hope you are all satisfied.

Laughter followed. The people dispersed.

The meeting in fact had settled little. A November 1878 case of witchcraft accusation raised again the division of power. The case began near the homestead of headman Mtoninzi who, three months earlier, had publicly criticised Shaw's rule only to receive the magistrate's sharp admonition. A 'man of some importance' had fallen ill. Accusations of witchcraft followed. Hope rescued the accused who had been 'very much injured from the tortures' inflicted by the witchdoctor and others, and arrested all the men with the exception of the 'wizard' Cekeso. Hope alleged that Mtoninzi 'encouraged' the men 'to torture her till she produced the charms', and thus had contravened colonial law.[44]

Hope demanded that Mhlontlo attend the trial. The accused 'admitted their guilt but said that Mtoninzi had said that I had given him authority to torture any one who might be "smelt out" provided he stopped short of killing them'. Unimpressed by this argument, Hope fined the men and sentenced them to hard labour, including Mtoninzi, once a chief, then colonial headmen, now a convict 'breaking stones and wheeling a barrow'.[45]

Hope's efforts to accumulate power for himself and for the Empire proceeded. In January 1879 he spoke to Mhlontlo concerning the Mguya that had just been performed at the chief's home. The Mguya, a central ritual moment for the Mpondomise, celebrated authority and fertility and re-affirmed the heroic status of chiefs as the descendants of men who slayed leopards and who brought nourishing rains. The chief explained to Hope that Orpen, the first magistrate, had allowed his people to conduct Mguya. He further explained that 'besides Doctoring the people to strengthen them in case of war', Mguya offered the opportunity for the chief to discuss pressing matters with his people. Nonetheless, Mhlontlo assured Hope 'that the ceremony ... had no political significance'.[46] The magistrate was concerned with what he considered to be the political implications of doctoring the army. In short, Hope feared conflict. He left the interview reassured of Mhlontlo's fealty.

Some nine months later, Hope attended a Mguya, at the chief's invitation. For Hope, the ensuing months had been taken up with the collection of hut taxes, land demarcations and resultant boundary and other land disputes, reports to his superiors and discussion of the Moorosi Rebellion taking place in near-by Basutoland, legal cases and the more mundane duties of bureaucrats living on the frontier.[47] Hope clearly knew that the ceremony related to issues of political authority; he saw his presence there as part and parcel of his magisterial duties, but also an indication of the superior position of the magistrate vis-à-vis the chief. What Hope did not appreciate was the fact that he was entering the most intimate domain of Mpondomise power and ritual, and especially the relationship between the ceremony and agricultural fertility and chiefship.

Confident of his position, Hope redoubled his administrative efforts. Hope began a campaign of assiduous collection of taxes, including arrears dating back to 1875. Mhlontlo complained in February. In May the issue had become serious enough for Hope to call for a meeting with the chief, accompanied by about 400 men.[48] Hope began the meeting by demanding the payment of 'all arrears'. Mhlontlo immediately countered by demanding 'to know where is the record of any meeting called by Mr. Orpen or Mr. Shaw to pay the Hut Tax for 1875'. From here the meeting became rancorous. The government 'has not shown us anything', pronounced one man, who spoke in *vino veritas*:

... or any reason why we should pay the Hut Tax, we have not obtained ground yet to show we have come under Government.... I have only paid Hut Tax once. I do not see the truth of the Government in not giving us the ground we wanted. This ground has been given to other chiefs. We would like to get some of our ground back. We must grumble, we always do grumble. I will pay Hut Tax when Mhlonhlo pays. Government has him round the neck and is strangling him.[49]

Others continued in much the same vein. 'We will never hear the truth of our words,' Zenzo asserted. 'How will people accept a law that has never been proclaimed?' At this point Hope read an extract from an 1874 meeting of Orpen and Mpondomise concerning hut taxes as a condition of British colonial supremacy. Zenzo promptly fainted.[50]

Hope began collecting taxes in July, beginning, significantly, with the chief. The chief and his people paid Hope £157 in two days, a considerable sum. '[S]ince then the people generally have come freely to the office' to pay their taxes. Hope 'received every assistance from the Chief Umhlonhlo in the collecting of the Tax and the discovery of defaulters'.[51]

In September 1879, one year after becoming magistrate, Hamilton Hope and his clerk attended a spring Mguya to bring rain and fertility to the land. Hope authorised the ceremony, to which he was invited by the chief. About 400 to 500 people attended the Mguya, most arriving by horse. In the morning they 'gathered in front of the cattle Kraal and had a dance'. In the afternoon Hope asked the chief 'to put his men through some military manoeuvres which he did with considerable skill and precision'.[52]

After a few men of influence spoke, the chief began his speech. He had called 'these sons of the great English Bull' to the ceremony. 'We are thankful', Mhlontlo said:

... that the Magistrate has had sufficient confidence in us to allow us to stretch our legs in a dance, for although our enemies are still saying that we wish to fight against the Government, we are not such fools, and our Mguyo is a time-honoured custom amongst us and we *guyn* [celebrate] in times of peace, and for our harvests.

Mhlontlo then instructed his people to pay their taxes. 'This is the chief thing that ensures you the protection of Government.'[53]

Ever the committed bureaucrat, Hamilton Hope now believed that his efforts to build the British Empire in the distant Transkei were finally bearing fruit. The land had been mapped, districts and sub-districts demarcated, the people counted and taxed. Hope saw the Mguya as a moment of submission, as affirming the political supremacy and power of the magistrate. What he scarcely understood was that Africans had been busily attempting to appropriate his power so as to bring rain. In doing so they were placing an important burden on the white official, and potentially exposing Hope to new kinds of critique.

For the spring Mguya failed to bring nourishing rains. By the end of the year large parts of the Transkei were experiencing a severe drought.[54] In December Mhlontlo complained of Hope's conduct in criminal proceedings, especially Hope's generous use of the whip. Again the chief returned to the earliest years of colonial rule. Mhlontlo asked 'that Mr. Orpen should be here, and we wish to talk to him ... as our first Magistrate + Governor. We wish to speak to him before our good Magistrate [Hope]'.

Crisis loomed by March 1880, when green maize is eaten and Africans throughout the Transkei celebrate first fruits ceremonies – a central moment in the creation and reconstitution of political society. The crops, as Hope later wrote, were an 'entire failure'.[55] Nor was this all. Mhlontlo's chief wife had fallen ill early in the spring and was 'slowly dying of a lingering disease'.[56] Hope was also unwell. He had been sick for some time and was finding his work 'very exhausting'.[57]

In March, as drought gripped the land and the chief's wife lay sick with a disease that lingered like the dry days, chief and magistrate again locked horns around the resolution of disputes. One of the chief's sisters had been slighted 'on her way down to her husband', an important moment in the marriage ceremony. Moreover, 'a lot of young men attacked and rather maltreated her [bridal] escort'.[58]

Mhlontlo leapt to action, fining the attackers and sending a leopard's tail to a man who had made insulting remarks to the bridal party. The brouhaha constituted a 'blood case' and thus involved fines. Not surprisingly, the magistrate learned of the conflict and, especially, that the chief had acted 'with his usual impetuosity'.[59] Hope informed the local headman that no one 'but myself had the power to enforce any fines' and was soon threatening people with humiliating flogging. But Hope went one step further. Not only did the magistrate order his chief constable to confiscate the leopard's tail, he had it returned to Mhlontlo.

Sending the leopard's tail, a sacred emblem among the Mpondomise, back to the chief was a great insult and outrage. The chief 'had flown' at the policeman 'in a great rage, refused to hear any message and ordered him off the premises with the tiger tail, which he was to take back to where he got it'. But the policeman refused, leaving the leopard's tail at the chief's residence. Only after some of the chief's men threatened him with death did the functionary take the tail away.[60]

The affair of the leopard's tail involved complex and highly charged meanings. For Hope, the chief's sending the leopard's tail meant that, once again, Mhlontlo was refusing to recognise British rule. For the chief, as for other Africans, the tail meant much more, particularly in the context of drought. It symbolised not simply chiefship but also, and importantly, the mytho-historical relationship between authority and the land. Not surprisingly, and indeed seemingly inexorably, the fracas of the leopard's tail led to a large meeting of the magistrate and his subjects, at which about 900 people attended, roughly twice the size of Hope's previous meetings with the Mpondomise. Chief Mhlontlo did not attend, though his principal praise singer and war doctor did. Both spoke. So, of course, did Hamilton Hope, who reiterated that only the magistrate could levy fines. He also took possession of the leopard's tail, the use of which he declared was illegal. Hope admonished the chief and ordered all assembled that they 'must look to the Magistrate for ... [their] orders'.

Coming armed as you did the other day. My Police have been insulted. The people have come here armed. No one must insult or come armed. I will tell you when to come armed.... There are some things I wish attended to. You must pay up your Hut Tax.[61]

The tax, Hope argued, was the 'grease of the wagon' of rule. The magistrate ended his disquisition by banning Sunday beer drinks.

Jara, the chief's praise singer, saw things somewhat differently. He pointed out the relative impotence of headmen. Soon the meeting began unravelling; Hope's threats to flog people did not help matters. The men in effect began arguing the case and, at the same time, protesting the position of headmen and the banning of Sunday beer drinks. One man pointed out how Hope and Mhlontlo 'were friends and they now seem at variance. Speak you wizards who did this.' Jara had spoken what had been kept silent: the use of magic in the creation of political conflict. For the drought, Mhlontlo's wife's illness and the rising political temperature all indicated the use of powerful and malevolent magic.

Hope concluded the meeting, returning to the issue of the powers of headmen. 'The Headmen wanting more power is an old tale,' he began.

All they want is to be able to 'eat up' people's cattle. You Headmen have power to settle garden disputes, to bring people to the office who have delayed in paying their Hut Tax, that is enough power for you to have, and that is all you will get.... I am over the Headmen, and not they over me.... 'Smelling out' [witchcraft accusations] I hear is in existence, if I find out such a thing I will inflict a very severe punishment.

Hope then announced he was going away, and that his clerk would be collecting hut taxes. He would return to his death. In the meantime, drought continued ravaging the area. Mhlontlo's crops had failed; he was forced to sell a considerable number of his cattle to purchase £200 worth of grain. His wife's illness progressed. But August is usually one of the driest months. Would the spring rains come?

Mhlontlo's wife died in early October 1880. By this time war had broken out in Basutoland and in neighbouring Griqualand East, in what has become known as the Gun War of 1880. Soon virtually all of Basutoland and much of the Transkei was in open rebellion, the largest conflict to have ever engulfed the region. By the middle of the month, the chief was busily 'organising his tribe and Doctoring them'. Hope reported seeing 'armed parties ... hovering round on the hills'. The question for the magistrate was whether the Mpondomise would rebel or would ally themselves with the British.[62] Heavy spring rains were falling. Hamilton Hope still felt unwell.

On 19 October Hope received a letter from the missionary Stephen Adonis warning him that Mhlontlo 'meant treachery' and that 'mutiny had been along intended and on a certain day [would be] carried out'.[63] Three days later the magistrate at nearby Maclear had 'grave reasons from reliable information' of 'an intended plot'.[64] Yet Hope pressed on to Sulenkama through a rain that, to him, seemed 'incessant'.[65] Clearly Chief Mhlontlo was rebuilding his power. Hope may not have fully known it, but by the end of the second week of October the magistrate was 'now dancing to' the chief's 'fiddle in every possible manner'. The chief was 'delighted to wait a little bit'.[66]

It was in a setting of quenching rains and incipient rebellion that Hope met his death before the largest assembly of Mpondomise the magistrate had ever witnessed. Mguya were moments when the institution of chiefship was exposed and potentially opened to criticism as well as reaffirmed and expanded. Hope, as chief, was overthrown so that Mhlontlo's chieftaincy could be reaffirmed. The morning before Hope's death Mhlontlo had sat apart, the once vanquished now exalted chief participating in and surveying the reconstitution of the chiefship and the return of social health before a grand and extremely charged political ceremony. Messengers moving between the army and the chief crawled to and from him, in movements of exaggerated deference.

Hope's murder, then, destroyed at least temporarily the colonial accumulation of power and the attempt to build legitimacy on the edge of empire. His demise, already indicated by his ill health, rebuilt the chiefship, strengthened the Mpondomise army in their coming war with the British and brought rain. Hope was not only killed but also was ritually murdered – or, better, sacrificed, a 'great bull' killed to renew society and polity.[67]

THE SPECTRAL STATE

Hamilton Hope had at his disposal the political technologies of the modern state. He used them assiduously. He mapped the land and created administrative districts based on the fiction of pure tribes. He counted people and property. He presided over legal proceedings. Hope also issued passes for Africans travelling out of the district. He communicated with his superiors through letters and the telegraph – an indispensable technology in addressing that 'great question of the government of the Natives'[68] – that had been installed in the magistracy the year before he assumed his command at Qumbu. Like bureaucrats elsewhere, Hamilton Hope pushed a lot of paper.

Even if the state's control remained weak, by the late 1870s its presence had become ubiquitous. The political technologies of conquest and colonial rule had a conspicuous place in the African resistance of the early 1880s. Rebels stole telegraph machines, telegraph wires and the paper upon which a bureaucratic order rested. Africans also appropriated colonial procedures, particularly the criminal trial. Mhlontlo became Hamilton Hope when the chief occupied the magistracy and oversaw a mock trial. This was not the only case of such mimicry. In Thembuland to the west warriors looted and burned to the ground the magistracy of Walter Stanford, who later became Chief Magistrate for Griqualand East, central member of the 1881 Native Laws and Customs Commission, under-secretary for Native Affairs, and Chief Magistrate of the Transkei, knight of the realm – in short, a man of exceptional status, to African and European alike. But not before a 'high festival in my office' overseen by the rebel chief Dalasile.

A blanketed warrior representing Ndabeni (myself) occupied the judicial bench. Another on a chair below was addressed as Lufele (Daniel). Then a mock prisoner was placed in the dock and the form of a criminal trial was mimicked with keen humour. Nor was Webb (Umquwu) the chief constable left out of the piece. At the conclusion of the dramatic entertainment, the offices, our houses, and the police huts, were set on fire. (MacQuarrie 1958: 131)[69]

We now know that the languages of the dominated were never simply their own. What is less clear is how the 'hidden transcripts' of resistance came to be written, as it were, using the material culture and institutional practices of a political order the colonised critiqued and contested (Scott 1990).[70] South Africa has a rich tradition of such appropriation, extending from the birth of the modern state in the nineteenth century well into the twentieth-century triumph of segregation and apartheid (see Crais 2002). Luise White (2000) has recently written of the stories Africans in East and Central Africa told each other about firemen and vampires, employees of the colonial state who people believed practised a most malevolent magic. White explores the emergence of vampire beliefs as a rich and malleable commentary on people's anxieties, their concern with evil and misfortune, and the ways they imagined themselves and others in the colonial period. What is especially striking in this envisioning of the world is the centrality of state institutions and practices. The most commonplace administrative features of the colonial state – firemen, police, game rangers, surveyors – helped sustain the most extraordinary conceptions of how the world worked.

Precisely because of these complications, precisely because colonial rule was never simply an act of foreign imposition, the state became an ineluctable part of the subaltern political imagination. Fascinated with modern power, especially the bureaucratic power of the state, Africans sought the locations of modernity's magic. This was not without irony. By entering into a conversation with modern power Africans participated in its dissemination. Resistance necessarily entails the production of difference in the constitution and reconstitution of political subjectivities, but these were ambiguous productions because of their intimate relationship to state formation. The inclusion of Hamilton Hope – his body and the world of which he was a part – into the political imagination of the Mpondomise also marked 'the assumption of subaltern status' (Sahlins 1995). A quintessential act of resistance became also the remembered moment of colonial subjugation.

Cannadine (2001) has ably demonstrated how the British transferred their conceptions of status and hierarchy to their relationships with indigenous rulers, and in so doing he has emphasised what they had in common with kings and princes, instead of what separated them. In the Transkei, and elsewhere in Africa, the recently colonised were doing much the same, by translating Europeans into their own conceptions of the world. What is particularly striking is the ways in which Africans believed Europeans, including bureaucrats, used malevolent magic, in short that officials were witches, or more precisely witch-chiefs. Michael Herzfeld has written that 'Bureaucrats work on the categories of social existence in much the same was as sorcerers are supposed to work on the hair or nail clippings of their intended victims' (1992: 62).[71] Much of a witch's insidious power stems from the panoptic surveillance of their victims. Unencumbered by ethical or moral obligations, their cool calculating behaviour has as its goal the attainment of a singular goal – selfish appropriation at another's tragic expense. Witches, and of course the modern state as well, depend on the accumulation of detailed and often intimate information. The very political technologies Hamilton Hope so energetically deployed awakened in Africans the spectre of witchcraft.

An interest in culture thus might usefully be turned to the study of politics, state formation and African resistance in the colonial era. Recent emphasis on the capillary forms of power, not surprisingly, led to a sense that the study of the state was old-fashioned. When scholars analysed the state in Africa they typically saw it as the 'geographical extension of the metropolitan state' (Mamdani 1976), its specificity determined by how the state grappled with capitalist development and, especially, the 'native question'. It is certainly true, as Fred Cooper (1996: 264) has argued, that the 'political base' of the colonial state, 'and the point from which the cultural and social background of its officers emanates, is distinct from the social formation in which it acts'. The death of Hope, however, suggests a more complicated picture, a blurring of the foreignness of colonial domination. Focusing on conquest as cross-cultural encounter offers historians a way of understanding the nature and daily exercise of domination and resistance and the imbricated histories of ruler and ruled, as Africans translated the European political world into indigenous concepts and practices, and Europeans intentionally or inadvertently wore the political mask of the very people they were busily conquering. In so doing it offers one way of transforming older approaches to both social and political history, by focusing on state formation and on the ways in which various historical actors made claims to dominance and control.

What of Mhlontlo? The chief fled into the mountains of Lesotho where he lived for some two decades in exile and as a fugitive. In 1903, however, the colonial authorities apprehended Mhlontlo. In a long trial ending in May 1904, Mhlontlo faced charges for the murder of Hope and the other white men. The case received widespread attention. Under colonial South Africa's bifurcated legal system, Africans were members of tribal groups and liable to customary law in civil matters. In criminal matters, however, Africans were tried as individuals and the law was, in theory at least, culture blind. Before the white man's court the chief's actions were in effect removed from their cultural context, a context in which a different set of rationalities had been operating. Not surprisingly, after deliberating only 25 minutes, the jury returned with verdict of not guilty. The chief, after all, had never laid a hand on the deceased. According to one account, the 'verdict was received with breathless interest and elicited shouts from the natives in Court, which were immediately suppressed'. Mhlontlo thanked the judge and, outside the court, received 'many congratulatory remarks and offerings from natives. So ended a trial,' the local newspaper concluded, 'which has evoked no small interest on account of the revival of a tragedy which at the time of its occurrence thrilled both Europeans and natives.'[72] In 1906 Mhlontlo returned to his home, not as a chief but as a simple commoner. He died in 1912, living on barren land, 'poor, in debt, and having to purchase grain for his family' (Beinart and Bundy, 1987: 121).

The death of Hope and the memory of Mhlontlo continue to breathe life into public discourse on the past and present during a time of important political transition and reconstruction in South Africa. Mpondomise tribal leaders have called for the 'restoration of its lost kingdom',[73] in effect a return to imagined pre-colonial borders and a heroic history. Increasingly people have spoken publicly of a Mpondomise past, of valorous chiefs and, especially, the loss of land at the hands of British conquerors. In August 2000, plans were being made to honour Mhlontlo to correct 'those historical imbalances and restore back to the community what is truly theirs.... His only crime was to resist oppression and the death of the then Qumbu magistrate, Mr. Hamilton Hope.'[74] People have invoked sacred symbols and have awakened a vision of politics that connected historical and political legitimacy to the land and the rains that originate high in the hills and mountains of Lesotho, a politics not of evil but of fertility and social health. Indeed, at one celebration, five molesnakes 'made a mysterious appearance at the laying of a tombstone'. The serpents' appearance was a harbinger of 'peace ... and an occasion for joy'. In welcoming the snakes 'prayers for rain were also offered. Before the end of the day, it was raining cats and dogs.'[75]

NOTES

1. A version of this chapter, with fuller citation of secondary sources, was published in the *American Historical Review*, 108(4) (October 2003): 1034–56. All archival sources are located in the Cape Archives Depot, Cape Town, unless otherwise noted.
2. For Africa see, for example, Mbembe (1992), Bayart (1993), Crais (2003). On ethnicity see Hamilton (1998). For a more traditional approach see Mamdani (1996).
3. See, for example, Appadurai (1993). See also Bayly (1996), Cohn (1996) and, most recently, Dirks (2001).
4. See, for example, Beidelman (1982), Comaroff and Comaroff (1991, 1997), Landau (1995). For one critique see Ranger (1997). Particularly in South African historical studies, political historians continue to analyse the state according to the promulgation of policies and the success or failure of its intervention in rural and urban society, terms very much established by the state itself. See, for example, Ashforth (1992), Bozzoli (1981), Dubow (1989), Posel (1991). And social historians remain largely preoccupied with detailing who did what to whom when, and how that who – defined as peasant, worker, tribesman, or defined on the basis of gender – reacted to European imposition. In the best work, the colonised are shown to have either accommodated themselves

to rule or reacted against an external imposition that remained intrinsically foreign. See, for example, Beinart and Bundy (1987), Hendricks (1990), Delius (1996).

5. See, for example, Wells and Joseph (1996), Joseph and Nugent (1994).
6. For an overview see Rogers (1933).
7. From the end of the nineteenth century the Transkei became especially important as a testing ground for new colonial policies ranging from indirect rule to agricultural management, particularly as Transkeian migrants came to represent a larger and larger proportion of an emerging migrant working class. In the apartheid era the Transkei represented the lynchpin for the 'homeland' policies of separate development. For background see Galbraith (1963), Peires (1981), Beinart and Bundy (1987), Crais (1992). See also Mamdani (1996).
8. On the African race for power see Lonsdale (1985). See also Lonsdale and Berman (1992).
9. I explore this story in greater detail in Crais (2002).
10. CMK 1/152, Hope to Chief Magistrate, Kokstad, 14 Oct. 1880. See also CMK 1/152, Hope to Chief Magistrate, Kokstad, 19 Oct. 1880; RM Maclear to Chief Magistrate, Kokstad, 22 Oct. 1880.
11. Hope to Davis, 19 Oct. 1880, in 'Historical Record of the Murder of Hamilton Hope', typescript originally compiled by W.C. Henman, photocopy in possession of author.
12. NA 20, Davis to Secretary for Native Affairs, 29 Oct. 1880.
13. See Michael W. Doyle, *Empires* (1986: 142) for statistical material on British imperial expansion.
14. CMK 1/152, Hope to Chief Magistrate, Kokstad, 22 Oct. 1880; Brownlie (1975: 82).
15. NA 20, Davis to Secretary of Native Affairs, 29 Oct. 1880; Brownlie (1975: 82).
16. NA 20, Davis to Secretary of Native Affairs, 29 Oct. 1880.
17. Brownlie (1975: 83); *Fort Beaufort Advocate*, 5 Nov. 1880, in 'Historical Record'.
18. Brownlie (1975: 83).
19. Emphasis mine. NA 20, Davis to Secretary of Native Affairs, 29 Oct. 1880.
20. Brownlie (1975: 84).
21. *Ibid.*; NA 20, Davis to Secretary of Native Affairs, 29 Oct. 1880.
22. *Ibid.*; (University of Cape Town [UCT]) BC 293, Stanford to ?, 23 Nov. 1880.
23. *The Eastern Star*, 23 Nov. 1880, in 'Historical Record of the Murder of Hamilton Hope'.
24. *Ibid.* 'The fowls of the air (aasvogels) should eat them, or the witch doctor's medicine would not act', *The Port Elizabeth Telegraph and Eastern Province Standard*, 26 Nov. 1880, in 'Historical Record'.
25. (UCT) BC 293, B116.39, Leary to Stanford, 29 June 1922. This also occurred in the Bhambata Rebellion of 1906–08 in Natal, where a European's body was mutilated to strengthen the warriors. See Carton (2000: 134).
26. CMK 1/94, Leary to officer commanding, 2 May 1881.
27. (UCT) BC 293, B116.39, Leary to Stanford, 29 June 1922; Brownlie (1975: 112, 84).
28. Brownlie (1975: 88). Hope was not the only magistrate whose power was mocked in the great rebellion of 1880–81. See below and Crais (2002: 39).
29. CMK 1/94, minutes of meeting, 23 Dec. 1879. The study of knowledge and colonialism has been of particular importance to scholars of Asian history. See, for example, Appadurai (1993). See also Bayly (1996), Cohn (1996) and, of course, Said (1978).
30. See Said (1978), Cohn (1996), Dirks (1992), Stoler (1997). On surveying see Burnett (2000).
31. *Black's Law Dictionary*.
32. (UCT) BC 293, D10, manuscript of Rev. E.J. Warner containing the history of his father, Rev. Joseph Cox Warner, n.d., t.s.

33. (UCT) BC 293, B2631, Edmonstone, Judge and Grant to Secretary for Native Affairs, 30 Dec. 1872. Early policy is described in CO 4521, Graham, 'Unannexed Tembuland', 16 Aug. 1881; CO 1156, Leonard, Opinion, 23 Apr. 1881.
34. CO 4521, quoted in Graham, 'Unannexed Tembuland', 16 Aug. 1881.
35. *Ibid.*
36. In 1877, the colony annexed Griqualand East and the region between the Kei and Bashee rivers. Griqualand East had received its first magistrate six years earlier; annexation formalised a prior process of colonial conquest, making de jure what was in many respects already de facto. In 1884 Mqikela, the Pondo paramount and son of Faku who had led Pondoland on the road of political centralisation, quite literally sold Port Saint Johns in return for a yearly subsidy. In 1885, the colony annexed Thembuland, Emigrant Thembuland, Gcalekaland and Bomvanaland. The following year saw the incorporation of the rest of the Transkei barring Pondoland, which was annexed to the colony in 1894. By this time with the exception of Pondoland the Cape had annexed the entire Transkei, a region of over 20,000 square miles. See also Brownlie (1923).
37. See CMK 1/94, Hope to Brownlie, 4 Sept. 1879; CMT 1/94, Hope to Davis, 6 Aug. 1879; CMT 1/53, Hope to Elliot, 24 July 1879; Crais (2002).
38. NA 158, Shaw, Report, Jan. 1878.
39. *Ibid.*
40. *Ibid.*
41. See Atmore (1970), Kimble (1982). The colonial administration had introduced a new policy aimed at disarming Africans.
42. This and the above quotations are from NA 158, minutes of meeting of 22 Aug. 1878.
43. *Ibid.*
44. NA 158, Hope to Secretary for Native Affairs, 26 Nov. 1878.
45. *Ibid.*
46. CMK 1/94, Hope to Chief Magistrate, Kokstad, 17 Jan. 1879.
47. See below and CMK 1/94, Hope to Brownlie (Chief Magistrate, Kokstad), 4 Sept. 1879; NA 18, Grant to Elliot, 5 Mar. 1880.
48. CMK 1/94, Hope to Brownlie (Chief Magistrate, Kokstad), 21 Feb. 1879; CMK 1/94, Hope to Chief Magistrate, Kokstad, 5 Apr. 1879; CMK 1/94, meeting of 3 May 1879.
49. CMK 1/94, meeting of 3 May 1879.
50. *Ibid.*
51. CMK 1/94, Hope to Chief Magistrate, Kokstad, 21 May 1879.
52. CMK 1/94, Hope to Chief Magistrate, Kokstad, 19 Sept. 1879.
53. *Ibid.*.
54. See, for example, NA 18, Cumming to Chief Magistrate, Tembuland, 10 Jan. 1880.
55. CMK 1/94, Hope to Chief Magistrate, Kokstad, 25 Aug. 1880.
56. *Ibid.*
57. CMK 1/94, Hope to Chief Magistrate, Kokstad, 13 Mar. 1880.
58. *Ibid.*.
59. *Ibid.*
60. *Ibid.*
61. CMK 1/94, meeting of 23 Mar. 1880.
62. CMK 1/152, Hope to Chief Magistrate, Kokstad, 14 Oct. 1880.
63. CMK 1/152, Hope to Chief Magistrate, Kokstad, 19 Oct. 1880.
64. CMK 1/152, RM Maclear to Chief Magistrate Kokstad, 22 Oct. 1880.
65. CMK 1/152, Hope to Chief Magistrate, Kokstad, 19 Oct. 1880.
66. A215, letter to Thomson, 19 Oct. 1880. Thomson was magistrate at Maclear.
67. CMK 1/94, Hope to Chief Magistrate, Kokstad, 19 Sept. 1879.
68. NA 158, Shaw, Report, 31 Dec. 1877.

69. See also 1/ECO 4/1/1, statement of Mangele, 8 Mar. 1881.
70. For Bakhtin the carnivalesque was '*the* ritual location of uninhibited speech ... the only place where *undominated discourse* prevailed' (Scott 1990: 175). See also Bakhtin (1984).
71. Ashforth (2000: 132) quotes a healer who says: 'People, they know that there *is* witchcraft. So if the government says "There is no witch," this means that they are protecting this witchcraft so that it must grow, grow, grow.'
72. *Graham's Town Journal*, 19 May 1904.
73. *Daily Dispatch*, 7 Nov. 1998; see also *Daily Dispatch*, 7 Jan. 1999.
74. *Daily Dispatch*, 25 August 2000.
75. *Daily Dispatch*, 24 Dec. 1999.

REFERENCES

Appadurai, A., 1993. 'Number in the Colonial Imagination', in C.A. Breckenridge and P. van der Veer, eds, *Orientalism and the Postcolonial Predicament: Perspectives on South Asia*. Philadelphia: University of Pennsylvania Press.
Ashforth, A., 1992. *The Politics of Official Discourse in Twentieth-century South Africa*. Oxford: Oxford University Press.
Ashforth, A., 2000. *Madumo: A Man Bewitched*. Chicago: University of Chicago Press.
Atmore, A., 1970. 'Moorosi's Rebellion: Lesotho, 1879', in R. Rotberg and A. Mazrui, eds, *Protest and Power*. New York: Oxford University Press.
Bakhtin, M., 1984. *Rabelais and His World*, trans. Helene Iswolsky. Bloomington: Indiana University Press.
Bayart, J.-F., 1993. *The State in Africa: The Politics of the Belly*. London: Longman.
Bayly, C.A. 1996. *Empire and Information: Intelligence Gathering and Social Communication in India, 1780–1870*. Cambridge: Cambridge University Press.
Beidelman, T.O., 1982. *Colonial Evangelism: A Socio-historical Study of An East African Mission at the Grassroots*. Bloomington: Indiana University Press.
Beinart, W. and Bundy, C., 1987. *Hidden Struggles: Politics and Popular Movements in the Transkei and Eastern Cape, 1890–1930*. Berkeley and Los Angeles: University of California Press.
Bozzoli, B., 1981. *The Political Nature of a Ruling Class: Capital and Ideology in South Africa, 1890–1933*. London: Routledge & Kegan Paul.
Brownlie, F., 1923. *The Transkeian Native Territories: Historical Records*. Lovedale.
Brownlie, W.T., 1975. *Reminiscences of a Transkeian*. Pietermaritzburg.
Burnett, D.G., 2000. *Masters of All They Surveyed: Exploration, Geography, and a British El Dorado*. Chicago: University of Chicago Press.
Cannadine, D., 2001. *Ornamentalism: How the British Saw their Empire*. Oxford: Oxford University Press.
Carton, B., 2000. *Blood from Your Children: The Colonial Origins of Generational Conflict in South Africa*. Charlottesville: University Press of Virginia.
Coetzee, J.M., 1980. *Waiting for the Barbarians*. New York: Penguin.
Cohn, B.S., 1996. *Colonialism and Its Forms of Knowledge: The British in India*. Princeton, NJ: Princeton University Press.
Comaroff, Jean and John Comaroff, 1991. *Of Revelation and Revolution: Christianity, Colonialism, and Consciousness in South Africa*. Chicago: University of Chicago Press.
Comaroff, Jean and John Comaroff, 1997. *Of Revelation and Revolution: The Dialectics of Modernity on a South African Frontier*. Chicago: University of Chicago Press.
Cooper, F., 1996. *Decolonization and African Society: The Labor Question in French and British Africa*. Cambridge: Cambridge University Press.
Cooper, F. and Stoler, A., eds, 1997. *Tensions of Empire: Colonial Cultures in a Bourgeois World*. Berkeley and Los Angeles: University of California Press.

Corrigan, P., 1994. 'State Formation', in G. Joseph and D. Nugent, eds, *Everyday Forms of State Formation: Revolution and Negotiation of Rule in Modern Mexico*. Durham, NC and London: Duke University Press.

Crais, C., 1992. *White Supremacy and Black Resistance: The Making of the Colonial Order in the Eastern Cape, 1770–1865*. Cambridge: Cambridge University Press.

Crais, C., 2002. *The Politics of Evil: Magic, State Power, and the Political Imagination in South Africa*. Cambridge: Cambridge University Press.

Crais, C., ed., 2003. *The Culture of Power in Southern Africa: Essays on State Formation and the Political Imagination*. Portsmouth, NH: Heinemann.

Delius, P., 1996. *A Lion Amongst the Cattle: Reconstruction and Resistance in the Northern Transvaal*. Portsmouth, NH: Heinemann.

Dirks, N., ed., 1992. *Colonialism and Culture*. Ann Arbor: University of Michigan Press.

Dirks, N.B., 2001. *Castes of Mind*. Princeton: Princeton University Press.

Douglas, M., ed., 1970. *Witchcraft Confessions and Accusations*. London: Tavistock.

Doyle, M.W., 1986. *Empires*. Ithaca, NY: Cornell University Press.

Dubow, S., 1989. *Racial Segregation and the Origins of Apartheid in South Africa, 1919–1936*. Oxford.

Evans, I., 1997. *Bureaucracy and Race: Native Administration in South Africa*. Berkeley and Los Angeles: University of California Press.

Foucault, M., 1991. 'Governmentality', pp. 87–104 in G. Burchell, C. Gordon, and P. Miller, eds, *The Foucault Effect: Studies in Governmentality*. Chicago, IL, and London: University of Chicago Press.

Galbraith, J., 1963. *Reluctant Empire: British Policy on the South African Frontier, 1834–54*. Berkeley and Los Angeles: University of California Press.

Geertz, C., 1973. *The Interpretation of Cultures*. New York: Basic Books.

Hamilton, C., 1998. *Terrific Majesty: The Powers of Shaka Zulu and the Limits of Historical Invention*. Cambridge, MA: Harvard University Press.

Hendricks, F., 1990. *The Pillars of Apartheid: Land Tenure, Rural Planning and the Chieftaincy*. Uppsala: Almqvist & Wiksell.

Herzfeld, M., 1992. *The Social Production of Indifference: Exploring the Symbolic Roots of Western Bureaucracy*. New York: Columbia University Press.

Joseph, G. and Nugent. D., eds, 1994. *Everyday Forms of State Formation: Revolution and Negotiation of Rule in Modern Mexico*. Durham, NC and London: Duke University Press.

Kimble, J., 1982. 'Labour Migration in Basutoland, c. 1870–1885', pp. 119–41, in S. Marks and R. Rathbone, eds, *Industrialisation and Social Change in South Africa*. London: Longman.

Landau, P., 1995. *The Realm of the Word: Language, Gender, and Christianity in a Southern African Kingdom*. Portsmouth, NH: Heinemann.

Lonsdale, J., 1985. 'The European Scramble', in J.D. Fage and R. Oliver, eds, *The Cambridge History of Africa, vol. 6*. Cambridge: Cambridge University Press.

Lonsdale, J. and Berman, B., 1992. *Unhappy Valley: Conflict in Kenya and Africa*. Athens: Ohio University Press.

MacQuarrie, J.W., 1958. *The Reminiscences of Sir Walter Stanford*, vol. 1. Cape Town: University of Cape Town.

Mamdani, M., 1976. *Politics and Class Formation in Uganda*. London: Monthly Review Press.

Mamdani, M., 1996. *Citizen and Subject: Contemporary Africa and the Legacy of Late Colonialism*. Princeton, NJ: Princeton University Press.

Mbembe, A., 1992. 'The Banality of Power and the Aesthetics of Vulgarity in the Post-Colony', *Public Culture*, 4(2): 1–30.

Patriarca, S., 1996. *Numbers and Nationhood: Writing Statistics in Nineteenth-century Italy*. Cambridge: Cambridge University Press.

Peires, J., 1981. *The House of Phalo: A History of the Xhosa People in the Days of Their Independence*. Berkeley and Los Angeles: University of California Press.

Posel, D., 1991. *The Making of Apartheid*. Oxford: Clarendon Press.

Ranger, T., 1997. 'Africa in the Age of Extremes: The Irrelevance of African History', in C. McGrath, K. King and J. Thompson, eds, *Rethinking African History*. Edinburgh: Edinburgh University Press.

Robinson, R. and J. Gallagher with J. Denny, 1961. *Africa and the Victorians: The Official Mind of Imperialism*. New York.

Rogers, H., 1933. *Native Administration in the Union of South Africa*. Johannesburg.

Sahlins, M., 1995. *How 'Natives' Think, About Captain Cook, for example*. Chicago: University of Chicago Press.

Said, E.W., 1978. *Orientalism*. New York: Vintage Books.

Sayer, D., 1994. 'Dissident Remarks on Hegemony', in G. Joseph and D. Nugent Joseph, eds, *Everyday Forms of State Formation: Revolution and Negotiation of Rule in Modern Mexico*. Durham, NC and London: Duke University Press.

Scott, J., 1990. *Domination and the Arts of Resistance: Hidden Transcripts*. New Haven, CT: Yale University Press.

Stoler, A.L., 1997. *Race and the Education of Desire: Foucault's History of Sexuality and the Colonial Order of Things*. Durham, NC: Duke University Press.

Stoler, A.L., 2002. *Carnal Knowledge and Imperial Power: Race and the Intimate in Colonial Rule*. Berkeley and Los Angeles: University of California Press.

Thorne, S., 1999. *Congregational Missions and the Making of an Imperial Culture in Nineteenth-century England*. Stanford, CA: Stanford University Press.

Todorov, T., 1982. *The Conquest of America*. New York: Oxford University Press.

Wells, A. and G.M. Joseph, 1996. *Summer of Discontent, Seasons of Upheaval: Elite Politics and Rural Insurgency in Yucatan, 1876–1915*. Stanford, CA: Stanford University Press.

White, L., 2000. *Speaking with Vampires: Rumor and History in Colonial Africa*. Berkeley and Los Angeles: University of California Press.

White, R., 1991. *The Middle Ground: Indians, Empires, and Republics in the Great Lakes Region, 1650–1815*. Cambridge: Cambridge University Press.

4 STATE FORMATION THROUGH DEVELOPMENT IN POST-APARTHEID SOUTH AFRICA

Knut G. Nustad

Clifton Crais demonstrated in the previous chapter how the expansion of the British Empire into the Transkei took place as a series of encounters between African chiefs and British bureaucrats. Hamilton Hope set out to secure this fringe of the British Empire by mapping the land, demarcating districts and sub-districts, and counting and taxing people. But this was much more than a simple exercise in mapping an already existing reality. Hope ordered the knowledge he produced according to a model of how he thought social reality in the Transkei *ought* to be: chiefdoms and pure tribes residing within clearly demarcated areas. But as Crais has pointed out elsewhere (2002), the British colonial state lacked the ability to inscribe its model of reality on the ground. It was not until the 1950s, with the victory of the National Party and the policy of apartheid, that the project begun by Hamilton Hope and his compatriots was finally realised. The apartheid policy followed the model of indirect rule – which had precedents in other parts of the continent – on a scale not previously seen. To create on the ground the fiction of territorially based 'tribes' in the 1950s involved tearing apart huge African urban communities, and returning urbanites to their rural 'homes', often desolate rural districts with which they had no connection. The apartheid state produced the kind of knowledge that it needed to realise its model of society. The project that Hope died trying to realise, was now continued by a huge, modern bureaucratic machine.

There was, then, both in colonial times and during apartheid, a close link between power and knowledge, between the knowledge produced and the underlying model of society that was implied by that knowledge. This chapter has two aims: first, I want to exploit this link between the knowledge produced and the underlying model of society that this knowledge implies, as a way into saying something about post-apartheid state-formation. For, as I will argue, the new democratic state is currently redefining the relationship between itself and its subjects. Whereas the apartheid state divided its people into citizens with inalienable rights, and subjects under the jurisdiction of, first chiefs, and later 'independent' puppet regimes, the new government is casting all South Africans as citizens under a neoliberal order.

But the more important aim of the chapter is to contribute to the overall discussion in this volume of finding ways of avoiding creating a fetish of the state. Through ethnography from a development project in Durban, I want to show that while a theoretical move from seeing the state as an entity to examining state-effects is a huge improvement, some further modifications of this perspective are necessary. Specifically, one needs to realise that state-effects are derived from a specific state formation, and, second, an analytical distinction needs to be introduced between effects as intended and as manifest.

To recapitulate from the Introduction, Trouillot (2001) argues that state power cannot be fixed to a particular place and that therefore a state cannot be defined as a circumscribed institution. Instead, focus must be shifted to state-effects, regardless of where these are produced. The state, therefore, is for him a 'set of practices and processes and their effects' and it is these that must be studied. The analytical task is to identify state-effects and where these are produced. Trouillot defines these effects as four: first, an isolation effect, 'the production of atomised individualised subjects molded and modeled for governance as part of an undifferentiated but specific "public"'; second, an identification effect, that is 'a realignment of the atomised subjectivities along collective lines within which individuals recognise themselves as the same'; third, a legibility effect, closely related to the knowledge described above, that is used to classify and regulate populations; and fourth, a spatialisation effect, the 'production of boundaries and jurisdiction' (2001: 126). These effects are forms of knowledge, and as such, they will serve as an illustration of both the benefits and problems with using knowledge production as a way into the study of the state.

DEVELOPMENT AND THE STATE

The following pages will use the largest post-apartheid development project in South Africa, the development of Durban's Cato Manor, as a case to study these processes. 'Development' is a particularly apt case for studying state formation, as the changing content this concept was given well reflects the overall model of the relationship between the South African state and its people, as perceived by those promoting it. In addition, development is about planned change, and development policies are therefore revealing about how authorities see the ideal relationship between people and the state.

Apartheid ideology was in many ways a culmination and a realisation of Hope's project, and as such should not be treated as a political exception (Mamdani 1996). It was the realisation of a model that tied the black population to a territorially defined tribal identity, where – according to the ideology – they should be allowed to develop along their own lines without interference. The idea was taken to its extreme when the South African government granted many of these entities independence and turned their inhabitants into citizens of desperately poor homelands. Under this model, the majority of the black population was subjected to a different kind of state, because of the perceived difference between them and the white population. An official publication stated, as late as 1974, that 'the Southern African Bantu are not and have never been a homogenous nation'. The white population, in contrast, constituted 'a new African nation which evolved in the same way as the new nations of the U.S.A., Canada, Australia and New Zealand' (Tapscott 1995: 177–78). Each 'ethnic group', according to this model, should therefore be left to develop at its own pace.

The development discourse changed with the election of P.W. Botha in 1978. After that time the National Party responded to growing resistance from the black population and from the international community by searching for a new paradigm. The new theme which emerged was a depoliticised version of development. 'Separate development' faded out of official language and was replaced with a search for 'appropriate development strategies'. It culminated with a partial adoption of neoliberal ideology: the market should regulate access to housing and to jobs. The different racial groups of the high-apartheid era disappeared from official rhetoric to be replaced with a Western development discourse. If black people were poor, this was not because of political repression but because of misjudged development policies: 'South Africa is using the same classical and Keynesian instruments and economic objectives as the West.... If the paradigm is the same, the same inadequacies can be expected' (Van der Kooy 1979: 21). As Tapscott notes, to claim that the pursuit of Western economic models was responsible for the poverty in the black homelands was obviously a gross distortion (1995: 187).

This conception of development was to a large degree taken over by the African National Congress (ANC). The state repression that followed Botha's area of reforms in the late 1970s and 1980s was immense and the liberation movement was reorganised, mainly through the United Democratic Front, to meet the challenge. This accounts partly for the failure of the movement to envisage and construct alternative economic policies. Tomlinson, writing in 1990, said that 'it is not too much of a caricature to claim that much progressive analysis of the post-apartheid future criticizes the current system at length, briefly considers the Freedom Charter, and concludes that "the people will decide"' (Tomlinson 1990: 5–6).[1] As Gumede predicted, this turned out to be a difficult task for the liberation movement, and particularly for the ANC when it had to prepare itself for assuming the responsibility of government.

Shortly before his release from prison in 1990, Mandela proclaimed that 'the nationalization of the mines, banks, and monopoly industry is the policy of the ANC and a change or modification of our views in this regard is inconceivable' (M. Murray 1994: 19). This was a restatement of the principles of the Freedom Charter. Some initiatives were taken to examine future economic policies after the ANC was unbanned; including the work of the Macroeconomic Research Group, hosted by Department of Economics at the University of the Witwatersrand (MERG 1993), which took as its point of departure the economic policy goals of the ANC and Cosatu (the Congress of South African Trade Unions) as they existed at the time and set out to create a macroeconomic framework to reach these goals. But the most important document to come out of the discussions in the first years was the *Reconstruction and Development Programme* (RDP) (ANC 1994). It was the result of widespread consultation with the NGO sector and the partners in the alliance (Cosatu, South African National Civics Organization [SANCO] and the South African Communist Party). As C. Murray and Williams (1994: 324) point out, the new South African government could not support further 'top-down' measures of reform. This approach to development was intimately associated with apartheid and the new government had to show that their policies constituted a radical break with those of the old regime. In the RDP, the ANC set out to outline an alternative ideology for development. One of the basic principles of the programme was that it would be based on a 'people-driven' process. This was the programme on which the ANC was elected in the first democratic elections. But in the last years the ANC has slowly abandoned this position, and there has been a change in focus from the integrated approach of the RDP to an 'orthodox economic stabilization package' (Michie and Padayachee 1997). Five years after Mandela argued for the nationalisation of important industries, there had been a complete shift to a free-market, neoliberal and growth-orientated policy.

The International Monetary Fund (IMF), which had severed links with South Africa in 1983, became involved again after 1990. In 1992, the IMF issued its first report (Lachmann and Bercuson 1992), which, according to Elling Tjønneland, could be summed up as 'growth first and redistribution later' (quoted in Padayachee 1997: 30). In its annual report for 1995, the IMF noted with pleasure that 'the most telling signal of the new government's economic ideology has been its broad advocacy of free trade' (quoted in Michie and Padayachee 1997: 20), and in July the same year, Mandela announced that the government must 'abandon its obsession with grand plans and make economic growth its top priority' (Michie and Padayachee 1997: 21).

A ministry was set up to oversee the development programmes that fell under the RDP, but it did not last long. In 1996 the RDP office was closed and responsibility for the projects spread to other departments. According to the ANC, this was done to make delivery more effective, but many, including one non-governmental organisation (NGO) leader and ANC activist that I spoke to,[2] saw in it the failure of the whole programme. This belief gained credence on the left with the publication of the *Growth, Employment and Redistribution* (GEAR) policy document on 14 June 1996.[3] It sets out to outline a 'strategy for rebuilding and restructuring the economy ... in keeping with the goals set in the Reconstruction and Development Programme'.[4] After outlining the strategy, the introduction ends on an optimistic note: 'We are confident that our social partners will join us in the combined efforts needed to achieve this goal.'[5] They were not, and GEAR has become hotly contested. Adelzadeh

(1996: 67) concludes that 'the proposed framework and policy scenarios represent an adoption of the essential tenets and policy recommendations of the neo-liberal framework advocated by the IMF in its structural adjustment programmes'. This, he argues, represents a recourse to the policy goals and instruments of the past apartheid regime (Adelzadeh 1996). Nattrass (1996) argues that GEAR gives primacy to market forces, and is more than anything else concerned with signalling the government's clear commitment to a market-orientated economic policy. Michie (1997) argues that trade should have been used to assist in the reconstruction and development of the economy; instead, GEAR accepted a 'free-trade line' wholesale (Michie 1997: 160). At the UN World Forum against Racism in Durban in 2000, 30,000 marched against the ANC's neoliberal policies.

Concomitant with this process, development projects have been continued. But their focus has been on local solutions to local problems, thus detaching the question of the huge gap between rich and poor from economic policies. This is in line with neoliberal ideology, which minimises the importance of the state's intervention in society. The question remains whether this can be linked to the micro processes of state formation as described by Trouillot. With this in mind, let us turn to the post-apartheid reconstruction of Cato Manor.

CREATING EFFECTS IN CATO MANOR

Durban's Cato Manor has had its share of experience with state power. It emerged as a mixed-race area in the 1930s, when Indian tenure workers who had finished their contracts bought land there – at that time just outside the city border. The pre-war industrialisation of Durban brought many black workers to the city, and many of these rented from the Indian landowners. Today Cato Manor is still remembered by many as the kind of society South Africa could have been had it not been for the separation of racial groups undertaken by the apartheid regime. Two incidents sealed the fate of Cato Manor. In 1949, a black kid was beaten up after stealing from an Indian street vendor. Onlookers intervened, and conflicts between Indians and blacks spread throughout the city. Cato Manor, with its huge concentration of people, was badly hit. This incident has been seen by some as a motivating factor for the Nationalist Party's commencing work on the Group Areas Act, the central legal instrument of apartheid. In preparation for 'rezoning' (in apartheid vocabulary) Cato Manor a white group area, people were moved into an emergency camp to await removal to the newly built townships of KwaMashu and Umlezi outside Durban. Many women, who were not offered new housing in the townships because they were not categorised as labourers, protested against the removals and might have succeeded had it not been for the second determining incident. The South African state financed the removal of black people from the white areas by taxes imposed on the beer sold in the municipal beer halls. Women protested by throwing men out these halls and by illegally brewing beer. On 24 January 1960, a group of police officers raided Cato Manor looking for illegal breweries, destroying the stock and beating people up. Suddenly the crowd turned on them, and nine policemen were killed. The public outcry that followed this sealed the fate of Cato Manor. By the mid 1960s, 120,000 people had been moved from the area.

For 30 years Cato Manor was a wasteland, the object of legal fights initiated by Indian lawyers contesting the state's right to confiscate the land from the Indian landowners. In the late 1980s people began moving back into the area. At first they hid their shacks well out of sight of the neighbouring white middle-class area of Manor Gardens. As the settlement grew, it became impossible to hide its presence. The police began removing shacks and chasing people away, but the squatters rebuilt their houses at night. Eventually, the squatters formed a community organisation, of the type referred to as a civic in South Africa, to resist removals and were helped in their struggle by ANC law students and Indian NGOs. Together these organisations and individuals formed a development committee, and later, when the ANC won elections in 1994, this committee was transformed into a development association with the responsibility for developing Cato Manor. It is the work of this association, the Cato Manor Development Association (CMDA) that I will use to examine state-effects. I want to show that, in this case, the establishment of control over the population in Cato Manor, which is what the creation of state-effects is all about, proved much more difficult than anticipated, and that the state as such failed to materialise as a reality in this setting.

THE CREATION OF A POPULATION

The development organisation attempted to create all four state-effects that were outlined above. On closer scrutiny, this should not come as a surprise. After all, what a development organisation is attempting to achieve is to intervene in a social setting and to transform it in a direction that it believes involves an improvement. This necessitates a large degree of control over the entity in which one wants to intervene, and it was exactly the emergence of 'the population' as an object of knowledge that made intervention and control on a grand scale possible in modern states. Hence, one of the first tasks the developers set themselves was to establish a clearly demarcated population. Cato Manor is a huge area, involving both established settlements and squatter areas. For the following discussion, I will rely on data from a fieldwork I conducted in the largest squatter settlement in Cato Manor, the informal settlement of Cato Crest.

Setting out to create a population, an object suitable for administrative manipulation, out of a squatter settlement, which by its very nature appears chaotic to an outsider, where people move in and out, renting a room in an established shack before obtaining a piece of land on which they can build their own structures, or simply drifting on; or maintaining a house in the townships and owning a shack in order to have a place to stay closer to work opportunities; or building a shack or a number of shacks for letting out; where a significant minority stays precisely because it is difficult for outsiders such as the police to penetrate, either because they are illegal immigrants or have escaped from prison, is a hugely complicated task. The CMDA and other organisations seeking to establish control over Cato Crest did nevertheless try.

Some background to what they wanted to achieve is necessary: housing and land were core issues in the first years of post-apartheid South Africa, and continue to be important issues today. The infrastructure of apartheid was built on the control of land and housing, on the denial of the right to stay in the city in the days of high-apartheid, and on the restrictions on affordable housing in the late-apartheid neoliberal reforms. Consequently, both land redistribution and especially the less politically sensitive issue of house building were high on the agenda of the new government. Each homeless South African was in principle given a housing subsidy of 17,500 SAR (South African rands, henceforth R), to be granted either individually or through a corporation such as a development agency. In practice, almost all the subsidies were given to development agents that managed the subsidies for the beneficiaries. This was also the case in Cato Crest. The first task, then, was to demarcate the population on whose behalf this subsidy was to be managed. In order to carry it out, an attempt was made to create all the four state-effects listed above.

At first, before it was decided that a development cooperation would be responsible for the area, Cato Crest had been given to a private developer, a company that planned to build houses for middle-class whites. The company, called the National Investment Corporation Ltd (NIC) served a 'First Site Vacation Notice'[6] to the residents, which read, 'Unfortunately you have chosen to construct your humble home on the land which NIC intends to develop for housing; however, it is NIC's intention to make your move in the future as convenient as possible and to this end NIC calls on your cooperation.'[7] The notice offered one of two alternatives: a replacement site elsewhere in Cato Manor or in one of the established townships outside Durban, or R 500 compensation.[8] NIC allocated numbers that were painted on the walls of the 132 shacks existing on 26 March 1991 and extended the offer to their residents.[9] Despite these efforts, the influx of people continued to increase. A week later, the Settlement Control Division of the Natal Provincial Administration, who were to guard NIC's interest in the area, found more than 200 completed shacks and 26 shacks under construction.[10] 'The squatters are moving in and building shacks all over the area. There is no control over the influx of squatters in the area', the officer complained in a report to his superiors.[11] This led NIC to issue a second and less polite warning on 11 April:

NIC appeals once again to all people who are building in this area to **stop immediately** and commence dismantling their structures. The only people who are permitted to remain are those who possess notices whose shacks were numbered by NIC a few days ago. **DO NOT IGNORE THIS NOTICE** if you do your structure will be demolished by NIC for you. If you resist you will be charged with trespassing. NIC repeats **DO NOT IGNORE THIS NOTICE** if you do your structure will be demolished by NIC for you. If you resist you will be charged with trespassing. By order ...[12]

Despite this, the number of squatters increased. According to the Settlement Control Division, 60 shacks were destroyed in the week following NIC's second warning, but at the same time more than 300 new shacks were under construction.[13] NIC now seemed to be aware that they were fighting a losing battle and that tougher measures would be required to get rid of the squatters. On 26 April the company issued a statement ordering all those not on its list to leave by 24 May.[14] Those not complying were threatened with a fine of R 2,000 or imprisonment for one year.[15] Still the influx of people into Cato Crest continued; only four days after the latest warning from NIC the population in Cato Crest had reached 400 families, and by now more shacks had been built since NIC's cut-off date than before.[16] NIC now employed a private security company, Kilosec Security, to stop the squatters from entering the area. The company found the area difficult to control; most of Cato Crest was still covered in thick bush and the squatters would drive trucks into the area at night and drop off building materials.[17] Twelve days before the demolition date, NIC issued a final warning, ordering people to demolish their houses.

The civic eventually managed to negotiate a settlement with the authorities and with NIC. According to one of the civic representatives, it was decided that the squatters would be allowed to stay, on condition that they prevented further influx into the area. To make sure that this agreement was upheld, an aerial photo was taken of the area. In a subsequent meeting, and the civic representative told me this with a smile, the developers drew a thick black line on the photo, a line that was to represent the spatial boundary of the area. Further, all buildings visible on the photo were allocated a registration number, and it was agreed that all houses found in Cato Crest that did not appear on the photo and had not been given a registration number, would be destroyed. Representatives of both the developers and the squatters then signed their names on the photo, thereby signalling their assent to the agreement. This was then followed by the survey. All the inhabitants of the buildings that appeared on the photo were registered and each building was painted with a registration number. The numbers consisted of the two letters cc (for Cato Crest) and a number, 1 to 245.

The next weeks were marked by an escalation of the conflict between the squatters and the authorities. One month after the agreement, 131 shacks had been demolished.[18] At first the demolition team from the Natal Provincial Administration (NPA) would satisfy themselves with pulling down the shacks and the squatters would rebuild them during the night. To prevent this, the NPA brought chainsaws and destroyed the building material before driving it to a waste dump.[19] NIC finally gave up on controlling Cato Crest. On 26 June, 40 squatters – mostly women with children – staged a sit-in protest at the Durban office of the Department of Home Affairs. The squatters utilised the history of Cato Manor in their protest; 'Cato Manor is our land and we are taking it back!' ran the slogan. One of the protesters told a newspaper that 'My grandfather's grave is there, and I am there to live. I am not moving.'[20] They handed a memorandum to the regional representative, demanding that the NPA stop demolishing their houses, and then left after negotiations with the police. They were permitted by the NPA to stay until a deal was negotiated and they were allocated numbers. A survey of Cato Crest was conducted on 13 August 1991 and revealed that 348 families, totalling almost 1,000 people, lived there, and that there were at this time 254 numbered shacks that corresponded to the aerial photograph.[21] These were now to constitute the population in Cato Crest. The situation stabilised for a time.

STATE-EFFECTS

This brief description reveals a number of interesting aspects of the state-effects that external authorities sought to create. First, the similarity of the approach of the agents external to Cato Crest underlines the point that state-effects are created also outside the boundaries of state institutions. The private construction company and the provincial authority both tried to create a stable population, defined within a boundary, tied to a building and not increasing. There was thus no difference here between the different agencies in the way in which they sought to transform the people living in Cato Crest into a population. Second, the tools that were employed were meant to achieve effects that appear to be picked straight out of the above definition of state-effects. There was an isolation of individuals through an individualisation of the persons living in Cato Crest at one specific date, 13 August 1991. These persons, and nobody else, were defined as members of the relevant population. There was an identification effect that defined all these people as members of a population with a right to stay in Cato Crest, and with a right to take part in a future development process, as opposed to those people seeking to settle in the area after this date. The identification effect was further strengthened by tying people to numbered houses. There was a legibility effect in the numbers provided. These were painted both on the houses and written on the photograph. A surveyor could then at a glance decide whether a house was included in the legal population, and know who was living there: their age, sex and number. There was spatialisation effect in the boundary drawn on the picture, defining the piece of land that is Cato Crest and within which a legal population might reside. All in all, these effects tied a known number of people, a population, to a known number of houses, to a known area of land. What was produced, in short, was a population that lent itself to easy surveillance by an outsider, thereby creating a legibility effect.

But what does the existence of these effects tell us about the development process? According to Trouillot, the answer is that the NPA and NIC are state bodies in as much as they sought to create these effects. But, as was argued in the Introduction, a closer scrutiny of the genealogy of Trouillot's four effects reveals they are derived from a specific form of state formation, and cannot be used to identify a generic 'state'. The existence of these effects also adds specificity to the claim by Foucault (1991) that governmentality works as a positive, generative force in that it creates subject positions. In the case of the development intervention in Cato Crest, the subject position that external agents sought to create was that of individualised citizens with rights to housing. But, as will become clear, other people also struggled to create alternative subject positions.

INTENTIONS AND EFFECTS

We have identified the four effects that Trouillot defined as state-effects, at least at the level of intention. But another aspect of the attempt to create state-effects leaps out of this material, that is, the difficulty with which these effects were produced. The people in Cato Crest did not passively let themselves be transformed into a population that could serve the interests of external agents. The effects created were achieved through overcoming processes that pulled in other directions. A focus solely on state-effects misses this crucial aspect, because it confuses model and reality. The transformation of an undifferentiated group of persons into a legible population presupposes that many characteristics of these persons, those that are of no interest to the agent that seeks to control them, are left out.

James Scott (1998) likens this process to a cadastral map. This is a powerful tool for achieving an overview of a huge area of land, and it works precisely because it leaves out what in other circumstances would constitute important information. Just as a 1:1 map that included all details would be useless, so the cadastral map highlights only the information that is useful for its users. Thus it is concerned with boundaries between units of land, thereby making it possible for official authorities to connect the land to people, and hence create a basis on which to calculate tax. For this purpose, the map overlooks what would constitute important information for a person concerned with cultivating the land, such as its orientation, altitude, climate, quality of soil, etc. The same holds true for the creation of a population. Certain aspects of reality, those that one seeks to control, are captured by the model, others are left out. What Trouillot overlooks is the way in which the residue – all that is left out of the abstractions – has an ability to interact with the formal abstractions. Scott similarly fails in this regard; he treats the state forms and the people's practices as two separate entities. Let me give one example from the above process: individualisation and identification were supposed to tie people to buildings and to land, thereby treating them as a part of a population with a stake in the development of Cato Crest. But persons are not reducible to the forms imposed on them.

In December 1991 between 40 and 50 women set up a huge tent in Cato Crest. At a meeting between the Cato Crest civic and the NPA, the NPA representative demanded to know where these women came from, as the agreement was that no one should be allowed to settle after the cut-off date.[22] The Cato Crest representative argued that these people had a right to stay because the women were already residents of the area and had set up the tent to accommodate their families and children who had returned home for Christmas.[23] The NPA nevertheless demolished the tent. It was rebuilt and demolished again and the occupants slept outdoors for a while (Attwood and Stavrou 1992). Finally, they were granted permission to stay over Christmas. This seriously undermined all attempts at controlling the influx into the area; the NPA officer in charge of demolition complained to his superiors, in a report dated 22 March 1992, that the 'big tent' was a 'bone of contention' and that he and his staff were approached daily by people whose shacks had been demolished but who had arrived in Cato Crest months before the erection of the tent.[24] The stress he was under was revealed in the last paragraph, which reads:

... with the declaration of a moratorium in Cato Crest, it has been absolutely impossible for my staff and myself to carry out our functions productively as we have been made the laughing stock of the Community and have been ridiculed by certain people to the community.[25]

Residents in Cato Crest argued using other parts of their identities than that seen by the external agents: no longer were they instances of a population ascribed to Cato Crest, but heads of families that wanted to spend the holiday with their loved ones. They thereby evoked other aspects of themselves than the one seen by the authorities, and, further, this evocation was based on a form of shared humanity that it was difficult to deny.

THE FORMAL AND THE INFORMAL

This means that we will have to divide up the process that Trouillot describes as the creation of state-effects: first, an agent seeks to order a group of people in such a way that it will be possible to produce knowledge of it as a population. But producing this knowledge of a population is little use if one cannot make the population correspond to the abstractions made of them. Scott cites the case of patronyms, first used by agents of the state to be able to trace property relations through generations, a task that was daunting when the last name was derived from the father's first name. As encounters with the state increased, these patronyms, at first only used by tax collectors and government officials, were then gradually internalised. This is how the process that Trouillot collapses into state-effects works.

It is necessary to subdivide this process to examine the present case, because the creation of state-effects failed between the first and the second part of this process. The numbers that were meant to enact the transformation of a chaotic mass of people moving in and out of an informal settlement to an ordered population tied to a development process, was hijacked by another political process that, instead of creating citizens in the new South African state, sought to create subjects of local leaders.

As part of the attempt to control the population of Cato Crest, the local civic, which had at first been instrumental in fighting against evictions, was assigned an important function: members of this body were to act as mediators between the developers and the population, embodying and representing the interest of the group. The civic was therefore meant to function as a manageable entity with which the developers could relate. The need for this demonstrates that the creation of a population was not a complete success – total legibility would have made it possible for the developers to deal with the population directly.

Dependence on this intermediary level was to prove the bane of the attempt to develop Cato Crest. In order to hold on to power as community representatives, the local leaders had to mobilise resources in some way, both to survive themselves and to be able to build up a group of loyal followers. The local leadership in Cato Crest soon split into two groups that would continue to fight for control over positions in the local political organisation. Why was it so important to gain access to these positions? The obvious answer is access to resources. Whereas for the developer, a community organisation represents a manageable manifestation of 'the community', for people living in the squatter settlement the organisation represents a link to the world of government and NGO funding and equipment. Such positions are extremely valuable resources in themselves, resources that exist because of the way the development process is structured.

Converting a position in a community organisation to material gains and power took a variety of forms. One group of strategies was to allocate jobs given by the developers to dependants and followers; another was to appropriate money and equipment from development organisations. A third very common strategy was the trading of registration numbers by people involved in the community organisations. As we have seen, the creation of state-effects cumulated in the registration numbers that were supposed to tie identities, people, houses and land together. To deliver the promised housing presupposed the establishment of some sort of order on the perceived chaos of the settlement. To this end, the developers sought to transform the people living in Cato Crest into a population. The CMDA was aware that it was not enough to impose a model on the people living in Cato Crest, the people would also have to conform to the model. Thus, while the numbers turned people into a population, the cooperation of people in this process was sought through the extension of recognition of the right to stay, symbolised by the registration number, on condition that the recipients managed to keep others out. The idea, then, was that those given the right to stay would see it as in their interest to keep other people out. This strategy would then stabilise the situation and enable the planners to estimate the number of people to include in their plans. There were four different attempts at ordering Cato Crest in this way. Each time new shacks were built, and when the number system lost all resemblance to the reality on the ground, the developers devised new formulae.

But these futile attempts at control underwent a transformation through their application. The numbers, in themselves, became commodities that obtained an exchange value. Ownership of a number not only gave freedom from police harassment, but also had an additional potential value. If the development of formal housing commenced, it guaranteed the number-holder a part in that process, and eventually a formal house. While the trading of registration numbers had taken place to a smaller degree when Cato Crest consisted of a handful of houses, trade became organised after the mass influx of 1993. As part of the agreement between the then active community organisation (the civic) and the provincial authorities, the organisation was charged with controlling the influx of people into the area. The civic initiated a system of 'marshals', people who were to allocate registration numbers to those already settled and make sure that no one arrived after the cut-off date. This put the marshals in a position where they had, on the one hand, a valuable commodity to offer (the number which symbolised legality) and on the other hand a sanction; they had the power to inform demolition teams from the provincial authority that a shack had been erected after the cut-off date. The marshals were quick to exploit the opportunity opened to them; they approached people building shacks and told them that they needed a registration number to stay. Prices for a number ranged from R 200 to R 500 (US $37–95). The marshals could demand a relatively high price because they had the sanction of informing the provincial authority that the house was being built illegally and therefore had to be destroyed.

What this example demonstrates is again that a focus on state-effects creates a short-cut between intentions and outcomes, and thereby creates too-dominant state agents. The development agency set out to create state-effects by creating a legible population of the people who moved in and out of Cato Crest. To this effect they allocated rights, registered houses and persons, demarcated a space within which to operate and allocated registration numbers. But the attempt at tying together space, houses, land and people failed because another association was created between these entities by another agent – the local leadership.

EFFECTS AND GIANTS: A STATE IN CATO CREST?

This case demonstrates the need for qualifying the idea of 'state-effects' in two regards. First, the identification of the four effects listed by Trouillot in any specific ethnographic setting does not point to the presence of a generic state. The effects that he pointed to are derived from a Marxist critique of a specific historically situated form of state formation: the capitalist state. Specifically, as Poulantzas (1968) and others have pointed out, the creation of atomised individuals and their alignment as autonomous legal entities, with equal rights as members of a nation-state, is tied to a bourgeois ideology that emerged together with capitalism. This does not make Trouillot's suggestion invalid, it only limits its applicability. Different historical trajectories produce states that create dissimilar effects.

Second, the case has demonstrated the need for opening up the process of creating state-effects. We need to distinguish between intentions and effects. This is important not only because the effects created were not what the development organisation intended, but also because the alternative constellation that emerged – the tying of subjects to local leaders – was dependent on the attempt. It was the instruments that the developers used to create state-effects that were translated into different devices. Instead of tying citizens to the state, the numbers tied subjects to local leaders.

Let me return to Radcliffe-Brown's ([1940] 1955) contention that there is no such thing as the state, that the state does not exist over and above the human individuals who make up society. The statement's validity, of course, hinges on the question of what a state is. If we follow the focus on state-effects to its conclusion, this would lead us to define the 'state' as any agent that produces state-effects. This follows from the proposition that state power has no institutional fixity and that state-effects never obtain solely in national institutions or in government sites.

This means that the state cannot be conceptualised separately from the effects it produces. Nagengast's state, an entity with the ability to 'determine the range of available social, political, ethnic and national identities' (1994: 109) does not exist, because it is the *production* of these effects that determines whether an agent is state-like. Whether an agent should be seen as a state can only be determined after the fact, from the effects that are produced.

This does not mean, of course, that there are no such things as states. Some actors are both giants, in that they control a large number of people, and states, in that they produce state-effects. In fact, the state-effects, as we have seen, are produced precisely because they facilitate the tying together of a huge number of people into a single entity, the population, that lends itself to governmentality. But one cannot start out by looking for criteria that distinguish such actors from other actors. This is because the focus here is shifted from society as a given to the processes that constitute a version of society. Thus the fact that an actor is a state actor is the end result, the outcome of a process. It follows that one cannot a priori distinguish between small scale and large scale, one will have to examine the processes that make it possible for some actors to achieve a large size. Then, after having examined the process, one can ask whether, in the process of achieving size, certain other characteristics are also achieved.

An agent becomes a state actor by establishing associations between people and objects, by translating the will of others into a single will for which it speaks. This turns the successful state actor into a centre of a web, where all communications between the different nodes have to pass through the centre. This was what the two central actors in the above material sought to accomplish. The developers wanted to be able to say that they represented that object, the population of Cato Crest, and acted on its behalf. The local leadership also wanted to act as the only node that connected people in Cato Crest to outside development resources. But theirs was a different form of association than that produced by a state actor. The local leadership did not try to construct a unified population; instead they tied some people together in networks of mutual dependence.

The CMDA attempted to create all the effects that define a state actor: individuation, identification, legibility and spatiality, but it failed. This underscores the point that a state actor's power cannot be explained by some inherent capacity that exists prior to and over and above interaction in the social world occupied by people.

NOTES

1. 'The Freedom Charter, Adopted at the Congress of the People, Kliptown, on 26 June 1955'. At the time of writing this document is available at http://www.anc.org.za/ancdocs/history/charter.html.
2. Interview, 17 May 1996.
3. 'Growth, Employment and Redistribution: a Macroeconomics Strategy', 14 June 1996. At the time of writing, this policy document is available on: http://www.polity.org.za/govdocs/policy/growth.html.
4. GEAR, p. 1.
5. *Ibid.*, p. 3.
6. All notices issued by NIC were written in Zulu and in English.
7. 'First site vacation notice', 26 March 1991. National Investment Corporation Ltd.
8. *Ibid.*
9. 'Re: Squatters – Cato Crest', 30 April 1991. Report from Brown, Settlement Officer, Department of Land Affairs, Durban, to D.P. De Beer, Senior Settlement Officer, Department of Land Affairs, Durban.
10. 'Re: Squatter Count Cato Crest', 4 April 1991. Report from Brown, Settlement Officer, Department of Land Affairs, Durban, to D.P. De Beer, Senior Settlement Officer, Department of Land Affairs, Durban.
11. *Ibid.*
12. 'Demolition Notice Warning', 11 April 1991. National Investment Corporation Ltd. Original emphasis.
13. 'Re: Squatters – Cato Crest', 15 April 1991. Report from Brown, Settlement Officer, Department of Land Affairs, Durban, to D.P. De Beer, Senior Settlement Officer, Department of Land Affairs, Durban.
14. 'Notice of Illegal Squatting', 26 April 1991. National Investment Corporation Ltd.
15. *Ibid.*
16. 'Re: Squatters Cato Crest', 30 April 1991. Report from Brown, Settlement Officer, Department of Land Affairs, Durban, to D.P. De Beer, Senior Settlement Officer, Department of Land Affairs, Durban.

17. 'Re: Squatters – Cato Crest', 13 May 1991. Report from Brown, Settlement Officer, Department of Land Affairs, Durban, to D.P. De Beer, Senior Settlement Officer, Department of Land Affairs, Durban.
18. 'Daily Sitrep, Cato Crest', 26 June 1991. Natal Provincial Administration, Department of Land Affairs, Squatter Control Unit.
19. Interview with Thandi, 6 June 1995; interview with Makhathini, 21 April 1995.
20. *Ibid.*
21. *Ibid.*
22. 'Minutes of the Temporary Squatters meeting held at Mayville 20 December 1991 at 3: 00'. Urbanization Support Unit.
23. *Ibid.*
24. 'Report: Cato Crest', 22 March 1992. Pearch, NPA, Urbanization Support Unit to Acting Deputy Director, Urbanization Support Unit, Durban.
25. *Ibid.*

REFERENCES

Adelzadeh, A., 1996. 'From the RDP to Gear: The Gradual Embracing of Neo-liberalism in Economic Policy', *Transformation* 31: 66–95.

ANC, 1994. *The Reconstruction and Development Programme.* Johannesburg: Umanyano Publications.

Attwood, H and S. Stavrou, 1992. 'Cato Crest Survey: Summary Document', unpublished report prepared by Data Research Africa.

Crais, C., 2002. *The Politics of Evil: Magic, State Power, and the Political Imagination in South Africa.* Cambridge: Cambridge University Press.

Foucault, M., 1991. 'Governmentality', pp. 87–104 in G. Burchell, C. Gordon and P. Miller, eds, *The Foucault Effect: Studies in Governmentality.* Chicago: University of Chicago Press.

Lachmann, D. and K. Bercuson, 1992. *Economic Policies for a New South Africa.* Washington, DC: International Monetary Fund.

Mamdani, M., 1996. *Citizen and Subject: Contemporary Africa and the Legacy of Late Colonialism.* Princeton, NJ: Princeton University Press.

MERG (Macroeconomic Research Group), 1993. *Making Democracy Work: A Framework for Macroeconomic Policy in South Africa. A Report to Members of the Democratic Movement of South Africa.* Bellville: Centre for Development Studies.

Michie, J., 1997. 'Developing the Institutional Framework: Employment and Labour Market Policies', in J. Michie and V. Padayachee, eds, *The Political Economy of South Africa's Transition: Policy Perspectives in the Late 1990s.* London: The Dryden Press.

Michie, J. and V. Padayachee, 1997. 'South Africa's Transition: The Policy Agenda', in J. Michie and V. Padayachee, eds, *The Political Economy of South Africa's Transition: Policy Perspectives in the Late 1990s.* London: The Dryden Press.

Murray, C. and G. Williams, 1994. 'Land and Freedom in South Africa', *Review of African Political Economy,* 21(61): 315–24.

Murray, M.J., 1994. *The Revolution Deferred: The Painful Birth of Post-apartheid South Africa.* London: Verso.

Nagengast, C., 1994. 'Violence, Terror and the Crisis of the State', *Annual Review of Anthropology,* 23: 109–36.

Nattrass, N., 1996. 'Gambling on Investment: Competing Economic Strategies in South Africa', *Transformation,* 31: 25–42.

Padayachee, V., 1997. 'The Evolution of South Africa's International Financial Relations and Policy: 1985–95', in J. Michie and V. Padayachee, eds, *The Political Economy of South Africa's Transition: Policy Perspectives in the Late 1990s.* London: The Dryden Press.

Poulantzas, N., 1968. *Political Power and Social Classes.* London: New Left Books.

Radcliffe-Brown, A.R., [1940] 1955. 'Preface', in M. Fortes and E.E. Evans-Pritchard, eds, *African Political Systems*. London: Oxford University Press.

Scott, J.C., 1998. *Seeing Like a State: How Certain Schemes to Improve the Human Condition have Failed*. New Haven, CT: Yale University Press.

Tapscott, C., 1995. 'Changing Discourses of Development in South Africa', pp. 176–91 in J. Crush, ed., *Power of Development*. London: Routledge.

Tomlinson, R., 1990. *Urbanization in Post-apartheid South Africa*. London: Unwin Hyman.

Trouillot, M.-R., 2001. 'The Anthropology of the State in the Age of Globalisation', *Current Anthropology*, 42(1): 125–38.

Van der Kooy, R., 1979. 'In Search of a New Economic Development Paradigm for Southern Africa: An Introduction', *Development Studies Southern Africa*, 2(1): 3–34.

5 NEGOTIATED DICTATORSHIP: THE BUILDING OF THE TRUJILLO STATE IN THE SOUTH-WESTERN DOMINICAN REPUBLIC

Christian Krohn-Hansen

The United States occupied the Dominican Republic from 1916 to 1924, in the process helping to create an effective national military institution in a country that had previously had none.[1] Among the members of the first class of native officers hastily graduated from the new military academy in 1921 was Rafael Leónidas Trujillo Molina. He was born in 1891 to a family of modest means and mixed ethnic stock, and raised in San Cristóbal, a small town near the capital. By the age of 39, he had become the leader of the modernised military that the United States had helped to establish, the Dominican National Army. Using his position to overthrow the elected government, he ruled the country from 1930 until his assassination in 1961. Many of Trujillo's brutal, corrupt and eccentric extremes indicate an almost complete dictatorship. His rule was marked by grotesque violence and abuse, and he and his family used state power to amass an unheard-of fortune. Under Trujillo, the state established a personality cult focused on the dictator, participation in which was compulsory throughout the country. Vast numbers of streets, buildings and monuments were named or renamed after him.

How, then, can an anthropologist usefully examine and write about the building of an authoritarian state? What is a dictatorship? Using the case of the Dominican Republic, this chapter outlines a set of answers to these questions. Here I offer an historical ethnography that sketches the creation and the construction of the Trujillo state in and around La Descubierta, a community situated in the south-western region of the country.[2]

The most influential literature on the Trujillo regime emphasises terror and deceit as almost the sole explanation for the protracted regime. Little has been said about life in the Trujillo state 'viewed from below'. What has been underscored is the dictator's ability to define most features of official policy and everyday life across the national territory from the top of the state. In what follows I will be writing against this sort of analysis. In my view, the typical notions of how authoritarian histories are produced have become confining and misleading. Hegemonic Western discourses on dictatorships express ethnocentrism, turning 'their' despotisms into fantasies of almost complete political savagery and irrationality, and much work on authoritarianism has strong elements of solipsism. What is needed is an understanding achieved with the aid of concrete history and ethnography.

To break away from a sterile and exoticising form of analysis, we must acknowledge two circumstances. First, we need to explode a deep-rooted myth – the myth which says that one man may wield total power. Even in dictatorships, state power is far more dispersed and transactional than is generally assumed. Second, even dictatorships must be viewed as sets of cultural processes. The past decades have seen the appearance of a new anthropology of modern state-building, with the focus of analysis on the cultural forms and practices that constitute states.[3] A growing number of researchers now recognise that much of the building of states involves the construction of meaning. I agree with this view, and in this chapter seek to show that political history under Trujillo cannot be understood in isolation from a cultural history.

That said, however, there is one more bit of baggage to be discarded: the common assumption that modern state formation is necessarily a set of processes that generate dramatically *new* types of subjects. True, some historical constructions of states may best be described as cultural revolutions, examples of simultaneously individualising and totalising processes that have produced new types of subjects (see Foucault 1979, 1991; Corrigan and Sayer 1985). However, not all states are like these. There are other examples, and these must be understood in other ways.

The Dominican Republic was never France or England. The past 150 years in the Dominican south-west reveal considerable cultural continuity. In the twentieth century, the communities of that region were increasingly incorporated into the postcolonial state. But the area's well-tried institutions were not in an antagonistic relationship to the building of the state. On the contrary, in this part of the country, the emergence of the state both depended upon and strengthened the most important pre-state cultural forms and practices of the region. The building of the postcolonial state consolidated and reinforced forms of masculinity and patronage; likewise with such institutions as the extended family and *compadrazgo*. The state was produced precisely by means of these cultural forms and practices. In the making of the state, pre-state forms were used in transformed ways and for new purposes. But the emergence of the state did not mean a cultural revolution.

We will consider each of these points in turn. The section which follows takes a closer look at a set of hegemonic ideas about dictators, showing how these ideas serve to mystify and are thus of little use. Next we turn to the building of the Trujillo state in the south-western part of the Dominican Republic.

DICTATORSHIP AND FETISHISM

The most influential literature on the Trujillo state has represented it as a sort of long-reigning dominance without a societal base that could render intelligible the power held by the leader and the longevity and stability of this particular dictatorship. A clear-cut example is Robert D. Crassweller's 1966 biography *Trujillo: The Life and Times of a Caribbean Dictator*, an influential yet not strictly scholarly work. The most cited treatment of the dictatorship is still this book, published only five years after the dictator's assassination (Turits 2003: 7). Crassweller's book is permeated and driven by an idea of the ruler as brutal, voracious and eccentric, and focuses only on the very top of the state-system.

A better example, though, is the work of influential political scientist Juan Linz, and the scholarly tradition that he helped establish. Linz used Trujillo's Dominican Republic in a classification of the types of non-democratic regimes in the world. In so doing he turned the Trujillo rule into an image – a nearly pure case of what he described as 'sultanism'. In the following, I will briefly sketch the Linz tradition's perspective on the Trujillo dictatorship and offer a condensed critique, for two reasons. First, Linz's ideas about the Trujillo state are still influential, and have continued to shape thinking about a decisive period in the history of the Dominican state. Second, I argue that the Linz tradition's ideas about the Dominican Republic articulate a powerful Western way of thinking about dictators. They express tenacious myths of modern state formations applied in many parts of the world.

Max Weber coined the term 'sultanism' to refer to an extreme form of 'patrimonialism', which in his scheme was a subtype of 'traditional' authority. He wrote: 'Where domination is primarily traditional, even though it is exercised by virtue of the ruler's personal autonomy, it will be called *patrimonial authority*; where it indeed operates primarily on the basis of discretion, it will be called *sultanism*' (Weber 1978: 232, italics in original). For Weber, the classic location of sultanistic authority was the Near East. Weber's terms have been applied extensively to contemporary politics in 'the Third World' – or in countries located outside Western Europe and North America. When, in the 1970s, Linz published an influential classification of so-called non-democratic regimes, his classification adopted Weber's term 'sultanism' (Linz 1975). In the 1950s, Linz had worked on Spain's Franco regime. He had realised that the model of the 'totalitarian' state then current, based on the history of Nazism and Stalinism, did not fit. The outcome was the conceptualisation of a new type, the 'authoritarian' regime. In an edited volume from 1998, *Sultanistic Regimes*, Houchang Chehabi and Linz describe how Linz thereafter discovered Trujillo, and how that resulted in the invention of yet another category – the sultanistic regime. An encounter with a Spanish exile was to convince Linz that:

... the authoritarian / totalitarian dichotomy did not exhaust the range of non-democratic regimes either. In the early 1950s Linz met his Spanish compatriot Jesús de Galíndez, a representative of the exiled Basque government, who had taught international law in the Dominican Republic. Although a republican émigré, Galíndez was treated courteously by Spanish diplomats in New York. But when he wrote a doctoral dissertation at Columbia University revealing some of the inside workings of the Trujillo regime, he confided to Juan Linz in 1955 that he feared for his life, and that he had deposited his manuscript in a safe place in case something happened to him. Soon afterward the dictator had Galíndez abducted in New York and taken to the Dominican Republic, where he was tortured to death. The contrast between Franco's non-democratic regime and Trujillo's rule led to the conceptualization of a regime type for which Linz borrowed Weber's term 'sultanism', since it too rested on the extreme development of the ruler's discretion.... Just as Franco's rule became the archetype of an authoritarian regime, Trujillo's became that of a sultanistic regime in Linz's 1973 classification of non-democratic regimes. (Chehabi and Linz 1998: 4–5)[4]

Apart from a chapter on Trujillo's Dominican Republic as the archetype, Chehabi's and Linz's *Sultanistic Regimes* from 1998 contains studies of the Batista state in Cuba, the Somoza state in Nicaragua, the Duvalier state in Haiti, the Pahlavi state in Iran and the Marcos state in the Philippines.

The sultanistic rule is claimed to have little social basis – so little that it seems to be almost without any at all: 'In the end the social bases of a sultanistic regime are restricted to its clients: family members of the rulers and their cronies' (Chehabi and Linz 1998: 20). According to the theory, it is this lack of a social basis and the resultant 'freedom' from social and cultural constraints that explains how the ruler can maintain his grip on power: 'The ability of sultanistic rulers to stay in power depends on their freedom from the need to forge alliances with civil society and to build coalitions' (Chehabi and Linz 1998: 20–21). Chehabi and Linz delimit the sultanistic dictatorship as follows:

It is based on personal rulership, but loyalty to the ruler is motivated not by his embodying or articulating an ideology, nor by a unique personal mission, nor by any charismatic qualities, but by a mixture of fear and rewards to his collaborators. The ruler exercises his power without restraint, at his own discretion and above all unencumbered by rules or by any commitment to an ideology or value system. (1998: 7)

These ideas about sultanism form a clear example of what Edward Said sought to counter when he published *Orientalism* (1978). The Linz tradition's representations of the Trujillo dictatorship and of despotic regimes in general seem mostly to constitute images of what 'we' – i.e. Western democracy – are believed *not* to be. In this way, a complex set of different political and social worlds becomes reduced, not just to pure difference, but indeed to savagery. The model of modern sultanism ignores and silences important differences between continents, regions and countries. It portrays the object of study as if 'it' were a single thing – *the* sultanistic regime. Nearly all features of the sultanistic regime are portrayed as expressions of a sole ubiquitous and constant essence or power – the omnipotence of the dictator. As Chehabi and Linz claim, 'The ruler exercises his power without restraint.'

The theory of sultanism thus produces sharply polarised and hierarchical ideas about the world, about the global 'core' and its 'others' and, however unwittingly, helps to naturalise and strengthen existing power differentials in the global system (Coronil 1996). However, as we shall see, this view of the Trujillo dictatorship as omnipotent sultanism bears scant relation to the complex historical transformations in political, economic, social and cultural life that resulted in the consolidation of the Trujillo rule's national control. Instead it constitutes a narrative that should be read as a Western Self's story of itself.

Foucault claimed that political theory should cut off the King's head (Foucault 1980: 97, 121). Yet many do not follow this advice. Instead they are obsessed with the idea that we must understand the ruler, and remain in practice convinced that this is sufficient for understanding state formation.

In his classic paper on the difficulty of studying the state, Philip Abrams ([1977] 1988) claimed that he was less radical than Radcliffe-Brown had been. In his Preface to *African Political Systems* ([1940] 1955), Radcliffe-Brown had maintained that the idea of the state was merely a source of mystification, and recommended that social analysis get rid of it. Less radical, Abrams ([1977] 1988: 76) nonetheless claimed that 'we must make a ruthless assault on the whole set of claims in terms of which the being of the state is proposed'. He proposed, not that we should try to eliminate the idea of the state, but that we should continue to take the *idea* of the state very seriously. The state, said Abrams, 'is the distinctive collective *mis*representation of capitalist societies. Like other collective (mis)representations it is a social fact – but not a fact in nature' ([1977] 1988: 75). With this I agree. A concrete configuration of social and political practices, the 'state-system' is the historical process out of which the idea of the state, a symbolic construct, is made.[5] Abrams' ideas rested upon a profound critique. Like Foucault, he rejected the value of work based on an intellectual separation of 'the state' and 'society'. By positing a veiling separation of the state and society, analysts have personified and reified the state. Analysts, politicians and citizens have provided the state with a misplaced concreteness (Alonso 1995: 115). They have fetishised it, turning complex historical processes into a person, a will, a spirit or a thing. The idea of the state, then, is above all an exercise in legitimation, 'the mask that prevents our seeing political practice as it is' (Abrams [1977] 1988: 82).

This is of importance for understanding the powerful Western discourse on dictatorships. Hegemonic discourses on dictators in the contemporary world continue to mystify. They continue to silence or reduce the need for understanding entire societies, or entire authoritarian histories. There is little need, so the argument in practice goes, to investigate a whole historically produced political and social formation. There is no need to inquire into how things work at the level of ongoing everyday practice, or deep down in the system. Instead, discourses on dictatorships often go to great lengths in personalising the state. They tend to construct an image of nearly perfect omnipotence, projecting the assumed total power onto a mythic figure, the dictator, and then demonising him. He is constructed not as God, but as Satan.

Key discourses on the Dominican Republic between 1930 and 1961 have represented Trujillo, the modern sultanistic despot incarnate, as almost all-powerful. The same discourses have unilaterally stressed his 'superhuman' capacity for producing tyranny – his capacity for deceit and exploitation. Crassweller, Linz and others helped to turn the history of the Dominican Republic between 1930 and 1961 into a fiction. They transformed the greater part of the history of the Trujillo state formation into an image of the activities of a single devil-like individual.

This faulty analysis is ironically mirrored in dictators' own representations of themselves. They often personalise the state to a striking degree. A dictator will try to construct, display and reify images of himself as all-powerful: not as a demon, but as a saviour. A dictator often attempts to represent himself not only as the source and the essence, but also as the very embodiment of the state. Dictatorships create a cult of the ruler. The cult turns complex political and social histories into a fiction, a bust, a monument, a myth and a name. The Trujillo state forged a personalist political ideology based on the all-encompassing figure of '*El Jefe*', or 'The Chief', whom it sought to deify. In 1936, the Dominican capital was rechristened 'Ciudad Trujillo'. Streets, bridges, squares, parks and buildings throughout the country were named or renamed after him and his family (Roorda 1998: 59, 97–98). By the close of the regime, 'an estimated eighteen hundred sculptures of the Generalísimo sat in public squares and buildings throughout the Dominican Republic, one for every ten square miles' (Roorda 1998: 97). The phrase '*Dios y Trujillo*' or 'God and Trujillo' appeared on state documents (Roorda 1998: 96). Where I carried out fieldwork in the early 1990s, villagers and peasants recalled how everyone had had to repeat '*Dios en el cielo y Trujillo en la tierra*', or 'God in Heaven and Trujillo on Earth'. In sum, one discourse sought to deify Trujillo; another sought to demonise him. Both, however, gave to the Trujillo state formation a mystifying concreteness. In Abrams' words, both transformed Dominican history between 1930 and 1961 into a mask.

DICTATORSHIP AND THE PRODUCTION OF HISTORY

The history of the Trujillo dictatorship is far less clear-cut than this. Let me try to explain gradually what I mean by this.

During the rule of Trujillo, as he accumulated spectacular wealth, the nation experienced egoistic decisions combined with scrupulous attention to constitutional facades and legal forms, and grotesque violence. From the beginning, Trujillo used his power to furnish himself with control of economic enterprises existing in the country. As he gained control of those enterprises, he abused the authority of the state to eliminate competition and build and consolidate monopolies. At the time of his assassination Trujillo is said to have controlled nearly 80 per cent of the Dominican Republic's industrial production and employed almost 60 per cent of the nation's wage-workers (Moya Pons 1998: 365). However, the bulk of the Dominican masses in 1961 were not wage labourers: they were rural people, or peasants. Trujillo and his family also gained control of vast land properties (Moya Pons 1998: 364–65).

Trujillo's political party was the Partido Dominicano, founded in 1932. It was the country's sole political party, and membership was virtually mandatory to avoid harassment by the authorities (Roorda 1998: 93). Trujillo also imposed a 10 per cent deduction from the salaries of the country's public employees; this money went to his political party (Moya Pons 1998: 360). Thousands of prisoners were sent to the regime's penal colonies established and run by the military. These were defined by brutality and terror and involved dreadful instances of forced labour for the state (Turits 2003: 193). Trujillo's general strategy was not that of elimination of opposition by assassination. Far more efficient was the spread of fear. Still, hundreds of Dominicans were liquidated by the regime during those 31 years. In 1946, a journalist listed 134 victims of political liquidation by Trujillo's rule (Hicks 1946: 228–30), but more must have died from diseases and abuse in state prisons (Turits 2003: 269, note 25). As noted, the regime abducted Galíndez from bustling New York City and killed him:

Galíndez was assassinated at the beginning of the end of the regime, when, in particular, Trujillo flailed out against all perceived opponents, arresting and torturing hundreds of mostly middle-class Dominicans in the major towns and cities and executing more than one hundred expeditionaries captured in an invasion led by anti-Trujillo exiles in 1959. (Turits 2003: 6)[6]

The dictator's most grotesque act of state violence took place some decades earlier. By the late 1930s, Haitian peasants had been settling for more than a century on abandoned agricultural lands on the Dominican side of the Haitian–Dominican border. In late 1937, the Dominican military slaughtered thousands of Haitian peasants in this frontier region; some 15,000 may have died in the massacre (Vega 1995: 341–53; Turits 1997: 486, note 137). Trujillo also expelled all Haitians from the country, with the exception of those working for the sugar plantations owned by foreigners. After the massacre and the evictions, the Trujillo state closed the border, launched a Dominicanisation programme in the frontier provinces, and embarked on a massive propaganda campaign to demonise its neighbour.

All this seems to support the theory of sultanism, but there is another history – a story of the dictator's regime that is very different from the one narrated above. When I carried out fieldwork in a community in the Dominican south-west in the early 1990s I was told this other story again and again by villagers and peasants. The community where my research was conducted, La Descubierta, is situated on the border that separates the Dominican Republic and Haiti. The twentieth-century history of La Descubierta typifies the Dominican south-west. And it is representative of the country's borderlands – the areas situated along the Dominican–Haitian border.[7]

In the Dominican south-west, people often described the Trujillo dictatorship as a crucial transition – from lack of progress, to a more civilised life. Many in La Descubierta claimed that the dictator had begun basic modernisation. Old people vividly recalled the dictator's use of terror and the 1937 Haitian massacre. Yet they argued that the region and the nation had needed development and Dominicanisation, and that Trujillo had taken care of both things. This is not to say that there was no cultural ambiguity. Most locals also recognised that Trujillo's regime had demanded sacrifices that had been too large – that the price paid by some had been too high. They claimed, for example, that Trujillo had been both unbelievably selfish and exceptionally cruel. A small minority would mostly condemn his rule. Most often, however, people said to each other that Trujillo had been right, that the political and social transformations that he headed had been not only necessary but also legitimate. The informal head of La Descubierta's largest extended family, a local leader of peasant stock, one day put it in the following manner:

They say that Trujillo was bad. But 85 per cent of the time Trujillo was a good president. And many times [now] we say 'Damn! Why isn't Trujillo alive?' [For example,] when we see a delinquency somewhere in the country. We are many who say 'For he was the man!'

In another conversation, he explained:

I was born in 1924. I'd say that those were the times of 'the crazy ones', or those who lacked civilisation [*A este tiempo yo diría que era el tiempo de 'los locos'*]. For they didn't know that one could study, what was a high school, a clinic. Where the Municipal Hall is now, my mother had three corals for goats.... We were pulled out from there by Trujillo. From that time until now it has been opened up.

Another leader in La Descubierta claimed: 'This region [the south-western region] was totally archaic. And no matter what people say, it is Trujillo who pulls us out and makes us take off.'

People remembered not only the dictator's terror. Villagers and peasants in La Descubierta recalled another history as well. They kept in mind how the Trujillo years had brought increased civilisation and development through the creation of the nation-state. Their main view, or story, was that, irrespective of how dictatorial a regime is, it may all the same change society in fruitful ways. No matter how undemocratic it is, it may still breed a sense of intensified progress and enhanced modernity.

The story from La Descubierta is far from exceptional. It is in accordance with the picture drawn by Malcolm Walker from a community in the Central Cordillera, called Villalta, where Walker carried out fieldwork from May 1967 until July 1968: 'As to Trujillo's tyranny', he writes, 'most Villalteros say they had little to fear so long as they had "respect"' (Walker 1970: 495, 1972). Even Jonathan Hartlyn, who has analysed Trujillo's rule in Chehabi's and Linz's *Sultanistic Regimes*, seems to acknowledge, albeit to a limited extent, that Dominican history may be more complex, or express a paradox:

In spite of Trujillo's brutality and venality, his apparent commitment to order, 'strong' government, state building, national integration, and economic nationalism helped to generate a degree of public acceptance among the most vulnerable elements of the population that lived under him. (Hartlyn 1998: 86)

Recently, the social historian Richard Turits has published *Foundations of Despotism: Peasants, the Trujillo Regime, and Modernity in Dominican History* (2003). Turits' work is original and impressive, and provides a powerful critique of the dominant narrative of the Trujillo dictatorship. His findings indicate that the often-nostalgic representations of the Trujillo years by people in the southern frontier is a picture applicable not only to these border areas, but also to the rest of the country. For example: 'Rather than its image as extreme, arbitrary, and irrational, in terms of everyday rural life, the Trujillo state has been remembered as orderly, efficient, responsive, and even honest' (Turits 1997: 20).

How should we understand these (most often peasant) memories? Many scholars have treated them as insignificant, or as products of ideological distortions, or even as false consciousness.[8] Turits has instead sought to profoundly investigate the Trujillo state's rural policies. His research reveals how the enduring and brutal regime mediated important economic and social changes, especially through agrarian policies that benefited the country's large independent peasantry. He shows how the dictatorship state carried out rural reforms that changed the nascent processes of restructuring in the countryside that had threatened Dominican peasants when Trujillo seized power – transformations energised by new property laws and the increased commercialisation of land and agriculture. By implementing agrarian policies that de facto sustained the peasants' free access to land during a phase of national economic growth, the dictator secured peasant backing as well as support from certain elite groups. In Turits' (2003: 81–82) terms, the dictatorship promoted a peasant-based or an alternative modernity.

Economic realities in the Dominican countryside – and the transactions, however unequal, between authorities and peasant masses under Trujillo – have never before been examined the way Turits has done. He writes:

I have found ... that Trujillo's efforts to achieve a type of rural populism and foster paternalistic policies were far more substantial than previously assumed.... Specifically, the regime distributed and maintained peasant access to large amounts of the nation's lands, and thereby helped secure political loyalty or acquiescence among the peasantry.... Judging by the statistics, as well as peasants' own recollections, the regime's efforts at economic development and land distribution were fruitful. (1997: 8, 10)

The bulk of the Dominican people remained rural. In the mid-1930s, 82 per cent of the population had been rural. In 1960, 70 per cent remained rural, still one of the highest percentages in Latin America and the Caribbean (Turits 2003: 265). The dictatorship's strategies to increase agricultural production and secure peasant access to land 'helped make Trujillo's Dominican Republic a virtually self-sufficient country in agricultural terms (save wheat), in contrast to the rest of the twentieth-century Caribbean and much of Latin America' (Turits 2003: 20).

For centuries, much of the rural population had lived a more or less independent existence of animal-raising and hunting, combined with shifting, slash-and-burn agriculture on tiny subsistence plots. But by the early twentieth century, peasants faced threatening transformations in property relations and land tenure arrangements. In the 1880–1930 period prior to Trujillo's dictatorship, the growing commercialisation of agriculture and rising land values in a few, limited areas had led to efforts to enclose, survey and claim land in most parts of the Dominican Republic. And new forms of individualised, private property were consolidated through legislation with the US occupation from 1916 to 1924. By the time Trujillo seized power in 1930, thousands of peasants had already been evicted by US-owned sugar companies that had gained control of enormous land areas in the eastern region. Confronting this historical situation, the Trujillo regime engaged in a massive agrarian reform that favoured rural dwellers and agriculturalists by offering them land and eventually property rights (Franks 1995; San Miguel 1997: 189–322; Turits 2003: 25–114).

The Trujillo state's reforms were put into effect also where I carried out research in the southern borderlands, and to this I will return. Let me, however, provide one illustration here. The Trujillo dictatorship offered support to rural people, on one condition: peasants had to cultivate the land as productively as the regime demanded. Laws that classified any peasant cultivating less than 10 *tareas* (0.63 hectares) of land as 'vagrant' were strongly enforced. In the 1980s, La Descubierta's most important leader during the Trujillo era, Jesús María Ramírez, wrote an autobiographical narrative of his years in the community.[9] His narrative, which takes us back to the time before 1920, describes a public meeting held in La Descubierta in 1935. The description is a testimony to the state's attempts to orchestrate campaigns across the country to increase agricultural production and secure peasant access to land. The dictatorship's land distribution campaign had started in 1934. It was then that the state commissioned an officer, Major Rafael Carretero, to travel to a part of the south-western region to examine and seek to resolve land tenure disputes there (Turits 2003: 90). Jesús María describes how, when Major Carretero arrived in La Descubierta in 1935, he summoned all the men of the community:

Major Carretero told us that vagrancy would be punished with public work and to show that you were not a vagrant, we who lived in the countryside had to have at least 10 *tareas* cultivated. He also said that he was going to organise a *Junta Protectora de la Agricultura* to distribute the neglected lands that were not being used by their owners. (Ramírez 2000: 58)

Between 1930 and 1961, the state's presence in everyday life grew dramatically across the national territory. The Haitian massacre initiated important change in the borderlands. The Dominican border region had been an ethnically mixed society. After the violent eviction, the Trujillo state established and policed a clear international border with Haiti. The regime also rapidly expanded the state infrastructure in the border provinces, creating agrarian colonies or settlements close to the demarcation line as well as building roads, schools and health-care systems, and establishing state bodies in the whole border region.

One of Trujillo's most frequently used slogans – 'My best friends are the men of work' – was not mere propaganda. Turits' central claim is that Trujillo's rule incorporated rural dwellers into economic markets, the national state and a common national community to a far greater extent than ever before in the Dominican Republic, and that this in turn laid the foundations both for the dictator's hegemony and for the often nostalgic representations of his regime even decades after its demise. I agree, but have an addition. All told, Turits' work seems to indicate that the history of the compromises between authorities and masses under Trujillo was mostly a history of material exchanges – almost purely an economic story. However, this does not seem entirely fair, for two reasons. First, as noted, he has produced a unique contribution. Second, Turits is aware that the story he has sought to uncover also has a cultural dimension. His work does mention and describe state cultural practices under Trujillo – namely, a variety of the regime's discourses and rituals. And it underscores that, for many, Trujillo's rule was legitimated in terms of a rural culture of '*respeto*' or 'mutual respectfulness' in interpersonal relations (Turits 2003: 208). Yet his work is none the less limited by the lack of what Sherry Ortner has called ethnographic 'thickness' (Ortner 1995: 190; 1999). Turits is thin when it comes to the enormous cultural complexity of local communities under Trujillo. He is also thin on the internal political processes of those communities. And he is thin on local forms of agency and leadership. In 1930, the overwhelming majority of the Dominican population was rural. Even three decades later, the proportion of the population that lived in the countryside was impressive. To a far greater extent than has generally been recognised, the dictatorship was made and remade by villagers and peasants. Local populations across the country helped to bring into being and build the Trujillo state. This they did by means of well-tried institutions in the Dominican countryside – institutions like the extended family, *compadrazgo*, and patronage. The most basic everyday forms and practices of the rural masses were neither threatened nor undermined under Trujillo. On the contrary, the construction and reconstruction of the dictator's rule both depended upon and reinforced those forms and practices.

The section that follows presents an ethnography of La Descubierta in the period from the first decades of the twentieth century to the demise of the dictator. I offer this ethnography in order to substantiate the claims made above, underscoring two points in particular. First, Rafael Leónidas Trujillo Molina *was* a dictator – but even under Trujillo's regime, power was far more dispersed and negotiable than has generally been assumed. The regime was built not only from the top of the state, but also by a myriad of actors who lived and worked at the grassroots level. This perspective is crucial. Many people participated in the construction of the 1930–61 state, and plenty of citizens felt they carried out and achieved a great deal.

As to the other point: the dictatorship's countryside-based or alternative road to modern state-building was far from a purely economically driven process (as if any economic system could exist in isolation from a corresponding symbolic system [see Sahlins 1976; Miller 1997]). It constituted also a deeply cultural process. We may say that people in the countryside forged an alliance with the dictator's regime. But this alliance was not only about rural dwellers' state-protected access to land, agricultural assistance and expanded infrastructure. The regime–countryside compromise also served to protect the greater part of a peasant way of life – central components of a world. The history of the Trujillo dictatorship is ambiguous, and Trujillo has two very different faces. Some have depicted him as savagery incarnate. In the late twentieth century, however, elderly Dominicans were telling another story. Many related how the Trujillo years had brought increased civilisation and development, and recalled the dictator as just, orderly, and even good. This late-twentieth century nostalgic discourse on Trujillo was a product of the dictatorship's patronage in a wider sense. The Trujillo rule had protected the mainstays of an entire social and cultural world.

THE APPEARANCE OF THE STATE IN THE SOUTHERN DOMINICAN BORDERLANDS, 1907–61

Two kinds of agrarian systems defined most of the eastern sector of Hispaniola, or Santo Domingo, up to the late nineteenth and early twentieth centuries: stock-raising based on extensive pasture-land usage, and agriculture of a slash-and-burn style on small plots. The cattle ranches, however, were far from advanced economic units. Population density was low and production for export to Europe tiny. Between the mid-1870s and 1930, sugar production for the world market in the Dominican Republic took off and then expanded at a dizzying pace. The south-east became transformed into the main sugar region of the country.

The emergence of a sugar industry in the east led to the marginalisation and ultimately the underdevelopment of the western parts of the country, or the borderlands (Baud 1987: 148). Deprived of state support (which was oriented toward the cane-producing areas) and drained of a part of its population (who were migrating to the new economic centres), the western region was left with the Haitian market as its main recourse. For the first four decades of the twentieth century, the people of La Descubierta and other parts of the Dominican western region were far more familiar with the Haitian capital Port-au-Prince than with the capital of their own country (Garrido 1970: 17; Ramírez 2000: 22–23).

The history of the island of Hispaniola as a tale of a political and social borderland – first between France and Spain, thereafter between Haiti and the Dominican Republic – begins in the early seventeenth century. But it was not until 1777 that the definitive boundary between France and Spain in Hispaniola was specified. The slave revolution led by Toussaint Louverture not only created Haiti, but also came to influence nearly all political life on the island thereafter. The eastern sector of Hispaniola was held, occupied and governed by Haiti from 1822 to 1844. After 1844, the year of Dominican independence, Haitian troops invaded the Dominican territory and were pushed back several times up to the second half of the 1850s. The frontier question remained disputed and unresolved until 1936. That year the first mutually accepted Dominican–Haitian treaty covering the demarcation of the two countries' common border was finally ratified, and the border has not been changed since then.

From 1907 onwards, the Haitian–Dominican borderlands saw an Americanisation of the border. The Dominican–American Convention of 1907, a product of efforts to reclaim proceeds for Dominican delinquent repayment of loans to international creditors and to restructure and formalise the country's state finances, turned over customs collection to the United States. Customs houses staffed by the United States were established along the Haitian–Dominican border. This new state control of the border established in 1907 imposed for the first time effective accounting on trade across the border, with fines for contraband activities. It meant that the Dominican state established itself where it previously had been most absent – in the midst of the everyday activities of residents of the Dominican border provinces (Clausner 1973: 146–62; Derby 1994: 489–90). Yet it was not until the late 1930s that the Dominican state firmly and massively established itself in the border region. Up till the beginning of the twentieth century, Haiti was militarily, economically and demographically the stronger of the two countries. In the course of the 1920s and 1930s, however, the Dominican Republic caught up with and surpassed its neighbour.

From the mid or late 1930s, the people of La Descubierta helped to build the Trujillo state in this part of the country. As the dictatorship's state-building project in the community unfolded, the region's most important pre-national-state forms – male hegemony, the extended family, *compadrazgo* and patronage – were put to use in new ways and for new purposes. They were employed to bring into being and construct the dictatorship's state-system in this region. In order to show this I will examine the Trujillo state-building project – not from the perspective of state bodies, discourses, and practices per se, but from the perspective of La Descubierta's local population and its relationship to the project of state-building.[10] In describing La Descubierta in the period from the first two decades of the twentieth century to 1961, I tell this local history with a focus on leadership and families. The most powerful extended family in La Descubierta during the greater part of the twentieth century was the Ramírez family, whose members had begun to develop power in the community from before the 1920s. The power of the Ramírez family was thereafter expanded under Trujillo, and preserved after his death. From the early 1920s to the late 1930s, the principal leader of La Descubierta was Emilio Ramírez Rosado. His nephew, Jesús María Ramírez, became the Trujillo state's most important leader in this region. These two were the main political leaders of La Descubierta from the early 1920s and up to the early 1960s.

How had the young Emilio Ramírez settled in the community and risen to power?[11] Some time before 1917, he and a brother left their wives and children in their native town Neyba, now capital of the neighbouring province to the east, and came to La Descubierta as members of a police entity, the Republican Guard. When the US forces dissolved the Republican Guard and created the Dominican National Police in 1917, the brothers refused to be members, and chose to settle down. A few years later they were joined by the wife of Emilio's brother and their children, including their son Jesús María, the later Trujillo leader and memoirs writer. However, Emilio was already living with a new woman. From the start after leaving the police, Emilio and his new wife had commercial success, while his brother remained a worker his whole life. Emilio owned a shop and raised stock, and from 1922 travelled regularly with his brother and Jesús María, the later leader, to Haiti in order to sell cattle. In the mid-1920s, Emilio closed his store and started to accumulate land in La Descubierta's lowlands, where he developed farming activities.[12]

Emilio's role as a political leader must be understood in this context of trade networks and relative economic power. Although he never possessed much, and slept in a hammock, in this frontier world of scattered animal-raisers and agriculturalists where hardly anyone knew how to write, his house became a centre to which all sorts of activities gravitated. Supplying locals with work and thus money, Emilio was consulted for advice on personal matters, trade and politics, and he offered hospitality to those who visited the community from outside. In 1924, the first presidential elections in the Dominican Republic were organised after the end of the US occupation. The Ramírez family backed Horacio Vásquez, who won and remained president up to Trujillo's coup in 1930. Emilio's role as a local leader is described by his nephew Jesús María in these terms:

The people came to consult him and he told them what to do in order to secure the triumph of Horacio Vásquez in the elections. He often travelled to the provincial capital and Neyba because of this, and the leaders of the Horacismo visited him to promote their candidatures in the community. (Ramírez notes; see in addition Ramírez 2000: 31)

The most influential *caudillo* in the south-western part of the Dominican Republic when Trujillo rose to power was José del Carmen ('Carmito') Ramírez, a kinsman of Emilio. Carmito, a big landowner with cattle ranches all over the San Juan Valley, lived in the vicinity of San Juan de la Maguana, to the north of the Neyba and La Descubierta areas.[13] After Trujillo's conquest of power in 1930, Carmito together with others – Horacistas, or supporters of Vasquez – went in exile to the Haitian capital, where Trujillo kept them under surveillance and negotiated with them (Vega 1988: 54–60, 105–22). Emilio also fled and spent some months in Port-au-Prince before he returned, accepting with other anti-Trujillistas the safety offered (Ramírez 2000: 51). Later, in the words of Emilio's daughter in the early 1990s, 'Trujillo sent for him, and he went, and they became friends.... Emilio and Trujillo became friends.' In brief, during the first years of the new regime, Emilio remained the leader of the community.

In the early 1930s, Dominicans in the southern borderlands continued to travel to Haiti to trade and carry out errands. Not so much changed in La Descubierta immediately after Trujillo had gained power in the capital. Jesús María Ramírez (2000: 54–56) writes that La Descubierta began to experience the Trujillismo as a political force in 1933. On 28 May 1933, the first political mass meeting in this region under the new regime was celebrated in Duvergé, another community situated in this part of the borderlands. The rally was part of a series of *revistas cívicas* or reunions organised in all parts of the country in order to demand the dictator's first re-election. Trujillo was present, as were representatives of communities from a wide area. The La Descubierta representatives were headed by Emilio, Jesús María and the community's military leader, a lieutenant.

Emilio died in 1943. However, even by the mid-1930s Jesús María had become La Descubierta's most influential man in practice. As a villager and ex-military man said of the dictatorship:

The principal of all was Jesús María Ramírez. He was the friend of Trujillo. If Trujillo wanted to know something about La Descubierta he sent for Jesús María Ramírez, there in the capital.... Jesús María was a respected man in the pueblo. He was so respected here that when there occurred whatever problem for you he ordered you see him in his home and he gave you advice there in his home.

People explained that the power of Jesús María was greater than that of La Descubierta's military, because, among the latter, there were mostly sergeants as highest-ranking commanders. In 1933, Jesús María bought his first land property. He thereafter continued to accumulate land and develop agricultural activities in La Descubierta.

After the regime's Major Rafael Carretero had held a public meeting in La Descubierta in 1935 to tell the community that every man had to have 10 *tareas* cultivated and that vagrancy would be punished, Jesús María was made head of the community's Junta Protectora de la Agricultura, the new state entity organised to distribute the neglected local lands not being used by their owners. Some land properties in La Descubierta and areas nearby were distributed. In the same period, Jesús María headed the construction of a public health clinic for La Descubierta. He recruited locals from various parts of the community to help him with the activities of the Junta and with carpentry work on the clinic (Ramírez 2000: 58–61).

In April 1938, Trujillo toured the region. On his way through La Descubierta, the dictator stopped. On the spot, he appointed Emilio as local judge and Jesús María, whom he then called 'the young man', as president of the local division of the Partido Dominicano, the state political party. At the same time Trujillo made the decision to elevate the administrative status of the village, to transform La Descubierta into an independent *común* or independent municipality. According to Jesús María's recollections, the dictator had then asked his uncle Emilio and him: 'Do you have the people you need to fill the public positions that will be created [as a consequence of the elevation to *común*]?' Jesús María had answered: 'Yes, sir' (Ramírez 2000: 64). After this, a friend of the Ramírez, a man from the village, was appointed as the first mayor of La Descubierta. Jesús María's cousin became municipal treasurer; another villager became the judge's (or Emilio's) secretary, while Jesús María's father was given the job as head of La Descubierta's Civil Status office. And another villager was appointed as Jesús María's secretary in the Dominican Party.

In the hills around La Descubierta, the state's violent eviction of the Haitians started immediately after Trujillo's April 1938 visit.[14] Soon thereafter the state launched its Dominicanisation programme – a systematic, massive attempt to increase the state's presence in the entire Dominican border region and to strengthen the incorporation of this region into the national community. As part of this programme, the state established a series of small agrarian colonies, or rural settlements, in the hills close to the demarcation line, aimed at preventing Haitians from repopulating the hills on the Dominican side. Jesús María Ramírez played an important part in the Dominicanisation programme. Sent first by the Ministry of Agriculture to the Pedernales area, a neighbouring province, in 1942 and 1943 to head the establishment of an agrarian colony there, he was later responsible for building four other small colonies close to the border in the hills of La Descubierta, between 1943 and 1945. These works consisted mainly in constructing wooden homes for peasant colonists. He used day labourers from the region. The regime also charged him with the building of houses for three military posts in the hills. As part of the Dominicanisation, Creole names of places, hamlets, and villages were changed by the Trujillo state throughout the country (Tolentino Rojas 1944: 328–33). Jesús María assisted in re-baptising parts of the highlands of La Descubierta – for example, Marrosó, Sabambón and Toussaint became Angel Felix, Sabana Real and Granada.

From 1943 to 1947, the regime's Dominicanisation programme changed La Descubierta. During these few years, La Descubierta saw the creation, not only of hill agrarian colonies and military posts, but also of a completely new road to Neyba, a new road in the community's highlands, an aqueduct, an electric power plant and schools. And the village nucleus got streets and a park, later followed by a church and a proper building to house the local chapter of the Dominican Party (Ramírez 2000: 83–90, 110).

The dictatorship's construction of roads, and of aqueducts and canals played a crucial part. Throughout world history, the establishment and development of public roads has been a key component of state-building. This is so because a system of roads has functioned both as a technology and as an idiom of connection and incorporation (see Harvey in this volume). Under Trujillo, travel and transport between La Descubierta and the rest of the country was dramatically altered in the 1940s and 1950s, particularly with the road to Neyba. Public works were largely carried out by members of local communities like La Descubierta through a public system of *prestación del servicio*, or forced or *corvée* labour for the state. Turits writes:

Formalised into law in 1907 ... *prestación del servicio* referred to public labor required in lieu of paying a road tax.... However, until Trujillo's rule, the level of resistance to this onerous obligation prevented it from running successfully on a large scale.... There was certainly some peasant resistance to this labor [also under Trujillo].... Yet overall, the state managed to secure peasants' cooperation in this onerous labor, which, in retrospect at least, elderly peasants [interviewed by him in the 1980s and 1990s] rarely condemned. (Turits 2003: 106)[15]

According to Jesús María Ramírez, the *prestación del servicio* or forced labour was far from popular, but was nonetheless used in La Descubierta during the initial phase of the dictatorship in order to improve many paths and tracks. Every man, he says, had to work on public labour for two days a month. A few, like him, could afford not to work on public labour; instead of working they paid a tax of 25 centavos for each day of *corvée* labour. Since this forced work was so disliked, he claims, the state stopped using it. Public works in this region were also carried out by means of paid day labour, and Jesús María argues that Trujillo's popularity in the area increased significantly when the regime in the 1930s substantially augmented the ordinary day wage for public works, from 25 to 80 centavos (Ramírez 2000: 57).

Jesús María Ramírez continued to work for the state in the first half of the 1950s, and remained La Descubierta's most influential leader up to the dictator's assassination. In 1950 and 1951 he was appointed provincial governor, first of his own province of Independencia and then of the neighbouring province of Bahoruco. In the first office he lasted less than a year and in the second only one month, however, presumably because of disputes with Trujillistas more influential than himself. We know at least that he was transferred from Independencia to Bahoruco after a conflict with a local man or rival supported by an officer from Trujillo's own family, Captain Danilo Trujillo, the dictator's nephew (Ramírez 2000: 108). While Jesús María Ramírez was governor of Independencia in 1950, he once received an unannounced visit by Trujillo. He showed the dictator around in the rustic, new provincial capital Jimaní,[16] and the two mapped and discussed state agrarian strategies, road work and aqueducts in the province. Jesús María then recommended three locally respected men and friends for the key posts as mayor of Duvergé, mayor of la Descubierta and president of the

Jimaní branch of the Dominican Party. Trujillo appointed the three on the spot (Ramírez 2000: 99–101). Although he lasted only one month in the second job as governor, Jesús María nonetheless maintained his authority in this part of the country, and was soon again assigned to work for the regime personally by Trujillo. In 1955, he was appointed General Supervisor of Agriculture for the whole frontier region.

Jesús María's tasks for the government were part and parcel of the dictatorship's comprehensive agrarian reforms (Ramírez 2000: 117–22; Turits 2003: 101). As La Descubierta's *caudillo* under Trujillo, Jesús María recruited people from the community to farm his own land, build roads and agrarian colonies, occupy public offices and run the La Descubierta branch of the Dominican Party.

Some family surnames were very common names in the community: Mella, Martínez, Alba, Barranco, Sanchez, Ares and Viñas.[17] Most locals bore some combination of two of these names. Jesús María employed members of one of the largest families in La Descubierta, the Barrancos, as his agricultural workers. Most of the Barrancos were landless. Through his patronage Jesús María tied them to his own family and hence to the regime. He recruited members from most families to carry out public works, organising and accomplishing these works with the aid of the socially acknowledged heads of these families, men who enjoyed respect in the community. A few of these highly respected villagers were offered public positions in the community. By the 1940s and 1950s, teachers and other public employees had to be recruited from other parts of the country as well, but the influence of the large local families and their informal heads remained strong.

A respected man in La Descubierta, a head of the Albas, worked closely with Jesús María as the general secretary of the local Dominican Party branch in the 1930s and 1940s, and then as head of one of La Descubierta's state offices, the Civil Status Office. The friendship between the two men, however, originated not in the Dominican Party, but in local everyday and ritual exchanges – in trade, fiestas and a shared passion for cockfights. When I lived in La Descubierta, this man, Jesús María's former right arm in the Dominican Party, was said to be the person in the community with the greatest number of *compadres*, more than a hundred. In his time, also Jesús María had had many *compadres* in La Descubierta.

The state-system in this part of the country was brought into being and built by means of previously established cultural and social forms – the forms of the local peasant population. These forms expressed ideas about gender, kinship and patronage. The authority of Jesús María resulted from and was nurtured by his friendship with 'The Chief'. But the respect that he enjoyed was also a product of other factors. His education was that typical in rural communities of the 1920s – only some three years of formal schooling. The leadership of Jesús María (and before him, his uncle Emilio) was a result of his participation in, and accumulation through, the pre-1937 trade with Haiti and agricultural activities in La Descubierta's lowlands. Jesús María possessed land, and he built and maintained relations of patronage based on this land. Like Trujillo, he acted like a patriarch. So did the rest of the informal heads of the extended families of the Dominican south-west. Jesús María's family background – his Ramírez name and descent – had provided him with a recommendation, a kind of capital with which he could produce trust and authority. As a dedicated enthusiast of cockfighting and of fiestas, he was enmeshed in the entire rural community. In the early 1990s, a man in his mid-60s described him in these terms:

He danced a lot. He drank a lot. Oh, when he drank rum, he lasted four days drinking rum and offering rum to everyone who wanted and food as well. He called on José, the musicians, and the whole pueblo went to dance and drink. He carried out up to 18 cases of rum, for everyone to drink. He made himself famous. I believe Trujillo gave him some help. He probably helped him with some money for those big parties.[18]

The Haitian slaughter in the Dominican borderlands in the late 1930s was by far the most extensive act of state terror carried out by the dictatorship. And yet, the bloodbath did not result in diminished support to the regime on the Dominican side of the border. On the contrary, many in the Dominican Republic backed or accepted Trujillo's massive imposition of a new community – a mono-ethnic nation – in the frontier.[19] In La Descubierta in the 1990s, an overwhelming majority claimed that the border areas and the country had needed the Dominicanisation. One elderly community leader, for example, had already accounted for Trujillo's eviction of the Haitians, when I asked whether many had been killed. He said. 'Not so many. You know how things are. If Trujillo doesn't do that, the Haitians take this. This place was already filled up with Haitians. After Trujillo repatriated them, he founded agrarian colonies. He repopulated.'

Old people in the southern borderlands in the early 1990s spoke openly of the regime's spread of fear. From time to time they acknowledged what had been almost unmentionable – the terror under the dictatorship. In this south-western part of the country, the most feared man during the Trujillo regime was an officer, Colonel José María Alcántara, whose name had become synonymous with fear. In the words of one old man in La Descubierta: 'When Trujillo wanted to set a pueblo straight, he sent Alcántara. And when the people knew that Alcántara was there, everybody walked trembling.' Alcántara was said to have mercilessly repressed the smuggling of the Haitian liquor *clerin* into the country.[20] A villager and local leader (whose father was Jesús María Ramírez's secretary in the Dominican Party in La Descubierta in the 1930s and 1940s) described the fear everybody felt under Trujillo:

You even feared those in your own home. You couldn't speak in this way [the way in which we talked] about Trujillo in your own house because you knew that someone could be listening outside the walls.... Fear was felt so much here during the era of Trujillo that you could arrive here [in La Descubierta] and, automatically, there would be people who looked at you as a stranger and asked 'and what does this man seek here?' If he sat down in the park, they would either hardly greet him, or for some reason [we would say that] he was an informer, or that he was an enemy of the regime. I remember that when I was in the army one spoke with one or two persons, two friends who at least played [the part of friend], but one trusted nobody. Also in the army, one felt that fear; yes, the Guards [too] lived with that fear.[21]

But as we have seen, people of La Descubierta remembered another history as well. What we must realise is to what extent the Trujillo regime managed to link this society to the national state-system, or the nation-state, and hence to the dictator's patronage after 1937. With Trujillo, the community was not only militarised and Dominicanised but also administratively elevated to the status of a municipality, and one significant result was the establishment of '*justicia*' or 'justice'. The community got its own municipal judge and court. People referred to Trujillo as *recto* or 'straight', and time and again would stress that he had secured order. A person could sleep in the streets without being robbed, and everyone had to work and produce. They emphasised that there were two things Trujillo did not tolerate – *el ladrón* or the thief, and *el vago* or the lazy one. Therefore the dictator was not bad or evil; rather he was, as they put it, bad with the bad. Or as a peasant in his 60s said, 'Trujillo had his law.'

TOWARDS A RECOVERY OF GLOBAL HISTORY:
THE HETEROGENEITY OF POLITICAL TRAJECTORIES

We should not unduly reduce historical heterogeneity. As Jean François Bayart has formulated it:

During this period of 'Euromania' [and fetishisation of the United States], it is perhaps more important than ever before to abandon ... theoretical provincialism, and to acknowledge the historical irreducibility, as well as the great political diversity, of the 'Third World'.... To whatever degree the economics of the 'South' have experienced capitalist 'internationalization', it cannot be presupposed that the emerging systems of inequality and domination will match those known in the West and Eastern Europe. (Bayart 1991: 52, 58)

Contemporary state formations constitute highly interconnected political trajectories, and these connections have helped to produce widely different results in different parts of the world. Today's world is best viewed as an historical, global web of interconnections. This has been, and continues to be, a relational process involving the simultaneous constitution of dominant and subordinate modernities (Coronil 1997: 388).[22]

Many studies of state formation are based on data either from the global core or from the areas conquered and controlled by a centralised European state during the nineteenth and twentieth centuries – as in Africa, Asia and the West Indies. However, there are important differences between these parts of the world, and Haiti, the Hispanic Caribbean and Latin America.[23]

The Dominican Republic was *not* ruled by a centralised European state during the nineteenth and twentieth centuries. Spanish colonialism in the eastern sector of the island of Hispaniola (today's Dominican territory) ended in 1795. Between 1822 and 1844, the former Spanish colony was controlled and governed by Haiti, the world's only republic established by ex-slaves. Up to the early twentieth century, the Dominican state apparatus remained weak, with very limited ability to implement its central decisions and to register and oversee the activities of the population. The Dominican Republic also lacked another key element in the master narrative of the appearance of the French or the English state – a self-aware modern bourgeoisie committed to the ideas of popular sovereignty that seized control of the state. Until Trujillo's rise to power, the state remained essentially in the hands of shifting groups of regional leaders and their clients. They were wedded, not to the democratising discourse of the Enlightenment, but to hierarchic notions of gender and race and to ideas about patronage. The country lacked a self-aware, democratic class. We may sketch this history in another way. What is today the territory of the Dominican Republic belonged for three centuries to the Spanish empire. Shortly before the French Revolution, French Saint-Domingue included nearly half a million black slaves – some 85 to 90 per cent of the colony's population. The slave revolution led by Toussaint not only created Haiti, it also gave form to important aspects of the building of the state and the making of the nation on the other side of the border. And since the late nineteenth century, Dominican society has been shaped by North American imperialism.

Analysts must work on concrete history. The long and brutal Trujillo regime promoted a countryside-based road to state-building. The dictatorship created and built a new state-system with the aid of masses who, to a striking degree, continued to be rural, raising cattle and tilling the soil. In practice, the regime's relationship to the countryside protected central features of a way of life. It was only after 1961, under the new Dominican authorities, that the country gradually became less insular and adopted a neoliberal model. State support for agriculture and the countryside was reduced, and the nation saw less self-sufficiency and a massive migration of all social strata from most parts of the country to the United States and beyond. All the same, the years under Trujillo continued to give form to the country. Joaquín Balaguer, who was serving as titular president in 1961 at the time of the dictator's assassination, had been among the intellectuals of the dictatorship ever since the 1930s. Balaguer ruled the country from 1966 to 1978 and from 1986 to 1996. In La Descubierta, the main representative of the Balaguer state was Miriam Mendez de Piñeyro, the niece of Jesús María Ramírez. Miriam was a leader and key state-builder in this part of the country from 1974 to 1998. Miriam and her local followers staffed the public sector in the same way as it had been staffed under Trujillo – with the aid of extended families and their informal heads, *compadrazgo* and patronage.

This is a story very different from the history of transformation of the Western centre as told by Foucault. And it is a far cry from the story narrated by Corrigan and Sayer. These empirical differences should not surprise us, however. They should be seen as part and parcel of a long global history – a history of Western colonialisms and their aftermaths.

CONCLUSION

The history of the Trujillo state is an ambiguous one. My aim in this chapter has been to show that if we want to understand this ambiguous political history better, we will need to examine it with the tools of ethnography. Even under this dictator's repressive regime, power was far more distributed, more transactional and more negotiable than has most often been assumed. The dictatorship was not simply imposed but was articulated in the everyday life of communities across the country. The Trujillo state-system was built not only from the top, but also at the grassroots level.

I am protesting against a long-established tradition. Many writers continue to transform modern state formations located outside the centre of the global system into myths of the untamed and the grotesque. Analysts and politicians commit the same mistake repeatedly, reproducing the narrative of the possibility of unlimited or absolute power. A Trujillo-like dictator, it is maintained, 'exercises his power without restraint, at his own discretion and above all unencumbered by rules or by any commitment to an ideology or value system' (Chehabi and Linz 1998: 7). But this draws a false picture. We must examine authoritarian histories – like other histories – on the basis of detailed explorations of power relationships, forms of agency and meanings.

Analysts should recast discourses on state-building in the contemporary world that presuppose a sharp separation between the West and its periphery. We need a perspective on the world as a historical web of interconnections. And we must also work carefully on culture. Much of what goes on in terms of state-building in the contemporary world manifests phenomena that are far from new. To be sure, state-building means change. But we still need anthropology's rich insights into cultural variation and cultural analysis. State-formation is a cultural process. It is shaped by, and it shapes, the myths of authority. Yet these myths of authority – or these cultural forms – vary enormously from one part of the global system to another. This chapter has shown that the Trujillo regime built a new state-system. It did so with the aid of masses who, to a conspicuous extent, continued to be villagers and peasants. The dictatorship's relationship to these masses helped in turn to protect and maintain key features of a way of life. The history of La Descubierta bears testimony to this. From the mid or late 1930s, the people of La Descubierta helped to create the Trujillo state in this part of the country. As the regime's state-building project in the region unfolded, its most important cultural forms – male hegemony, the extended family, *compadrazgo* and patronage – began to be used in new ways. They were employed to build the new state-system in this part of the country. A new state-system, yes – but the emergence of the Trujillo state did not mean a cultural revolution.

NOTES

1. I would like to express my profound debt to social historian Richard L. Turits, from whose pioneering work on the Trujillo regime I have benefited enormously. As will become apparent, I could not have written this chapter had it not been for Turits's recent thought-provoking examinations of Dominican history (Turits 1997, 2003). I have also been inspired by the work by Lauren Derby (1999, 2003). Knut Nustad has read drafts and discussed them with me; I extend special thanks for his comments and support.

2. I carried out 13 months of fieldwork in La Descubierta in 1991–92. In 1997, I spent three months in the Dominican capital and in various regions of the country; I worked in libraries, travelled and talked with people. In 2000, I spent two weeks in the Dominican capital. In the period from mid 2002 to mid 2004, I spent between seven and eight months collecting data among Dominican immigrants in New York City. The analysis in this chapter is based on the whole of this contact with Dominicans, and on the literature.

3. For some important works, see Geertz (1973, 1980); Foucault (1979, 1980, 1991); Abrams ([1977] 1988); Corrigan and Sayer (1985); Herzfeld (1992); Alonso (1994); Joseph and Nugent (1994); Nagengast (1994); Nugent (1997); Steinmetz (1999); Hansen and Stepputat (2001); Aretxaga (2003). See also the essays by Crais and Shore in this volume.

4. Galíndez's study was later published in Spanish and in English (Galíndez 1958, 1973). The book contains valuable information on the regime, but it deals almost exclusively with the elites, not the masses.

5. For more along these lines, see Mitchell (1999).

6. On the Trujillo dictatorship's terror and repression, see Vega (1985, 1986).

7. On the south-western region and the Dominican borderlands, see for example Garrido ([1922] 1975); Palmer (1976); Baud (1993a, 1993b); Derby (1994); Turits (1997: 427–577); Ramírez (2000); and Lundius and Lundahl (2000).

8. For a telling example of this type of approach, see the otherwise fascinating *Peasants and Religion: A Socioeconomic Study of Dios Olivorio and the Palma Sola Movement in the Dominican Republic*, a monumental study from the country's south-western region by J. Lundius and M. Lundahl (2000, particularly pp. 162, 507–11, 514, 517, 522–23). For other examples, see Inoa (1994: 211–12, 222–24, 228), Cassá (1990: 597), and Kryzanek and Wiarda (1988: 37–41).

9. Jesús María Ramírez wrote some 400 pages of notes about his life in La Descubierta. He was born in Neyba in 1909, moved to La Descubierta in 1921, left the community in 1964, wrote the notes about his life in the Dominican capital in the 1980s, and died in 1988. In the early 1990s I was given access to parts of the notes by his daughter, who said she was in the process of shortening and revising the notes for family circulation and possible publication. The revision was done to protect her father's reputation, and consisted in eliminating repetitions, imposing a stricter chronology on the narrated events and checking information against other sources. In 2000, Jesús María's story was published in Spanish in Santo Domingo, as a book of some 150 pages: Jesús María Ramírez, *Mis 43 años en La Descubierta (My 43 Years in La Descubierta)*. In this chapter, I refer to both the book and the notes. The reference to the book is Ramírez (2000). The reference to the notes is Ramírez (notes). The latter have been used only where I was unable to find in the book what I found in those notes, to which I had been granted access. All quotes from Ramírez's book and notes in this chapter are my translation.

10. I have drawn this distinction between two types of approaches from Nugent (1997: 11).

11. My reconstruction of La Descubierta's history is based mainly on two kinds of sources: oral history produced through my 13 months of fieldwork in the early 1990s, and the written narrative of Jesús María Ramírez.

12. The Dominican Republic experienced processes of land consolidation during the first decades of the twentieth century (Inoa 1994: 1–18, 86–101; Baud 1995: 153–65; Franks 1995; San Miguel 1997: 199–220; Turits 1997: 14–16, 259–332). We should view the fact that Emilio began to accumulate land property in lowland La Descubierta in light of these national processes.

13. For more on Carmito and Carmito's father, Wenceslao Ramírez, who was the most powerful man in the south-west around the turn of the century, see Lundius and Lundahl (2000: 41, note 26).

14. The Haitian massacre under Trujillo started in the northern borderlands in October 1937. The following year the dictator ordered the expulsion of thousands of ethnic Haitians from the southern border areas, and many lost their lives in this military action.

15. For more on the Trujillo regime's use of forced labour for public works, see Inoa (1994: 105–52), San Miguel (1997: 266–88) and Turits (2003: 300–301, note 100).

16. One part of the Dominicanisation in this part of the country was the creation and establishment of Jimaní – a completely new frontier town situated closer to the Haitian–Dominican border than either Duvergé or La Descubierta. Jimaní, founded in the early 1940s, became the new administrative centre of the province.

17. Mella, Martínez, Alba, Barranco, Sanchez, Ares and Viñas are not the actual family surnames, but pseudonyms. In this chapter, I have used the real names of all members of the Ramírez family, but all other names from La Descubierta have been changed.

18. On the part played by a broad range of notions of masculinity in the everyday production of political legitimacy in the Dominican Republic, see Krohn-Hansen (1996); also Derby (2000).

19. This is not the place for a lengthy Dominican history of official and popular anti-Haitianism. For an examination of Haitians in the Dominican popular imagination prior to 1937, see Derby (1994). Derby (1994: 489) concludes that the 1937 massacre was state sponsored and executed for reasons entirely exterior to the border, but that 'the massacre', as she puts it, nonetheless 'made sense in a Gramscian way to [Dominican] border residents'. For more on the 1937 massacre, see Turits (1997: 427–577, 2003: 144–80). For more on Dominican official and popular discourses and practices, see Moya Pons (1986), Mateo (1993), Krohn-Hansen (1995, 2001), Martínez (1997), Torres-Saillant (1999a, 1999b), Sagás (2000) and Howard (2001).

20. La Descubierta's *caudillo* Jesús María Ramírez and the feared José María Alcántara were friends. They first met in the armed forces in 1929, and remained friends after that (Ramírez 2000: 91, 115, 135). For more on this infamous officer under Trujillo, see Turits (2003: 193, 257).

21. Also Jesús María Ramírez portrays the terror and the lack of certainty and trust under the dictator. He describes situations and incidents where he became frightened or terrified and profoundly feared that particular representatives of the regime would be able to hurt him or a friend (Ramírez 2000: 91–116).

22. I agree with those who insist that Foucault short-circuits empire – the facts and implications of colonialism (Stoler 1995: 5–6, 14). As Clifford (1988: 264–65) has put it, Foucault has been 'scrupulously ethnocentric'.

23. In this and the next paragraph, I draw heavily on Nugent (1997: 316–23). For a work on the Haitian state, see Trouillot (1990). For analyses of Cuba and Puerto Rico, see Ortiz ([1940] 1995) and Duany (2002).

REFERENCES

Abrams, P., [1977] 1988. 'Notes on the Difficulty of Studying the State', *Journal of Historical Sociology*, 1(1): 58–89.

Alonso, A.M., 1994. 'The Politics of Space, Time and Substance: State Formation, Nationalism, and Ethnicity', *Annual Review of Anthropology*, 23: 379–405.

Alonso, A.M., 1995. *Thread of Blood*. Tucson, AZ: University of Arizona Press.

Aretxaga, B., 2003. 'Maddening States', *Annual Review of Anthropology*, 32: 393–410.

Baud, M., 1987. 'The Origins of Capitalist Agriculture in the Dominican Republic', *Latin American Research Review*, 22(2): 135–53.

Baud, M., 1993a. 'Una frontera-refugio: Dominicanos y haitianos contra el estado (1870–1930)', *Estudios Sociales* (Santo Domingo), 26(92): 39–64.

Baud, M., 1993b. 'Una frontera para cruzar: La sociedad rural a través de la frontera dominico–haitiana (1870–1930)', *Estudios Sociales* (Santo Domingo), 26(94): 5–28.

Baud, M., 1995. *Peasants and Tobacco in the Dominican Republic, 1870–1930*. Knoxville: University of Tennessee Press.

Bayart, J.-F., 1991. 'Finishing with the Idea of the Third World: The Concept of the Political Trajectory', pp. 51–71 in J. Manor, ed., *Rethinking Third World Politics*. London and New York: Longman.

Cassá, R., 1990. *Movimiento obrero y lucha socialista en la República Dominicana (desde los orígenes hasta 1960)*. Santo Domingo: Fundación Cultural Dominicana.

Chehabi, H.E. and J.J. Linz, 1998. 'A Theory of Sultanism 1: A Type of Nondemocratic Rule', pp. 3–25 in H.E. Chehabi and J.J. Linz, eds, *Sultanistic Regimes*. Baltimore, MD, and London: Johns Hopkins University Press.

Clausner, M., 1973. *Rural Santo Domingo: Settled, Unsettled, Resettled*. Philadelphia, PA: Temple University Press.

Clifford, J., 1988. *The Predicament of Culture*. Cambridge, MA, and London: Harvard University Press.

Coronil, F., 1996. 'Beyond Occidentalism: Toward Nonimperial Geohistorical Categories', *Cultural Anthropology*, 11(1): 51–87.

Coronil, F., 1997. *The Magical State: Nature, Money, and Modernity in Venezuela*. Chicago, IL, and London: University of Chicago Press.

Corrigan, P. and D. Sayer, 1985. *The Great Arch: English State Formation as Cultural Revolution*. Oxford: Basil Blackwell.

Crassweller, R.D., 1966. *Trujillo: The Life and Times of a Caribbean Dictator*. New York: Macmillan.

Derby, L., 1994. 'Haitians, Magic, and Money: Raza and Society in the Haitian–Dominican Borderlands, 1900 to 1937', *Comparative Studies in Society and History*, 36(3): 488–526.

Derby, L., 1999. 'The Dictator's Two Hidden Bodies: Hidden Powers of State in the Dominican Republic', *Etnofoor*, 12(2): 92–116.

Derby, L., 2000. 'The Dictator's Seduction: Gender and State Spectacle during the Trujillo Regime', pp. 213–39 in W. Beezley and L. Curcio, eds, *Latin American Cultural Studies: A Reader*. Wilmington, DE: Scholarly Resources.

Derby, L., 2003. 'In the Shadow of the State: The Politics of Denunciation and Panegyric during the Trujillo Regime in the Dominican Republic, 1940–1958', *Hispanic American Historical Review*, 83(2): 295–344.

Duany, J., 2002. *The Puerto Rican Nation on the Move*. Chapel Hill, NC, and London: University of North Carolina Press.

Foucault, M., 1979. *Discipline and Punish*. New York: Vintage Books.

Foucault, M., 1980. *Power/Knowledge*, ed. C. Gordon. New York: Pantheon Books.

Foucault, M., 1991. 'Governmentality', pp. 87–104 in G. Burchell, C. Gordon and P. Miller, eds, *The Foucault Effect: Studies in Governmentality*. Chicago, IL, and London: University of Chicago Press.

Franks, J., 1995. 'The *Gavilleros* of the East: Social Banditry as Political Practice in the Dominican Sugar Region, 1900–1924', *Journal of Historical Sociology*, 8(2): 158–81.

Galíndez, J. de, 1958. *La era de Trujillo: Un estudio casuístico de dictadura hispanoamericana*. Buenos Aires: Editorial Americana.

Galíndez, J. de, 1973. *The Era of Trujillo: Dominican Dictator*, ed. R.H. Fitzgibbon. Tucson, AZ: University of Arizona Press.

Garrido, V., 1970. *En la ruta de mi vida 1886–1966*. Santo Domingo: Impr. Arte y Cine.

Garrido, V., [1922] 1975. 'Común de San Juan', pp. 223–36 in E. Rodríguez Demorizi, ed., *Lengua y folklore de Santo Domingo*. Santiago: Universidad Católica Madre y Maestra.

Geertz, C., 1973. *The Interpretation of Cultures*. New York: Basic Books.

Geertz, C., 1980. *Negara: The Theatre State in Nineteenth-century Bali*. Princeton, NJ: Princeton University Press.

Hansen, T.B. and F. Stepputat, eds, 2001. *States of Imagination*. Durham, NC, and London: Duke University Press.

Hartlyn, J., 1998. 'The Trujillo Regime in the Dominican Republic', pp. 85–112 in H.E. Chehabi and J.J. Linz, eds, *Sultanistic Regimes*. Baltimore, MD, and London: Johns Hopkins University Press.

Herzfeld, M., 1992. *The Social Production of Indifference: Exploring the Symbolic Roots of Western Bureaucracy*. Chicago, IL: University of Chicago Press.

Hicks, A., 1946. *Blood in the Streets: The Life and Rule of Trujillo*. New York: Creative Age.

Howard, D., 2001. *Coloring the Nation: Race and Ethnicity in the Dominican Republic*. Oxford: Signal Books.

Inoa, O., 1994. *Estado y campesinos al inicio de la era de Trujillo*. Santo Domingo: Librería La Trinitaria.

Joseph, G.M. and D. Nugent, eds, 1994. *Everyday Forms of State Formation*. Durham, NC, and London: Duke University Press.

Krohn-Hansen, C., 1995. 'Magic, Money and Alterity among Dominicans', *Social Anthropology*, 3(2): 129–46.

Krohn-Hansen, C., 1996. 'Masculinity and the Political among Dominicans: "The Dominican Tiger"', pp. 108–33 in M. Melhuus and K.A. Stølen, eds, *Machos, Mistresses, Madonnas: Contesting the Power of Latin American Gender Imagery*. London: Verso.

Krohn-Hansen, C., 2001. 'A Tomb for Columbus in Santo Domingo: Political Cosmology, Population, and Racial Frontiers', *Social Anthropology*, 9(2): 165–92.

Kryzanek, M.J. and H.J. Wiarda, 1988. *The Politics of External Influence in the Dominican Republic*. New York: Praeger Publishers.

Linz, J.J., 1975. 'Totalitarian and Authoritarian Regimes', pp. 259–63 in N. Polsby and F. Greenstein, eds, *Handbook of Political Science*, vol. 3. Reading, MA: Addison-Wesley.

Lundius, J. and M. Lundahl, 2000. *Peasants and Religion: A Socioeconomic Study of Dios Olivorio and the Palma Sola Movement in the Dominican Republic*. New York and London: Routledge.

Martínez, S., 1997. 'The Masking of History: Popular Images of the Nation on a Dominican Sugar Plantation', *New West Indian Guide*, 71: 227–48.

Mateo, A., 1993. *Mito y cultura en la era de Trujillo*. Santo Domingo: Editora de Colores.

Miller, D., 1997. *Capitalism: An Ethnographic Approach*. Oxford: Berg.

Mitchell, T., 1999. 'Society, Economy, and the State Effect', pp. 76–97 in G. Steinmetz, ed., *State/Culture: State Formation after the Cultural Turn*. Ithaca, NY, and London: Cornell University Press.

Moya Pons, F., 1986. 'Los Historiadores y la Percepción de la Nacionalidad', pp. 253–64 in F. Moya Pons, *El pasado dominicano*. Santa Domingo: Fundación J.A. Caro Alvarez.

Moya Pons, F., 1998. *The Dominican Republic: A National History*. Princeton, NJ: Markus Wiener Publishers.

Nagengast, C., 1994. 'Violence, Terror, and the Crisis of the State', *Annual Review of Anthropology*, 23: 109–36.

Nugent, D., 1997. *Modernity at the Edge of Empire: State, Individual, and Nation in the Northern Peruvian Andes, 1885–1935*. Stanford, CA: Stanford University Press.

Ortiz, F. [1940] 1995. *Cuban Counterpoint: Tobacco and Sugar*. Durham, NC, and London: Duke University Press.

Ortner, S., 1995. 'Resistance and the Problem of Ethnographic Refusal', *Comparative Studies in Society and History*, 37(1): 173–93.

Ortner, S., 1999. 'Thick Resistance: Death and the Cultural Construction of Agency in Himalayan Montaineering', pp. 136–63 in S. Ortner, ed., *The Fate of 'Culture'*. Berkeley, CA: University of California Press.

Palmer, C.E., 1976. 'Land Use and Landscape Change along the Dominican–Haitian Borderlands', PhD dissertation, Department of Geography, University of Florida.

Radcliffe-Brown, A.R., [1940] 1955. 'Preface', pp. xi–xxiii in M. Fortes and E.E. Evans-Pritchard, eds, *African Political Systems*. London: Oxford University Press.

Ramírez, J.M., 2000. *Mis 43 años en La Descubierta*. Santo Domingo: Editora Centenario.

Roorda, E., 1998. *The Dictator Next Door: The Good Neighbor Policy and the Trujillo Regime in the Dominican Republic, 1930–1945*. Durham, NC, and London: Duke University Press.

Sagás, E., 2000. *Race and Politics in the Dominican Republic*. Gainesville, FL: University Press of Florida.

Sahlins, M., 1976. *Culture and Practical Reason*. Chicago, IL, and London: University of Chicago Press.

Said, E., 1978. *Orientalism*. New York: Pantheon Books.

San Miguel, P., 1997. *Los campesinos del Cibao: Economía de mercado y transformación agraria en la República Dominicana, 1880–1960*. San Juan: Editorial de la Universidad de Puerto Rico.

Steinmetz, G., ed., 1999. *State/Culture: State Formation after the Cultural Turn*. Ithaca, NY, and London: Cornell University Press.

Stoler, A.L., 1995. *Race and the Education of Desire*. Durham, NC, and London: Duke University Press.

Tolentino Rojas, V., 1944. *Historia de la División Territorial de la República Dominicana*. Santiago: Editorial El Diario.

Torres-Saillant, S., 1999a. 'Introduction to Dominican Blackness'. Dominican Studies Working Papers Series, 1. CUNY Dominican Studies Institute, City College of New York.

Torres-Saillant, S., 1999b. *El retorno de las yolas: Ensayos sobre diáspora, democracia y dominicanidad*. Santo Domingo: Ediciones Librería La Trinitaria y Editora Manatí.

Trouillot, M.-R., 1990. *Haiti: State against Nation: The Origins and Legacy of Duvalierism*. New York: Monthly Review Press.

Turits, R.L., 1997. 'The Foundations of Despotism: Peasants, Property, and the Trujillo Regime (1930–1961)', PhD dissertation, Department of History, University of Chicago.

Turits, R.L., 2003. *Foundations of Despotism: Peasants, the Trujillo Regime, and Modernity in Dominican History*. Stanford, CA: Stanford University Press.

Vega, B., 1985. *Nazismo, Fascismo y Falangismo en la República Dominicana*. Santo Domingo: Fundación Cultural Dominicana.

Vega, B., 1986. *Control y represión en la dictadura trujillista*. Santo Domingo: Fundación Cultural Dominicana.

Vega, B., 1988. *Trujillo y Haití*, vol. 1 (1930–37). Santo Domingo: Fundación Cultural Dominicana.

Vega, B., 1995. *Trujillo y Haití*, vol. 2 (1937–38). Santo Domingo: Fundación Cultural Dominicana.

Walker, M.T., 1970. 'Power Structure and Patronage in a Community of the Dominican Republic', *Journal of Inter-American Affairs*, 12(4): 485–504.

Walker, M.T., 1972. *Politics and the Power Structure: A Rural Community in the Dominican Republic*. New York and London: Teachers College Press.

Weber, M., 1978. *Economy and Society*, vols 1 and 2, ed. G. Roth and C. Wittich. Berkeley, CA: University of California Press.

Manuscripts

Ramírez, J.M., notes. Excerpts from Jesús María Ramírez's unpublished autobiographical notes.

6 THE MATERIALITY OF STATE-EFFECTS: AN ETHNOGRAPHY OF A ROAD IN THE PERUVIAN ANDES

Penelope Harvey

THE ROAD FROM CUSCO TO PUERTO MALDONADO

The 484 km of road that connects Cusco to Puerto Maldonado is traversed by the huge Volvo trucks that provision the mining towns of Peru's gold- and timber-rich Amazonian region.[1] Every day migrant workers enter and leave the *'selva'* (lowland forest) perched on top of heavy loads of wood, gasoline or foodstuffs, crouched under huge, smelly tarpaulins, sometimes carrying no more than a tiny bag, sometimes moving numerous sacks of produce, commercial goods, or personal possessions sewn into white flour sacks to protect the contents from damage or theft. These heavy vehicles carve deep ruts in the road, which the smaller lorries negotiate as best they can as they move passengers and goods between Cusco and the outlying areas of this region of southern Peru provisioning small businesses and households along the route. Doing fieldwork in Ocongate, a small town some 120 km from Cusco, I got to know this road and the people who travelled along it: the migrant workers from the city as well as the *selva*, people working in construction or domestic service, those on leave from salaried employment, from university, from the army or those who needed to travel to the city to deal with financial, legal or medical matters, to visit family, to buy and sell goods.

Travelling required patience and stamina. There were often hours of waiting involved as the trucks piled up with people and goods. We frequently drove around the edges of the city for hours getting ready to depart, visiting workshops, wholesalers, gas stations or simply waiting for passengers. Drivers would not leave until their trucks were full. The contours of the passenger accommodation changed as beer crates, car batteries, kerosene drums, sacks of clothing, rice or vegetables were piled in and travellers adjusted themselves, trying to find a spot where they could achieve a modicum of comfort for the 5–10 hour journey. Sometimes I got a seat in the cab and could sit alongside the driver. The cab was warmer, drier and less dusty; *cumbia*, *salsa* and *huayno* tapes would be played over and over again filling the gaps in conversation and providing a soundtrack to the journey. Drivers charged extra for this more comfortable accommodation, but ability to pay could not secure the seats which were often reserved for personal friends, family or *compadres*, and respected members of the driver's community. Up on top there was often a more raucous sociability as passengers teased each other, entertaining themselves as they reacted to incidents along the way. But such scenes depended on who was travelling, on the weather and the state of the road, and the mood could equally be quiet and sombre, with individuals crouched under ponchos or plastic sheeting.

During the 1980s and 1990s when I travelled this road with some frequency, the lorries were stopped at the checkpoints that surrounded the city. Here police and sometimes army personnel would scrutinise passengers and their baggage. They looked for goods that should not be moved without state licence – *coca* and hard woods particularly – and for people who were travelling without proper proof of citizenship – perhaps avoiding military service, perhaps a subversive, most likely somebody who had simply not managed to complete the bureaucratic procedures which result in legal status and who was thus liable to be fined or open to veiled requests for money. As the lorries slowed down at these checkpoints passengers were accosted by people selling fruit, bread and cooked food – urban luxuries to carry to the countryside, sustenance for the journey itself. In contrast to the slow rhythm of the departure, stops at the checkpoints would be hurried and tense – the exchange of goods frantic and urgent.

Urcos, a town some 40 km from Cusco was a turning point in the journey. The lorries often made a final provisioning stop here. Passengers grabbed a quick meal or made a few final purchases before the lorries turned left off the tarmac piste, and began the long slow ascent up the hillside to the pass high above the Cusco valley. Now the lorries only stopped if they needed water to prevent over-heating, or if a passenger whistled to climb on or off. In the dry season the roads are dusty and passengers riding on top are soon coated in a greyish-white powder. The climate is harsh, very cold or very burning. The tiny bridges that carry the road over the many small streams and gullies in the mountainside are rickety. The deep ruts made by the heavier lorries can easily upset a smaller vehicle. The journey is dangerous, particularly in the rainy season when landslides often occur. The ruts are deeper and the road more slippery and there are many accidents and fatalities. Small wooden crosses by the side of the road mark places where people have died, creating a macabre reminder of how precarious it is to travel.

At the pass there is a small shrine. People crossed themselves as they reached that point. If given a chance they climb down to offer a prayer at the chapel or pile a stone on the cairns that surround the shrine. I once travelled with a dance troupe returning from a pilgrimage; they climbed down and offered dance and music at this point. More usually people offer coca and quiet contemplation. The lorries then begin the first descent, looking for short-cuts, veering off the road to avoid the long meandering loops that closely follow the contours of the mountain, purportedly the result of greedy engineers, paid by the metre. Finally, another police post, papers checked again, loads inspected and fines exacted for anything not in order. From this point onward there are more frequent stops to let people off, as there are more numerous small settlements alongside the roads.

This short stretch of road from Cusco to Ocongate provides far more than a means of moving between two places. The connectivity afforded by this road is complex and its impact differentially experienced. The advent of motorised transport drew previously distant places experientially closer as journey times became shorter (Schivelbusch 1977). But the Peruvian road reminds us that such time/space compression (Harvey 1990) is discontinuous and uneven. Indeed, for some parts of this route the trucks move between points more slowly than those on foot, who can follow the precipitous but more direct pathways up and down the steep mountainsides. Some modes of transport are infinitely more 'efficient' than others. The NGO workers who travel in small four-wheel drive jeeps can usually get from Cusco to Ocongate in 3–5 hours. By lorry the journey time was more usually 5–10 hours, and if the road was blocked in any way the journey times became indeterminate, with passengers often spending the night huddled in the freezing cold waiting for a spare part to be delivered, or a landslide to be cleared. Even on a single vehicle some will travel 'faster' than others. Some passengers are forced to wait for hours while others are able to coordinate arrival and departure times more precisely.

Nor should we assume that the technological developments behind contemporary transport systems in Peru have produced the kinds of modern subjectivity that are sometimes attributed to them. As we have seen, road travel in Peru only partially separates the traveller from the environment through which they are passing, and even the most committed local entrepreneur stays deeply in touch with the animate powers of the landscapes through which they move (Harvey 2001, 2003). This continual awareness of the road itself is inevitable when they are in such a poor state of repair and demand the attentive engagement of drivers and passengers in ways that smooth tarmac highways do not. Furthermore, the vehicles themselves need constant attention and manifest the signs of fatigue and exhaustion that historians of transport have assumed disappeared with the demise of horse-drawn carriages (Schivelbusch 1977: 12). Thus while some can find a modicum of travelling comfort and pass a journey relatively passively in relation to their mobility, others feel every pot-hole, note every cross by the roadside and even climb on and off at frequent intervals to mend the road, fill the radiator with water and actively coax the vehicle towards its destination.

In what ways then does a focus on this road allow me to approach the Peruvian state ethnographically? Does the singularity and specificity of this road exemplify the scalar difference that has made ethnographic approaches seem limited and inappropriate in relation to the study of extensive, translocal forms of modern power? Or might the road in some way encapsulate the challenges that all ethnographers of 'the state' have to address and thereby provide a concrete manifestation of the kinds of 'state effects' (Mitchell

1991) that ethnographers *can* realistically expect to describe and analyse. My suggestion is that roads inevitably lead us to 'the state', but indirectly. The circuitous and somewhat tangential approach is important because it leaves space for disruption of the ethnographer's prior assumptions about the form and the location in which 'the state' might appear.

My argument in this chapter is that Andean roads give us a particularly interesting window on the Peruvian state as they manifest state presence yet also reveal the weakness of the national communications infrastructure and the very limited possibilities for the exercise of political control by a centralised administration. And while it is clear that roads channel people and their possessions along particular routes and encourage particular forms of economic practice that are not always beneficial to local people (Wilson 2004), state control of the roads is far from absolute. After all, when even the lorries don't stick to the roads we should be wary of exaggerating the effects of these particular technologies of state.

ETHNOGRAPHY OF THE STATE?

Recent anthropological approaches to the state have articulated the dilemmas involved in turning 'the state' into the object of ethnographic study. It is the kind of object that dissolves on close inspection and affords the ethnographer no tangible vantage point: 'there is obviously no Archimedean point from which to visualise "the state", only numerous situated knowledges' (Haraway 1988). Bureaucrats, for example, imagine it through statistics (Hacking 1982), official reports and tours, whereas citizens do so through newspaper stories, dealings with particular government agencies, the pronouncements of politicians, and so forth (Gupta 1995: 392). The state, in similar ways to many of our previously treasured modernist categories (society, culture, nation, identity, etc.) has been revealed as complex, in the sense that it is comprised of 'things that relate but don't add up' (Mol and Law 2002: 1). Subsequent attempts to 'add things up' are quickly recognised as ideological, imaginary, illusory or at least partial and provisional.[2]

However, complexity and attempts at standardisation *can* be studied ethnographically. One useful approach has been to focus on processes of scaling (see Strathern 1991, 1995; Ferme, 2001). As Nustad argues in Chapter 4, agency frequently entails a scaling process whereby the state agent comes to occupy a position at the centre of a given population, thereby imposing a hierarchical structure of control through which populations are known and acted upon in specific ways. How state actors achieve the appearance of size is an important aspect in the production of state-effects. Ferme's interest in the language and practices of scaling, and the processes of magnification or scaling up within dialectical relations of large and small provide an excellent example of ethnographic thinking about these issues (Ferme 2001). Another more common approach to complexity and standardisation has been to step back from fine-grained ethnography to focus instead on discursive forms, and some feel that this is the most viable way forward for anthropological approaches to the state. Gupta (1995), for example, argues that anthropological commitment to 'a physics of presence' has hampered ethnographic work on the state. While accepting his arguments on the importance of using various discursive forms as sources for an anthropology of the state, it is equally important to stress that such sources can only be deployed *ethnographically* if reconnected to particular lives in particular places. Thus, far from abandoning or watering down the importance of co-presence, I argue to the contrary, that a renewed commitment to spatial proximity is necessary for a truly dynamic ethnography of the state, despite the obvious difficulties. Indeed, I would go further and argue that in many ways it is the inherent problems of 'location' in relation to the state that give ethnographic methods their critical purchase. By approaching the state through the study of particular concrete material effects, ethnographic methods can generate a critical position by standing outside the state's own version of itself, revealing the concrete effects of its supposedly ephemeral power and challenging claims to ideological singularity. This approach appears to be counter to the important theoretical trends (discussed in the introduction to this book) that have worked to disarticulate 'the state' from privileged places and to focus instead on dispersed disciplinary power and specific state-effects.

Navaro-Yashin (2002), following Žižek, has drawn attention to the fact that increased theoretical awareness of the ephemerality of 'the state' does not seem to have diminished the pervasive sense of located singularity that surrounds the notion of state agency. She looks to the material effects of statecraft to explain this situation.

The signifier state can remain intact, in spite of public consciousness, because a material and tangible world has been organized around it.... Even when we have come intellectually to disentangle the state, we need to keep on treating it as a reality, because there exists a reality that has been activated through this symbol. (Navaro-Yashin 2002: 171)

In a somewhat different vein Mitchell (1991) has argued that the ephemerality of the state is also central to what are recognised as state-effects. Thus in addition to the problems of an enduring self-evident state, despite widespread recognition of translocality, distributed agency and experiential multiplicity, we must add an integral dynamic of absence, externality or concealment, for the state is a conceptual entity that is also systematically elusive and indirect. Location is thus not a problem simply because of dispersal, but because as 'social effect' the state is generated from beyond the space that it claims to inhabit. In this context, the promise of ethnography is to relocate an elusive conceptual entity that thrives on collapse into a generic absent force and on notions of scalar discontinuity.

This dynamic relationship between presence and absence characterised my initial understandings of 'the state' in the southern Peruvian Andes. The mechanisms of the bureaucratic state reached into the town of Ocongate where I did fieldwork, most noticeably in the presence of the town hall, with its elected and nominated officials, the local judiciary, and the employees of various government ministries – education, transport, communications, agriculture and health. There was also a police post in the town and the very occasional appearance of military personnel. Ocongate is a District Capital (of the Province of Quispicanchis, Department of Cusco). It is the location for state ritual and for the delivery of state services. It was here that people came to vote, to receive 'aid' and to begin the bureaucratic trails required for any more sustained engagement with government agencies (Lund 2001). This was a place where people performed the state into being in their daily lives, exploring possibilities, striving to inhabit clear bureaucratic categories but often struggling to do so convincingly. Such practice was visible in the Independence Day celebrations,[3] and the numerous occasions when people either made or were made to listen to patriotic speeches, sing the national anthem and salute the Peruvian flag, as they queued patiently to exercise the right to vote, and as they turned up to register births, marriages and deaths.

   In Peru more generally the contemporary state had been made visible in a particular way in the 1980s and 1990s, through the war with Shining Path. This war was explicitly waged by Maoist guerrillas against the state, although in practice it revolved around the violent control of people's daily lives and non-negotiable demands for collaboration, to which the army responded by the often brutal suppression of people assumed to be aiding their enemies. The war revealed a crisis in 'legibility' (Scott 1998). The state did not know who the enemy were, they did not know how to locate or suppress them. Shining Path did not care about whether the people they killed and tortured were their enemies or not. They simply needed to show that the state was not able to protect people. State legitimacy was under threat. It could offer no effective protection. Agents of state were particularly subject to attack but so too were the so-called revisionist forces, the political parties, trade unions, indeed anybody who tried to imagine forms of governance that left the modern state intact. The war with Shining Path was not the only problem that the Peruvian state faced. Peru's sovereign territories were under threat from neighbouring Ecuador, and from the various regions of the rainforest where the combined forces of drug traders and corrupt military officials made it impossible to enforce the law. Subject to the interests of capital and to the demands of the international financial community, it is clear that the state had little autonomy in financial matters either. The attempts in the 1980s to nationalise the banks and to reject the terms and conditions of the IMF brought rapid financial ruin and deep political instability to the country. Deep-seated political corruption and the collapse of the traditional political parties strengthened the image of a financially and morally bankrupt state. When President Fujimori suspended the Constitution in 1992, for most people, it was business as usual!

   This visibly absent state characterised public life in Ocongate. Here overt corruption (although certainly visible) was less relevant to people than the sense of abandonment, and the obvious poverty and unreliability of the state. When I lived there in the 1980s the school was bare, the telephone didn't work, there was no electricity and the road was in an appalling state of disrepair. Teachers were often absent and the police drunk, isolated and paranoid. By the end of the 1990s there was electricity and the school had had some refurbishment, even the town hall had been moved into a new building – but it was still an all-but empty building. The road had got worse than ever – and people still lived with a sense of marginality. Even the war hadn't really come their way.

Yet this was no stateless society (Clastres 1987). On the contrary, one of the key axes of differentiation within Latin Americanist anthropology is precisely between those regions such as the Peruvian Andes where the state is tangible, even in its absence and those, such as large parts of Amazonia, where the state seems irrelevant, despite its traceable effects (Gow 1991). In the Peruvian Andes the state has survived scandal and disruption, incapacity and weakness. Yet the notion of a potentially effective external power is kept alive. This raises further questions. How is it possible that a modern nation-state that has existed constitutionally for over 500 years can still be seen as an external power? How is this form of power produced and reproduced in the mundane activities of people's everyday lives? And how do these internal and external dimensions of state power coexist and relate to each other?

People in Ocongate sustain their sense of the state despite its obvious shortcomings. There is no paradox here as, while state power is clearly constitutive of people's contemporary environments, this locus of agency is also understood as external to them. Those people who *I* identified as agents of the state in Ocongate do not really embody the state for local people. They are seen variously as *compadres*, relatives, neighbours, friends (*familiares, conocidos* or *vecinos*).[4] Occasionally these people were referred to as 'the authorities' (*las autoridades*), usually by those who do not know them well and have to engage via them in bureaucratic practice or state ritual. Such engagements are always embarrassing and slightly humiliating, and express a social distance and sense of strangeness. Nevertheless, local people who become state employees or officials are generally thought to have done well – taken an opportunity, perhaps managed to get a salaried job, perhaps taken advantage of connections. But their presence doesn't exactly bring the state into the town. The effect is almost the opposite: such locals become more distant, more like outsiders. Outsiders themselves sometimes become friends, but often they remain external to local concerns.

As anthropologists we commonly appeal to the state in two quite different ways. On the one hand the state appears as an unmarked and self-evident reference to the apparatus of government and to regulatory regimes which create lasting effects on the particular localities where we come to study. Here the state is invoked as part of the basic context, which frames the particular ethnographic realities we are focused on. The state can be attributed powerful agency but remains an abstract shadowy presence, somehow out of view and therefore not available for analysis. Where the state does appear within the ethnographic frame, it is either in a particular institutional guise, or as an idea. In my own work I have explored both these dimensions within the particular locality of Ocongate – looking at the school, the judge's office, the town hall and Spanish language as sites of state practice, but also discussing the state as external power, a source of local fascination and/or disdain, capricious, dangerous but nevertheless with a promise of transformational possibility, efficacious should it want to be (Harvey 1997, 2001, 2003). My current interest is to look in a more focused way at the materiality of the state in an attempt to produce a site for the ethnographic study of state power that will reveal the varied 'faces of the state' (Navaro-Yashin 2002), its intrinsic externality (and the consequent experience of absence), and its simultaneous pervasive presence in people's daily lives.

Studying the state in this way throws up the question of what it means to know something ethnographically. An ephemeral and complex object such as the state clearly presents various problems for ethnography. How do particular ideas about the state relate to the more generalised contextual notions that are often invoked to historicise or contextualise ethnographic accounts? How can the self-evident partiality of ethnographic knowledge relate to wider regional or theoretical debates about politics and public life? Strathern has written that 'the apparent dilemma of ethnography is that it generates too much specificity'. The issue then is how such specificity is handled. Here we need to address issues of scale. If we think of the specific (often translated as the local) in terms of a scaled relationship of encompassment, then there can be no ethnography of the state, as that which we could describe (the local) would always be 'less than' the object we are trying to focus on (the state). Furthermore, this model buys into the story that the bureaucratic state tells about itself, namely that local administrative units are small and lesser versions of national administration (which is more because it is the sum of the parts). To reproduce this story is to study the fetish on its own terms. Such idioms of scale place the state elsewhere and thus produce the ethnographic dilemma of how to locate the object of study.

In this chapter I argue, following Navaro-Yashin (2002) and Ferme (2001), that the materiality of state-effects is crucial to anthropologists, because such materiality provides a focus that allows us to exercise the kind of critical awareness that ethnography affords. I approach ethnography as a particular mode of attentiveness that entails, but is not defined by, spatial proximity to the object of study. Discursive forms such as media reports, everyday talk, official language and the whole panoply of transnational symbolic 'languages' and branded commodities are crucial components in such an approach, but the challenge for the ethnographer is to force these entities to appear in an embedded rather than abstracted form – to recover the impurities and reveal the collaborations that counter the illusion of abstraction without dismissing the reality that such illusion can acquire in people's everyday lives. Crucially, I argue that ethnography, even of a multi-sited kind, has to work through the dynamics of spatial proximity.[5] The challenge for an ethnography of any state is thus to identify material traces which can be engaged ethnographically and which open out, rather than close down, further perspectives on the structures and practices through which this particular mode of power is effected and reproduced.

With these ideas in mind I return to the road, and to the idea of carrying out an ethnography of the state by looking 'elsewhere' and suggest that the state of the roads offers an interesting perspective on the state. This approach leaves open how 'the state' appears as self-evident to the people I was living with. It also allows incompatible notions of 'the state' to appear alongside each other as there is no need to hold the state together analytically as a coherent object. Roads can invoke both the presence and the absence of the state. They are concrete material entities that reveal multiple agencies, produced through particular circumstances and relationships, and used and claimed in ways that planners and politicians never envisaged. They are immobile material entities yet they draw attention to mobility; they have fixed geographical coordinates yet they extend beyond and exceed named places and thus have an air of the translocal about them; they are the outcome of modern technological practice yet people in the Andean town of Ocongate, on whom I base this analysis, also talked of them in relation to the land and alternative understandings of knowledge and power.

Wilson (2004) has pointed out how roads can operate as technologies of standardisation and control, offering single, institutionalised routes through the landscape, often explicitly created by governments to enable the neoliberal economy to the detriment of alternative possibilities. Roads provide tangible evidence of both technical and political capacity. They materialise state and corporate ambition, and transform particular territorial spaces into sites of fantasy and projection for politicians, planners and local people. The social, political and economic implications for those connected and for those bypassed by such singular routes are considerable, and most road-building projects are bitterly fought over as people compete for the benefits and struggle simultaneously to avoid the effects of the territorialising projects of the state and/or private capital that road-building entails.

As a concrete space of ethnographic focus roads also have the advantage of holding together the imaginative and the concrete in a quite explicit way. Not only do they operate as powerful discursive tropes of connectivity alongside their existence as concrete located material forms. They also conjoin technological and territorial forms. The acknowledged translocality of the modern state is evidenced by the continual movement of people and things, but such movement has also drawn forth a more explicit concern by governments with control of technological spaces alongside the traditional concerns with territorial spaces (Barry 2001). Following Callon and Latour (1981) Barry recognises that, 'The macro order of the state is built up from a complex network of localised technical practices and devices. To understand how modern government is possible we need to understand the spatial connectedness of technical devices (Barry 2001: 12).

To approach the state by way of an ethnographic analysis of a road thus requires some historical work to uncover the ways in which successive governments have tried to display technological and political capacity through the control of particular territorial spaces. Within this framing of the modern state, communications systems take on a crucial role, apparently holding a state together, by reassembling multiple versions of reality and creating and maintaining clear-cut distinctions between inside and outside (Slater 1998). Modern politics cannot be reduced to spatial politics, but a spatially constituted state remains one of its most self-evident forms (Slater 1998; Radcliffe 2001). Once again roads offer an interesting perspective on these practices as they both engage and transgress territoriality, linking 'transnational flows and penetrations of different kinds of power', to 'the territoriality of politics within national boundaries' (Slater 1998: 381). In this respect it is not surprising that roads become key sites of political struggle appropriated alternately by the military, by revolutionary groups, by popular protesters and by social outcasts who lay claim to marginal spaces through assault and theft.[6]

In the following section I will use the road from Cusco to Ocongate to look historically and ethnographically at how political connections have been made and maintained over time. Clearly the road network in and of itself doesn't deliver national integration (Thévenot 2002) so we need to look with more precision at what connections roads do bring into being, and how these connections are made and maintained. What are the state-effects of the Cusco/Ocongate road?

BUILDING THE ROAD FROM CUSCO TO OCONGATE: HISTORIES OF CO-PRODUCTION

'In the post-colonial period, the project of Latin American nation building has been a profoundly spatial project, in which a lack of physical integration has been compounded by regional conflicts over the nature of the state project' (Radcliffe 2001: 124).

The major road-building projects in Peru began in the 1920s. Massive investments were made in an attempt to integrate the national economy and expand state bureaucracy. It was a time when central government was making a concerted effort to 'promote citizenship, individual rights and equality before the law, as the only legitimate basis of national life' (Nugent 2001: 267). Until this time the Peruvian state had been unable to exercise any direct control over its territories. Since the founding of the modern state in 1824, government had been forced to make alliances with aristocratic families and with the landowners, who, in areas such as the Ocongate region, controlled all aspects of the state apparatus and used these institutions quite openly to support their own ends. The Leguia government dealing with the post-First World War world, the opening of the Panama Canal, diminishing British influence and the rise of US investment in Latin America, sought explicitly to create 'a tranquil economic and political climate for US investors' (Stein 1980: 53). By the 1920s there was a veneer of popular participation in Peruvian state politics, but most people were systematically blocked from the opportunity to participate as citizens. They were kept illiterate, not allowed to speak Spanish and not allowed to display any of the symbolic apparel of modern life. In the large hacienda which borders on the town of Ocongate the peasants were not allowed to wear long trousers, or to ride horses as such acts were taken by the landowners as claims to equal status. By the 1930s local traders were in a position to take advantage of changing markets and the rule of the landlords was challenged. In Ocongate local *mestizo* traders, in armed struggle, managed to move the market place away from the main house of the hacienda and down to Ocongate itself. These struggles, facilitated indirectly by the commercial opportunities that the road networks afforded, meant that people felt that their rights to citizenship and participation in the nation had been won. It was something they valued, even though it took several decades for the Agrarian Reform of 1969 to deliver hacienda land for local use.

The state initiative was seen as a collaborative project in other ways. As the road comes into Ocongate it crosses the river. There are two bridges. The original stone bridge is no longer wide enough for today's lorries and is now only used by pedestrians, animals and bicycles. But it is this bridge that captures the local imagination and there are various stories associated with it. Many people told me that an old man and an old woman had been buried alive in the foundations, as an offering to the Earth, to appease the sense of aggravation and violent intrusion that the road-building process entailed and to prevent the bridge from collapsing. Building roads in the Andes is akin to mining.[7] Dynamite is used to blast through the rock to create the high passes, to widen the valley floors and to carve flat surfaces along the steep mountainsides. The sense of both disturbing and eating away at the core of the land requires sacrificial recompense, to ensure the safety of future travellers. Those who told me the stories of human sacrifice explained that the bridge would not stay up without this payment. The engineers had been unable to complete the road, unable to make the link between Ocongate and the city of Cusco, without the active cooperation of the Earth forces.

The road from Cusco to Ocongate was completed in 1936. Men from today's older generation provided their labour via a much resented conscripted labour road-building programme.[8] To this narrative of state co-option of local people's labour further sinister motives for the expansion of the road system could be added; a means by which the state is engineered into the landscape, with the possible consequences of being able to control local populations more readily, particularly in relation to taxation and control of labour (Fairhead 1992). The ease and speed with which people and goods can be channelled constitute a serious threat to more fragile alternative modes of livelihood (Wilson 2004).

The 1920s and 1930s were times of struggle primarily between the state and regional oligarchies over land and labour, struggles in which local people were not necessarily supportive of the ultimate goals of either of these more powerful interest groups. Modernising elites were pushing for a transition from land to communications as the central organising principle of the modern state.[9] Such a move was generally supported by local people. The road offered new opportunities and access to markets that allowed them to circumvent the landowner's control of the local economy, and the road also gave them access to symbols and practices of the more autonomous modern liberal subject. The fact that the road did not always *deliver* benefits to local people did not diminish these gains. In many ways, 'modernisation' was achieved via state conscription of local labour, for ends that were not necessarily in the interests of local people. For example, the army was brought in to put down the assault on the hacienda, so people knew that the road delivered outside interference as well as opening up options for them. Nevertheless, the road was primarily seen as liberating. Furthermore, the conscripted labour had the effect of making the road 'local' in ways that might not otherwise have been felt so strongly. People had the sense that *they* had worked to bring the road into the local landscape, the rock was blasted to make the connections possible, and those who paid with their labour, and with their lives in many cases, were also local people. Those who wanted roads so fervently certainly deeply resented the ways in which they were compelled to build them, but this did not dampen their enthusiasm for the road itself.

The road thus provides a complex site through which people negotiate their relationships with power. The road connects centres of political and economic power but takes people through a sacred and powerful landscape on the way. This relationship between state and landscape is objectified in the contrasting points of hiatus that punctuate journeys, as people respect both ecological and bureaucratic checkpoints: showing papers to the police and making small offerings to the landscape deities and Catholic saints at the high passes. The road is of the land and wrested from the land. It is contested space, the site of violent confrontation both by politically motivated actors in past and recent times, and by the voracious agency of the land itself, as it claims a return for the existence and the use of the road. Many die on these roads. It is also the source of great anxiety for other reasons. Local people know that while in one respect the road connects Ocongate both to the current extractive domains of the rainforest and the Andean and coastal cities of Cusco, Arequipa and Lima, Ocongate is not in fact a necessary link on this wider route. The town itself is no longer a source of wealth, nor a significant locus of consumption. It is a focal point for trading activity, but as such it is also in many ways marginal to the regions on which it depends for survival: the hinterland where wool and meat is produced, the lowlands from which gold and timber are extracted and the urban capitalist enterprises which finance local trade. The road could take a different route, and the fear is that the decision to re-route the road could be taken at any time by bureaucrats and officials who care nothing for the fortunes of one small place in the mountains. After all, Ocongate's loss would be another's gain.[10]

This discussion of the road shows how people in Ocongate, from various walks of life, looked for the state to take a more active role in their area. They fought for enhanced connection to centres of power and the state apparently responded, providing the infrastructure and the desired connection. The effects of these collaborations are complex. Prakash (1999) argues that technical projects such as these are central to the ways in which modern states display their efficacy. Governments can manifest state power through technical projects. But in Ocongate people were clear that while this was indeed the case, the road was also produced *in collaboration with them*. Road-building required a combination of expertise. Once built, the road itself *does* leave people open to state control. These projects *do* render people more legible, they *can* be monitored and controlled more easily. But this is not all it does. It also affords other more horizontal less centralising effects. In this respect we have to acknowledge that many people are prepared to accept this compromise with power. Demonstrable connection to external sources of power affords recognition and meets certain desires for legitimation. In this framework the state appears in yet another guise, as object of desire and fantasy and people's fears are as likely to focus on abandonment as on control.

THE STATE AS OBJECT OF DESIRE

In 1997 Ocongate was visited by Fujimori, then president of the Republic. His visit was unannounced and totally unexpected. The mayor had not even been in town. Many of the villagers were up on the sports field beside the school, waiting for groups of dancers to return from a pilgrimage to an important local shrine. This religious festival had grown enormously since the 1980s. I was told that local religious sponsors now compete openly in the feast that they offer the returning pilgrims. Fujimori was in luck, for it would only be at such times that such an array of local specialities would be available. The ritual sponsors were persuaded to give over portions of food to the president and his entourage. Once fed, and apparently in fine spirits, Fujimori then set off on a bicycle down the main street from the school to the central square. I was told that he was quite horrified that the town had such a small and inadequate school and promised that he would provide the funds for a new building. Before leaving in his helicopter he was also told that the road from Cusco to Ocongate was in a terrible state of disrepair. One of the local notables had a broken arm at the time from a recent road accident and again Fujimori had apparently responded to these very personal circumstances with a promise of immediate repairs. People were impressed by the fact that he refused to sign any record of these agreements; they were required to accept and trust his word. And he had indeed delivered. This visit was a source of tremendous local pride. The president had conferred something very special on them and, while some other towns in the region had also been visited in subsequent years, the prize of the school was seen as a quite exceptional one. The sense that their festival preparations had enabled them to respond to a surprise visit to such good effect had obviously added to their sense of local achievement.

I found this story extraordinarily significant for it brought together several things that had preoccupied my thoughts on earlier research visits. The presence of the president in the community was about the most tangible evidence of a connection between the village and the state apparatus imaginable. This connection was one that had always preoccupied people; it was tenuous, problematic. Despite the pride and excitement, the president's visit could not of course overcome that feeling. He came and left very quickly. They had talked to him, he had smiled at them, responded to their most immediate needs, and ridden a bicycle down their main road, but he had then gone off in a helicopter without even leaving the vital trace of their agreement in his signature. The school is there of course, but there always was a school of sorts. They would have preferred to have had the agreement objectified in writing. People are used to the obsessive literacy of state practice, and it must have been somewhat disturbing for the president to have left without signing the official record book, the *Libro de Actas*. People expect their relationship to state power to be hierarchical, unequal. The fact of the president having been there was as important in its own way as the legacy of his visit, but he had not left them his signature in his official capacity, just some signed photographs and calendars.

It was as if the appearance of the president re-scaled the state in ways that parallel the ethnographer's dilemma. Proximity to Fujimori allowed an intimate connection, but simultaneously detached Fujimori the man from the more abstract source of state power and revealed how no single individual can sustain the 'bigness' that the notion of the external state evokes. While in Ocongate the president was visibly dependent on local people. They fed and entertained him, lent him a bicycle to visit their main square, engaged him in talk about the problems and deficiencies they experienced in daily life. In this context the signed photographs and calendars took on a problematic and ambiguous meaning. For while treasured as evidence of personal connection to the president, the suggested intimacy also worked against the processes of abstraction whereby the power of the state is enhanced by distance and scalar difference. In contrast to this treasured, yet problematic intimacy, the mode of Fujimori's arrival and departure distanced him from the people of Ocongate. He had not used the road. Air travel afforded him a temporal connectivity to urban centres and sites of governmental procedure that was not available to local people. Fujimori's visit to Ocongate thus displayed how state officials and local people co-produce both the intimate sense of interdependence and the structures of hierarchical distance through which the modern state is constituted.

CONCLUSIONS

Defining 'the political' as 'the antagonistic dimension that is inherent in all human society' and 'politics' as 'the ensemble of practices, discourses, and institutions that seek to establish a certain order and to organize life' (1998: 386), Slater explores the dynamic tension that lies at the heart of all political process. In ways reminiscent of Kapferer's (1998) interpretation of Deleuze, Slater stresses how politics is always interrupted by the political and, in turn, is continually acting on the political to depoliticise it, to control, rationalise and order. The political, in turn, continually reasserts its presence, as the 'irremovable inner periphery at the heart of politics' (1998: 386).

This way of formulating the relationship between politics and the political helps me to reconnect the road from Cusco to Ocongate to the state as an object of ethnographic attention. As 'state-effect' the road was in one sense produced through a particular territorial politics. But this moment of state ordering also revealed the fragility of the territorial order. The roads were built at a time when the Leguia government was explicitly increasing its dependence on foreign capital and foreign technical expertise, and simultaneously negotiating with emergent regional governments. In this context and subsequently, the development of effective communications has assumed great importance as a way in which successive governments have tried to demonstrate their ordering capacity, stabilise the social environment and connect the otherwise dispersed regional fragments into a coherent whole. But of course such order can never be fully achieved or finalised. And in a region such as the Andes, that tension between politics and the political is played out through relationships that exceed any simple dichotomy between state and society, for the ethnography reveals not simply the fragility of the spatial order, but the existence of competing spatial orders or ways of creating territorial coherence.[11]

The road from Cusco to Ocongate connects territories where incompatible spatial politics are not even recognised or acknowledged. For some travellers, the animate landscape, the Christian saints, the state checkpoints, the pot-holes, the accident spots and the road-building and maintenance programmes are experientially continuous, for others (such as Fujimori) they are not experienced at all! Fujimori's helicopter allowed him to keep his distance from the experience of these people's everyday life, as effectively as statistics flatten the realities that they supposedly depict.

In studying the state, the ethnographer's task is to find ways to uncover the workings of the state, and in particular the ways in which this abstract and so-often absent social agent can appear in such a concrete way in people's lives. But to focus on the production of 'state-effects' is to address the dynamics of political agency of a pre-existing, and thus apparently non-political entity. Slater (1998: 385), uses Butler's work to make the point:

... agency can be viewed as belonging to a mode of thinking about persons as instrumental actors who confront an external political field, and 'if we agree that politics and power exist already at the level at which the subject and its agency are articulated and made possible, then agency can be *presumed* only at the cost of refusing to inquire into its construction' (Butler 1992: 13).

My focus on the road was intended to show that an ethnography of the state can uncover these social processes by assuming a tangential approach. Indeed a tangential approach may well be the only option, given the ways in which the state is entangled in mundane sociality. We cannot know where the state will appear from, or in what guise. Fujimori dropped out of the sky after all. I am suggesting that the ethnography of the state requires ethnographers to think across a range of practices – some ordered, some highly dispersed and messy. But rather than thinking of ethnography as attention to the local or small-scale, we should instead look at how attention to detail reveals the complexity of relationships and challenges the uni-dimensional plane which scalar models create and depend on. Even the one brief example of a relatively short stretch of road reveals the relational dynamics through which the 'bigness' of the state is constituted and reproduced in people's lives, while simultaneously affording glimpses of a range of other perspectives on how states exist through mundane personal relationships.

Finally, I want to suggest that the importance of emphasising ethnography's detail is that it enables an interesting shift to occur in how we perceive the dilemmas of the contemporary Peruvian state. For as long as the local is seen as 'less than' and 'encompassed by' wider national or transnational contexts, there is always going to be the problem that local issues are in the end irrelevant to wider concerns. This of course is the fear of irrelevance that the model also produces in people in Ocongate. However, if the focus is on complex relationality rather than scale – then local dilemmas and solutions offer models and ways of understanding how social entities (such as states) can cohere without the need to posit coherent systems. In other words, attention to detail obviates the need for encompassing theory (or scalar models), which requires all constitutive elements to be of a kind, compatible and coherent. My work on contemporary information technologies in Manchester has shown the importance given to the ideal of commensurability in modern communication systems. Indeed, the key technical challenge for communications systems is to facilitate the seamless flow of information (Harvey and Green 2002). The beauty of an ethnographic attention to detail lies in the possibilities afforded for the recognition that incompatibilities are inherent in such systems and continually reassert themselves (Green et al. 2005). This observation is in many ways an anthropological commonplace. We know that modernity is enduringly incomplete and that modern economies depend on the continual need to 'repair', 'replace' and 'improve', which in turn requires ongoing technical solutions to the discontinuities that human relationships produce.

The focus on the road has also made it possible to address the ways in which people think about the state as simultaneously translocal and as centred elsewhere. State rituals, epitomised by the visit of Fujimori, can make the state appear, revealing concrete relationships, but in so doing they also emphasise the tenuous connections that local people have to it, feeding anxieties and desires. For these same people also know, from other contexts, that the state is constituted through multiple agencies, organisations, levels, agendas and centres, and act in the knowledge that state power is both arbitrary and contingent, potentially transformative yet also intrinsically fragile. As Ferme reminds us: 'Ultimately the key to many of these processes of enlargement is embedded in details, in clues that are secreted away from direct apperception' (2001: 10). The trick for ethnographers and local people alike is not to be beguiled for too long by the state's own version of itself and to look instead at the details through which things come to seem as they do.

NOTES

1. I am grateful to the ESRC Centre for Research on Socio-Cultural Change who are currently funding a period of research leave in which I am developing the roads project.
2. See, for example, Anderson (1983), Abrams (1988), Taussig (1993, 1997), Gupta (1995) and Hansen and Stepputat (2001).
3. Harvey (1997) is an essay which illustrates the incomplete 'thraldom' (Navaro-Yashin 2002) in state-orchestrated ritual, and the counterpoint of an alternative state imaginary which draws together the indigenous and state powers into relationships of active engagement for the benefit of local people.
4. It could be argued (following Nustad, this volume) that these actors fail to achieve the status of state actors, as the scaling process requires them to be visibly centred elsewhere.
5. Interesting ethnographic discussions on the location of the state include: Harney (2002) who, drawing on his experience of a period in office in a short-lived radical leftist Canadian government, locates the state beyond particular governments in the specific interests that allow particular governments to continue or not; Gupta (1995) locates the state in the interface between local officials and discursive tropes; while Navaro-Yashin (2002) locates the state as 'elsewhere', in daily life rather than in official offices of state.
6. Unfortunately there is insufficient space to elaborate at length, but it is worth noting that roads were also integral to Inka statecraft, although this was not primarily a territorial state but one which operated through the control of labour and the symbolic control of space, by which outlying regions were connected symbolically through sight lines (Zuidema 1964) to the imperial city of Cusco located at the centre of the Inka world (Urton 1990). During the period of Spanish colonial rule, spaces and territories were conceived in new ways, but space was still differentiated by qualitative means and different settlements were seen as different in kind (Orlove 1993). Standardised measures of population size or geographical location were only introduced during the Republican period, and it was only at this juncture that all spaces were rendered commensurable (Orlove 1993).
7. On mining, see Nash (1979), Taussig (1980), Sallnow (1989).
8. Leguia's government introduced a hugely resented programme of conscripted labour for road construction, the *conscripcion vial*.
9. Pat Joyce's (2003) work on the 'communication state' has been very useful to me in thinking about these issues.
10. There has indeed been a continual discussion over the past few decades on the possibility of building what became known as the Interoceanic Highway to connect

Brazil with the lucrative markets of Asia. The various suggested routes included more than one that would cross through southern Peru – the Cusco–Maldonado road was under consideration, but had by no means secured definitive favour. Any competing road would immediately divert the majority of the traffic, and affect the livelihoods of people in towns such as Ocongate. Local fears of bureaucratic decisions were thus quite well founded (Llosa 2003).

11. I am unable to expand on these competing spatial orders within the confines of this chapter. More detail is given in Harvey (2001).

REFERENCES

Abrams, P., 1988. 'Notes on the Difficulty of Studying the State', *Journal of Historical Sociology*, 1(1): 58–89.

Anderson, B., 1983. *Imagined Communities: Reflections on the Origin and Spread of Nationalism*. London: Verso.

Barry, A., 2001. *Political Machines: Governing a Technological Society*. London: Athlone.

Butler, Judith, 1992. 'Contingent Foundations: Feminism and the Question of "Postmodernism"', in J. Butler and J. Scott, eds, *Feminists Realise the Political*. London: Routledge.

Callon, M. and B. Latour, 1981. 'Unscrewing the Big Leviathan, or How Actors Macrostructure Reality and How Sociologists Help them Do So', in K. Knorr-Cetina and A. Cicourel, eds, *Advances in Social Theory and Methodology: Toward an Integration of Macro and Micro Sociologies*. London: Routledge & Kegan Paul.

Clastres, P., 1987. *Society Against the State: Essays in Political Anthropology*. New York: Zone Books.

Fairhead, J., 1992. 'Paths of Authority: Roads, the State and the Market in Eastern Zaire', *European Journal of Development Research*, 4(2): 17–35.

Ferme, M., 2001. *The Underneath of Things: Violence, History and the Everyday in Sierra Leone*. Berkeley and Los Angeles: University of California Press.

Gow, P., 1991. *Of Mixed Blood: Kinship and History in Peruvian Amazonia*. Oxford: Clarendon Press.

Green, S., P. Harvey and H. Knox, 2005. 'Scaling Place and Networks: An Ethnology of the Imperative to Connect through Information and Communications Technologies', *Current Anthropology*, 46(5).

Gupta, A., 1995. 'Blurred Boundaries: The Discourse of Corruption, the Culture of Politics, and the Imagined State', *American Ethnologist*, 22(2): 375–402.

Hansen, T.B., and F. Stepputat, eds, 2001. *States of Imagination: Ethnographic Explorations of the Postcolonial State*. Durham, NC: Duke University Press.

Harney, S., 2002. *State Work: Public Administration and Mass Intellectuality*. Durham, NC: Duke University Press.

Harvey, D., 1990. *The Condition of Postmodernity: An Enquiry into the Origins of Cultural Change*. Oxford: Basil Blackwell.

Harvey, P., 1997. 'Peruvian Independence Day: Ritual, Memory and the Erasure of Narrative', pp. 21–44 in R. Howard-Malverde, ed., *Creating Context in Andean Cultures*. New York: Oxford University Press.

Harvey, P., 2001. 'Landscape and Commerce: Creating Contexts for the Exercise of Power', pp. 197–210 in B. Bender and M. Winer, eds, *Contested Landscapes*. Oxford: Berg.

Harvey, P., 2003. 'Elites on the Margins: Mestizo Traders in the Southern Peruvian Andes', in C. Shore and S. Nugent, eds, *Elite Cultures: Anthropological Perspectives*. London: Routledge.

Harvey, P. and S. Green, 2002. 'Anthropologists Among the Evaluation Technologists', paper presented to AAA, New Orleans.

Joyce, P., 2003. *The Rule of Freedom: Liberalism and the Modern City*. London: Verso.

Kapferer, B., 1998. *Legends of People, Myths of State*. Washington, DC and London: Smithsonian Institution Press.

Llosa, E., 2003. *La batalla por la carretera interoceánica en el sur peruano: ¿localismo o descentralismo?* Documento de Trabajo No. 129. Lima: Instituto de Estudios Peruanos.

Lund, S., 2001. 'Bequeathing and Quest: Processing Personal Identification Papers in Bureaucratic Spaces (Cuzco, Peru)', *Social Anthropology*, 9(1): 3–24.

Mitchell, T., 1991. 'The Limits of the State: Beyond Statist Approaches and their Critics', *American Political Science Review*, 85(1): 77–96.

Mol, A. and J. Law, 2002. 'Complexities: An Introduction', pp. 1–22 in J. Law and A. Mol, eds, *Complexities: Social Studies of Knowledge Practices*. Durham, NC: Duke University Press.

Nash, J., 1979. *We Eat the Mines and the Mines Eat Us: Dependency and Exploitation in Bolivian Tin Mines*. New York: Columbia University Press.

Navaro-Yashin, Y., 2002. *Faces of the State: Secularism and Public Life in Turkey*. Princeton, NJ: Princeton University Press.

Nugent, D., 2001. 'Before History and Prior to Politics: Time, Space and Territory in the Modern Peruvian Nation-State', pp. 257–83 in T.B. Hansen and F. Stepputat, eds, *States of Imagination: Ethnographic Explorations of the Postcolonial State*. Durham, NC: Duke University Press.

Orlove, B., 1993. 'Putting Race in its Place: Order in Colonial and Postcolonial Peruvian Geography', *Social Research*, 60(2): 301–36.

Prakash, G., 1999. *Another Reason: Science and the Imagination of Modern India*. Princeton, NJ: Princeton University Press.

Radcliffe, S., 2001. 'Imagining the State as a Space: Territoriality and the Formation of the State in Ecuador', pp. 123–45 in T.B. Hansen and F. Stepputat, eds, *States of Imagination: Ethnographic Explorations of the Postcolonial State*. Durham, NC: Duke University Press.

Sallnow, M., 1989. 'Precious Metals in the Andean Moral Economy', pp. 209–31 in J. Parry and M. Bloch, eds, *Money and the Morality of Exchange*. Cambridge: Cambridge University Press.

Schivelbusch, W., 1977. *The Railway Journey: The Industrialization of Time and Space in the 19th Century*. New York: Berg.

Scott, J.C., 1998. *Seeing Like a State: How Certain Schemes to Improve the Human Condition Have Failed*. New Haven, CT: Yale University Press.

Slater, D., 1998. 'Rethinking the Spatialities of Social Movements: Questions of (B)orders, Culture, and Politics in Global Times', pp. 380–401 in S. Alvarez, E. Dagnino and A. Escobar, eds, *Culture of Politics, Politics of Cultures: Re-visioning Latin American Social Movements*. Boulder, CO: Westview Press.

Stein, S., 1980. *Populism in Peru: The Emergence of the Masses and the Politics of Social Control*. Madison: University of Wisconsin Press.

Strathern, M., 1991. *Partial Connections*. Savage, MD: Rowman & Littlefield Publishers.

Strathern, M., 1995. *The Relation*. Cambridge: Prickly Pear Press.

Taussig, M., 1980. *The Devil and Commodity Fetishism in South America*. Chapel Hill, NC: University of North Carolina Press.

Taussig, M., 1993. 'Maleficium: State Fetishism', in M. Taussig, *The Nervous System*. New York: Routledge.

Taussig, M., 1997. *The Magic of the State*. New York: Routledge.

Thévenot, L., 2002. 'Which Road to Follow? The Moral Complexity of an "Equipped" Humanity', pp. 53–87 in J. Law and A. Mol, eds, *Complexities: Social Studies of Knowledge Practices*. Durham, NC: Duke University Press.

Urton, G., 1990. *The History of a Myth: Pacariqtambo and the Origin of the Inkas*. Austin: University of Texas Press.

Wilson, F., 2004. 'Towards a Political Economy of Roads: Experiences from Peru', *Development and Change*, 35(3): 525–46.

Zuidema, R.T., 1964. *The Ceque System of Cusco*. Leiden: E.J. Brill.

7 CONTRADICTORY NOTIONS OF THE STATE: RETURNED REFUGEES IN GUATEMALA

Kristi Anne Stølen

Every Monday morning at 8 o'clock, the primary school children in the returnee community of La Quetzal gather outside the school building to salute the Guatemalan flag.[1] The headmaster, himself a local returnee resident, gives a short speech reminding the children of the importance of belonging to the Guatemalan nation and of their responsibility in making their country a good place to live. Painted in big letters on the wall behind the children is the name of Jacobo Arbenz – for many Guatemalans the sole truly democratic president in the history of their country, and the only one who sought to improve the situation of the poor. In 1954, he was overthrown in a military coup supported by the US government. Every week during my fieldwork in La Quetzal I would observe this scene from my window in the house next door: Jacobo Arbenz and the flapping flag, accompanied by the thin voices of the children singing the national anthem.[2]

This is but one of the many manifestations of the striving of returnees to reintegrate into the Guatemalan nation-state after more than ten years in exile in Mexico. The name of Jacobo Arbenz, visible to anyone who visits the community, demonstrates their identification with a different kind of society and government than those that forced them to leave in the early 1980s.

This chapter presents an ethnographic account of state formation from the margins, based on long-term fieldwork among the returnees of La Quetzal. Using an historical perspective, it analyses the changing relations between these peasants and the state during various stages of migration, within Guatemala as well as between Guatemala and Mexico, and attempts to access the process of production of ideas and images about the modern state. As we shall see, these ideas and images of these peasants are complex and contradictory, and change over time. Their crossing of the Mexican border not only made them aware that they belonged to a nation-state, it also provoked changes in the interstate relations between Mexico and Guatemala – which in turn challenged state–society relations in both countries. Through interaction with non-governmental organisations (NGOs) and international organisations in the camps, the refugees were introduced to new forms of organisation and ideas about the state, which they came to use in negotiating their return and resettlement. While focusing on the Guatemalan refugees,

I will explore how and through what discourses and techniques, channels and networks, intermediaries and brokers the various images and understandings of state, nation and citizen are produced and transmitted.

CHANGING NOTIONS OF THE STATE

The state has recently been rediscovered as an object of inquiry by a broad range of scholars and development practitioners. Social anthropologists have contributed with studies of what the state looks like to those who view it from a variety of local perspectives (Nugent 1994; Hansen and Stepputat 2001). These studies, focusing on the micro-politics of everyday state-making, examine the mythologies, paradoxes and inconsistencies of the state. They show that the authority of the state is constantly challenged from the local as well as the global level, and that growing demands to confer rights and recognition on more and more citizens, organisations and institutions also undermine the idea of the state as a source of social order and an embodiment of popular sovereignty (Shore 2001; Trouillot 2001). Many of these studies are inspired by Abrams' (1988) important theoretical unpacking of the state. He rejected the dominant view of the state as a distinct social unit separated from and 'located' over and above the social – which has been how Marxist and political scientists alike have commonly conceptualised the state. The following quotation summarises Abrams' concept of the state:

> The state is a state-system in Miliband's sense; a palpable nexus of practice and institutional structure centred in government and more and less extensive, unified and dominant in any given society. And its sources, structure and variation can be examined in a fairly straight-forward way. There is, too, a state-idea, projected, purveyed and variously believed in different societies at different times. And its modes, its effects and variations are also susceptible to research. (Abrams 1988: 71)

Abrams emphasises the ambiguity of the state. This idea of ambiguity is central in the perspective developed by Hansen and Stepputat in their suggestively titled *States of Imagination* (2001). They argue for a broad perspective that can embrace the ambiguities of the state as both illusory *and* a set of concrete institutions, as both distant and impersonal ideas *and* localised and personified institutions, as both violent *and* benevolent and productive. Modern forms of state are in a continuous process of construction, they argue, and this construction takes place through the invocation of a bundle of widespread and globalised registers of governance and authority (2001: 5). To understand the modern state, we need to look behind the facade of its formal institutions (although these should not be ignored either) and explore the more diffuse ways that 'power' and 'governance' work – including the everyday rules and normalising technologies that govern conduct and render populations governable in the first place (Shore, 2001: 30).

Study of the migration trajectory, during which my informants interacted in various ways with state and non-state institutions, may help us to understand the multifaceted character of state–society relations. What does it mean for people to be citizens of a state that, more or less explicitly, suspects them of opposing its authority? And what happens when they learn that they have rights – as human beings, as refugees and as indigenous people? To answer these questions, we must give consideration to the subtle, non-violent techniques of social domination, focusing on how power works through everyday state and non-state agency; how it arises from routinised practices of government operating at the level of the individual and local community. We should also look into the conditions under which institutional authority is accommodated, and when, why and how it is opposed.

In encounters with state and other powerful institutions, individuals tend to ascribe to people labels with implications for various levels of social interaction. The most conspicuous labels carry negative meanings, such as 'illegal migrants', 'subversive' or 'terrorists', but also seemingly positive or neutral labels such as 'returnee' or 'repatriated' may be equally forceful in this process. People also label themselves, and in so doing invest labels with their own meanings. When power is mediated and contested by particular social groups, domination involves both control and conviviality; it is about wielding power and yielding power. In this regard, I am particularly interested in how people draw upon their experiences of migration, transnational communication and networks to generate alternative forms of organisation that attempt to shape policies and change the relations between state and society.

A SHORT HISTORY OF PEASANT–STATE RELATIONS IN GUATEMALA

Until the armed conflict in the 1970s, the state had only a limited direct presence in the lives of Guatemalan peasants, even though they were deeply affected by its policies. This was due mainly to the poor development of material infrastructure and institutions and the lack of centralisation of power that characterised the Guatemalan state. Throughout history the relationship between indigenous peasants and the state has been mediated by different non-state actors such as the Catholic Church, landowners and local *ladino* elites, and eventually the international aid community (Smith 1990; Stepputat 2001; Stølen 2004).[3] The fact that most of Guatemala's peasantry have been illiterate as well as being unable to speak the dominant language also prevented direct communication with representatives of the state, most of whom only spoke Spanish. Thus, their position in relation to state institutions has traditionally been one of marginalisation and exclusion. In the 1980s this culminated with the counter-insurgency campaign that resulted in the flight of approximately 200,000 people from Guatemala to Mexico, the majority of whom were poor indigenous peasants. Some 46,000 were registered as refugees and settled in camps; the rest were undocumented migrants who dispersed among the Mexican population, vulnerable and subject to deportation (Salvadó 1988; Zinser 1989).

After six years of difficult negotiations between the URNG[4] and the government, a final peace agreement was signed in December 1996. This agreement marked the end of 36 years of internal armed conflict in Guatemala, and initiated a period of transition from conflict to rehabilitation and development. The peace accords also provided a new and broader framework for dealing with returnees and displaced populations in Guatemala. This transition to more democratic forms of government implies a reconstruction of the state as the guarantor of democratic rights and obligations. Through these processes, citizenship was reformulated and measures taken to benefit and protect those groups and individuals who had been marginalised, victimised or excluded under the previous regime (Sieder 1998).

Stepputat (2001) claims that the exclusion of the Indian peasants has been associated with the formation of the postcolonial state in Guatemala, more specifically with the expansion of coffee production and the liberal reforms implemented under the government of Rufino Barrios (1873–85). The most important elements in these reforms were the liberal land reform that privatised and individualised land, and the concept of vagrancy – in practice meaning forced labour for those who did not possess enough land to be considered productive. These reforms (labour and land) divided Guatemalan society into property owners with political rights, and lessees who were subjected to forced labour on the private properties. In other words, society became divided into citizens and subjects, the former being the 'white' landowners and local *ladino* elites in towns who mediated relations between the Indian community and the state.

Even though the structure of state formation was in place with the liberal reforms, it had only a limited capacity for surveillance. For that, the state depended on alliances with local elites. Public order depended on *ladino* militias and locally appointed volunteers taking turns to do one year of service. Not until the 1930s, with the dictatorship of General Ubico (1931–44), was there a real strengthening and centralisation of the state. Ubico engaged in road construction using forced labour and also appointed representatives of the central state in towns, opening the way to new negotiations and alliances between the central state and the Mayan elites of the towns against the local *ladino* elites. At the village level, where most Indian peasants lived, the state was present only sporadically, if at all. The landowners and their Indian tenants, as well as those Indians who still possessed communal land, largely lived and worked with little or no contact with state institutions. Such contacts took place in towns or cities and through the compulsory public works. This situation continued until the 1960s, interrupted only by the reforms associated with the 'ten-year spring' from 1944 to 1954 under the governments of Arévalo and Arbenz. Even though labour migration between the Highlands and the southern coast had been common in certain areas since the expansion of coffee production in the late nineteenth century, the majority of the Indian population in the Highlands continued to live in mono-ethnic, mono-linguistic rural communities. Only the bigger pueblos and departmental capitals had mixed populations, normally dominated by Spanish-speaking *ladinos* and members of the majority ethnic group (Stepputat 2001: 287–91).

Stepputat argues that, from the liberal reforms in the late eighteenth century to the present, the relationship between the Indians and the Guatemalan state has been characterised by negotiations concerning their conditions of exclusion and their possible re-inclusion – and not by antagonism and resistance, as maintained by Smith (1990). Smith argues that the main political dialectic in Guatemala is located not in relations between peasants and landlords or workers and capitalists, but in the relations of power and culture embedded in the two institutions of *state* and *community*, a relationship that has always been antagonistic. According to Smith, the state never gained legitimacy within the Indian communities, and was able to control them only through coercive means. The army's counter-insurgency campaign in the early 1980s was the ultimate attempt by this weak but despotic state to eradicate the basis for the autonomous Indian community once and for all (Smith 1990: 11–17).

In contrast to Smith, my findings, based on what my informants told me about their relations and perceptions of the state over time, support the view put forward by Stepputat. It is not a relation characterised solely by antagonism and resistance, even though this was a dominant feature during the years of exile. Avoidance of any contact, as well as active engagement in order to become included into the Guatemalan state, is no less common. The latter is especially remarkable in the current situation, where the returnees have been using the peace accords as well as national and international networks to renegotiate their citizen conditions and thereby contribute to creating a new, democratic state.

In the following, I will analyse the changing perceptions of the state held by my informants during the various stages in their migration trajectory: as poor peasants in the Highlands, as settlers in Ixcán, as refugees in Mexico and, finally, as returnees in El Petén.

FROM HIGHLAND PEASANTS TO COLONISERS OF THE TROPICAL LOWLANDS

While living in the Highlands my informants had scant contact with state institutions. Few had access to health and education services, because there were no schools or health clinics within reasonable distance or because parents did not send their children to school. Those who had been hacienda serfs had almost no direct contact with state institutions, as this relationship was mediated by their patron. Those who were poor 'independent' peasants explained that they tried to keep any contact with state representatives to a minimum: it often involved humiliation and bad treatment, because they were poor and illiterate Indians who could not speak the official language. This is illustrated in the following episode told by one of my oldest informants, Juan Pedro, a *Chuj*, now in his mid 80s:

I come from a family with many children and almost no land. Because we had no land we were obliged to participate in the system of '*jornadas*', which means that you had to do compulsory work.[5] The authorities, always *ladinos* in those days, called upon us once a year and gave us a piece of paper. Since I could not read and did not understand one single word of Castilla [local term for Spanish] I had to go with somebody who could help me to do this paperwork. Each time we finished a job, the patron wrote down the number of days in his service and signed the paper. We had to continue like this until we had reached 150 days. If they caught us without the papers in order, proving that we had complied with our obligations, we were punished.

Even though the state was represented at the local level through the *alcalde auxiliar*, (representing the municipal mayor), whose duties included maintaining law and order and reporting violations, my informants did not feel protected by the law. Impunity was the order of the day, as illustrated in Mateo's story:

When I was ten, my father was killed. One night he went to a cantina to have some drinks. This was what they told us. Some men started to quarrel and one of them was killed. My father got very upset and said that he would report what he had seen. This was probably why he was killed. When we got to know that he had disappeared we made a report to the *alcalde auxiliar*, who called upon people to find him. After three days they found his body on a slope by the river, with his throat slit. They had apparently tried to throw him into the river, but the bushes had blocked the way. His killers were never punished, even though everybody knew who they were.

My informants associated the state institutions with the powerful people, '*los del poder*'. This started to change when my informants joined the colonisation programmes in Ixcán from the late 1960s. It was widely recognised that land distribution was a major problem in Guatemalan agriculture, and that it led to under-utilisation of lands and to rural under-employment (Hough 1982; Berger 1992). Through economic incentives of the Alliance for Progress, the USA encouraged Guatemala to institute land reforms as a way to head off revolution. However, since there was no political will to change the distribution of land, any efforts to improve the situation of the rural poor and thereby alleviate pressures for land reform focused on incorporating marginal lands into agricultural production.[6]

The Catholic Church was a main actor in the colonisation of Ixcán and helped to shape the colonisation policy of the state in the new settlement areas. In Guatemala, as in the rest of Latin America, the Catholic Church had traditionally been allied with the power elites. Its activities had concentrated on the spiritual life of the people, together with continuous attempts to wipe out traditional Mayan religious practices. The Second Vatican Council (1962–65), where the role of the Church in the modern world was redefined, produced important changes in liturgy and rites as well as in the relationship between clergy and lay people. No longer could the Church turn a blind eye to political abuses in return for a guarantee of its privileges and rights, from now on it was expected to be at the forefront of protest against the infringement of freedoms and rights (Ker 2002). Inspired by the theology of liberation, younger priests started to change their work methods: they became teachers, instant agricultural or other kinds of experts, and used their skills to improve the living conditions in indigenous communities. The colonisation projects in Ixcán were a product of this new involvement of the Church in the everyday sufferings of their parishioners (Morrisey 1978; Arias 1993).

The majority of my informants had fled to Mexico from cooperatives in Ixcán, cooperatives that had been organised at the initiative of US priests from the Diocese of Huehuetenango and Spanish priests from the Diocese of Quiché as part of these colonisation programmes. The programmes were supported by the government and planned in close collaboration with state institutions such as INTA (the National Institute of Agrarian Transformation), the Department of Cooperatives and the Ministry of Education. The inspiration came from the Moshavim settlements in Israel – agricultural cooperatives based on family units of production (Morrisey 1978; Falla 1992; Dennis et al. 1988). Land was abundant and fertile, and the settlers learnt to grow new cash crops in addition to the traditional subsistence crops of maize and beans.

These settlement projects offered a unique economic opportunity to landless and exploited peasants. After a few years of hard work and many sacrifices, the settlers began to experience a degree of prosperity that they had never known before. By the mid-1970s, most cooperative centres had public services like primary schools and health centres in addition to the services offered by their cooperatives (AVANCSO 1992: 38). Through their participation in the colonisation programme, my informants were introduced not only to a new religious ethic, but also to a new economic ethic – that of justice and development. The equal distribution of land, the participation of peasants in church and community institutions and activities demonstrates an impulse towards egalitarian democracy. The cooperatives were granted a high level of autonomy in internal affairs as long as they followed certain pre-established rules, most of them in accordance with the Law of Agrarian Reform (Morrisey 1978).

Even though relations and negotiations with state institutions were mediated by the priests, who operated as project coordinators, local cooperative leaders were gradually drawn into the mechanisms of dealing with the various institutions. Already at this point my informants had started to develop new ideas about the state, seeing it as not only violent and repressive, but also benevolent and productive. After all, it was the state that had handed over to them the land that they were allocated. State institutions like INTA and the Department of Cooperatives assisted in surveying and granting land titles to the cooperatives as well as providing technical assistance in the production of new crops. Once the cooperatives had constructed school buildings, the Ministry of Education assigned teachers to the cooperatives. During the first years of settlement, even the army was seen as quite benevolent and supportive, as illustrated in Gilberto's story:

In the beginning our relationship with the army was peaceable. They were just around, greeted us and talked to us in a friendly way. The soldiers even helped me to prepare the site for building the house on my plot of land. I asked the colonel to do me a favour, and he agreed and sent a number of soldiers to do the work. When the violence arrived, I had just bought the iron sheets and the nails to make a proper house. I had everything to start building.

These new perceptions of the state were, however, interrupted by the armed conflict. When my informants talk about their past in the cooperatives in Ixcán, they often conclude by saying: '*then the violence arrived and destroyed everything*'. They associate the arrival of the violence with the first important guerrilla action in the area in June 1975, when EGP (Ejército Guerrillero de los Pobres) guerrillas killed the powerful landowner known as the Tiger of Ixcán. This action attracted a permanent military presence, and with it the establishment of military detachments and the appointment of military commissioners in the settlements (Falla 1992). It triggered off a nightmare of death, destruction and displacement for my informants. The EGP, whose long-term objective was to overthrow the military government and take control of the state, attempted to start building a network of peasant support in this area, where the local structures of the state were still highly vulnerable (EGP 1982; CENSA 1983). Even though the EGP did not succeed in this, the army retaliated by defining the settlers as guerrilla supporters and therefore targets of the military counter-insurgency campaign (Payeras 1982; Le Bot 1995).

Since the armed forces could not manage to defeat the guerrillas, who could hide in the almost impenetrable jungle, they decided to 'drain the sea from the fish' – the fish being the guerrillas operating in the region, the sea being the peasants who lived and farmed there. In February 1982, violence escalated dramatically as the army carried out a scorched-earth campaign in Ixcán. The troops crossed the region from east to west, destroying communities and fields, and indiscriminately killing the civil population (Schirmer 1998).

The continuation of Gilberto's story illustrates the changes in the relationship between the settlers and the armed forces:

Later the soldiers, those *cabrones* [sons of bitches], destroyed everything on my site. They punctured my iron sheets. They destroyed the fruit trees, the plants, they killed my animals and burnt the house; nothing was left. They pinioned me and took me to the military base in Playa Grande. More than two months I had been a prisoner in the military camp, when I managed to escape.... When the catechists and the evangelists talk about hell, I don't know what they are talking about. What I know is that Playa Grande was a hell.

Gilberto accused the EGP of provoking his capture and the terrible suffering inflicted upon him by the army:

What sons of bitches, the guerrillas!! They had nailed a placard on a tree close to the entrance of my house where they had written *Viva EGP!* [Long live the EGP!] I had not seen this placard, if I had, I would have taken it down immediately. Of course, when the soldiers saw that placard they thought that I was a guerrilla soldier and they came to get me. They could not capture the real guerrilla soldiers because they were hiding safely in the jungle. These people [the guerrillas] were irresponsible – really *cabrones*.

My findings largely confirm the conclusions reached by David Stoll (1993) in his study in the Ixil towns in the Highlands: the peasants became involved in the armed conflict against their will. The peasants of Ixcán, who for the first time had obtained land and prospects for a better life, had no interest in a revolution. They were forced to take part in the conflict by the army as well as by the guerrillas.[7] At first they were reluctant to leave the land they had worked so hard to obtain and make productive, so they tried to adapt to the situation of terror and violence while remaining in their villages. Later, with the escalation of violence, they hid in the jungle for shorter or longer periods of time (Falla 1992). When the internal refugee situation finally became untenable, they crossed the border to Mexico, where they eventually became refugees. Crossing the border was to become a revealing experience for them.

BECOMING GUATEMALANS

My informants explained that before they fled to Mexico they had not thought about themselves in national terms, as being Guatemalans, or in ethnic terms as being *mam*, *k'ichee'* or *q'eqchi'*. They defined themselves in terms of their place of origin, the municipality or village where they were born, or of their new place of settlement. Their vision was a local-centric one. Informants also reported that they did not realise the significance of nationality and national borders, because there was nothing that marked the boundary, and the landscape, the villages and the people on both sides were similar. Some of the returnees who came from certain Highland areas had not even known that borders existed. Gerardo, who used to live in the Ixil region in the Central Highlands, told me the following:

When I lived in the Highlands I did not know that there were other countries in the world than Guatemala. I did not know about the existence of Mexico before I arrived in Ixcán in 1988. In Quintana [here he is referring to the refugee camp] I learnt that there are hundreds, maybe thousands, of countries in the world. There I also learnt why there are different countries, and why the borders exist. Now it is difficult to understand that I could be so ignorant.

Even though Mexico had not signed the international convention on refugees, the Mexican border represented the definition of their condition. With the arrival of the UNHCR (United Nations High Commission on Refugees) in 1982, the Guatemalan refugees were granted a status that permitted them to stay temporarily in Mexico. However, only those who settled in refugee camps were granted such status, while the others – an estimated 150,000 – were defined as undocumented economic migrants subject to deportation. Many of these were seasonal labourers who decided to remain in the Mexican state of Chiapas until the situation in Guatemala changed (Salvadó 1988; Zinser 1989).

For my informants, the border became a question of life and death. Before crossing they lived in constant fear of the Guatemalan army, who labelled them 'subversives' and would kill them without mercy and in the most cruel way. They had seen this happen to others. After crossing the border they were no longer defined as subversives, objects of extermination, but as displaced people or refugees, entitled to assistance. The latter was associated with registering as a refugee and living in a camp. There they also realised that the meaning of being 'indigenous' changed. In Guatemala they had experienced discrimination and exploitation in interaction with non-Indians. But now, in the refugee context, being an Indian was no longer something negative: everybody was entitled to the same treatment independent of race, colour or religion. They had entered an area of influence of international law based on a concept of universal human rights that implies a specific kind of subject – the individual citizen – all of whom are equal.

These new ideas about state–citizen relations were acquired though encounters with non-state institutions as well as with Mexican state agencies. This supports what Trouillot has argued: to identify state practices, processes and effects, we have to look beyond the central sites of national governments (Trouillot 2001: 131–32).

ENFORCING NATIONAL BORDERS

Crossing the border implied not only changes for the refugees, it also altered the relations between the states of Guatemala and Mexico and produced a reinforcement of the border between them. Until 1824, when Chiapas became part of Mexico, it had belonged to Guatemala. That is why its history and its ethnic and cultural characteristics are more similar to Guatemala than to the rest of Mexico. When the border between Chiapas and Guatemala was established in 1882, the people living in these regions did not recognise the division, because life and people were similar on both sides. Mexicans and Guatemalans continued to cross the border, assisting each other in agricultural work, exchanging goods and services, or simply visiting relatives. According to one estimate made by church workers at an early stage of the refugee influx, about one-third of the refugees had relatives in Mexico prior to their entry – which probably also contributed to the sense of continuity across the national border (Zinser 1989: 108).

The first refugees arrived in Marqués de Comillas, Chiapas, in mid-1980. In the course of 1981 the exodus intensified, and by the end of that year some 5,000 people had arrived. During the same period, refugees also started to appear in other parts of Chiapas. With the scorched-earth campaign in 1982, the exodus exploded: by the end of 1982, the number of refugees in Chiapas had increased to more than 30,000. By the end of the following year, the number of refugees officially recognised by the state of Chiapas approached 46,000 (Kauffer 1997: 91–93). Camps were established spontaneously in *ejidos* (communal land) or private properties with the consent – even the support – of the *ejido* members and the landowners.

The reactions of the Mexican authorities towards the refugees show clearly that states are not homogeneous entities beside or above society. Mexican state institutions varied in their attitudes towards the refugees. Foreign affairs authorities were sympathetic towards the progressive political tendencies in Central America. To a certain extent, they supported revolutionary movements, and favoured the reception and the good treatment of the Guatemalan refugees. The defence authorities, in contrast, were worried about security in the border areas and did not welcome the presence of the refugees.

Between 1981 and 1984, the Guatemalan armed forces regularly violated Mexican national sovereignty, entering Mexican territory in search of supposed guerrilla soldiers in the refugee camps. According to Aguayo (1985), a total of 68 military incursions took place between 1980 and 1983, resulting in several kidnappings and casualties among the refugees and the local population, in addition to material damage in the camps and beyond. This represented a threat to Mexican national security and revealed the dilemma faced by the Mexican authorities: they wanted to prevent a rupture with Guatemala despite the incursions, at the same time as their acceptance of Guatemalan refugees constituted an implicit denunciation of the Guatemalan regime. The Mexican government also faced internal problems produced by social unrest in the border areas due to increased pressure on the land, followed by heated political debate at the local and national level by political groups and civil organisations mobilising to pressure the government to protect the refugees. For the Guatemalan government, the refugees were defined as subversives; thus, they not only represented a threat to national security, they also bore witness to a state that had lost control over its own population.

Once again the Church became a mediator between the peasants and the state. The Catholic Church in Mexico, especially the diocese of San Cristóbal de las Casas in Chiapas headed by Bishop Samuel Ruiz García, played an influential role in shaping Mexico's response to the Guatemalan refugees. From the beginning of the refugee influx, the Church provided assistance to the Guatemalans, displaying a particular sensitivity to their special needs. The bishop, priests and nuns of the diocese became strong advocates on behalf of the refugees, which created a difficult and at times conflictual relationship between the local church and the state. The diocese of San Cristóbal, deeply inspired by the theology of liberation, had a long history of work in the region, especially with indigenous people. Moreover, they had experience with international collaboration, which facilitated rapid fundraising.

NEGOTIATING REFUGEE CONDITIONS

In the camps the refugees were not treated as passive recipients of aid. From the very beginning, they were encouraged to become involved in making their own living, not only as far as food production and the building of shelters and certain infrastructure were concerned, but also by creating new forms of cooperation for mutual benefit, taking advantage of opportunities open to them as a consequence of international assistance. The strategy of some of the relief organisations, especially the diocese of San Cristóbal, was to recruit personnel among the refugees: these individuals were then trained, gradually learning to run important parts of the relief work. Generally, the Guatemalan refugees became very well organised despite their precarious and poor conditions, and they became proactively involved in shaping conditions in the camps. This inspired funding agencies, especially the UN and INGOs (international NGOs), to extend their support beyond emergency relief, which in turn contributed to a more integral and coherent process of social and economic development (Kauffer 1997).

The camps enjoyed a high degree of autonomy in internal affairs. The old authority structures were eroded and new leaders appeared, individuals more in line with the needs of the camp community. Education promoters, catechists and health workers assumed leadership positions because they could speak Spanish and could function as mediators in negotiations with aid agencies and Mexican authorities. Under this new camp leadership, decisions were made only after an assembly where all adult camp dwellers were invited to participate and discuss every issue concerning the community.

Because of persistent border violations, the Mexican government decided to move the 46,000 camp refugees from Chiapas to the states of Campeche and Quintana Roo on the Yucatán peninsula. Although many refugees had long requested to be relocated further away from the border, the majority in fact refused to move. This brought them into direct and bitter confrontation with Mexican authorities. Over the next two years, a combination of persuasion, threats and confrontation was used in order to relocate some 12,000 to Campeche and 6,700 to Quintana Roo. The rest remained, under rather precarious conditions, in camps in Chiapas, dispersed within Mexico, or returned to Guatemala (Zinser 1989: 82).

My informants were among those who, after serious resistance, had agreed to resettle. They talk about the relocation as one of the most dramatic events during the period of exile. Despite the tensions and aggressions created by the Guatemalan military presence in the area, most of them were strongly opposed to moving. In the first place, they were concerned about the security situation. Disturbing rumours started to circulate about the fate of those who had moved. According to some rumours, they were relocated in order to be killed by the Mexican army; others painted an equally frightening scenario – deportation to Guatemala, where they were handed over to the Guatemalan army. According to some informants, these rumours were fomented by the guerrillas, who feared the loss of contact with the refugees, even though they officially supported the relocation (Delli Sante 1996). The confrontation with regard to resettlement revealed the refugees' inherent lack of trust in state authorities.[8]

With hindsight, my informants consider the move a success, an assessment shared by several aid agencies (Franco 1999: 79). After having overcome the initial phase of precariousness and hardship, they realised that the transfer was for the better. The new camps were constructed to resemble villages rather than camps. Housing standards were improved, and people got access to land to cultivate their own food and even products for sale; there was also potable water, electricity, good access roads and transport, and above all a variety of possibilities for earning cash income. Public services were improved considerably, especially in education and health. The UNHCR, in collaboration with the Mexican refugee council, implemented programmes to help the refugees to integrate and become self-sufficient. These programmes were based on a combination of subsistence farming, casual wage labour within the state and income-generating projects within the settlements themselves (Stepputat 1989).

Through the participatory organisation in the camps as well as through more formalised training offered by aid organisations, the refugees learnt new techniques of governance: not only registration and control, but also the techniques involved in committee work, meetings, negotiations, representations, planning, projects and other practices aimed at improving their lot. They also gained a high level of political awareness, as reflected in their interaction with Mexican and Guatemalan state institutions during the years of exile, particularly during the negotiations and preparations of return. In this process, the refugees learnt about the existence of rights, of human rights, women's rights and citizen rights, about the existence of national constitutions and international conventions, and they learnt how to claim their rights. This knowledge was new to most people, even though some of the ideas about democracy and participation were known to those who had held leadership positions in the cooperatives in Ixcán. During the many meetings, courses and workshops in the camps, the returnees took part in defining the conditions and forms of services that the modern state should provide, and in negotiating the limits to state control and surveillance. These were skills and knowledge that would become crucial in the negotiations that later led to their return to Guatemala. This once again illustrates the point stressed by Trouillot, that in the globalised world of today, state-effects never obtain solely through national institutions or in government sites (2001: 132). In the Guatemalan context, as in the South more generally, NGOs as well as trans-statal institutions are central actors in creating ideas about the state, and these in turn are used by the citizens in alliance with international actors to reshape state institutions.

NEGOTIATING THE CONDITIONS OF RETURN

Even though most of my informants considered their stay in Mexico a temporary one, they had no concrete plans for returning – until 1992, when the government and representatives of the refugees in Mexico signed an agreement for a safe and assisted return to Guatemala. They were deeply sceptical of the repatriation efforts initiated in 1986, following the election of President Vinicio Cerezo, which marked the return to civilian rule after three decades of military dictatorship (Zinser 1989; Riess 2001). The camp refugees did not accept the conditions of repatriation offered to them, mainly for security reasons. They knew that people who had been repatriated had not been allowed to settle in their home areas but had been relocated to model villages under strict military control.[9] Those who settled in rural areas were obliged to participate in the so-called civil self-defence patrols (PACs), established as another counter-insurgency measure.[10] Moreover, they knew that the image created of them in Guatemala was that they were guerrillas or guerrilla supporters and that the refugee camps were insurgency sanctuaries – and this image represented a threat to their safety in Guatemala.

However, these repatriation initiatives called for a response from the refugees and inspired increased organisational activity in the camps. Wanting to determine the conditions under which their return should take place, the refugees established Permanent Commissions (CCPP) in 1987 to represent them in direct negotiations with representatives of the Guatemalan government and state institutions, including the armed forces. The CCPP was a representative body elected by direct vote of all adult refugees living in the camps. It did not replace the existing camp leadership, who continued to administer the internal affairs of the camps. The CCPP did, however, gain considerable power and granted the refugees a countrywide representation (Zinser 1989: 76–77).

In early 1989, following an elaborate process of discussion and consultation, the CCPP formulated their conditions for the return to Guatemala (CCPP 1989; de Rivero 2001). However, the mutual lack of trust, especially the reluctance of the Guatemalan authorities to recognise the CCPP as the legitimate representative of the refugees and a relevant negotiating partner, delayed progress towards the negotiation table. Not until March 1991 were peace negotiations initiated between the refugee organisation and representatives of the Guatemalan government and armed forces, mediated by the Roman Catholic Church and the UNHCR. After one and a half years of difficult discussions, an agreement was signed on 8 October 1992. The first return under the terms of these accords took place in January 1993.

In the agreement, the Guatemalan government committed itself to facilitating access to land for those refugees who decided to repatriate. This was an important achievement and probably the most important motivating factor for return, at least for my informants. Another essential condition often mentioned by the returnees was the exemption from military service, and that members of the armed forces were forbidden to enter the returnee communities. International verification and monitoring, particularly by the United Nations and the international monitors who settled in the returnee communities, was also an important element in this process.[11] The latter reveals the deep scepticism that was felt towards the Guatemalan state. The agreement that prevented the entry of the armed forces was to be monitored on a daily basis by foreigners who were to live in the returnee community and thus would be able to witness and report any violations to the relevant UN authority. A distinction was made between *retorno* (return), which referred to the collective returns under the terms of the 1992 accords, and *repatriación* (repatriation), the term used for the smaller groups who chose to return outside the 1992 framework and who were given the basic assistance laid out under the 1987 Tripartite Pact signed during the government of Cerezo. For my informants, this is a very important distinction. They will correct anyone who refers to them as 'repatriated', explaining that they are different from those who returned in an individualistic and/or unorganised way, whereas they were organised. Organisation plays a central role in the self-identification of the returnees.[12]

BELONGING TO A TERRITORIALISED NATION

Conversations about their motives for returning revealed that my informants also conceived of Guatemala as being something above and beyond despotic rulers, a territorialised space for all Guatemalans. Expressions like '*Quería volver a mi tierra, estar en tierra ajena es muy duro*' (I wanted to return to my land; to be on the land of others is very hard) were quite common. *Mi tierra* does not refer to a specific place, but to anywhere in the Guatemalan national territory that could provide enough land to secure a livelihood. Most people say that they did not want to return to the places they left: first, because they had been occupied by others, people brought in by the army after the refugees left; second, because there was not enough land to support the sons and daughters who by now had married and established their own families in exile.

However, the decision to return was not an easy one. Memories of the past were terrifying, and not all the refugees had enough confidence in the new government to go back. Moreover, many people felt that they had managed to achieve a good life in Mexico, materially as well and socially. This was especially the case with several women who said that they themselves would have preferred to stay, but felt that they had to join their husbands. The fact that the Mexican government decided to grant permanent residence and eventually citizenship to those who opted to stay also played an important role in this decision. Some of my informants said that their doubts were so overwhelming that they changed their minds several times before finally deciding to join the return to El Petén. And many refugees decided to remain in Mexico and become Mexican citizens.

BUILDING A NEW COMMUNITY

As noted by Nugent (1994) there is a tendency in the literature on state–society relations to argue on the basis of an implicit model that sees state and community as two essential and bounded entities in opposition to each other. The first is basically expanding, transforming and coercive; the other is basically conservative and actively resists any imposed transformations. Several studies, including Nugent's recent study from Peru (2001), have challenged this view, showing that it is only one of several possible 'junctures' of state–community relations. Such relations may also be characterised by marginalised communities actively involved in producing themselves as a community of citizens (Hansen and Stepputat 2001; Stepputat 2001). In the following, I argue that state–community relations may be characterised by both resistance and active engagement in inclusion.

The process of peace negotiations referred to above reveals the state–returnee relationship as one characterised by resistance, especially against military control of the returnee community. This is reflected in the ban on military presence in the returnee communities and the exemption from military service, as well as the monitoring by UN forces and international personnel. At the same time, it is also characterised by a striving to become a community of citizens through the extension of state institutions and through new administrative techniques of community organisation. The latter is reflected in the way their new settlement, La Quetzal, was to be constructed.

The construction of La Quetzal was very different from the more spontaneous ones so common in El Petén during recent decades. It was realised after two years of detailed planning assisted by different development agents, the most important being NGOs. Rejecting what they defined as the dominant liberal model of development as one that concentrates wealth and impoverishes the majority of the population, the returnees created a new model of cooperative-based agricultural communities. According to this model, returnee communities should embody the following principles: recognition of human rights; inclusive and participatory democracy; and an efficient and sustainable communitarian economic base that protects natural resources.[13]

A first step in implementing this communitarian model was to make an inventory of available resources. The farm was carefully surveyed to mark borders, rivers, mountains, swampland and a site for the village centre. Types of soil were classified and samples sent to a laboratory for analysis. A forest inventory was also made to identify the economic potential of the jungle. The results were presented to members of the cooperative in several workshops, as part of the overall discussion on how the land should be used. Some of my informants, who were not in leading positions, came up with the idea that the farmland should be divided so each family could have its own individual plot of land. This was how cooperatives normally used to be organised in Guatemala. With reference to the inventory, the cooperative leaders and their advisers argued that this would not be feasible, because of the ecological characteristics of the region and because most of the land was located within the protected area of the Maya Biosphere Reserve.[14] These arguments supported their ideological conviction that individual solutions alone do not lead to development. It was decided, however, that each family should be given the opportunity to produce its own food. Each family was assigned 5 hectares for this purpose – two plots of 2 hectares each for *milpa* (maize field) and 1 hectare of swampland for rice production.

As in the case of the villages in Nentón, Huehuetenango, described by Stepputat (2001), the design of the new settlement was made in the image of the town. Before the return, a '*plan de urbanización*' was designed by an international NGO, but this was not something that was imposed on the villagers. On the contrary, the design of the hamlet is an expression of their desire to create a formal site of governance. After only a few days, a temporary school and a health clinic were functioning in the returnee village, long before the construction of houses started. More formal school buildings were constructed later, as was the current health clinic. A venue for public assemblies was soon in place, as was the two-storey building to house the offices and other cooperative bodies. Later, a bus station and a sports field were built. A park has been planned but is still to be completed. Making and implementing plans is an important element in the cooperative concept of 'being organised'.

Organisation is one of the key labels used by the returnees to differentiate themselves from their neighbours. Organisation is seen a prerequisite for development, not only because staying together makes you stronger (a very important point in negotiations with the state as well as other non-governmental actors), but also because it is seen as an aspect of being 'modern'. When people talk about organisation, they refer to the bureaucratic way of organising, with the cooperative as the ultimate example.

The cooperative Unión Maya Itzá is the backbone of the community. It was established in June 1994 – almost one year before the return to Guatemala – to facilitate the purchase of land and other preparations. Being organised in cooperatives was a prerequisite for getting access to land and credits, as agreed in the peace negotiations. The cooperative is a complex bureaucratic organisation, governed by the general assembly which delegates responsibility for the daily running of the institution to a board of directors – *junta directiva* – elected once a year.[15] The *junta directiva* consists of five ordinary members, plus one representative of each of the committees of education and of 'vigilance'.[16] The level of activity within the cooperative is very high. Nowadays, meetings of the *junta* are not organised as frequently as during the first months after the return, when the members met every day to resolve current problems. However, more people are attending, as the number of cooperative committees increases. In addition to the committees of education and vigilance there are now 13 other committees appointed by the cooperative, responsible for the following activities: labour, agriculture, forestry, poultry, vegetables, apiculture, tailoring, *xate*,[17] credit, transport, marketing, eco-tourism and project planning – each committee with its own chairman, vice-chairman, secretary, treasurer and *vocal*. In addition to the committees working within the frames of the cooperative, several committees are active at the community level and involve specific segments of the population. These are referred to as *sectores*, six in number: for women, youth, education promoters, health promoters and midwives, catechists and parents of school children. Some of the *sectores* are affiliated to formal organisations operating at the municipal, regional or national level. The *sectores* are also formally organised, with chairman, vice-chairman and three members.

Meetings are many, and people do attend – men more frequently than women, several times a week, sometimes more than once a day. The cooperative with its *junta* and 15 committees mobilises many people, as do the different *sectores*. The community is also visited by many people who require attention from members of the *junta*, the different committees or *sectores* – there may be representatives of NGOs and other donor or potential donor organisations, visitors from other communities who come to 'learn about the experience of the returnees', journalists, etc. If one walks through the village centre, especially in the afternoon, it is common to see people meeting in five or six different places. Attending a meeting takes time – because few people arrive on time and one never knows when the meeting will start, and also because discussions tend to be lengthy, as all those present are to have the chance to express their opinions and then reach a consensus without having to vote.

From the above we may conclude that the construction of a new community in Guatemala has been strongly influenced by the new forms of organisation and new ideas about what a modern state should be, learnt while its members were in exile and engaging in interaction with NGOs and transnational institutions. The language used and the bureaucratic positions established are clear evidence of this.

NEGOTIATING INCLUSION

One of the slogans of the returnees, 'Struggle to return, return to struggle' bears witness to the refugees' proactive approach towards the peace agreements. According to de Rivero (2001) this has been a key factor in the development and enjoyment of rights and in the higher levels of assistance that the returnees have obtained from governmental, non-governmental and international organisations – as compared to the 'repatriated', who are dispersed or unaware of the benefits of the accords. Some of the returnees' achievements have been made through tough confrontations with Guatemalan state institutions, others by more moderate means. The first confrontation took place even before leaving Mexico, when they occupied the Guatemalan consulate in Chetumal in protest against attempts by the

Guatemalan state to obstruct their collective return. They won this round, and a date of return was settled.

Another confrontation took place a few months after they came to El Petén. During the negotiations for return, they had been promised that the road connecting La Quetzal to the main road would be improved before they arrived, to permit transit during the rainy season. When the first heavy rains fell a few weeks after they arrived, the road became totally impassable. In June 1995 dozens of returnees – men, women and children – occupied the regional offices of CONAP (the national entity in charge of the protected areas in Guatemala) in the departmental capital. Neither threats nor persuasion made them leave until an agreement was signed between the returnees and the state institution responsible for the repair of the road. This action contributed to improving relations with their nearest neighbours, who had been quite sceptical about their settlement in the area. This action, as well as other similar ones, was set in the language of rights, equality and order.

Other less dramatic confrontations and negotiations have taken place over the years. In most cases, state institutions have been persuaded or pressed to comply with the accords.

EDUCATION AS A VEHICLE OF INCLUSION

A different example of active involvement in state formation by the returnees is related to education. Wilson (2001) has indicated that, for the bureaucracy of the modern state, the school has become the emblem that demarcates the territory effectively covered by the state, an institution that relies on ideas about state, nation and citizen. It is at school that the children learn to become citizens – by saluting the flag, standing to attention at hearing the national anthem and learning about national history, geography and ceremonial events (Wilson 2001: 313). Unlike what Wilson describes from Peru, where education has been promoted by the central state to integrate members of the peripheral population, the education system of the La Quetzal returnees was developed by non-state agents in the periphery and then incorporated into the central state system through negotiations.

Since the establishment of the camps, education has been defined as a privileged road to personal and social development for the refugees, introduced and promoted by the aid agencies shortly after the establishment of the camps in Mexico. To begin with, the children had Mexican teachers, but very soon the training of education promoters, recruited among the refugees, was initiated by UNHCR and other international agencies, first with the objective of having Guatemalan teachers in the camps, later to prepare teachers for the return.

Thanks to the efforts of the education promoters, the primary school was functioning a few days after the arrival in El Petén, in the rather ramshackle buildings raised by members of a working brigade, who had come in advance of the other returnees. Since then the education services have improved, both quantitatively and qualitatively. Today they comprise pre-primary and secondary level (*ciclo básico*) in addition to primary education with 18 promoters/teachers altogether. During the first years, the promoters received their salaries from Fondo Nacional para la Paz (FONAPAZ), a government agency established to assist the peace process, since they were not recognised by the Ministry of Education. Through the national organisation of rural teachers AMERG, who negotiated with the government, they were recognised by the ministry on condition that they complete a competence-building programme, a two-year programme designed so that it can be combined with the education promoters' teaching obligations. By the end of 2000, the programme was completed and the first teachers were officially recognised by the Ministry of Education. The achievement in education in La Quetzal is widely recognised in the area, and the school, especially the *ciclo básico*, receives children from other communities in the region.

A similar process has taken place with regard to health care. Here, the negotiations for inclusion have been more complicated because the local health-care system is differently organised and far better than is normal in El Petén (Stølen 2000). According to my informants, the Ministry of Health has been reluctant to accept it, because it fears demands for similar services from other communities. The returnees, on the other hand, believe that if they agree to adapt their system to the government standards, this will mean a deterioration. These negotiations were not completed when I finished my fieldwork.

COMMUNITY AND IDENTITY

In situations of displacement, a common ethnic identity may be an important cultural resource in the building of networks and, more generally, in dealing with the experience of social rupture. In other cases, new forms of identification may develop. This has been the case in La Quetzal, where identification seems to be based primarily on the shared experience of violence and collective return. In the following, I will briefly discuss how ethnicity is dealt with in the returnee community.

La Quetzal is multi-ethnic and the majority of people are of various indigenous origins. Eight Mayan languages are spoken, in addition to Spanish.[18] Locally, people identify themselves and are identified by others with reference to language. Those who do not speak an indigenous language are referred to as *castellanos*, unless their parents are known to speak an indigenous language. I would often hear comments like: 'She is a *mam*, but does not speak the language.' The dichotomy of *ladinos–indígenas*, common in other parts of the country, is not used here, because these terms are considered to be labels belonging to the discriminatory past. This ethnic differentiation is observed only internally and only in certain contexts. In contact with the outside, people from La Quetzal are referred to – and refer to themselves – as *retornados*.

Those who do not identify themselves as *castellanos* speak of themselves as indigenous: they want their children to speak their mother-tongue and learn certain traditions – the good traditions – like those related to food, life-cycle rituals such as engagement and marriage, but not at any price. Most of them have suffered from not speaking Spanish, a language they later learnt in exile. They have also suffered the burden of illiteracy. Therefore, they give high priority to their children attending school and mastering Spanish. They are critical of the bilingual education efforts that a private university assisted by USAID has tried to introduce in the community.[19] In their view, this teaching, because of the lack of teachers as well as pedagogical materials, only distracts attention from what they consider the most important vehicle for progress – fluency in Spanish. Most adults have suffered shame and humiliation for not speaking the dominant language, the language of the state. They also observe that they have spoken their Mayan language for centuries, and intend to continue doing that. What they find difficult to understand is why some organisations should now insist on the need to read and write it.

In returning to Guatemala, the refugees did not want a return to the past, to Maya religious and government traditions. They have rejected the attempts made by the *Q'eqchi's*, the biggest and (according to some) the most conservative group, to revitalise the traditional hierarchies of *cofradías*, because this is seen as belonging to the dark side of their history. They want to be modern, to be active cooperative members, have well-functioning schools and health centres, a progressive church concerned with their everyday problems and not only the spiritual ones, and they want to participate in the economic and political life of the country. Those familiar with the Pan-Mayan movement believe that the focus on the indigenous, in opposition to the *ladino*, tends to create new forms of conflict and racism. My own observations indicate that the wishes of at least some Indians are far removed from the position held by leading Maya intellectuals. The returnees see themselves as indigenous people who want to be modern citizens of the Guatemalan state, at the same time as they maintain and adapt certain important Maya values and traditions.

CONCLUSION

From the analysis of the migration trajectory of these returnees, we have seen that their ideas and images of the state are complex and at times contradictory. They change over time, depending on the changing historical junctures of state–society relations. Their relations have certainly been characterised by antagonism and resistance, as suggested by Smith. This was especially salient during the years of violence and exile. However, we have also seen that they are characterised by active involvement aimed at becoming included as fully fledged citizens of the Guatemalan state. Non-state actors have been instrumental in bringing about the preconditions for the creative engagement of the returnees with state institutions. First, the Catholic Church organised new settlements and cooperatives in Ixcán in the

1970s, providing organisational training, and new concepts and forms of reflection, though this was largely limited to male cooperative and church leaders. Representatives of this 'new' Catholic Church not only introduced them to a new religious ethic but also a new economic ethic of justice and development. When the armed conflict accelerated in the late 1970s, the settlers were caught in the crossfire between the army and the guerrillas. There was little room for manoeuvre, since most of them happened to live in areas singled out for the scorched-earth campaign implemented by the Guatemalan army.

Crossing the border to Mexico was an eye-opener for the refugees in more than one sense. For the first time, they started to conceive of themselves as Guatemalans. They discovered that they were citizens of a nation-state, and they gained awareness of their conditions of exclusion. In the refugee camps, they entered an area of social life dominated by a global aid culture, represented by UN and various Mexican and international aid and solidarity organisations. Here they were introduced to and trained in modern forms of government, couched in the language of democracy and rights. Participation and organisation became guiding principles in community life. Through this modernising experience, the refugees became involved in defining the conditions and forms of services that the modern state should provide, and they developed a capacity for critical assessment of the kind of order installed by state institutions. This became particularly salient during later negotiations of their collective return.

Today, these returnees hold contradictory notions of the state. On the one hand, they see the state as violent and repressive – and this view is reflected in their avoidance of and/or resistance to certain state practices and institutions. Pertinent examples are their negotiated exemption from military service, and the rule prohibiting members of the armed forces from entering the returnee communities. A further example was the presence of international verification and monitoring personnel during the first years after return. These attitudes build on the decades of non-recognition and exclusion that were produced by the violent forms of state repression in their villages. On the other hand, the returnees also see the state as benevolent and productive. It is the object with which one negotiates rights, somehow representative of the will of the people; it is also a provider of services, and the returnees strive to become included. This can be seen in the way their new community has been set up – spatially, in the image of a small town, and organisationally, in the image of modern bureaucracy.

The majority of the returnees are actively engaged in this modernising experience, and this is a point that does not fit in well with the idea of the all-penetrating state. These efforts, based on a discourse of recognition and rights, in turn presuppose the appropriation of ideas of human dignity and equality acquired during the years of exile. Without the invaluable support of non-state agents, the returnees would not have gained the negotiating power that they hold today. The organisational capacity and fighting spirit that characterise the returnee community of La Quetzal have been developed and maintained through the alliance with the international aid community. This alliance has proven an invaluable resource in their work to contribute to the creation of a new nation-state – as symbolised in the schoolyard by the flag and anthem, and name of Jacobo Arbenz.

NOTES

1. I would like to thank the editors of this volume for very useful suggestions on an earlier draft of this chapter. I am also grateful to Eduardo Archetti, Santiago Alvarez, Laura Golbert and Rosana Guber for constructive comments.
2. I carried out anthropological fieldwork between 1998 and 2001, spending between one and two months three times a year in La Quetzal. My project was part of a research and teaching agreement between the University of San Carlos and the University of Oslo, financed by the Committee for Development Research and Education of the Norwegian Council of Universities.
3. *Ladinos* are popularly assumed to be descendants of Spanish/Indian liaisons (i.e. *mestizos*) but are in fact mostly ethnic Mayans who have assimilated the national language and culture (Smith 1990: 72).
4. The URNG is a coalition of the three guerrilla groups – the EGP, FAR and ORPA – and the Guatemalan Communist Party (PGT) established in 1982. It was the government's counterpart in the peace negotiations.
5. He refers to the Law against the Vagrancy enacted by the government of General Ubico in 1934. This law obliged landless peasants to work at least 150 days on the lands of others. The number of days worked had to be registered in a specific document called *Libreta de Jornaleros*.
6. Colonisation of new lands was a bleak substitute for land reform. It could not solve the acute man/land problem in Guatemala. According to an evaluation carried out in Ixcán Grande, such projects were too complicated, too costly and too slow. Moreover, there was not enough public land available (Hough 1982).
7. According to the Truth Commission, 93 per cent of the killings registered were committed by the army, 7 per cent by the guerrillas (CEH 1999). In contrast to the torture, killing and massacres carried out by the army, in some areas directed indiscriminately against the civilian population, the killing of the guerrillas was generally selective and directed at military personnel or civilians accused of collaborating with the military and thereby defined as traitors who deserved to die. A number of internal executions also took place (Payeras 1982; Macías 1999; Ramírez 2001).
8. Sánchez Martinez (1999) and Carrera Lugo (1999) give a more detailed description of the relocations to Quintana Roo and Campeche respectively.
9. During the counter-insurgency campaign, the army created model villages grouped in several development poles established in the departments of El Petén, Alta Verapaz and Quiché, where people lived under strict prison-like control.
10. The Patrullas de Autodefensa Civil (Civil Self-Defence Patrols), or PACs, were created by the army in 1982 to fight real or alleged enemies of the state. Some 1,000,000 men, most of them members of indigenous groups, served in the patrols at the height of their power during the 1980s (Salomon 1994).
11. In November 1994 the United Nations Mission for the Verification of Human Rights and the Compliance of the Obligations of the Global Agreement on Human Rights in Guatemala (MINUGUA) began its work.
12. In the refugee camps Stepputat (1994) observed that 'organisation' had a negative connotation as opposed to 'freedom'. In La Quetzal, however, the connotation is positive, and the term is used in opposition to 'individualistic'.

13. For more detailed information about planning of the return, see van der Vaeren (2000).
14. The Maya Biosphere Reserve (MBR), comprising 1.6 million hectares (4 million acres), includes about 40 per cent of El Petén. It is divided into three zones that have varying degrees of environmental protection. Core Zone areas (784,000 ha) are set aside for absolute protection of biodiversity. No human settlements are allowed here, and only research and eco-tourism are permitted (Beletsky 1998).
15. This does not mean that all the board members are in office only for one year: in fact, they are expected to stay in office for two years. Withdrawal after one year has to be approved by the general assembly and requires a good reason.
16. The vigilance committee (*comité de vigilancia*) is responsible for overall supervision of the activities of the cooperative.
17. *Xate (Chamaedorea spp)* is a type of wild palm gathered in the jungle for export. Florists use it to accompany flowers when making bouquets. It has the special attribute that after having been cut it stays fresh for two to three weeks without water.
18. There are altogether 21 different language groups in Guatemala. The following Mayan languages are spoken in La Quetzal: *q'eqchi'*, *q'anjob'al*, *mam*, *k'ichee'*, *popti'*, *chuj*, *ixil* and *ch'orti'*, in addition to Spanish, the *lingua franca* spoken with varying degrees of fluency by the majority of the population.
19. This programme comprised four of the most spoken languages in the community. Those who were monolingual in Spanish or any of the other Mayan languages had to choose one of the four.

REFERENCES

Abrams, P., 1988. 'Notes on the Difficulty of Studying the State', *Journal of Historical Sociology*, 1: 47–77.

Aguayo, S., 1985. *El éxodo centroamericano. Consecuencias de un conflicto*. Mexico: SEP.

Arias, A., 1993. 'Changing Indian Identity: Guatemala's Violent Transition to Modernity', pp. 230–57 in C. Smith, ed., *Guatemalan Indians and the State 1540–1988*. Austin: University of Texas Press.

AVANCSO, 1992. *Donde está el futuro? Procesos de integración en comunidades de retornados*. Guatemala City: Asociación para el Avance de la Ciencias Sociales en Guatemala (AVANCSO).

Beletsky, L., 1998. *Belize and Northern Guatemala (Tikal)*. San Diego, CA, and London: Academic Press.

Berger, S.A., 1992. *Political and Agrarian Development in Guatemala*. Boulder, CO: Westview Press.

Carrera Lugo, L., 1999. 'Creación de nuevos asentamientos en Campeche y el programa multianual', pp. 85–87 in *Presencia de los refugiados guatemaltecos en Mexico*. Mexico City: UNHCR & COMAR.

CCPP, 1989. *El retorno de los refugiados guatemaltecos en el extranjero. Ponencia de las CCPP presentada a la Comición Nacional de Reconciliación para el diálogo nacional*. Ciudad de Guatemala.

CENSA, 1983. *Listen Compañeros: Conversations with Central American Revolutionary Leaders*. San Francisco, CA: CENSA/Solidarity Publications.

Comisión para el Esclarecimiento Histórico (CEM) (1999). *Guatemala: Memory of Silence*. Report of the Commission for Historical Clarification. Conclusions and Recommendations, Guatemala.

Delli Sante, A., 1996. *Nightmare or Reality: Guatemala in the 1980s*. Amsterdam: Thela.

Dennis, P., et al., 1988. 'Development under Fire: The Playa Grande Colonization Project in Guatemala', *Human Organization*, 47(1): 69–76.

EGP, 1982. *Entrevistas al Comandante en jefe del Ejercito Guerrillero de los Pobres: Rolando Morán hechas por Marta Harnecker y Mario Menéndez.*

Falla, R., 1992. *Masacres en la selva: Ixcán, Guatemala (1975–1982).* Guatemala: Editorial Universitaria.

Franco, L., 1999. 'Un episodio controvertido en la historia del refugio: La Reubicación a Campeche y Quintana Roo', pp. 78–80 in *Presencia de los refugiados guatemaltecos en Mexico.* Mexico City: UNHCR & COMAR.

Hansen, T.B. and F. Stepputat, eds, 2001. *States of Imagination: Ethnographic Explorations of the Postcolonial State.* Durham, NC: Duke University Press.

Hough, R.L., 1982. *Land and Labor in Guatemala: An Assessment.* Washington, DC: AID/Development Associates.

Kauffer, F., 1997. 'Chíapas y los refugiados de la década de los ochenta: de la conformación de la frontera al desarrollo de un espacio fronterizo', *Perspectivas Históricas/ Historical Perspectives/Perspectives Historiques*, 1(July–Dec.): 89–124.

Ker, I., 2002. 'What Did the Second Vatican Council Do For Us?', *The Catholic Herald*, 11 October.

Le Bot, Y., 1995. *La guerra en las tierra mayas: Comunidad, violencia y modernidad en Guatemala (1970–1992).* Mexico: Fondo de Cultura Económica.

Macías, J.C., 1999. *La guerrilla fué mi camino.* San Salvador: Editorial Piedra Santa.

Miliband, R., 1969. *The State in Capitalist Society.* New York: Harper Books.

Morrisey, J., 1978. 'A Missionary Directed Resettlement Project among the Highland Maya of Western Guatemala', PhD Dissertation, Department of Anthropology, Stanford University, Stanford, CA.

Nugent, D., 1994. 'Building the State, Making the Nation: The Basis and Limits of State Centralisation in "Modern" Peru', *American Anthropologist*, 96: 333–69.

Nugent, D., 2001. 'Before History and Prior to Politics: Time, Space, and Territory in the Modern Peruvian Nation-State', pp. 257–83 in T.B. Hansen and F. Stepputat, eds, *States of Imagination: Ethnographic Explorations of the Postcolonial State.* Durham, NC: Duke University Press.

Payeras, M., 1982. *Los días de la selva.* Ciudad de Guatemala: Piedra Santa.

Ramírez, C., 2001. *La guerra de los 36 años: Vista con ojos de mujer de izquierda.* Guatemala City: Editorial Oscar de León Palacios

de Rivero, J., 2001. 'Reinventing Communities: The Resettlement of Guatemalan Refugees', *Forced Migration Review*, 11(October): 8–11.

Riess, S., 2001. '"Return is Struggle, not Resignation": Lessons from the Repatriation of Guatemalan Refugees from Mexico', *Journal of Humanitarian Assistance*, 21: 1–25.

Sánchez Martinez , F., 1999, 'Recepción y autosuficiencia de refugiados en Quintana Roo 1984–1989', pp. 82–84 in *Presencia de los refugiados guatemaltecos en Mexico.* Mexico City: UNHCR & COMAR.

Salomon, J.A., 1994. *Institutional Violence: Civil Patrols in Guatemala 1993–1994.* Washington, DC: Robert F. Kennedy Memorial Center for Human Rights.

Salvadó, L.R., 1988. *The Other Refugees: A Study of Non-recognized Guatemalan Refugees in Chiapas, Mexico.* Washington, DC: Hemispheric Migration Project/Center for Immigration Policy and Refugee Assistance, Georgetown University.

Schirmer, J., 1998. *The Guatemalan Military Project: A Violence called Democracy.* Philadelphia: University of Pennsylvania Press.

Shore, C., 2001. 'Nation and State in the European Union', pp. 25–51 in R. Kiss and A. Paládi-Kovács, eds, *Times, Places, Passages: Ethnological Approaches in the New Millennium.* Plenary Papers of 7th SIEF Conference, Budapest.

Sieder, R., ed., 1998. *Guatemala after the Peace Accords.* London: ILAS, University of London.

Smith, C.A., 1990. *Guatemalan Indians and the State: 1540 to 1988.* Austin: University of Texas Press.

Stepputat, F., 1989: *Self-Sufficiency and Exile in Mexico: Report on a Field Study among Relocated Guatemalan Refugees in South-East Mexico, August–November 1988*. Geneva: UNRISD.

Stepputat, F., 1994. 'Notions of Organisation, Freedom and Traditions among Guatemalan Refugees', pp. 58–73 in F. Wilson and F. Stepputat, eds, *People in Politics: Debating Democracy in Latin America*. Copenhagen: CDR.

Stepputat, F., 2001. 'Urbanising the Countryside: Armed Conflict, State Formation and the Politics of Place in Contemporary Guatemala', pp. 284–312 in T.B. Hansen and F. Stepputat, eds, *States of Imagination: Ethnographic Explorations of the Postcolonial State*. Durham, NC: Duke University Press.

Stølen, K.A., 2000. 'Creating a Better Life: Participatory Communitarian Development among Guatemalan Returnees', *SUM Working Paper*, 2003.3. Oslo: University of Oslo, Centre for Development and Environment.

Stølen, K.A., 2004: 'The Reconstruction of Community and Identity among Guatemalan Returnees', *European Review of Latin American and Caribbean Studies*, 77(Oct.).

Stoll, D., 1993. *Between Two Armies in the Ixil Towns of Guatemala*. New York: Columbia University Press.

Trouillot, M.-R., 2001. 'The Anthropology of the State in the Age of Globalization', *Current Anthropology*, 42(1): 125–38.

van der Vaeren, P., 2000. *Perdidos en la Selva*. Amsterdam: Thela.

Wilson, F., 2001. 'In the Name of the State? Schools and Teachers in an Andean Province', pp. 313–44 in T.B. Hansen and F. Stepputat, eds, *States of Imagination: Ethnographic Explorations of the Postcolonial State*. Durham, NC: Duke University Press.

Zinser, A., 1989. 'Repatriation of Guatemalan Refugees in Mexico: Conditions and Prospects', pp. 57–114 in M.A. Larkin, F.C. Cuny and B.N. Stein, eds, *Repatriation under Conflict in Central America*. Dallas: Center for the Study of Society in Crisis.

PART III

A VIEW FROM STATE BODIES

8 COUNTING ON STATE SUBJECTS: STATE FORMATION AND CITIZENSHIP IN TWENTIETH-CENTURY MEXICO

Helga Baitenmann

This chapter is an effort to rethink state–society relations in light of what can be loosely characterised as a new generation of state-formation studies.[1] In the last decade or so, a number of scholars have revisited old (mainly Europe-centred) questions about state-building, seeking to explain state formation in a number of other geographical regions.[2] In the case of Latin America, for example, one can identify two general trends. One group, primarily made up of historians and anthropologists, is likely to debate the work of Antonio Gramsci, the Subaltern Studies Group and James Scott's *Weapons of the Weak*. Another group of scholars, comprised generally of sociologists, is more likely to discuss Barrington Moore, Theda Skocpol, Charles Tilly and James Scott's *Seeing Like a State*.[3] In broad terms, one can say that the first group focuses on how subaltern groups resist, appropriate or help construct the nation-state, while the latter is generally more concerned with how state rule is accomplished.

This chapter pursues a dialogue between these two currents. In some ways, this was one of Gilbert Joseph and Daniel Nugent's goals in their influential edited volume on everyday forms of state formation in Mexico. They invited scholars to think about how to 'simultaneously examine the formation of orders of domination and orders of resistance' by considering in relation to each other James Scott's work on everyday forms of resistance (1976, 1985, 1990) and Philip Corrigan and Derek Sayer's work on English state formation (1985).[4] As William Roseberry noted in his contribution to the volume, contributors ended up placing the works in partial opposition to each other: '"the moral economy" of the peasantry and other subordinate groups as opposed to "the great arch" of the triumphal state' (1994: 355). Perhaps it was not surprising that many scholars writing on post-revolutionary state formation in Mexico found Gramsci's concept of hegemony a particularly good lens through which to assess the longest lasting regime in Latin America, concluding that the success of the Mexican post-revolutionary state lay in its ability to establish a common moral and social project between rulers and ruled.[5]

Overall, the historiography since the mid-1990s on post-revolutionary state formation in Mexico has consciously distanced itself from earlier state-centred analyses in order to recover local political culture and subaltern agency throughout rural and urban Mexico.[6] We find, among many other examples, Juchitecan residents challenging the directives of the central state (Rubin 1997), Michoacán peasants consistently distorting elite conceptions of order (Becker 1995) and Namiquipan *serranos* using discourses of honour for counter-hegemonic purposes (Nugent and Alonso 1994).[7]

For the most part, this mode of research fits into what has been termed the 'new cultural history of Mexico'. The achievements and shortcomings of this academic trend (which includes topics other than state formation), have been amply discussed elsewhere.[8] However, one concern that merits revisiting is how the notion of agency ('a central issue in discussions of resistance and the study of subaltern groups') in Eric Van Young's words, 'add[s] too many degrees of freedom to individual thinking and action' (1999a: 244). This chapter reintroduces some of these limits to agency in the process of state formation in Mexico. In order to do so, it revisits theories concerned with how state rule is accomplished.

Some of the most interesting current theories of state formation suggest that the line of separation between state and society 'objectifies what is in fact a mobile demarcation, subject to continual construction and deconstruction' (Steinmetz 1999: 12). Like Philip Abrams ([1977] 1988) before him, Timothy Mitchell distinguishes between networks of institutional arrangement and political practice and the ideational construct of the 'state' (which the former creates) (1999: 76). Inspired by the work of Michel Foucault, Mitchell believes that modern 'methods of organisation, arrangement and representation ... create the effect of an enduring structure apparently external to those practices' (1991a: 91, 92; see also 1999: 76–78). Disciplines produce what appears to be a binary order: 'on the one hand individuals and their activities, on the other an inert "structure" that somehow stands apart from individuals, precedes them, and contains and gives a framework to their lives' (1999: 89).[9] As opposed to the idea of the state as a sovereign authority above and outside society setting external limits to behaviour, disciplinary power works 'not by constraining individuals and their actions but by producing them' (1991a: 91–92, 1991b: xi). As Corrigan and Sayer argue for English state formation, new subject identities are produced through the categorisation, regulation and routinisation of everyday life. The power of these everyday state routines and rituals lies in their capacity to produce new individual and collective identities (Corrigan and Sayer 1985: 141).

Most often, scholars have studied how Foucault's disciplines are found in the organisation of the garrison, the school, the clinic or the prison. This chapter focuses on the network of institutional mechanisms and quotidian administration through which the Mexican agrarian reform was implemented in the early 1920s and then dismantled in the 1990s. Most specifically, this chapter examines census-taking and the creation of state subjects and citizens.[10]

If states make their power visible 'through the gradual extension of "officialising" procedures' (Cohn 1996: 3) then one of the most important and widespread state rituals is the effort of state agents to count and classify the population living within a state's territorial boundary. Whether scholars adopt a more Weberian notion of the state having the 'cognitive capacity' to administer a population,[11] or a more Foucaultian perspective for which the central characteristic of the modern state is its increasing capacity for surveillance, 'making society legible' – in the words of James Scott – is a hallmark of modern statehood (Scott 1998: 2–3, 65, 76–77, 81; Caplan and Torpey 2001: 1). An analysis of the use of agrarian censuses during Mexico's twentieth-century agrarian reform shows that, in two periods more than a half century apart, state agents employed the same techniques of registration and classification to change the meaning and content of subjecthood or citizenship during two massive social engineering projects: the post-revolutionary agrarian reform created in 1915, and the neoliberal land-titling programme begun in 1992. In the case of the post-revolutionary agrarian reform, the censuses officialised a new form of rights-bearing individual (the agrarian-rights subject), while the census undertaken as part of the land-titling programme was an effort to create citizens with rights to landed property regulated by the market. In both instances, state agents employing apparently neutral administrative procedures profoundly changed the content of citizenship in Mexico.

The remainder of this chapter is divided into four sections. The first part shows why the agrarian reform was – and continues to be – an integral part of state formation in Mexico. The second and third sections explore the use of the census in two moments of Mexican twentieth-century history. Here, the discussion illustrates how the architects of Mexico's agrarian reform used census-taking to create new state subjects in the aftermath of a long, bloody and profoundly multifaceted social conflict. They principally did so by dividing the rural population into two categories: those who were legally recognised as agrarian-rights subjects (*sujetos de derecho agrario*), and those who were excluded from the land reform scheme. The analysis then shows how the Mexican government is now in the process of privatising the agrarian sector by using the very agencies and administrative tools established to construct the agrarian sector more than half a century earlier; indeed, the architects of the 1992 neoliberal land-titling project used census-taking to transform the post-revolutionary agrarian-rights subject into a new type of citizen. This discussion draws on fieldwork observations and archival material from the Central Veracruz region to illustrate some of the ways in which the individuals affected by the reforms responded or participated in these state projects.[12]

The concluding section discusses why state-building and the creation of subjects or citizens are part of the same process. It demonstrates that, despite multiple and complex local and regional struggles throughout rural Mexico, in the end rural dwellers internalised the categories constructed by state agents (and implemented through census-taking) in their pursuit of agrarian reform – whether that process was portrayed as revolutionary or neoliberal.

AGRARIAN FORM AS STATE FORMATION

The Mexican Revolution, according to Alan Knight, was a historical watershed in which the state had to be reconstructed and reinvented:

The Revolution both encouraged and made possible a prodigious effort of nation and state building, probably unequalled in Latin America; an effort which involved education, art, radio, rhetoric, the press, mass mobilisation, sport, social reform, and party organisation. (Knight 1994: 153–54)

A key part of this state-building project – and perhaps with the exception of the post-revolutionary education project, the most far-reaching in its consequences, certainly in rural Mexico – was the agrarian reform.

In 1915, five years after a wide-ranging revolutionary movement had begun and long before a central political authority could be forged, one faction of the revolutionary elite began what would become one of the first massive national (as opposed to colonial) transformations of the rural sector. What would be known as 'the agrarian reform' was originally based on General Venustiano Carranza's Law of 6 January 1915.[13] This law was ground-breaking in several ways: it recognised the collective (rather than individual) right to own land, nullified all illegal land seizures made under the Liberal laws of the nineteenth century (which were aimed at privatising communal Indian and Church property), mandated the return of usurped lands to the communities that had lost them and promised land to the landless.[14] In January 1917, delegates to the constitutional convention included the Law of 6 January 1915 in Article 27 of the new Constitution, which became one of the most important symbols (as well as guiding principles) of the post-revolutionary state.

In order to distribute land, the architects of the post-revolutionary agrarian reform created a new body of law, a hierarchical administrative structure and a series of intricate administrative tools and practices that remained operational for over seven decades. Agrarian legislation – comprised of hundreds of statutes, decrees and regulations – became a distinct body of law practised by a new cadre of government legislators and jurists. In order to implement these laws, state planners constructed a multi-level administrative apparatus under the jurisdiction of the federal executive, with separate agencies at state and national levels, diverse administrative offices, consultative bodies, agrarian registries and archives. This bureaucracy was headed by the National Agrarian Commission, under the Ministry of Development; a Local Agrarian Commission in each state or territory; and agrarian committees representing rural dwellers petitioning for land at the village level. Over the course of seven decades, this agrarian reform bureaucracy employed thousands of fieldworkers (trained in specialised schools) and a legion of government bureaucrats.

Between 1915 and 1992, an increasingly complex agrarian bureaucracy expropriated and redistributed over half of Mexico's land to 3.5 million individuals (and their families), organising them into almost 30,000 land and labour arrangements known as *ejidos* and agrarian communities (Secretaría de la Reforma Agraria 1998: 313). For over seven decades, this massive redistribution of land greatly altered human settlement and agricultural production patterns.

During the 1980s and 1990s, many Latin American governments began to privatise their land reform sectors. In late 1991, the government of Mexico decided to demonstrate its commitment to the neoliberal agenda (including the adoption of the North American Free Trade Agreement), by privatising the agrarian sector and promoting the freedom to hold and dispose of personal property. On 6 January 1992 (the 77th anniversary of Carranza's agrarian law) President Carlos Salinas de Gortari (1988–94) oversaw the amendment of Article 27 of the Mexican Constitution, formally ending the state's historical commitment to land distribution.[15] This bold move was accompanied by a series of laws that, for all practical purposes, privatised the post-revolutionary Mexican ejido.[16]

Rather than simply amending the Constitution and decreeing new laws, leaving the ejido sector to disintegrate gradually, the Salinas team sought actively to dismantle previous land reform arrangements. It did so not by taking apart the agrarian administrative apparatus, but rather by revamping what had become a profoundly inefficient and corrupt bureaucracy.

In order to implement the new agrarian reform, the government decentralised the Ministry of Agrarian Reform (a direct descendant of the National Agrarian Commission designed in 1915) and restructured several agrarian agencies like the Agrarian Attorney General's Office (Procuraduría Agraria) in order to undertake a massive titling programme of agrarian parcels and urban plots on ejidos. Several government agencies participated in the programme – principally (but not exclusively) the resuscitated Agrarian Attorney General's Office, with new regional offices in every state and large numbers of 'visitors' or field staff; the National Institute of Statistics, Geography, and Informatics (Instituto Nacional de Estadística, Geografía e Informática, INEGI); and the National Agrarian Registry (Registro Agrario Nacional, RAN).

Like the post-revolutionary surveyors before them, the new field personnel of the Agrarian Attorney General's Office became key figures who implemented a national project at the local level, using the same techniques of power that had for decades been employed to create ejido subjects. The officially stated purpose of the titling programme was to give each land reform beneficiary a certificate to his or her parcel and a title to his or her urban plot.[17] For this purpose, each ejido would be measured and mapped and a new census would be taken. In doing so, government officials created a massive and precise registration and classification process, comparable in size and scope only to the national electoral registry created in Mexico in the 1990s. By the turn of the twenty-first century, consecutive governments had made substantial advances in the land-titling programme. By 2005, government officials had completed technical work in 89 per cent of ejidos nationwide and 95 per cent of ejido residents had joined the programme (Procuraduría Agraria n.d.). At no time before did government officials measure and map more land and count more people in one single government programme.

An analysis of the use of censuses during Mexico's twentieth-century agrarian reform shows that, in two periods more than a half century apart, state agents employed the same techniques of registration and classification to change the meaning and content of subjecthood under the two state projects. What kinds of subjects were created in the 1920s and 1930s and then again in the 1990s? How were land beneficiaries picked and classified? What meaning did these classifications have? Who played a role in the categorisation of individuals? These are among the questions that inform the next two sections of this chapter.

THE CONSTRUCTION OF THE POST-REVOLUTIONARY 'AGRARIAN-RIGHTS SUBJECT'[18]

In order to redistribute land, post-revolutionary agrarian law established limits to rural property. Land exceeding these limits was distributed to newly formed 'agrarian committees' in the form of ejidos, a collective form of land ownership.[19]

The endowment process began after a town's agrarian committee forwarded a land petition to the governor or military commander of the state. In response, the state's Local Agrarian Commission sent a surveyor to conduct a census and make an inventory of petitioners' properties. Upon receiving a formal recommendation from the commission, the governor would issue a resolution. If positive, the surveyor would measure land and mark the boundaries of the endowment so that the agrarian committee could distribute plots on a provisional basis. Although the state-level agrarian bureaucracy was in charge of day-to-day tasks, the federal executive had the ultimate say. The definitive endowment would be granted only after the National Agrarian Commission had made its own assessment and formally delivered its written findings to the president. The final step in the process would later be known as the 'presidential resolution'. Resolutions would not take effect until they were published in the *Diario Oficial*, the federal government's official publication.

The agrarian reform was implemented by a cadre of *ingenieros agrónomos* (surveyors) who were what Benedict Anderson called 'the pilgrims of the imagined national community' (Baitenmann 2002: 4; Cotter 2003: 4). In Mexico, they largely belonged to the middle class that had welcomed Francisco I. Madero's efforts to oust [dictator] Porfirio Díaz. They were graduates of the National School of Agriculture, and many joined the revolutionary armies. Their expertise had been shunned by hacienda owners who refused to hire them, and most of them allied with the revolutionary state in the making. Local Agrarian Commissions hired them to survey haciendas in order to redistribute land. Not only did the land reform project offer them job opportunities, but also most surveyors believed that they were constructing a more just society; indeed, many risked their lives trying to do so.[20] According to Joseph Cotter:

For agrónomos the Revolution and the new regime that it created opened a window of opportunity: a chance to create a new world order in rural Mexico. Some agrónomos recognised that the agraristas were natural allies because both benefited from State action to transform rural society: the latter by obtaining land; the former by helping them acquire it and by managing new ejidos. (Cotter 2003: 49)

What surveyors reported in writing was often incorporated (literally copied) by the Local Agrarian Commission into its recommendation, and then duplicated in the National Agrarian Commission's ruling. Ultimately, many presidential resolutions employed data and language that originated with a surveyor in the field. The National Agrarian Commission and the federal executive had the final say, but because little was known in Mexico City about most small towns across the country, decisions on submitted land petitions were often based not on the factual accuracy of information contained in these reports but on overall logic.

Basic operating procedures for land endowments included counting and classifying people, registering properties, measuring space and marking boundaries – the techniques of power essential to state building. Agrarian officials created state routines designed to turn the agrarian reform into a nationally uniform process, with seemingly impartial tools such as engineering formulas used for surveying and mapping the boundaries of the new ejidos.[21] One of these state routines was census-taking.[22]

The census was the single most powerful instrument of the endowment process. The post-revolutionary reform could not have been implemented without prior knowledge of census-taking, which had a long history in Mexico. Particularly after 1763, the Spanish colonial administrative apparatus was expanded and 'the stream of colonial reports on local population submitted to Spain for administrative, fiscal, military and religious purposes swelled to a flood' (Platt 1998: 7, 66). Prior to the agrarian census, national censuses were taken in 1885, 1900 and 1910. Starting in 1916, officials designed and printed the first agrarian censuses in order to register all residents in a locality and select the new agrarian-rights subjects from the broader population. With the census, state officials created a new subject of the state that did not formerly exist: the agrarian-rights subject (*sujeto de derecho agrario*). This meant that they were not simple land beneficiaries (*agraciados*); they were a new category of rights-bearing individuals with the lifelong right to receive land from the state.

The agrarian censuses were similar to earlier population censuses in that they included names of all members of a community, and information concerning their sex, age and civil (marital) status. However, agrarian censuses also included three new categories: occupation, an inventory of property (specifically, livestock and land), and an additional space to record 'observations and motives of exclusion'. Censuses in the 1920s additionally recorded whether or not individuals lived in the locality, if they possessed over 1,000 pesos and whether or not they worked in agriculture.

Categories of Inclusion and Exclusion
Except for people's names, agrarian officials used all categories of information to bestow agrarian rights on some and to exclude others from the endowment process. This subsection explains why these categories were selected and how they served to determine who would become an agrarian subject of the post-revolutionary state.

For the revolutionary group in power in 1915, the agrarian reform was not intended to promote farming more generally, but rather to be a school or training ground for what they considered to be unproductive Indians and peasants (*campesinos*). Therefore, the census category 'profession' was included in order to limit the distribution of land to those who already made a living from farming. However, individuals who worked the land had to be poor and landless in order to qualify for agrarian rights. As a consequence, the category 'profession' was directly linked to that section of the census where property (in the form of land and cattle) was recorded. According to the 1920 Law of Ejidos, potential beneficiaries were family heads who lacked enough land to earn twice the average daily wage (*jornal*) prevailing in the region.

The census category 'place of origin' was also used to include or exclude individuals from the land reform project. One of the central characteristics of Mexico's post-revolutionary agrarian reform was that it recognised the collective rights of communities to demand and receive from the government enough land to satisfy the needs of their residents. If the communities were too large (and ostensibly urban enough to provide other forms of employment), or too small to be a legally recognised town, they would not be considered legitimate collective-land solicitors – even if they had landless farmers among their population.[23] Alternatively, if a community received collective land rights, state officials wanted to stop the landless living in other towns from migrating to the endowed population centres in order to claim land. Therefore, during most of the agrarian reform, a year's residence in the endowed community was a prerequisite for individual land rights.

Sex and marital status were closely linked, and together these elements were employed in such a way that the agrarian reform became a profoundly gendered state scheme. Agrarian law in twentieth-century Mexico was an unusual combination of nineteenth-century jurisprudence, revolutionary ideals (mainly urban and white or *mestizo*) and indigenous demands for the restitution of usurped lands. None of these influences was gender-neutral. Legal scholars, politicians and revolutionaries who played roles in the construction of the Mexican agrarian reform during the first decades of the twentieth century shared the ambition of changing the structure of land tenancy in favour of the creation of family farms (see also Deere and León 2001: 3). Therefore, lands granted or restituted by the government were considered 'family patrimony' (Baitenmann, 1997: 294). This meant that agrarian rights would be granted to 'heads of family' (*jefes* or *cabezas de familia*) responsible for providing for a household. Heads of family were automatically presumed to be male (if a man lived in the household) because the foundations of post-revolutionary agrarian reform were laid at a time when the Civil Code of 1870 and the revisions of 1884 were still in effect, and these laws largely subjected wives and children to the pater familias's control. And, as laws had done since colonial times, agrarian law empowered the woman only 'in default of the male spouse'; only widows and single women with children could be heads of family and enjoy agrarian rights.[24]

Age was also a category for inclusion (or exclusion) in the agrarian reform. Like other forms of subjecthood, full membership depended upon the attainment of adulthood. Like marriage, military conscription and electoral rights, agrarian rights were endowed to those legally considered adults. With the Agrarian Regulatory Law (*Reglamento Agrario*) of 1922, the minimum age of 18 years was established for men. From this date on, clear differences were established between the rights of men and women, based solely on sex and age. Whereas women could become family heads only when they were sole family providers, land endowments for men were solely contingent on adulthood and no longer on their responsibility to support one or more family members.

Census-Taking in Central Veracruz during the 1920s and 1930s

Local-level agency was important. As this subsection illustrates for the case of Central Veracruz, landowners, government agents, communities and factions within communities, all played important roles in the unfolding of the agrarian reform. By focusing on the agrarian census, one point becomes clear: no matter how complex and multifaceted local, regional and national struggles were, in the end a number of individuals became the new agrarian rights-bearing subjects of the post-revolutionary state.

Starting in the 1920s, censuses had to be conducted in the presence of three parties: a representative of the National Agrarian Commission, a municipal authority and a representative of the landowner.

Agrarian officials were often the driving force behind the agrarian reform. Although peasants in the sate of Morelos had risen during the revolution to demand land, not all rural dwellers wanted to be included in the agrarian reform project. In Central Veracruz, agrarian officials found many reluctant potential land beneficiaries. One case in point was the land grant for the town of Rinconada. Here, in April 1917, Rodolfo Cuevas, the chief of the civil administration board (the equivalent of a municipal president), requested a land grant for Rinconada.[25] However, when surveyor Luis Marín arrived in October 1917, he found that several of the communities refused to participate in the census-taking. Residents claimed they feared being attacked by rebel groups.[26] Nevertheless, by December 1917, Cuevas managed to produce a population census for Rinconada. It included 590 names, their civil status, age, place of origin and information on literacy.[27] For the smaller towns refusing to participate, Surveyor Marín created a special census only for those who in the end did agree to participate in the land distribution project. It included names, the number of family members, the amount of land they owned (all responded they had none), whether the person was an owner or renter of land, the amount of rent paid and who the property was rented from.[28] In October 1918 Carranza granted land to Rinconada and several of the neighbouring localities within existing hacienda borders as part of a package conceived by the Local Agrarian Commission.[29]

Communities like Chavarillo were more proactive. Although most residents declined to identify themselves as *agraristas*, in the end, they actively participated in the first agrarian census, identifying 76 potential agrarian-rights subjects. They held regular assembly meetings even before receiving a provisional endowment, and they pressured the Local Agrarian Commission to undertake the administrative tasks necessary for a land grant.[30]

Property owners could also influence the land reform process. For example, reducing the number of individuals listed in the census was a widespread strategy aimed at decreasing the amount of land to be expropriated. Landowners could argue that certain individuals were under age, not heads of family, were engaged in lines of work other than agriculture or had recently settled in the community. In 1923, for example, Manuel Ibarra, administrator of the Agricultural and Manufacturing Company of El Encero, S.A., reviewed the agricultural census of the petitioning town El Chico and found 16 women who – in his words – could not be considered heads of family engaged in agriculture because they were housewives ('*dedicadas a quehaceres domésticos*').[31]

Most often, participation in the agrarian reform either created or intensified local power struggles. Ben Fallaw notes in his work on Yucatán that observers often reduce complex political and social contexts in post-revolutionary Mexico to 'a story of a simple class and moral conflict, one in which the post-revolutionary state sides with the oppressed against the hacendado class, and victory is measured in hectares of land granted' (Fallaw, 2002: 645, 681). Archival material and oral history from Central Veracruz illustrate that factions commonly labelled 'revolutionary' and 'reactionary' were difficult to differentiate on the ground. Although some landowners did hire armed guards to kill agraristas in an effort to prevent the expropriation of their lands, local struggles (fuelled by regional and national political divisions) were far more complex and fluid.

During the agrarian reform, many towns and regions split violently into those who supported and those who opposed the process. San Marcos de León was a case in point. In September 1914, a group of 90 men and one woman from San Marcos asked the governor not for a land grant, but for his help in purchasing uncultivated lands at the neighbouring La Providencia hacienda, 'none other than for the development and progress of the community'.[32] After Carranza decreed the agrarian reform Law of 6 January 1915, the town split between those who wanted to pursue a land grant and those who refused to participate in the agrarian reform.[33] Therefore, when local leaders decided to petition for a land grant in 1921, they had to bring in people from Teocelo and Coatepec in order to inflate the agrarian census because many local residents declined to become involved.[34] Many of the so-called agriculturalists listed in the census were workers employed at the neighbouring 'La Purísima' yarn factory. Two of the leaders, Pedro and Manuel Torres, had been previously employed at a coffee-processing plant in Teocelo.[35] In June 1921, calling themselves 'emancipated peasants' (*campesinos emancipados*) and forming the Union of Free Peasant Workers (Sindicato de Obreros Campesinos Libres), they filed a formal land petition.[36]

In November 1921, Jesús Medina, surveyor from the Local Agrarian Commission, arrived in San Marcos to take the census and coordinate the election of agrarian committee representatives. Three months later, in the workers' meeting hall at 'La Purísima', petitioners received a provisional endowment.[37] Apart from La Providencia, a relatively small property of 379 hectares, the government also expropriated part of the neighbouring Zimpizahua and Mahuixtlán haciendas. Many of the San Marcos residents who had refused to participate in the agrarian census were renters living on the Mahuixtlán property who were now being displaced from their lands.[38] They angrily confronted the new grantees and shot at them, crying 'Long live the Mahuixtlán hacienda' and 'Death to the Bolsheviks, shameless bandits!'[39] Fifty-eight *colonos* from San Marcos were forced off their rented lands after the partial expropriation of the hacienda.[40] They were given two months to harvest their coffee and move on so that land reform beneficiaries could begin cultivating what was now theirs to farm.[41]

Regardless of the complex local and regional histories of *how* each ejido was formed, in the end state agents created new subject identities through the state's techniques of registration and classification. Ultimately, rural Mexico was divided into state subjects endowed with agrarian rights and the rest of the rural population, which – similarly poor and landless – did not acquire this particular subject status.

THE CONSTRUCTION OF THE NEOLIBERAL CITIZEN

In the early 1990s, government officials decided to end the state's responsibility to distribute land to the rural poor and opened the way for the privatisation of the ejido sector. When evaluating these policies a decade later, two things are clear. First, as with other neoliberal government programmes ostensibly intended to reduce the role of state institutions in the economy, the massive land-titling programme greatly enhanced state capacity in rural (and urban) Mexico (Snyder 2001). And second, state capacity was enhanced, once again, through a massive recategorisation of the population.

By the end of 1996, nearly all ejidos in Central Veracruz (as well as in many other regions and states) had enrolled in the neoliberal land-titling programme. The programme managed to advance quickly in a relatively short period of time, primarily because it utilised the same techniques of registration and classification that, for most of the century, government agents had used to distribute land. Agrarian censuses became the heart of the land-titling programme that would essentially privatise the agrarian reform sector.

The land-titling programme had several implications for the ongoing process of state formation in Mexico. First, the ruling elite, the old cadre of agrarian officials and the new land-titling recruits could redeem the idea of the state in the eyes of rural dwellers after a long history of inefficient and corrupt practices by state agents and ejido representatives. Second, on the basis of registration and classification techniques, agrarian officials would once again create new subject identities.

Redeeming the State through the Neoliberal Project
In many ways, the titling programme was a way for the Salinas government to 'redeem the apparatus of the state' (Hansen 2001: 229), to restore the idea of the state 'as a producer of impartial and universal justice'. If Thomas Blom Hansen is correct in that 'there is a constitutive split between a profane dimension of the state – incoherent, brutal, and partial – and a sublime state principle' (Jensen 2001: 108), then the decades-long agrarian reform had shown the profane face of the idea of the state all too clearly. As the number of land grants increased dramatically nationwide during and after the 1930s, a large number of overburdened and underpaid agrarian officials became increasingly negligent and corrupt.

Ejidatarios in Central Veracruz, for example, had to deal with an increasingly fraudulent process. Surveyors incorrectly measured ejido boundaries, endowed the same lands to two or more ejidos and often failed to call for the renewal of ejido boards, enabling some representatives to stay on longer than legally permitted.[42] Most consequential, surveyors increasingly began demanding bribes for their work.

By the 1960s, the agrarian bureaucracy had accumulated an administrative backlog (*rezago*) so severe that it became impossible to resolve. Numerous efforts to restructure bureaucratic procedures and alleviate these problems mostly made matters worse. For example, from 1970 to 1976 the number of agrarian personnel tripled. Paradoxically, the increase in personnel had a negative impact on the agrarian reform process. Agrarian bureaucrats were among the worst-paid public servants (some had to survive without pay for up to eight to ten months at a time), and many had no proper schooling or professional training. As a result, agrarian reform procedures were plagued with errors. (For instance, many documents were misplaced in what was already an archaic filing system.) In Veracruz, administrative mismanagement was so serious that government officials did not even know exactly how many ejidos there were in the state.[43] Nationally, by the early 1990s there were an estimated 150,000 incomplete administrative procedures.[44]

The problem was compounded by the inordinate number of bureaucratic and administrative steps required in issuing agrarian certificates. Agrarian certificates, which legitimated individual agrarian rights, required 34 different administrative procedures involving nine internal branches of the Ministry of Agrarian Reform, as well as the special offices of the Presidency and the Ministry of Interior (Zaragoza and Macías, 1980: 603). As a result, in 1970 almost half of all ejidatarios lacked agrarian-rights certificates. Without them, individuals were vulnerable to the dealings of the ejido board of representatives, infamous in rural Mexico for their abuse of power.

The Messiness of Everyday Life
Most scholars doing fieldwork in ejidos have noted the abuse of power by members of the *comisariado* (board of representatives) and the continuous breaking of agrarian rules – primarily in the form of sales and rentals of land parcels (both illegal in this form of property removed from the market). What is striking is that the rules that are broken are precisely those rules created in 1915 for the new subjects of the post-revolutionary state. The domain of the illegal was created in 1915 as well, and it is part and parcel of this state project. Moreover, ejido members created their own internal categories to deal with the messiness of everyday life – forms of classification that were also directly derived from the agrarian reform categories created in 1915, based upon who was a subject of the post-revolutionary state and who was not.

In most ejidos there were several categories of individuals: ejidatarios or agrarian-rights subjects, *avecindados* or *libres* (non-ejidatarios residing in the ejido's urban settlement), *comuneros* (ejidatarios without parcels but with collective rights to land) and *posesionarios* (individuals with only de facto use rights to a land parcel, oftentimes the result of an illegal purchase of ejido land). In Chavarrillo, Veracruz, for example, there were five types of residents: *derechosos* (beneficiaries), *herederos por derecho* (heirs of beneficiaries), *hijos de derechoso* (offspring of beneficiaries), *avecindados* (residents without agrarian rights), and *prestamistas* (residents without rights who rented land) (Casas, 1993: 28, fn. 3). In this ranking system, citizenship rights were determined by agrarian rights (see also Azuela de la Cueva 1995).

A Big Project of Incorporation
As noted, the land-titling programme was implemented through an apparently neutral administrative tool, the census. Perhaps the most important characteristic of the post-1992 censuses was their accuracy and reliability. Agrarian bureaucrats – largely young, recently trained engineers, agronomists and social workers – approached their tasks with more technologically sophisticated techniques of state; mapping was done on the basis of satellite-transmitted images,[45] and censuses were compiled in computerised form. These new censuses permitted a thorough spring-cleaning of agrarian records. All individuals claiming to legally *or illegally* hold ejido parcels for cultivation, or ejido plots to build houses on, were added to a master census conducted by the Agrarian Reform Registry. Individuals could then rectify their information if they had been incorrectly registered in earlier documents or disclose changes in the registry system (recording events such as

deaths, sales and inheritance transfers). Everyone legally or de facto working a parcel of ejido land would have their use rights properly officialised.

The genius of the new titling programme lay in that, instead of stripping ejidatarios of their agrarian rights, state officials first legalised the de facto or the illegal (*posesionarios*, or those with access to a land parcel but without agrarian rights) in ejidos. By validating the rights of *posesionarios*, the land-titling programme legalises the illegitimate.[46] All those living and working on ejidos without prior agrarian rights became new agrarian subjects – without the right to claim land, but with certificates that formalised their previously illegitimate status. In this manner, the project was perceived as one of incorporation or expansion of the agrarian population. (Only later, after the titling programme was completed, could ejidatarios vote to privatise the ejido.) As the land-titling programme progressed, tens of thousands of individuals without prior agrarian rights became agrarian state subjects. As a result, at no other time in history did the Mexican state have as many agrarian-rights subjects as during the implementation of the land-titling programme.

At the Estación Alborada ejido in Veracruz, for example, there were 57 agrarian-rights subjects before the titling programme; after the titling programme, almost twice as many (108) additional individuals (formerly *posesionarios*) were added. The Mahuixtlán ejido had 74 agrarian-rights subjects before the titling programme and a total of 356 thereafter.[47] Censuses from 14 other ejidos in the region show that, in most ejidos, the numbers of agrarian-rights subjects tripled after the land-titling programme.

Local Responses to the Land-Titling Programme

Local responses varied across Central Veracruz. Ultimately, however, even those who were philosophically opposed to the neoliberal project accepted the land-titling project, largely as a result of the state's powerful (and now more technologically sophisticated and accurate) techniques of registration. The new Agrarian Reform Registry counted and registered everyone living and working on ejido lands. Whether or not individuals wanted to participate in the titling programme, individuals realised they had *already* been included in the neoliberal project.

A number of ejido communities joined in actively. In Veracruz, El Chico is a case in point. An ejido located only a few kilometres southeast of the state's capital, Xalapa, El Chico is surrounded by middle-class housing complexes built for urban residents fleeing congested city life. Because of the severe coffee crisis of the late 1980s and early 1990s, as well as a rise in real estate prices, many ejidatarios sought to sell their ejido parcels. According to the president of the ejido board, in the early 1990s approximately 30 per cent of all ejidatarios were trying to sell their parcels.[48] Therefore, when representatives of the Agrarian Attorney General's office held elections to decide whether to join the titling programme, 74 of the 77 ejidatarios voted in favour (the remaining three were absent). In October 1993, El Chico became the first ejido in the state of Veracruz to complete the land-titling programme. In January

1994, El Chico residents were invited to the annual celebration in Medellín de Bravo that marks the anniversary of the Law of 6 January 1915, where then President Salinas, the Agrarian Attorney General and the Governor of the State of Veracruz gave each agrarian-rights subject a certificate.[49]

Other ejidos were divided between those who wanted to preserve the collective ideals of the ejido and those who basically wanted to rid themselves of the ejido authorities (infamous in most ejidos for their corrupt and abusive practices). In the summer of 1993, government officials implementing the titling programme arrived in San Marcos. They informed ejido members that Article 27 of the Constitution had been reformed. The purpose of these reforms, they explained, was to give the ejido full autonomy and ejido members security regarding land ownership. Carlos Conde, then president of the *comisariado*, emphatically explained that if they joined the programme, land would be privatised and the ejido, as an organisation, would fall apart. Furthermore, he warned that, as holders of private property, they would have to pay higher taxes to a municipal government that had not been accountable to San Marcos for the most part. That day, government officials held elections and the majority of ejidatarios voted against entering the programme.

A year later, when a new ejido president was elected, government agents re-established contact with San Marcos. The national press had been critical of the titling programme for its sluggish pace and government officials needed to show results. Although ejidatarios in San Marcos agreed to discuss the matter once again – this time in private – government officials made a surprise appearance on the day of the assembly meeting. They had been invited by Alejandro Mestizo, the new president of the *comisariado*, who gave long speeches in favour of the titling programme because, he said, with the new laws, their ejido documents were now worthless.

Government and ejido officials sat at a table placed in front of the large meeting hall facing the assembly members. According to ejido member Zeferina Martínez, they placed them there so that they could see who raised his or her hand and who did not.[50] Only half of the 202 ejidatarios were present. And since only 27 of them raised their hands in favour of the programme, the president proceeded to call the roll, updated by the Agrarian Reform Registry. One by one, every ejidatario had to move to the front of the hall and cast a vote. Only two ejidatarios openly refused to sign. Luciano Torres, who was opposed to the privatisation of the ejido on philosophical grounds, nevertheless instructed his daughter to sign in favour of the programme.

Most strikingly, even ejidos with a deep sense of agrarian history joined the land-titling programme. Chavarillo residents, for example, were conscious participants in electoral politics (usually in support of an opposition party), had a history of relatively successful production cooperatives and were active participants in the coffee producers' movement of the 1980s, which challenged the government for not protecting the price of coffee. Early on, Chavarillo residents voted against the land-titling programme, and they tried to conduct business as usual. In 1994, they continued to hold assemblies on the last Sunday of every month.[51] One of the most politically active young leaders believed that they were going to be the last ejido in the region: 'We'll be like a tourist theme park: "the last ejido in the region".'[52] Nevertheless, by 1996 ejido members had already completed the various administrative steps of the land-titling programme. In the end, having proper state registration was more important than post-revolutionary principles.

If the global wave of neoliberal policies has changed the content of subjecthood in Mexico, it has done so by strengthening the administrative capabilities of the state, including revamping inefficient bureaucracies, modernising techniques of registration and classification, and employing new generations of surveyors and engineers. The 1992 land-titling programme amounts to the most sweeping agrarian reform (in the sense that the nature of property, in the form of land, is profoundly altered) in the entire history of Mexico. Whether taking land from large landowners to give to the landless, or granting agrarian rights to *posesionarios*, both the 1915–92 and the post-1992 reforms changed the idea of subjecthood or citizenship. If the agrarian rights-bearing individual had the collective and individual right to demand land from the state, the new citizen has the individual right to partake in the landed property market.

CONCLUDING REMARKS: THE ENDURING POWER OF STATE RITUAL

This study of the day-to-day implementation of Mexico's agrarian reforms (both post-revolutionary and neoliberal) sheds light on the multiplicity and complexity of local struggles and negotiations. In the end, however, rural dwellers internalised categories that were established by a revolutionary or ruling elite – and implemented by state agents through the census.

The rituals of state employed in Mexico's pursuit of agrarian reform (whether post-revolutionary or neoliberal) had an enduring power: the capacity to create subjects or citizens, and, in so doing, the giving and taking away of rights with real material implications (in this case land). According to Derek Sayer:

This was the point of *The Great Arch*'s insistence that 'the state' lives in and through its subjects: we were not arguing an 'incorporation' thesis at the level of ideology and belief, but pointing to precisely the materiality of everyday forms of state formation. (1994: 377)

In the case of the agrarian reform (post-revolutionary and neoliberal), subjecthood and citizenship have important material implications.

If Fernando Escalante is correct in arguing that Mexican citizenship is historically specific (that is, not a copy of European citizenship), then it is also true that the content of Mexican citizenship is fluid (Escalante 1992).[53] In contrast to the agrarian reform begun in 1915, in which the architects of the post-revolutionary state created a clearly defined and separate category of state subject (the agrarian-rights subject), those who designed the new agrarian reform initiated in 1992 sought to transform these separate subjects into liberal and universal citizens with rights to private property. Whereas the post-revolutionary agrarian-rights subject had the right to demand land from the state,[54] the neoliberal citizen has the right to participate in the market.[55]

A massive categorisation and recategorisation of individuals and their rights was possible because of the power of the enduring power of state rituals. The 'myth of the state' is upheld with the perception that state routines are neutral or objective. Although numerous scholars, journalists and artists (among others) have scrutinised the Mexican Revolution from all possible angles, no one has questioned the use of the census and its power of categorisation to determine who among the poor and the landless would become a state subject, and who would be excluded from a social engineering project. And although supporters and critics of the neoliberal land-titling programme have debated its content and progress, neither side has questioned the authority of state agents to conduct the massive censuses that are recategorising *en masse* Mexico's rural (and increasingly urban) ejido population.

NOTES

1. I thank Kevin Middlebrook, Knut G. Nustad and Christian Krohn-Hansen for their comments. This chapter draws partly on research conducted for the author's doctoral dissertation, for which the support of the Wenner-Gren Foundation for Anthropological Research is gratefully acknowledged. During this time, William Roseberry was a great source of encouragement; I dedicate this essay to Bill's memory.

2. For example, see the collective projects found in Joseph and Nugent (1994), Steinmetz (1999), Centeno and López-Alves (2001), Hansen and Stepputat (2001), Dunkerley (2002), Crais (2003), Davis and Pereira (2003). For Latin America specifically, three monographs that should also be mentioned are Nugent (1997), López-Álves (2000) and Centeno (2002). Monographs on state formation in Mexico are mentioned below.

3. To some extent, they all engage Michel Foucault, Karl Marx, Max Weber and Émile Durkheim.

4. James Scott's *Seeing Like a State: How Certain Schemes to Improve the Human Condition Have Failed* (1998) had not been published.

5. See the contributions in Joseph and Nugent (1994), Mallon (1995), Vaughan (1997) and Wells and Joseph (1996).

6. For an overview of earlier state-centred analyses, see, for example, Knight (2001: 178–79) and Rubin (1996).

7. On the role of workers in post-revolutionary state formation, see, among others, Bortz (2000).

8. See, for example, Knight (1996), Brunk (1997: 605), the special issue of the *Hispanic American Historical Review* (1999) and Van Young (1999b).

9. For a key text on the rituals of state and bureaucratic power, see Herzfeld (1993).

10. According to Kertzer and Arel (2002: 2), the most important means by which officials count and classify a population is the census.

11. For Latin America, see, for example, Whitehead (1994: 46–47) and Knight (2002).

12. The area of study is confined to the eleven municipalities that constitute the coffee-producing region of Central Veracruz. Here, the author found 104 grant petitions (74 granted and 30 denied) and 49 petitions for grant extensions (*ampliaciones*) (15 granted and 34 denied). Of the 104 grant petitions, only one requested a restitution;

this community was given a land grant instead. Most *ejidos* in the region were granted in the 1920s and 1930s.

13. General Venustiano Carranza, First Chief of the Constitutionalist Army, was faced with the prospect of losing the civil war to the armies of Francisco Villa and Emiliano Zapata. He issued the Law of 6 January 1915 in an effort to expand his political base by gaining the support of agrarian reform advocates. The longevity of the reform was unintentional because its architects saw it as a provisional strategy intended to turn rural dwellers into efficient family farmers.

14. The law distinguished between communities that had been illegally despoiled of their lands (which would be restituted) and rural dwellers with no or little land (who would receive a grant from the state). For an in-depth study on the lack of empirical studies on how land was usurped during the Porfiriato, see Kourí (2002).

15. For all practical purposes, the reforms have privatised the ejido. For detailed explanations, see Pérez Castañeda (1995, 2002).

16. Before 1992, ejidatarios had two joint social property rights: the right to a parcel, and the right to lands held in common. With the Agrarian Law of 1992, these joint rights were divided into two separate ones, and each was radically transformed. Rights to individual parcels were transformed into private rights (*derecho de propiedad en sí mismo*), which allowed individual holders to use or dispose of lands as they saw fit. However, the 1992 law is contradictory with respect to common lands. In theory, lands in common are inalienable, but in practice and except for woodlands, they can be divided if all ejidatarios agree to do so (Pérez Castañeda, 1995: 458–96). Thus, Article 48 established that common land (except in the case of woodlands) could be individually parcelled under certain conditions. Articles 56 and 57 permit ejido assemblies to parcel common lands, and article 60 permits their '*cesión*' (a euphemism for '*enajenación*') (Pérez Castañeda, n.d.: 103). In essence, this means that ejidos cannot legally 'sell' land held in common because it cannot be privatised by ejidatarios or *comuneros*. Nevertheless, ejidatarios can 'transfer' land held in common (in a monetary transaction), and once the land is transferred to a non-ejidatario, it becomes private property (Pérez Castañeda n.d.: 97–121).

17. Programa de Certificación de Derechos Ejidales y Titulación de Solares Urbanos, or Procede.

18. This section draws in part on Baitenmann (1997: ch. 6).

19. The term *ejido* (whose significance varies historically as well as geographically) was commonly used to denote communal land use, and the term was adopted for the land grants made by the post-revolutionary government. Ejido land could not be sold, mortgaged or transferred in any other way than by inheritance to a family member. With the Agrarian Codes of 1934, 1940 and especially 1943, a number of basic principles concerning ejido tenure and organisation were gradually clarified. The ejido became a collective entity with its own patrimony, its own legal standing (*personalidad jurídica*), and its own administrative and representative organs (general assembly and *comisariado ejidal*), under the control of the agrarian bureaucracy. Endowed population centres (*núcleos de población*) became permanent corporate owners of ejido lands. Although woodlands, pastures and water sources would be managed communally, arable lands could either remain under communal control or be fractioned into individual parcels. Both communal land and individual parcels could be worked individually or cooperatively. In 1934 the Agrarian Code differentiated between two types of land endowments: the *dotación*, or granting of land by state fiat to rural dwellers with no ancestral claims to land, and the restitution (*restitución*) of lands to those communities that could prove that their communal lands had been usurped during the implementation of nineteenth-century liberal laws.

20. Some joined Carranza in Coahuila, others joined General Pancho Villa in Chihuahua, and still more joined General Emiliano Zapata's Agrarian Commission of the South (see Calderón Arozqueta 1993: 11–13). Archival material from Central Veracruz points

to many incidents in which surveyors risked their lives. For example, one engineer had to flee the Coatepec region in 1915 because of rebel attacks (ACAM exp. 2, Xico, Telegrama dirigido por el Gobierno Constitucionalista del Estado de Veracruz a Jalapa o donde se encuentre, al Sr. Adalberto Palacios, Jefe de la Comisión Agraria del Estado, 25 noviembre 1915). In Banderilla, from at least 1918 until 1920, topographic work was made difficult by the presence of outlaws (*bandoleros*), and it often had to be suspended (see, for example, ACCA exp. 5085, Banderilla, Informe del Ingeniero encargado de la Delegación de la CNA, 2 April 1918; and ACAM exp. 59, Banderilla, de la CLA al Ingeniero de Gortari, 6 July 1920). That same year, an engineer working in Tlalnehuayocan asked for a civil guard escort of eight to ten men because the region had been invaded by outlaws (ACAM exp. 93, Tlalnehuayocan, al Presidente de la CLA, del agente de la CLA, Manuel Jiménez, 1 June 1918). In 1920, another engineer asked for a detachment of 25 soldiers because there were anywhere between 40 and 60 rebels in the region (ACAM exp. 59, Banderilla, del Ingeniero Salvador de Gortari, and Presidente de la CLA, 26 April 1920).

21. There were also standardised instructions for surveyors to streamline the land reform process, blueprints for the *pueblos* that included the appropriate language for soliciting land, ready-made forms asking the bureaucracy to send an official and pre-written petitions soliciting legal opinions. There was even a form for reporting livestock theft.

22. In 1917, Circular 15 of the National Agrarian Commission instructed surveyors to conduct censuses and write reports on the types of lands that could be expropriated and made available for distribution, their values and the amounts that would be required for a family to make a living. See *Circular Número 15*, 'Sobre los datos que deben recabarse en los expedientes de dotación de ejidos', 24 January 1917 (Fabila 1984: 301–02).

23. Laws excluded towns that were too small to receive formal recognition as a town (*congregación*, *poblado*, etc.) as a way to prevent renters living on hacienda lands from claiming land – a concession made to landowners up until the 1930s.

24. For a detailed gendered analysis of civil laws, see Arrom (1985: 305–06, 309). In post-revolutionary agrarian law, the term 'family head' (*jefe de familia*) was explicitly employed for the first time in the 1920 Law of Ejidos. In 1921, Circular 48 from the National Agrarian Commission specifically included single or widowed women with dependants in the category of family head. Fowler-Salamini also found that municipal census-takers during the Porfiriato equated *jefes de familia* with male heads of household and imposed a particular view of gender roles by allowing women only one occupational category: *doméstica* (housewife) (1994: 60–61). For a gendered analysis of the agrarian census, see Baitenmann (n.d.).

25. ACAM exp. 19A, Palo Gacho, Resolución del Presidente de la Comisión Local Agraria Froilán del Castillo, 21 enero 1918. The towns mentioned were Palo Gacho, Rinconada, Plan del Río, and Carrizal. Coscorrón and Buena Vista were included as well, but residents refused to participate (see ACAM exp. 19A, Palo Gacho, December 1917).

26. ACAM exp. 19A, Palo Gacho, del Delegado de la Junta de Administración Civil de Rinconada al Presidente de la CLA, 24 December 1917. In Veracruz, local groups in the region splintered into Zapatista, Villista and Carrancista factions. See Nelly León Fuentes, 'Conformación de un capital en torno al café 1890–1940' (BA thesis, Universidad Veracruzana, 1983, 56). Villista bands roamed the Huasteca, while Zapatistas sought refuge in the Sierra Madre Oriental mountain range west of the Xalapa–Coatepec region. From there, they were able to launch periodic attacks on Carrancista forces camped out in villages surrounding the two cities (see Hoffmann 1992: 63).

27. Padrón General de la Congregación de Rinconada, Municipio de El Chico, Cantón de Jalapa, 16 December 1917, signed by Rodolfo Cuevas (ARAN). It is interesting that literacy was included as a category given that it did not determine agrarian rights.

190 *State Formation*

28. Censo Agrario de la Congregación de Palo Gacho, 21 December 1917, signed by Rodolfo Cuevas (ARAN); Censo Agrario de la Congregación de Plan del Río, 22 December 1917, signed by Rodolfo Cuevas (ARAN).
29. ACAM exp. 19A, Palo Gacho, del Delegado de la Junta de Administración Civil de Rinconada al Presidente de la CLA, 24 December 1917; and ACAM exp. 19A, Palo Gacho, Dictamen de Carranza y de la CNA, 24 October 1918.
30. ACCA exp. 10387, Chavarrillo, Censo General y Agrario, por el Ing. comisionado Alvaro Fernández, s.f., 1930; ACCA exp. 10387, Chavarrillo, del Presidente del Comité Onónimo Valdés al C. Daniel Santa Maria, 11 January 1931; and ACCA exp. 10387, Chavarrillo, Al Presidente de la CLA, del Presidente del Comité, 12 February 1931.
31. The final ruling, however, excluded only three women. See ACAM exp. 208, El Chico, folio 142–52, Dictamen de la Comisión Local Agraria, 6 April 1923; and Sánchez Gómez (1979: 56).
32. '[N]o tratando más que del engrandecimiento y progreso de la Congregación' (ACAM exp. 179, San Marcos, de la Junta Directiva de Agricultura, al Gobernador del Estado, 24 September 1914).
33. There are indications that, by 1917, there were several factions within San Marcos (ACAM exp. 179, San Marcos, de la CLA al Grupo Primero de la Congregación de San Marcos de León, 15 June 1917).
34. The general census registered 746 inhabitants, and the agrarian census registered 116 agriculturalists (ACAM exp. 179, San Marcos, Reporte del ingeniero ayudante al Presidente de la CLA, 17 December 1921).
35. Life history, Luciano Torres (son of Manuel Torres), San Marcos de León.
36. See, ACAM exp. 179; 14 June 1921; Padrón de la Congregación de San Marcos de campesinos emancipados; ACAM exp. 179; 1 July 1921; Padrón de los socios del Sindicato de 'Obreros Campesinos Libres' de San Marcos; and ACAM exp. 179, San Marcos, Solicitud, 17 June 1921.
37. ACAM exp. 179, San Marcos, Acta de Posesión provisional, 14 February 1922.
38. ACAM exp. 179, San Marcos, Reporte del Ingeniero Ayudante, a la CLA, 17 December 1921.
39. ACAM exp. 179, San Marcos, del Sindicato de Campesinos de San Marcos de León, adherido a la CROM, a la CLA, 23 February 1922. In 1922, as many as 61 renters from the Mahuixtlán hacienda went to the CLA to protest the invasion of their lands by the new grantees (ACAM exp. 179, San Marcos, de arrendatarios de la Hacienda Mahuixtlán, a la CLA, 23 February 1922).
40. ACCA exp. 5135, San Marcos, del Procurador de los Pueblos, al Gobernador Tejeda, 27 December 1922.
41. ACCA exp. 5135, San Marcos, del Presidente de la CLA, al Presidente de la CNA, s.f. October 1922. Some grantees claimed that, for two years after the provisional possession, the manager of Mahuixtlán gave out free land parcels in order to complicate the expropriation efforts. It later turned out that, indeed, many of the tenants' *fincas* were uncultivated. See ACCA exp. 5135, San Marcos, del Secretario Gral. de la CNA, al Procurador de los Pueblos del Edo. de Veracruz [transcriben escrito del CPE de San Marcos], 18 January 1923; and Hoffmann (1992: 155). It is difficult to determine how many renters actually lost cultivated lands.
42. There are numerous examples of this. See, for example, ALCA, Emiliano Zapata: El Palmar, del Secretario de la Liga de Comunidades Agrarias y Sindicatos Campesinos, a Pablo Hernández, Delegado del Departamento Agrario, 10 December 1948.
43. In the 1990s, official figures varied between 3,337 and 3,424, a difference of 87 ejidos. INEGI contended that there were 3,337 granted ejidos and agrarian communities; the Veracruz delegate of the Agrarian Reform Ministry publicly announced that there were 3,424. The first figure comes from Instituto Nacional de Estadística, Geografía e Informática (1991: 1); the second from *El Financiero* – Sección Golfo, 8 July 1993, IX

44. UAM study by Beatríz Canabal and Joaquín Flores Félix, cited by Lourdes E. Rudiño, 'Crean un espacio fértil para la discusión del artículo 27 las demandas del EZLN: Especialistas', *El Financiero*, 14 February 1994, 36.
45. This is a satellite-based radio navigation system called Global Positioning System.
46. It is interesting to note that the illicit is a space where women have had a greater presence (Baitenmann, n.d.).
47. ADDAT Estación Alborada, Emiliano Zapata Municipality, 22 September 1994, ARAN; ADDAT Mahuixtlán, Coatepec, Municipality, 11 April 1999, ARAN.
48. Interview with Manuel García, El Chico, 13 July 1994.
49. Field visit, Medellín de Bravo, 6 January 1994.
50. Life history, Zeferina Martínez, San Marcos de León.
51. Interview with Pascual Ruíz, Chavarrillo, 1 August 1994.
52. Interview with Cirio Ruíz, Xalapa, 13 July 1994.
53. Abel and Lewis, for example, briefly identify some of the patterns and variations in the content of citizenship in Latin America (2002: 4–15).
54. Even though the post-revolutionary agrarian reform is always discussed in terms of its collective nature, rights to land in ejidos were, in most cases, profoundly individual. One exception involves the concept of family patrimony. For a detailed discussion of the post-revolutionary construction of agrarian family patrimony, see Baitenmann (n.d.).
55. Those individuals recorded on the new land-titling censuses are now the potential renters, buyers, sellers, and debtors that development agencies are closely monitoring. See, for example, the joint World Bank and Secretaría de la Reforma Agraria study by Deininger et al. (2001).

REFERENCES

Abel, C. and C.M. Lewis, 2002. 'Exclusion and Engagement: A Diagnosis of Social Policy in Latin America in the Long Run', in C. Abel and C.M. Lewis, eds, *Exclusion and Engagement: Social Policy in Latin America*. London: Institute of Latin American Studies.

Abrams, P., 1988 [1977]. 'Notes on the Difficulty of Studying the State', *Journal of Historical Sociology* 1(1): 58–89.

Arrom, S.M., 1985. 'Changes in Mexican Family Law in the Nineteenth Century: The Civil Codes of 1870 and 1884', *Journal of Family History* 10(3): 305–17.

Azuela de la Cueva, A., 1995. 'Ciudadanía y gestión urbana en los poblados rurales de Los Tuxtlas', *Estudios Sociológicos* 13(39): 485–500.

Baitenmann, H., 1997. 'Rural Agency and State Formation in Postrevolutionary Mexico: The Agrarian Reform in Central Veracruz (1915–1992)', PhD diss., New School for Social Research, New York.

Baitenmann, H., 2002. 'Gendered Explorations of the State: The Agrarian Reform in Twentieth-Century Mexico', paper delivered at the workshop 'Explorations of the State: Considerations from Critical Anthropology/Ethnography', University of Oslo, 25–26 October.

Baitenmann, H., n.d. Gendered Explorations of the State: Agrarian Reform in Twentieth-Century Mexico. (manuscript).

Becker, M., 1995. *Setting the Virgin on Fire: Lázaro Cárdenas, Michoacán Peasants, and the Redemption of the Mexican Revolution*. Berkeley: University of California Press.

Bortz. J., 2000. 'The Revolution, the Labour Regime and Conditions of Work in the Cotton Textile Industry in Mexico, 1910–1927', *Journal of Latin American Studies* 32(3): 671–703.

Brunk, S., 1997. 'Review of *Setting the Virgin on Fire*', *Americas* 53(4): 605–07.

Calderón Arozqucta, R., 1993. 'La formación de profesionales para el desarrollo rural: el caso de la agronomía en México', MA thesis, Universidad Autónoma Metropolitana-Xochimilco.

192   *State Formation*

Caplan, J. and J. Torpey, 2001. 'Introduction', in J. Caplan and J. Torpey, eds, *Documenting Individual Identity: The Development of State Practices in the Modern World*. Princeton, NJ: Princeton University Press.

Casas, C., 1993. 'Familia y poder: La identidad de una comunidad del centro de Veracruz', BA thesis, Department of Anthropology, Universidad Veracruzana.

Centeno, M.Á., 2002. *Blood and Debt: War and Nation-State in Latin America*. University Park, PA: Pennsylvania State Press.

Centeno, M.Á. and F. López-Alves, eds, 2001. *The Other Mirror: Grand Theory through the Lens of Latin America*. Princeton, NJ: Princeton University Press.

Cohn, B.S., 1996. *Colonialism and Its Forms of Knowledge: The British in India*. Princeton, NJ: Princeton University Press.

Corrigan, P. and D. Sayer, 1985. *The Great Arch: English State Formation as Cultural Revolution*. New York: Basil Blackwell.

Cotter, J., 2003. *Troubled Harvest: Agronomy and Revolution in Mexico, 1880–2002*. Westport, CT: Praeger.

Crais, C., ed., 2003. *The Culture of Power in Southern Africa: Essays on State Formation and the Political Imagination*. Portsmouth, NH: Heinemann.

Davis, D.E. and A.W. Pereira, eds, 2003. *Irregular Armed Forces and their Role in Politics and State Formation*. Cambridge: Cambridge University Press.

Deere, C.D. and M. León, 2001. *Empowering Women: Land and Property Rights in Latin America*. Pittsburgh, PA: University of Pittsburgh Press.

Deininger, K., et al. 2001. 'Mexico's "Second Agrarian Reform": Implementation and Impact', paper presented at the 'Foro Internacional: Ordenamiento de la Propiedad y Sistemas Catastrales' Procuraduría Agraria, 26–29 November, Mexico City.

Dunkerley, J., ed., 2002. *Studies in the Formation of the Nation State in Latin America*. London: Institute of Latin American Studies.

Escalante Gonzalbo, F., 1992. *Ciudadanos imaginarios*. Mexico City: El Colegio de México.

Fabila, M., 1984. *Cinco siglos de legislación agraria 1493–1940*. Mexico City: Secretaría de la Reforma Agraria and Centro de Estudios Históricos del Agrarismo en México.

Fallaw, B., 2002. 'The Life and Death of Felipa Poot: Women, Fiction, and Cardenismo in Postrevolutionary Mexico', *Hispanic American Historical Review* 82(4).

Fowler-Salamini, H., 1994. 'Gender, Work, and Coffee in Córdoba, Veracruz, 1850–1910', in H. Fowler-Salamini and M.K. Vaughan, eds, *Women of the Mexican Countryside, 1850–1990*. Tucson: University of Arizona Press.

Hansen, T.B., 2001. 'Governance and State Mythologies in Mumbai', in T.B. Hansen and F. Stepputat, eds, *States of Imagination: Ethnographic Explorations of the Postcolonial State*. Durham, NC: Duke University Press.

Hansen, T.B. and F. Stepputat, eds, 2001. *States of Imagination: Ethnographic Explorations of the Postcolonial State*. Durham, NC: Duke University Press.

Herzfeld, M., 1993. *The Social Production of Indifference: Exploring the Symbolic Roots of Western Bureaucracy*. Chicago, IL: University of Chicago Press.

Hispanic American Historical Review. 1999. 'Mexico's New Cultural History: ¿Una lucha libre?' 79(2).

Hoffmann, O., 1992. *Tierras y territorio en Xico, Veracruz*. Xalapa: Gobierno de Estado de Veracruz.

Instituto Nacional de Estadística, Geografía e Informática. 1991. *Atlas Ejidal del Estado de Veracruz: Encuesta Nacional Agropecuaria Ejidal, 1988*. Aguascalientes: Instituto Nacional de Estadística, Geografía e Informática and Institut Français de Recherche Scientifique pour le Developpement en Cooperation.

Jensen, S., 2001. 'The Battlefield and the Prize: ANC's Bid to Reform the South African State', in T.B. Hansen and F. Stepputat, eds, *States of Imagination: Ethnographic Explorations of the Postcolonial State*. Durham, NC: Duke University Press.

Joseph, G.M. and D. Nugent, eds, 1994. *Everyday Forms of State Formation: Revolution and Negotiation of Rule in Modern Mexico*. Durham, NC: Duke University Press.

Kertzer, D. and D. Arel, 2002. *Census and Identity: The Politics of Race, Ethnicity, and Language in National Censuses*. Cambridge: Cambridge University Press.

Knight, A., 1994. 'Peasants into Patriots: Thoughts on the Making of the Modern Mexican Nation', *Mexican Studies/Estudios Mexicanos* 10(1): 135–61.

Knight, A., 1996. 'Review of *Peasant and Nation: The Making of Postcolonial Mexico and Peru*', *Times Literary Supplement*, 4849 (8 March), 30.

Knight, A., 2001. 'The Modern Mexican State: Theory and Practice', in M.Á. Centeno and F. López-Alves, eds, *The Other Mirror: Grand Theory through the Lens of Latin America*. Princton, NH: Princeton University Press.

Knight, A., 2002. 'The Weight of the State in Modern Mexico', in J. Dunkerley, ed., *Studies in the Formation of the Nation State in Latin America*. London: Institute of Latin American Studies.

Kourí, E.H., 2002. 'Interpreting the Expropriation of Indian Pueblo Lands in Porfirian Mexico: The Unexamined Legacies of Andrés Molina Enríquez', *Hispanic American Historical Review* 82(1): 69–117.

López-Álves, F., 2000. *State Formation and Democracy in Latin America, 1810–1900*. Durham, NC: Duke University Press.

Mallon, F.E., 1995. *Peasant and Nation: The Making of Postcolonial Mexico and Peru*. Berkeley: University of California Press.

Mitchell, T., 1991a. 'The Limits of the State: Beyond Statist Approaches', *American Political Science Review* 85(1): 77–94.

Mitchell, T., 1991b. *Colonising Egypt*. Berkeley: University of California Press.

Mitchell, T., 1999. 'Society, Economy, and the State Effect', in G. Steinmetz, ed., *State/Culture: State-Formation after the Cultural Turn*. Ithaca, NY: Cornell University Press.

Nugent, D., 1997. *Modernity at the Edge of Empire: State, Individual, and Nation in the Northern Peruvian Andes (1885–1935)*. Stanford, CA: Stanford University Press.

Nugent, D. and A.M. Alonso, 1994. 'Multiple Selective Traditions in Agrarian Reform and Agrarian Struggle: Popular Culture and State Formation in the Ejido of Namiquipa, Chihuahua', in G.M. Joseph and D. Nugent, eds, *Everyday Forms of State Formation: Revolution and Negotiation of Rule in Modern Mexico*. Durham, NC: Duke University Press.

Pérez Castañeda, J.C., n.d. *La propiedad y el nuevo derecho agrario en México*. Manuscript.

Pérez Castañeda, J.C., 1995. 'Las reformas a la legislación agraria en el marco de la propiedad territorial', in R. Alejandro Encinas, ed., *El campo mexicano en el umbral del siglo XXI*. Mexico City: Espasa Calpe.

Pérez Castañeda, J. C., 2002. *El sistema de propiedad agraria en México*. Mexico City: Editorial Palabra en Vuelo.

Platt, L.D., 1998. *Census Records for Latin America and the Hispanic United States*. Baltimore: Genealogical Publishing Co.

Procuraduría Agraria. 2003. *Procede*, www.pa.gob.mx/Procede/info_procede.htm (accessed 25 July 2005).

Roseberry, W., 1994. 'Hegemony and the Language of Contention', in G.M. Joseph and D. Nugent, eds, *Everyday Forms of State Formation: Revolution and Negotiation of Rule in Modern Mexico*. Durham, NC: Duke University Press.

Rubin, J.W., 1996. 'Decentering the Regime: Culture and Regional Politics in Mexico', *Latin American Research Review* 31(3): 85–126.

Rubin, J.W., 1997. *Decentering the Regime: Ethnicity, Radicalism, and Democracy in Juchitán, Mexico*. Durham, NC and London: Duke University Press.

Sánchez Gómez, R.C., 1979. 'Afectación agraria y población beneficiada en la hacienda El Encero', *Anuario* II (Universidad Veracruzana).

Sayer, D., 1994. 'Everyday Forms of State Formation: Some Dissident Remarks on "Hegemony"', in G.M. Joseph and D. Nugent, eds, *Everyday Forms of State Formation:*

Revolution and Negotiation of Rule in Modern Mexico. Durham, NC: Duke University Press.

Scott, J., 1976. *The Moral Economy of the Peasant: Rebellion and Subsistence in Southeast Asia*. New Haven, CT: Yale University Press.

Scott, J., 1985. *Weapons of the Weak: Everyday Forms of Peasant Resistance*. New Haven, CT: Yale University Press.

Scott, J., 1990. *Domination and the Arts of Resistance: Hidden Transcripts*. New Haven, CT: Yale University Press.

Scott, J., 1998. *Seeing like a State: How Certain Schemes to Improve the Human Condition Have Failed*. New Haven, CT: Yale University Press.

Secretaría de la Reforma Agraria. 1998. *La transformación agraria: orígen, evolución, retos y testimonios*. Mexico City: Secretaría de la Reforma Agraria.

Snyder, R., 2001. *Politics after Neoliberalism: Reregulation in Mexico*. Cambridge: Cambridge University Press.

Steinmetz, G., ed., 1999. *State/Culture: State-Formation after the Cultural Turn*. Ithaca, NY: Cornell University Press.

Steinmetz, G., 1999. 'Introduction: Culture and the State', in G. Steinmetz, ed., *State/Culture: State-Formation after the Cultural Turn*. Ithaca, NY: Cornell University Press.

Van Young, E., 1999a. 'The New Cultural History Comes to Old Mexico', *Hispanic American Historical Review* 79(2): 211–47.

Van Young, E., 1999b. 'Making the Leviathan Sneeze: Recent Works on Mexico and the Mexican Revolution', *Latin American Research Review* 34(3): 143–65.

Vaughan, M.K., 1997. *Culture and Politics in Revolution: Teachers, Peasants, and Schools in Mexico, 1930–1940*. Tucson: University of Arizona Press.

Wells, A. and G.M. Joseph, 1996. *Summer of Discontent, Seasons of Upheaval: Elite Politics and Rural Insurgency in Yucatán, 1876–1915*. Stanford, CA: Stanford University Press.

Whitehead, L., 1994. 'State Organisation in Latin America since 1930', in Leslie Bethell, ed., *Cambridge History of Latin America*, 6(2).

Zaragoza, J.L. and R.M. Macías, 1980. *El desarrollo agrario en México y su marco jurídico*. Mexico City: Centro Nacional de Investigaciones Agrarias.

9   'A SPEECH THAT THE ENTIRE MINISTRY MAY STAND FOR': ON GENERATING STATE VOICE

Iver B. Neumann

As noted in the introduction to this volume, two trends in recent anthropological scholarship on the state have been to study it through its effects, and to deny its separateness from society.[1] My chapter goes against the grain on both counts. First, the field in which I worked was a state ministry. I study what went on in that field, and do not privilege the effects that it may or may not have had outside that field itself. Second, a key point that emerges from my ethnography is that my informants are less interested in these effects than they are in relating to one another. Using speech-writing as an example, I want to demonstrate that this particular state organisation is definitely separate from society in the sense that it engages in practices that are centred around itself, rather than towards its interface with society.[2]

The Durkheimian school has so far answered the question of why the state appears to be separate from society in two different ways. Durkheim's (1996: 3) own evolutionary answer was that 'the State is a special organ whose responsibility it is to work out certain representations which hold good for the collectivity'. The functions of the state, understood as the social brain to society's body, have multiplied with time, giving it a more multiplex steering role vis-à-vis society and strengthening the entire organism. A second answer began to germinate with Mauss's scrutiny of body techniques as the key element of habitus, which was then developed, among others, by Bourdieu, and also by Foucault's work on bio-power. The one who linked these insights directly to the question of why the state appears to be separate from society was Timothy Mitchell (1999), who stresses the 'larger than life' effect of the disciplined bio-mass that is the state. These two answers have to vie with the most popular explanation, which is provided by Max Weber and refined by neo-institutionalists, and may be paraphrased as follows: the state appears monolithic to society because its work follows certain impersonal, rational and standardised routines which gives it a *sui generis* quality. In this chapter, I will draw on ethnographic work carried out within the apparatus of the Norwegian state in order to provide an answer that is definitely Weberian, in the sense that it stresses routines, but that draws on the Durkheimian school and its Foucauldian stepchild inasmuch as it stresses how the bureaucratic process is certainly impersonal and routinised, but disciplinary rather than rational. The state appears monolithic because it produces acts – speech acts and other acts – in standardised and impersonalised ways. Once left to its own devices, the state will reproduce texts and acts of the same kind that it has produced before.

DRAFTING A SPEECH

'The Asia adviser has ordered a speech in connection with the royal couple's visit to China. I thought this might be a good opportunity for you, Iver, to try your hand at speech-writing.' We are at a morning meeting in the Planning and Evaluation Unit, an organ of the Norwegian Ministry of Foreign Affairs (MFA) subordinated directly to the secretary general, on a par with the ministry's ten departments. The secretary general is the senior civil servant in the ministry, and only outranked by its politicians. Like the ten departments, the Planning and Evaluation Unit is headed by a director general, and it is he who gives me a two-page order slip from the ministry's Asia adviser. He and the other regional advisers are all former ambassadors; with only eleven director general positions and around a hundred foreign postings headed by people with the status of ambassador, the ranks hold more ambassadors than there are regular jobs at the ambassadorial level, and so positions like those of area advisers are filled by personnel with the grade of ambassador. I am also an adviser, employed for a year and a half, brought in, or so I was told, to 'furnish a different perspective' and to be an intellectual jack-of-all-trades. I was picked because I was a researcher in the Norwegian Institute of International Affairs, another institution that is part of the close-knit foreign policy establishment of a small state. I had participated in the public debate, given occasional lectures in the ministry's in-house academy and even worked as a guard and interpreter in the Norwegian Moscow embassy as a very young man. When the head of the Planning Department offered me the job, I accepted on the express condition that I could study diplomatic practice while I was there. This was immediately agreed. Initially, my colleagues used to joke about my interest in what to them was routine and hence unexciting work (one even demanding jocularly that he wanted to pick his own alias when I wrote up), but my interest was also welcomed, since it meant less work for the rest of the unit. Drafting a speech, then, seems to be an obvious task for the new adviser.

The speech turns out to be the King's, to be delivered in 20 minutes to a party of businessmen from Hong Kong gathered around a luncheon table by the Norwegian Consulate General. Along with the order slip there is a half-page note from the consulate in Hong Kong. It states that the consulate was established in 1907, as one of the first after Norway left its personal union with Sweden in 1905; that Norway and Hong Kong have always had good business relations; that Hong Kong is mentioned in particular in the Foreign Ministry's two-year-old Asia plan. There is also some advice on what the focus of the speech should be.

The Planning Unit's number two is Assistant Director General Ranveig S., who is a fellow slavist I already knew well before entering the ministry. She has become my mentor. It so happened that she returned from a foreign posting to the second-highest position in the unit just as I joined it, and we have had ample opportunity to re-establish contact during the first weeks, when we shared an office. Ranveig says that above all I have been given the task of writing this speech in order to familiarise myself with the workings of the ministry. She explains how I should proceed. I should 'go and talk to' the various 'in-house' sections in order to draw out their input. In this particular case, it is of the essence to 'establish rapport with' the Office of Foreign Economic Affairs, she explains. Why so? Because the Office, and the department of which it is a part, are the closest thing in the regular organisation grid to being directly responsible for the issue area concerned. Once I have 'established rapport with' them – that is, once I have spoken to them, received their input and established a feeling of consensus amongst us – I may proceed to write the speech and put it in the director general's pigeonhole. He will then read it, perhaps annotate it, and then return it to me. I will subsequently correct it, send it to the Translation Section to be language-washed, and then it will finally be signed off. Does that mean that I should send it to the archive? No, Ranveig explains, not entirely. I will deliver the finished speech to the unit secretary, who will then write a covering note and make three copies (an original, a blue copy for the general archive and a yellow copy for the unit's manual archive). She will also, when necessary, make copies for the rest of the unit. In any case she will put a copy of the end-product in my pigeonhole. Finally, it may also be wise for me to keep a copy of the processed text, and perhaps I should also make some copies for the colleagues who have contributed their input and for the Secretariat of the foreign minister.

'So I'll find out who is the officer in charge of the case in the Office of Foreign Economic Affairs and send him or her an e-mail', I say. Well, says Ranveig, it would be a good thing if 'you went and spoke to the officer in charge'. The process, she seems to imply, should not be an anonymous one. Diplomats, it seems, believe in the face-to-face. Of course I take her advice. I draw up an outline of the speech, print several copies, make additional copies of the order slip and the note from the consulate in Hong Kong, check who is the officer in charge at Foreign Economic Affairs, call him to announce my arrival, and then walk the 300 metres of corridor from the Northern Building in Victoria Terrace, home of the three main buildings of the ministry, to the Southern Building, where the Foreign Economic Affairs Section is located. I have a chat with the officer in charge. Norway and its political community is a tight-knit affair; I have never met the man before, but it soon turns out that a friend of mine was once his colleague. We chat. 'When do you think you can send me the speech?', I say. 'I think I can manage a little something for you in the mail by tomorrow', he says. Two days later there is a brown pigeon-post envelope in my pigeonhole, containing half a page of text and a floppy disk. I sit down to write the speech, print it out, pick it up and head for the unit secretary. I have this speech here, I say, now what? 'Send it up to Harald', she says. Director General Harald J.'s office is located next to the rest of the unit's offices, but his pigeonhole sits on top of a vertical stack of pigeonholes. Even in sections where the pigeonholes are organised horizontally, with the director general's always to the far left, one 'sends up' drafts to be read through. The 'up' refers to social space, not necessarily to the physical world of offices or pigeonholes.

Harald knocks on my open door as he steps over the threshold, putting the speech on my desk. I scramble to my feet. 'This is fine', he says. 'Just send it over to the Asia adviser when it's finished.' Since it is the secretary who takes care of the practicalities when the speech is to be signed off, I take his meaning to be that I should walk the 200 metres over to the Middle Building and deliver the cover note, the speech and the floppy disk to the Asia adviser in person. We talk a little about something else, he leaves and I have a look at the draft, which he has annotated with a red pen. The corrections are what I would have called stylistic: word sequence, a certain weakening of the first person singular, an adjustment of a formulation about the expected 'HR' (human rights) situation after the transfer of Hong Kong to Beijing's jurisdiction. I decide simply to implement the suggested corrections, finish the speech, store it on the ministry's central disk drive and put the entire thing in the pigeon mail (this time I don't need to make a printout, because the secretary and I are among the younger generation in the ministry, who use its new intranet). The following day it is back in my pigeonhole all completed, I call the Asia adviser and announce my arrival, and then I walk the 150-metre corridor over to the Middle Building and up to the attic where the division of which he is a part is located. We talk a little about the possibility of a war between Taiwan and China and the consolidation of the regime after the generation shift in the Beijing leadership. He is going to accompany the royal couple, so I wish him a good trip. He thanks me for the speech. The following day I get a Norwegian-speaking but definitely English voice on the phone, she is calling from the translation office (which is situated in another part of town, which is to say that it is impractical for her to walk over and talk to me in person). No stylistic objections, she says, but there is an ambivalent point on page five. We resolve it, and the conversation comes to an end.

POST-SPEECH PUZZLES

The speech has been sent off and the job is done, but there are two things that bother me about the whole thing. Although I have been brought into the ministry to be an all-rounder, the economic sphere is my Achilles' heel as a political analyst, and one of the parts of the world I know least about is China. Seen in this light, the assignment seems to have been an odd one. I raise this in the canteen at lunch. At table with me is an old friend from university who is now a trusted civil servant, and a number of his office

colleagues. They all chuckle, and one of them says 'Welcome to the Foreign
Ministry, that's how it is for all of us. Here in the Foreign Service our role
model is that of the potato: we must be able to cover all needs and fit in with
everything. You see, you have to be a generalist.' When on later occasions I
mention to people from the Foreign Ministry, and also to foreign diplomats,
that my first experience of speech-writing came in an area where my expertise
was definitely at its weakest, they all react in a similar fashion.

The other thing that bothers me about the Hong Kong speech is the fact
that whereas the writing job itself – that is, the thinking and writing up – took
less than two hours, everything else taken together took around ten hours.
Counting input, reading, annotation, secretarial aid, etc., all in all it must
have taken the ministry around 30 hours to produce that little 20-minute
luncheon speech. I pour this out to Ranveig. She says this is a totally reasonable
and respectable allocation of resources. I ask her about the director general's
corrections – is it common to receive only stylistic corrections? She takes a
look at them and says, these are not only stylistic comments – human rights
is a sensitive area where it is important to be consistent. 'Yes', I say, 'but there
is not even a nuance of difference in meaning between the director general's
formulation and mine.' 'Perhaps not', replies Ranveig, 'but it is important that
the ministry sends consistent signals, and the director general's formulations
are more appropriate.'

So, although the speech is not what diplomats call 'operative' – meaning
it has no direct bearing on what they think of as day-to-day policy-making
– but rather a decorative speech, this distinction is not of the essence. For
all speeches, a number of genre demands seem to apply, and these demands
are part of that stock of shared practices that has been called the diplomatic
culture (Bull 1977; Der Derian 1996). I understand that the distinction I have
made between style and content does not necessarily apply as expected in my
current working environment. The point is rather that the text is diplomatic,
that is to say that it is adapted to the genre in general, and adapted to the
formulations that have been used previously about this cluster of issues in
particular. Writing a ministerial speech is something other than writing
an analytical political speech. In my previous work as an academic I had
of course been aware of this, in my capacity as a reader of such speeches,
but my awareness had always been directed towards finding new political
signals. Here I am instead working at a practical level (cf. Giddens 1984). It
is a question not of seeing but of doing, of achieving the opposite of newness,
that is, of learning the art of writing a speech so that it conforms to a series
of earlier greeting speeches, as well as to previous speeches on economic
relations with Hong Kong and relations with China, and to all former speeches
given by ministry personnel for that matter.

A few weeks later I come across a review of the speech in the Foreign
Ministry's daily press clippings, taken from a commercial magazine. When
I mention this at the morning meeting of the Planning Unit, however, I am
surprised to find that no one is interested.

TRANSNATIONAL ALLOCATIONS OF SPEECH-WRITING

A couple of weeks later the director general, the higher executive officer of the unit and I are on our way to London to have political talks with the Planning Unit of the British Foreign Office. 'Political talks' is an informal institution, which recurs at several different levels, whether at a political level between ministers, state secretaries or occasionally even between political advisers, the heads of departments, or, as in this case, between the heads of the planning units. One meets to discuss affairs in general. Still, a list of more or less specific topics for discussion is often prepared in advance. The existence of a series of such informal institutions is yet another reason why specialists on international politics routinely talk about the existence of 'diplomatic culture' (see Eriksen and Neumann 1993). In addition to discussions on current political affairs, talks at the civil service level present themselves as occasions for colleagues to exchange experiences where organisational planning is concerned. As a general institution of diplomacy, the planning unit came into existence after the Second World War, when the British Foreign Office and also the US State Department decided to resume the planning they had carried out in order to win the peace, but now in a more general form (Rostow 1964). Through political talks, among other things, the idea spread to the foreign ministries of other countries. The establishment of the Planning Unit in the Norwegian Foreign Ministry in 1973 was thus part of a trend. In a sense, the three of us from the Planning Unit in the Norwegian Foreign Ministry are on our way to visit the Mother Institution. The practices of a Ministry of Foreign Affairs not only emerge within a specific state apparatus, for the MFA is not only a ministry amongst other state ministries, it is also part of a series of world MFAs. This series is the site of a continuous and constitutive flow of ideas, norms and practices. As the example of the establishment of departments of planning demonstrates, innovation is most often diffused from a hegemonic centre to other units in the series, but there also exist examples of flows having taken other courses. While these flows are of course transnational, their specific *intergovernmental* character should be stressed. There is no lack of examples of institutional transnational flows that involve other units (the introduction of electronic communication being a recent case in point), but the major flow is state-to-state.

At the time I gave this conversation little thought – in retrospect I think this was probably because at that point I first and foremost directed my attention towards how the contradictions between the various parts of the Foreign Ministry were reflected in the most minute of details. Thus I understood both the British 'we' and the Norwegian '*vi*' as referring to the planning units, in opposition to 'the others' in the ministry and in particular to the Department of Public Relations in the British Foreign Office and the Secretariat in the Norwegian Foreign Ministry. In accordance with both political science theory about 'bureaucratic infighting' (Allison 1971) and Michael Herzfeld's (1992) emphasis of the 'interests' of various bureaucratic units, I saw the worry of the planners over the loss of the speeches as yet another turf battle between the various parts of an organisation. However, like all pronouns, 'we' is what linguists call a 'shifter', which means that what it signifies depends entirely upon context. In light of what occurred later on, I wonder whether the 'we' in the talks with British Policy Planning should not rather be understood as the ministries in their aspect of unitary bureaucracies, as distinguished from the political leadership and their 'spin doctors' (that is to say the advisers who are specialists at pitching things at the media) and party political leadership.

THE SPEECH AS MINISTERIAL VOICE

This thought first occurred to me when I was working on another speech a month later. The speech-writing tasks were increasingly distributed by Principal Officer Hallgrim S. in the Secretariat of the foreign minister, who had contacted my director general to inquire about whether the Planning Unit could write a speech which the Foreign Minister was to give to the employees of the Department of Press, Culture and Information.

At the Planning Unit's morning meeting, my director general asked whether I would like to write the speech. I was a little startled. The foreign minister is a career diplomat, and is going to give a speech to colleagues whom he mostly knows personally. Nonetheless the task of writing the speech is not given to his Secretariat, but to the Planning Unit. This does not conform to the notion of 'turf battles'. In order to write such a speech well, one would need a certain familiarity with the information habits of the Norwegian MFA. One would also need to know something about the web of relations and the flows of information between the minister and the section in question. Since it would be bad taste for the section to write a self-congratulatory speech, the logical place for it to be hatched would be the ministry's Secretariat. The Planning Unit is a less likely choice. And since I was among those, both in the Planning Unit and perhaps even in all the ministry, who had least experience in the field, I was a downright unlikely choice. Still, I accept the offer, but add that it might be best for number two in the unit, my mentor Ranveig S., to supervise my work. This is accepted. My first draft is an account of how public relations units came into existence as a part of the democratisation of diplomacy in the wake of the First World War, how one goes about image-building, how the point is to get the population in one's own country and the elites and populations of other countries to accept the representations or 'pictures' of Norway that the Public Relations Section produces. Ranveig and I sit down together for the rewrite, we tighten it up and fill it in, and then we sign it off. However, a few days later we hear that the foreign minister put our draft aside as 'too analytic', and instead gave a loosely prepared feel-good speech. This is a format at which the foreign minister excels. A few weeks later I am present at the annual Christmas party for members of the Foreign Ministry chapter of the academics' trade union. There the foreign

minister gives a dazzling feel-good speech, notwithstanding that this is his
fourth speech that day.

This incident taught me a bit more about speech-writing in the ministry. Not
even feel-good speeches are treated as the minister's, or even the Secretariat's,
own portfolio. Every speech concerns the entire ministry, regardless of
form, place of delivery, etc. Furthermore, when it comes to the question of
authorship, special competence for the task at hand is not of the essence,
and even if people with such competence are at hand, it does not mean that
normal procedures for speech-writing are set aside. To this one may add that
speed and efficiency are less important than observance of right procedure,
for a later incident illustrates how it is first and foremost politicians, and not
the Foreign Ministry's own people, who treat speeches as something that
must be produced in a flurry. Half a year after the incident with the feel-
good speech, when I and a number of colleagues were on vacation, one of
the state secretaries found herself in acute need of a speech on the Foreign
Office and cultural promotion. Consequently, her Secretariat in the shape
of Hallgrim tipped her off that there might be something in the Planning
Unit's archive. The speech was excavated and given, clearly as an emergency
solution. The state secretary herself was, I later heard from the Secretariat,
greatly satisfied with the speech, but I had the feeling that Hallgrim and
the Secretariat only accepted this procedure as an emergency solution. The
unease that was caused, both by the genesis of this speech and also, on other
occasions, when a speech was simply fished out and given without being
hatched specifically for the purpose, constituted an analytical challenge for
me. This unease showed that from the diplomat's perspective it was not the
quality of the speech as judged by the political leadership that was decisive
– although that was what everybody said when you asked them what the
main criterion was for judging speeches. Also, this incident demonstrated
that there were other things than turf battles at stake. There was a different
logic in the ministerial writing process, in addition to the desire to produce
things that the political leadership would be satisfied with, and the desire to
be better than the other diplomats at doing so. What was that?

NEGLECT OF AUDIENCE, NEGLECT OF ANALYSIS

The thought that first struck me was that this must have to do with the
difference in the degree of audience receptivity. The striking thing about
the conversation in London had been that neither the Norwegian nor the
British diplomats had any time for the argument that one had to start work
on a speech by thinking about the audience. This could not be due to an
entirely general insensitivity to the importance of targeting the speech at the
audience, as shown by the incidents within the ministry, when the foreign
minister chose to give a feel-good speech rather than an analytic speech
for his employees in the Office of Public Relations, and when, in spite of
an overwhelming workload, he chose to tailor-make his own speech for the

annual Christmas party. Could there be a partial insensitivity to audience demand, which only applied to non-diplomats? No, diplomats themselves spend much time as audiences for the speeches of other foreign ministries and institutions, when they participate in various meetings, and in particular when they are posted abroad and their main task is to follow and report on the development of the politics of the host country. 'The speeches were mostly of the Merry Christmas and Happy New Year type', as it was put with an uncharacteristic lack of discretion in a report from a foreign posting. As a segment of an audience, diplomats are (at least) as irritated as others by lack of sensitivity to the audience.

When a new opportunity to participate arose, I grabbed it with both hands. This time it was the Foreign Ministry's main speech in a Norwegian context, the annual foreign policy account to Parliament (for a discussion of this other state locus, see the chapter by Marit Melhuus in this volume). Principal Officer Hallgrim S. in the Secretariat had given it to the Planning Unit, and the director general of the Planning Unit had delegated it to me. I suggested and had it accepted by both the Secretariat and my own unit that we should try to structure the speech around a uniting narrative, so that the speech itself would transmit a clear message. If things were done in this fashion, the ensuing speech would stand in stark contrast to previous speeches of this type. Having gone through the dossier where they were kept, I noted with confidence that they were indistinguishable from one another and from other types of text the ministry produced, such as notes and white papers. So, with the aim of breaking this invariance, I set to work. I asked for input from the Offices, read the statement of purpose that had been put forth by the current governmental coalition upon their accession to power, as well as the previous speeches of the ministry's political leadership. I found that the two topics that kept recurring in the most recent documents were values and globalisation. On this basis I decided to structure the entire speech around the notion of 'ethical globalisation'. This would allow me to include most of the topics and ideas that the various sections had come up with, but in different forms that I could relate to the government's main message about the importance of values and the insistence of the foreign minister that Norway maintain a high ethical profile in its foreign policy. I submitted the draft to the morning meeting in the Planning Unit, and proceeded to tone down and edit in response to criticism. Then I passed it on to Hallgrim S. in the Secretariat.

Two weeks later the phone rang. Hallgrim told me that the foreign minister had brought the draft along on two trips, but that he had only had time to read it the preceding day. When he had reached page two and the introduction of the term 'ethical globalisation', he had put the speech aside as being too analytical. The question was whether I could write a new draft more similar to previous speeches? I said I would discuss this with my director general. So I went and knocked on his door. 'We had to expect this', he said. 'This is not how things have been done before.' 'Alright', I said, 'but perhaps it would be wise if somebody else in the unit completed the task, so that we are certain that we hit that ministerial slant.' So it went. The minister went to Parliament and made a speech similar to the accounts of previous years. The speech did not start a debate in the press or in the foreign policy milieu, and the country's main broadsheet, *Aftenposten*, noted in an editorial that there was nothing new in the speech. I never heard this commented on in the ministry, and when I cautiously tried to get people in the canteen to express an opinion on the comment in *Aftenposten*, it was shrugged off. The negative reception of the speech was simply not an interesting conversation topic. I had managed to confirm that analysis was unimportant in the Foreign Ministry system, that the audience's reception was of little or no interest to the ministry and that the established patterns were difficult to break, but I had learned little else.

It was difficult for me to deal with the ministry's disavowal of analysis. When I let go of the annual account to Parliament, and thus the possibility to learn more about how a speech gets a more ministerial slant, it was not least because I experienced this as equal to excluding the analytical aspect. I chose to let go of it because I already had another speech on the books, the Johan Jørgen Holst memorial lecture. Instituted to honour a previous foreign minister, former speeches had been given by Henry Kissinger and the world's leading military historian, Sir Michael Howard. The memorial speech was to be published in an academic journal and delivered to an audience of researchers and international diplomats. This time, I thought, an analytical perspective must after all be inevitable? I wrote a draft of which the purpose was to display a number of contradictions in Norwegian security policy after the Cold War, trace the causes back to the uneven adaptation of various aspects of our defence and security policy to the new geopolitical situation, and announce a few moves that might reduce the tensions within the policy and make it seem more proactive. After a discussion in the Planning Unit I once again sent a draft to the Secretariat.

ALWAYS REPEAT

This time I had a response within a few hours. The draft had happened to end up in the hands of the ministry's assistant secretary general in charge of security policy. When he had finished reading it, he had immediately walked over to Hallgrim S. in the Secretariat, and said that he had 'almost had angina pectoris' from reading the draft. 'Alright', I said, 'what happens now?' Hallgrim's response to the ranking security officer had been to suggest a meeting in his office the following day, with someone from the Security Policy Section, himself and me. The director general of the Department of Security Policy and a couple of his closest colleagues attended the meeting. It turned out that the department had two main objections to my draft. First, a lack of detailed information about developments in certain sub-areas, both their own and areas that were the responsibility of other sections of the ministry. Second, the direct language. In spite of having thought that I had learned that diplomats think of style as content and an indirect approach as a virtue, still my draft was too direct. I immediately succumbed to this, but as far as the details were concerned I decided to go for a confrontation. 'Who needs that information in this context?' I asked, and pointed out that the audience would be coming in order to get an overview of the situation and the general drift of the plans. We needed an eagle's view from above, and not a snake's view from below. 'No', was the answer, it was not possible to give a speech on Norwegian security without mentioning the importance of the US security guarantee, nuclear waste in the North, etc. If such things were not mentioned, it would be a signal that they were not given priority.

So, the policy had to be repeated, if not it would be weakened. This is of course an entirely valid argument. It takes hard discursive work to keep things as they are (Garfinkel 1967). Making the world seem to be stable when it is in fact in constant flux, means that having power among other things involves having the ability to freeze meaning. This has to be done by constantly repeating specific representations of things, actions and identities, until what one repeats is naturalised to such an extent that it appears doxic (Bourdieu 1972). One can only refrain from repeating representations if they are already embedded in other representations that are repeated, so that they are confirmed indirectly. That was not the case on this occasion, so I did not feel that I could argue against the need to repeat the policy in general. Instead I argued that it would be a closed forum for the informed, and that spending a lot of time on repeating the official line would be an ineffective way of spending resources. We should rather concentrate on saying something that would catch the interest of an audience consisting of academics and foreign diplomats, and I thought that would be something conceptual. This was rejected. It was not the 'conceptual', but the 'operational' that interested diplomats, and that should therefore be at the centre.

This was also an unassailable argument. I was being made subject to diplomatic identity-building, according to the formula that 'you academics' concentrate on the conceptual, while 'we diplomats' concentrate on the operative. Thereafter the context of the speech was defined as being merely incidentally and quite unconsequentially an academic arena; it was defined as being mainly a diplomatic arena. The space I had created for my innovative moves had thus effectively been erased. I said that I had written the speech on the basis of the idea that the conceptual would be the main thing in a speech to academics, but that the speech would obviously have to be written differently if it were written with a different function in mind. The director general leaned forward and said, 'The draft is interesting enough, it is impressive that anyone would make an attempt at such a thing.' The meeting died away, and I was asked to coordinate the rest of the speech, even though Hallgrim would be far better placed for the task. The meeting was resolved, but Hallgrim started a conversation with me about something else, and when the two other participants had left, he said smiling: 'We might have avoided the risk of sick leave if we had polished the first draft a little.'

I headed down the corridor for my own office. So if Hallgrim and I had sat down and polished the text before it had reached the assistant secretary general, both the risk of angina pectoris and the need for clarifying meetings would have been less. What was most interesting was the way the conflict had been handled: as soon as it was clear that the result would be what the assistant secretary general had decided, consensus-building and the re-establishment of collegial harmony were the main objectives. Instead of going straight to my own office, I knocked on my mentor Ranveig's door and told her the story, and also my own reflections on it. 'Is it not this inclination towards consensus that eliminates the space for creativity and debate in the ministry?', I asked. 'Well, is it better up at Blindern [the university campus], where people don't speak to each other at all?' came the reply. No, I said, but in this case the result will be a less good speech. 'It is important for everyone to be in on it, so that we get a speech that the entire ministry may stand for,' said Ranveig S.

At the following morning meeting I gave my account of the issue. The director general slumped back in his seat and said that now the fate of another initiative taken by the unit, in which we depended on the goodwill of the Department of Security Policy, was open to doubt. No more was said about the speech, but I had finally found an answer to my question about what this 'other' was that makes audience reception subsidiary when speeches are written in the Foreign Ministry. Of course the Foreign Ministry has a need to inform. It would be incorrect to claim that the Foreign Ministry is uninterested in the speeches it writes. But in addition to this there is a powerful imperative that says that the entire ministry should be comfortable with what is written in the name of the ministry. The tougher the fight, the more important the need to participate in the mutual preening of ruffled feathers afterwards, not only in order to maintain the outward appearance of unity, but also to maintain the collective capacity to act in unity. This is not specific to foreign ministries, but also seems to go for a number of other state organisations where unity is seen as being of the essence. For example, from Khrushchev's time onwards, historians have highlighted a clear tendency to hand the responsibility for implementing a joint decision to those who had been the most opposed to it. Such a practice would have been impossible within a modern foreign ministry; as a functionally divided organisation, its flexibility would not suffice. But exactly since such alternative integrative practices are not available, the mutual preening of feathers becomes that much more important. The fact that in this case it was the director general who emphasised how one turf battle might affect the next one, while it was the assistant director general who emphasised consensus, is in principle incidental. In no way was it due to a lack of awareness of the importance of turf battles on the part of the assistant director general. Only a few weeks before our conversation she came to me to ask about something in connection with a speech she herself was writing, and told me that 'Only an hour after Hallgrim had sent the draft to that Office they were at his door complaining, but he has become so accustomed to it that he simply ignores them.' The point is that by getting caught up in the importance of these turf battles, as I did when I wrote my first speeches, I missed all the other mechanisms that delimit how deep, comprehensive and decisive diplomats let these turf battles become. The expectations inculcated by a training in political science had blinded me to a lot of other things that were also going on.

When I had discovered this, I suddenly remembered how a diplomat friend once joked that he and his colleagues never fell out with one other, for it might well happen that they would end up as the only two Norwegian civil servants posted to Abidjan (most Norwegian posts have only two career diplomats). It struck me that there was no logical reason why this integrative and conflict-evasive way of organising speech-writing should only apply between diplomats who work in different offices, but that it most likely also applies within each office. That, after all, was the case in my own unit. One way of finding out about whether this also held true for other parts of the ministry would be to inquire about how the writing of the new parts of the Holst memorial speech were going in the Department of Security Policy. So the next time I saw somebody I knew in the Security Policy Section, I asked him how much time it had taken to write the speech, and who had done it. He estimated the section's work on the speech at about 22 hours: he himself had spent eight hours on it, X had written about one field and Y about another, Z had written a few bits and the director general had read through the entire draft twice. The section as such had thus followed the same model as the ministry as a whole: everyone who was seen as having a claim to chime in had been invited to do so.

This mode of working takes time. The next time I met Hallgrim S., I asked him to give an estimate of how long the ministry as a whole had worked on the foreign minister's speech. He put the efforts of his colleagues and himself at about 40 hours, the foreign minister's at about three, that of the entire ministry at about 120 hours, 'and in addition there are section meetings and canteen talk'. As far as the larger speeches are concerned, it is thus not only metaphorically that the entire ministry stands behind them.

CONCLUSIONS

The fact that, during 15 years as a reader of politician's speeches prior to my stint in the Foreign Ministry, I had not thought about the complexity of the genesis of speeches, speaks volumes about how isolated from the microphysics of power one in fact is as an academic, even when one is seemingly in constant interaction with practitioners. It also says a good deal about the advantage of participant observation as a form of data collection about social processes, and about the enormous advantages of researchers who have personal experience of the field they are researching. Those who know a little about practical politics know that the foreign minister's speeches seldom can be read as the result of a simple tug of war. They are also the result of a process in which different points of view and emphases are patched together in a manner that everyone can live with.

It is the task of a Foreign Ministry, which by definition consists of widely different units, to join together in a higher unity in such a way that the seams between them come to be as invisible as possible. Each section mediates in relation to various human collectives outside the ministry. If a foreign ministry is to maintain its unity, as must each and every organisation, it must maintain its own integrative processes. In the case of the Norwegian MFA, speech-writing turned out to be one such process. It is among other things because speech-writing is so important as a common ministerial concern that informing and convincing the audience of the message in each speech is not held to be important. Speech-writing is first and foremost a question of ministerial identity-building. Information and argumentation is important enough, but the organisation's self-confirmation and the cementation of working relations between each part of the organisation and between each employee are of greater importance. When ministerial employees returned from speech-writing courses, they related that the lecturer – whether it was an employee of the Prime Minister's Office or an American professional speech-writer – had emphasised the unity of the speech, and that it can only be unitary if there is one person who supervises its writing and has the final say. The expression for this is that one person should 'sit on the lap of the minister' (that is, have his ear). The American president has a crew of speech-writers consisting of a domestic and a foreign section. While Roosevelt gave around 80 speeches a year, Clinton averaged about 500, and thus he found it necessary to leave the writing to a dozen employees who worked directly for him, independently of the State Department. In the British Foreign and Commonwealth Office, since the foreign secretary made the speeches part of his political arsenal, they have also been torn away from the bureaucracy. If a future Norwegian foreign minister were to insist that the speeches he or she were to give should first and foremost be politically effective in relation to domestic and foreign political groupings, then the Norwegian Foreign Ministry would also have to give up its speech-writing procedures. As noted above, this has already happened in the case of the British Foreign Office. It has also happened in a number of other Norwegian ministries. To an increasing degree, it even happens in the Secretariat of the human rights minister within the Foreign Ministry itself. These developments, however, seem to have no effect on how speech-writing proceeds inside the (rest of) the Norwegian Ministry of Foreign Affairs. One may conclude that, as long as diplomats take care of speech-writing, the speeches will continue to look like the Foreign Ministry's notes and white papers, for the simple reason that all such types of text are produced in the same manner. They are all texts that the entire ministry may stand for, and thus they are not first and foremost expressions of the points of view of particular politicians or instantiations of particular fields, but instantiations of the ministry as such.

When the entire ministry can stand behind a speech, it is because the speech *is* the ministry. In his chapter, Cris Shore stresses the role of well-known symbols of state formation such as flags, anthems, etc. When viewed from a particular locus such as a state ministry, the list of working state symbols appears to be considerably longer. The ethnographic material presented here also brings out how, in order to stay in business, even a well-established state like the Norwegian one must perpetually go about the discursive work of polishing those symbols and fighting for their relevance. The ministry exists, among other things, because it purports to speak in one voice, and it is therefore important that this voice rings as unequivocally, as often and as clearly as possible. That is why the number of speeches that are not written by the entire ministry is minimised, and notes that have no place in the bureaucratic scale are weeded out. As long as the politicians themselves do not intervene, nothing new will emanate from the Foreign Ministry. From the point of view of the bureaucrat, it is thus only when the system *does not work* that something new is produced, because the fact that something new is produced means precisely that the system has failed. Civil servants in the Foreign Ministry do not find this paradoxical. On the contrary, they see it as evidence that the civil service is functioning as it is supposed to. To many people on the outside it is a mystery why the Foreign Ministry never produces anything new, when by continuing as previously, one increasingly and undeniably loses out in the competition with other policy generators. Nonetheless, because of the structure of its discourse, the Foreign Ministry will continue to produce speeches that the entire ministry can stand for until the political leadership forces through greater audience-targeting by changing the routines for writing speeches. The change can only come from the outside. If the Norwegian Foreign Ministry follows the British Foreign Office in this question, the reaction of the diplomats to any change will probably constitute no more than a lament that the old *modus operandi* is being abandoned. The question of whether there are in fact exogenous reasons for such a change of routine, would probably go undiscussed. The British example indicates that diplomats do not learn lessons in this regard, but rather rest content with lamenting the loss of the speech-writing function.

Contrary to Durkheim's conception of the state/society nexus, the state does not give guidance to society. It speaks in its own voice, into thin air. It is only when politicians explicitly and specifically drown out the ministerial voice and let their own voice ring out that we may talk about speech-making as a society-oriented practice. Contrary to Mitchell's conception of the state as biomass (1999), what we have here is an untidy reality of disjointed groups of people who come together as a body not by dint of its biomass, but by dint of voice. Mitchell is right to stress the larger-than-life quality of the state, though, for the voice is being listened to not because it interpellates subjects, but because those subjects already assume that it comes from somewhere important. And, contrary to Weber's conception, the state appears monolithic to society not because it follows certain impersonal, rational and standardised routines. Its routine speech-making is highly personal. To Weber, rationality in this context seems to have meant effective maximisation of gain in relation to society. Far from being rational in this sense, I have demonstrated that speech-making is irrational, in the sense that society or societal groups do not even appear to be its target. Furthermore, speech-writing is certainly standardised, but this standardisation is exactly what accounts for its character of being a celebration of a state self, rather than a rational practice in the Weberian sense.

May we conclude that the state does not exist? We certainly may not. By dint of being a reality studio, the state is as real as any other collective actor. There is no reason whatsoever not to treat it as a social fact. Neither is there any reason to doubt its capacity to act once it is mobilised. In these cases, however, such mobilisation did not take place, even when there was a societal demand for it. In these cases, the Ministry of Foreign Affairs functioned as just another contingent organisation. My conclusion is a negative one. Change is not generated from within this particular state institution. It has to come from without, and if not *from* above, then at least *via* above. Attempts to change the *modus operandi* of a state organ from within may simply be eliminated by the very ordering of existing discursive practices. Only politicians may initiate change that may, if pressure is hard and consistent, change the discursive order. When it comes to presentation of self in everyday life, the state seems to respond to society only via its politicians.

NOTES

1. I should like to thank the editors, Thomas Hylland Eriksen and Jim Scott for comments.
2. Based on previous work on Norwegian state-building (cf. Neumann 2002), I would also stick to this as a general view.

REFERENCES

Allison, G., 1971. *Essence of Decision: Explaining the Cuban Missile Crisis.* New York: Scott, Foresman.

Bourdieu, P., 1972. *Esquisse d'une théorie de la pratique, précédé de trois études d'ethnologie kabyle.* Genève: Droz.

Bull, H., 1977. *The Anarchical Society: A Study of Order in World Politics.* London: Macmillan.

Der Derian, J., 1996. 'Hedley Bull and the Idea of Diplomatic Culture', pp. 84–100, in R. Fawn and J. Larkins, eds, *International Society after the Cold War: Anarchy and Order Reconsidered.* Basingstoke: Macmillan.

Durkheim, E., 1996. *Professional Ethics and Civil Morals*, 2nd edn. London: Routledge.

Eriksen, T.H. and I.B. Neumann, 1993. 'International Relations as a Cultural System: An Agenda for Research', *Cooperation and Conflict*, 28(3): 233–64.

Garfinkel, H., 1967. *Studies in Ethnomethodology.* Englewood Cliffs, NJ: Prentice-Hall.

Giddens, A., 1984. *The Constitution of Society: Outline of the Theory of Structuration.* Cambridge: Polity.

Herzfeld, M., 1992. *The Social Production of Indifference: Exploring the Symbolic Roots of Western Bureaucracy*. New York: Berg.

Mitchell, T., 1999. 'Society, Economy and the State Effect', pp. 76–97, in G. Steinmetz, ed., *State/Culture: State-Formation after the Cultural Turn*. Ithaca, NY: Cornell University Press.

Neumann, I., 2002. 'This Little Piggy Stayed at Home: Why Norway is Not a Member of the EU', pp. 88–129 in L. Hansen and O. Waever, eds, *European Integration and National Identity. The Challenge of the Nordic States*. London: Routledge.

Rostow, W.W., 1964. 'The Planning of Foreign Policy', pp. 41–55, in E.A.J. Johnson, ed., *The Dimensions of Diplomacy*. Baltimore, MD: Johns Hopkins University Press.

10 'BETTER SAFE THAN SORRY': LEGISLATING ASSISTED CONCEPTION IN NORWAY

Marit Melhuus

LEGISLATION – AN ETHNOGRAPHIC SITE

In the introduction to their book *States of Imagination*, Hansen and Stepputat (2001) suggest that in order to study the state one should study 'how the state tries to make itself real and tangible through symbols, texts, and iconography ... and study how the state appears in everyday and localized forms' (2001: 5). They propose that the state be studied from '"the field" in the sense of localized ethnographic sites' (2001: 5). In what follows I will explore aspects of the state by examining a specific legislation and its concomitant legislative process. These two phenomena constitute my ethnographic site. The legislation in question is that which concerns the regulation of new reproductive technologies and assisted conception in Norway.[1]

Although it is true that international conventions are increasingly impinging on national legislation, with the aim of harmonising regulations, in the case of assisted conception it is the variations in regulations and provisions that are symptomatic. Within Europe, for example, Italy has (until very recently) had no legislation whatsoever, Spain has a very liberal legislation and the Nordic countries vary as to what the law provides, Norway being the most restrictive Denmark the most permissive.[2] A central characteristic of the Norwegian legislative processes with regard to assisted conception is the explicit will to govern. In matters relating to biotechnology applied to human beings, state intervention was deemed necessary. On this question there was no disagreement in Parliament. The disagreements concerned the extent of the regulation, that is, the content of the law. I will return to this below.

There is no doubt that states make themselves visible and felt through legislation (for a different tack on legislation and its profound effects, see Baitenmann on Mexican agrarian reform, this volume). Hence, I would argue that national legislation may articulate national concerns, and that legislative processes represent an interesting ethnography for exploring the attributed meanings, limits and articulations of the state. As such, legislation and laws represent key institutions as well as institutional practices. They are not only techniques of governance, but also embody the very language of stateness (to use Hansen and Stepputat's phrase) and, by implication, the mythical quality of the state as something abstract, above and beyond the mundane routines of everyday life. Yet not only are laws (routinely) made by people in specific positions, they also have direct implications for people's lives. As Mitchell indicates, the details of a legal process 'all of which are particular social practices, are arranged to produce the effect that the law exists as a formal framework, superimposed above social practice' (1999: 90). Legislative processes are therefore interesting both in what they articulate or disclose and in what they produce.

In what follows, my focus is primarily on processes that occur within government, that is, within what is perceived as part of the workings of the state apparatus. Analytically, my approach is twofold. On the one hand I am interested in the making of the law, as well as its specific content. This implies examining a series of events and social practices, ideas and values informing the law, including motivation, culminating with the vote in Parliament. On the other hand, I am interested in the effect of the law (and the legislative process), not only as producing a framework but also as generating a moral universe, the boundaries of which coincide with those of the nation-state. Obviously, these two processes occur simultaneously; that is part of the point I wish to make. However, by introducing an analytical distinction between practices and effect, it is possible to trace how practices that create a formal framework (in this case a law) at the same time create a moral state which in turn projects an image of its morality, recreating a world-view which glosses the contradictions intrinsic to its very creation. This position presumes that the practices themselves are understood as morally embedded.

However, not all legislation will have the same effect. It may well be that the case that I bring to the table is especially revealing due to the very nature of the matter at hand. New reproductive technologies are evocative in ways that perhaps other subjects of legislation would not be. They broach ontological, epistemological and ethical issues. Hence, the boundaries produced by the law are at once both moral and territorial. They make visible the limits of accepted practices within the field of assisted conception. The very explicitness of these limits also makes visible the potentiality of transgression. Paradoxically, another effect of the legislation is to confine the range of individual agency and choice regarding matters of conception within the Norwegian state, while simultaneously encouraging subversive practices: people travel abroad to obtain the treatment otherwise prohibited in Norway. In some ways the law – and its making – can be seen as a sociocultural space where specific moral limits are made explicit and are transformed into policy. The stakes are high as the elements involved not only go to the core of the liberal state and its dilemma (individual freedom vs state control) but also strike at the very cords of life itself and what it is that creates meaningful relationships. These have to do with such things as the status of the embryo, the question of rights, the significance attributed to biogenetic bonds, the issue of knowledge production and competence-building, and questions related to the public health system.

It was the rapid development in biomedicine and biotechnologies that prompted the legislators to act, lest matters get out of hand. However, it does not follow from a general agreement about the need to regulate that the law must necessarily be restrictive. Moreover, it is an open question whether the restrictions that were put in place can be understood in terms of the nature of the issues at hand (e.g. that egg donation breaks fundamentally with Norwegian understandings of motherhood) or whether the restrictive laws reflect a very guarded attitude to new technologies and developments in science (see Halvorsen 1998 whose arguments tend toward the latter). Nevertheless, the law regulating assisted conception can be seen to both challenge and reflect the moral basis of the liberal order as understood by (a majority of) Norwegian politicians, not only projecting a particular kind of society (where there is room for all, see discussion below) but also underscoring the significance of the individual unequivocally located in a heterosexual family, allowing no room for doubt about what constitutes the basic family relations. To this end, the meanings of biogenetic bonding and child rights were evoked. The law was passed on the basis of a precautionary principle – 'better safe than sorry' – which was explicitly iterated, subsumed under an overarching concern for ethics. The law not only affects the involuntary childless and their options, but also those researchers and medical practitioners involved in issues of infertility.

The issues I want to examine are complex, as are the varying sources and data they are based on. There is not one thread that can easily be followed to a logical conclusion. However, my hope is to be able to indicate some clusters of concerns that this legislation addresses directly or indirectly which will throw light on ways the state is conceptualised and projected. As mentioned, the Norwegian law regulating assisted conception is one of the most restrictive in Europe. This is in itself an interesting datum worth exploring. Moreover those involved in making – and passing – the law looked upon it as an exceptional case. Finally, the provisions in the law are revealing insofar as they articulate fundamental values in Norwegian society while at the same time indicating central points of contention.

A PROCREATIVE UNIVERSE

My overall topic is procreation and my field of inquiry has been what I have called a procreative universe. My ethnography is based on research in Norway and my case explores issues related to assisted conception. Over the past few years, I have traced the different social fields that in one way or another comprise or feed into the phenomenon of assisted conception. This has included fieldwork and interviews among the involuntary childless, interviews with various experts on infertility or related issues (such as practising medical doctors, bureaucrats, biologists, bio-engineers, bio-ethicists, etc.); visits to infertility clinics and a sperm bank; attending public hearings organised by the Biotechnology Council as well as parliamentary debates. It has also included collating a vast amount of documents as well as media coverage (from the 1950s onwards) of what might loosely be termed 'infertility events'.[3]

In the course of this (field)work I have also interviewed former and present members of Parliament who have been central spokespersons on issues related to assisted conception (12 in all). They are former ministers of health and members of Parliament who have sat on the Social Affairs Committee of the Norwegian Parliament ('Sosialkomitéen') in the periods when the laws regulating assisted conception have been passed. As members of Parliament, they have had the possibility of direct and explicit influence on the shaping of policy through their involvement in the making of relevant legislation. These are by virtue of their position powerful people who also acknowledge the influence they have had on its making. Thus, in addition to the information that can be found by examining the official records, my present account takes into specific consideration the personal and subjective views of politicians who have in some way been involved in the making of this law.

These interviews were carried out in 2001–02, years after the 'original' events (the laws were passed in 1987 and 1994), yet at a time when proposals for a new law were being discussed. Some of those interviewed were no longer 'in politics' and others were actively engaged in other issues. Hence, I was asking them to recall a time and process which was not necessarily at the top of their agenda. The value of these accounts lies not in their historical accuracy – or a person's ability to remember correctly – but rather in what they project of personal involvement, ideas and reflections on a turbulent political issue with reverberations down to this day. The interviews convey self-perceptions regarding influence on the outcome, as well as the atmosphere surrounding the debates (be it in Parliament or in the committee). These interviews are also revealing with respect to issues of contention and to grasp the perceived need to regulate – that is, the sense of urgency that prevailed. By focusing on the thinking of these central decision-makers, I hope to convey some of the explicit (and implicit) reasons for why the law took the shape it did.

Procreative practices do not merely reflect personal decisions relegated to the domestic and intimate spheres of social life. As basic elements in processes of social reproduction, they address broader aspects of the social order. Thus, they are a public concern with political implications. This is the case whether attention is directed at local meanings/practices of gender, marriage, descent, inheritance or whether it is the more general problematic of demography and population control that is being addressed.

In this context, I am concerned with a very specific instance of family planning – that which faces the involuntary childless the moment they decide to take specific action to overcome their infertility. This planning involves the active engagement of various other agents and agencies in order to succeed. The procreative world of the involuntary childless involves scientific knowledge, technologies, advanced and specialised practitioners, often foreign donor substances, in short extensive and expensive treatments often based on methods and research many of which are not permitted in Norway. It is access to this procreative universe that the law seeks to regulate. In its actuality and its potentiality, this procreative universe kindles and provokes the imagination of many people, reflecting a broad public concern and dissonant values. It has opened up what many perceive as a private and intimate sphere of their lives to extensive public scrutiny.

Assisted conception is not talked about in terms of either demography or family planning. Yet it has become a concern of state affairs, not only in Norway. The uses of biotechnology for assisted conception are perceived to raise profound ethical questions, and as a political issue, they are placed over and above the ordinary realm of politics. This is at least a perception held in Norway (see also Warnock Committee 1985; Brekke 1995; Fox [1993] 1997; Franklin 1997, esp. ch. 2; Sirnes 1997). This has to do with the fact that practices of assisted conception involving new reproductive technologies (NRT) have fundamentally challenged basic assumptions about nature, upsetting 'the natural order of things'.[4] The questions that these technologies and their accompanying practices raise go to the core of basic values in Norwegian society, involving such fundamental notions as the natural, motherhood, identity, rights as well as ideas about development, technology, control, the role of research and the role of government. Moreover, the law itself reveals tensions inherent to the liberal state: putting in place regulations which curb individual freedom and choice in matters as personal as the way one chooses to have – or make – a baby.

THE LAW – IN BRIEF

Norway passed its first law regulating assisted conception in 1987. This law was also among the first in the world. A precondition for passing the law was that the government would continue its work on these issues. Hence, in 1994, a revised proposal (the Act Relating to the Application of Biotechnology in Medicine) was put before Parliament. With this Act, assisted conception came under the same law as other medical biotechnological procedures. Yet again, Parliament stipulated that the law be evaluated after five years. But it was not until 2002 that new proposals for revising the law were put forward and these were passed in 2003.

The Act of 1994 permits sperm donation by anonymous donor, but does not permit the donation of ova; it only permits treatment of heterosexual couples (married or cohabiting); it does not permit the combination of *in vitro* fertilisation (IVF) with donor sperm. Embryos cannot be stored for more than three years and storage of oocytes is prohibited. Research on embryos is prohibited, as is the use of techniques 'aimed at the production of genetically identical individuals' (chapter 3 a, section 3a–1). The Act also includes provisions on primary sex selection, pre-implantation and prenatal diagnosis as well as genetic testing after birth and gene therapy (chapters 2, 4–7). Only clinics authorised by the government may give assisted conception treatment.

The latest revisions to the law include rescinding the anonymity of the sperm donor; permission for the storage of oocytes; the extension of the period of storage of embryos (from three to five years). The other restrictions will be upheld, most notably the prohibition on egg donation; the limiting of treatment to heterosexual couples; as well as the ban on research on embryos.

The preamble to the law of 1994 states that:

> ... the purpose of this law is to ensure that the application of biotechnology in medicine is utilised in the best interest of human beings in a society where everyone plays a role and is fully valued. This shall take place in accordance with the principles of respect for human dignity, human rights and personal integrity and without discrimination on the basis of genetic background, on the basis of ethical norms relating to our Western cultural heritage. (Section 1–1; purpose of the act)

This preamble is formulated so as to underscore an ethos about the all-inclusive society.[5] Phrased positively, the preamble does not warn about the dangers of selective breeding nor does it question issues of abnormality or birth defects, but rather stresses that in our society there is room for everyone. Nevertheless, there is no doubt that an underlying fear of '*sorteringssamfunnet*' – that is, a society that classifies people according to particular (genetic) traits – motivated the move to legislate. The new reproductive technologies along with other advances in biomedicine and biotechnology were and are viewed as conducive to this possible development (i.e. of selective breeding) through selection of gametes and techniques of screening (whether by pre-implantation or prenatal diagnosis).[6]

Although the immediate event that prompted legislation was the birth of the first IVF child in Norway in 1984, issues related to biogenetics were already on the public agenda in the early 1980s. Theologians and medical experts were involved in extensive ethical debates with regard to new reproductive technologies and prenatal diagnosis, where the status of the foetus was a central concern (see Rådet for medisinsk forskning 1983; Kirkerådet 1989; Brekke 1995: 113 ff). In 1982–83, issues pertaining to the new reproductive and genetic technologies reached formal political channels in relation to the organisation of public services within genetic medicine. These debates concerned ethical questions as well as questions of priority within the public health system (see Kirkerådet 1989; Hellum et al. 1990; Brekke 1995: 114). In the wake of these debates, the government was asked to put forward a proposition with suggestions for the regulation of assisted conception. The result was the law of 1987. At the same time, Parliament asked the government to present a proposition concerning ethical guidelines for research and development of biotechnology and gene technology. In 1988, an Ethics Committee was constituted; it submitted its report in 1990.[7] This in turn laid the ground for the white paper presented to Parliament in 1993 on biotechnology related to human beings, which formed the basis of the 1994 law.[8] In the meantime, the Biotechnological Council was appointed in 1991 as a free advisory board under the Ministry of Health and Social Affairs.

Although there was a series of events in the 1980s and 1990s with direct impact on the legislative processes, there is also an historical background that must be taken into account in order to obtain a fuller understanding of the predominating mentalities and values, not least the application of a precautionary principle. Most significantly, this has to do with a fear of eugenics. Under no circumstance would the government permit socio-technical developments that in any way make possible any form of systematic selection of humans. Hence, influences on the prevailing attitudes to legislation (from the 1980s to the present) can be traced to the early 1900s when ideas of racial hygiene were gaining prominence, through the 1930s (when some of these ideas were put in practice) and the Second World War and the Nazi ideology of racial supremacy and into the post-war period (for different elaborations of these themes, see Roll-Hansen 1980; Aasen 1990; Seip 1994; Nielsen 2000).

In terms of the nature/nurture divide and what it is that constitutes a person, there is a gradual shift away from the weight placed on inheritance and hereditary traits prior to 1939, to the weight placed on environment and social milieu in the post-war period.[9] The attempt to regulate artificial insemination by donor (AID) in the 1950s is a case in point. Contrary to the predominant position permeating public discourses in 2003 (with regards to AID), which is singularly grounded in child rights and the best interests of the child (this will be discussed in more detail below) the arguments for and against of the 1950s centred on marriage, the good home and love (the latter two being preconditions for the former) in addition to the question that anonymous sperm donation involves a lie. The conjugal relation was the nexus around which other relations gravitated. In fact, marriage as an institution was taken for granted, as was the rule of *pater est*. This was the moral ground upon which the other arguments rested. The most controversial issue (then as now) was that of the anonymity of the donor. In retrospect, it appears that the arguments stressing the significance of non-biological relatedness had a certain persuasive power which has since been lost.[10] Today, with the increasing focus on biogenetics, biocentrism has come to dominate certain discourses, at the expense of sociocentric notions. There are voices that claim that the pendulum has now swung back and that we are witnessing an era of 'new eugenics' (see Nielsen 2003); yet social practices indicate that attitudes are much more nuanced (see Howell 2003). It is therefore paradoxical that the Norwegian law, with its good intentions and an explicit avoidance of certain practices that are considered unethical, nevertheless grounds fundamental arguments (in support of the law) in biology and genetics. The law presumes an idea of the natural, and reiterates (albeit in a somewhat altered guise) underlying notions of kinship in Norway, that is, blood is thicker than water. The heterosexual family appears as the natural unit within which significant relatedness is maintained. Insofar as this family unit is not based on biogenetic bonds, the presumption is that this knowledge should be made known.

One final point regarding the relevant context of the law in question: it cannot be seen isolated from the question of abortion. The legislation related to abortion is a tangential process which has direct relevance for the questions that assisted conception provokes (see Syse 1993).[11] This is reflected in the ethical and ontological issues (e.g. the moral status of the foetus and its relation to its mother) as well as in the dilemmas these laws raise with regard to the liberal state. Put succinctly: whereas abortion is based on a principle of self-determination, assisted conception (as well as prenatal screening) is not. Hence, as some are prone to point out, there is a lack of consistency between these two laws.

I have stated that there was consensus in Parliament about the need to regulate. However, both the objective of regulation and the content of the legislation was contested and hotly debated. Moreover, questions related to the new reproductive technologies and biotechnology shifted the traditional political axis (left–right) in Parliament. In addition, there was not necessarily agreement within the different political parties. Therefore, alliances were sought across party lines. Keeping this in mind, it is nevertheless possible to say that at a general level, there was (and is) a major divide between the so-called 'technology optimists' with a more permissive attitude to the technologies (positive to science and the contribution of science to the betterment of society) on the one hand, and the more conservative, restrictive attitudes on the other. Whereas the former are, by and large, represented by the Labour Party, part of the Right Party and the Progress Party (Fremskritts partiet – a far right, populist party), the latter include first and foremost the Christian Democratic Party, the Centre Party and the Socialist Left Party.[12] This political constellation is reflected in the proposals for the law of 1987 as well as in the ensuing revisions.

Although it was a Labour government that put the first law before Parliament, it did not win a majority for all its provisions. The issues of contention covered almost all the provisions in the law, from research on embryos through anonymity of sperm donors, to egg donation, the combination of IVF with donor sperm and the freezing of embryos. In some cases the margins of the vote were small: for example, in the case of research on embryos, 46 voted for while 48 voted against; while 49 voted for restricting treatment to married couples, 45 wished to allow treatment to stable cohabiting couples.[13] When the entire law was finally voted on, the Christian Democratic Party and the Centre Party voted against the whole law, which is very unusual. The law was passed with 67 votes for and 27 against.

AN EXCEPTIONAL SITUATION

Most of the politicians involved in the formulation of the 1987 law stated that the making of this law was in many ways an exceptional situation. To my mind, the elements that contribute toward this qualification are the following:

1. This was a new law. Being the first time that assisted conception was to be regulated in Norway made the process unique and significant. One even phrased it in terms 'of making history'.
2. The field that was to be regulated was one that, on the whole, people were ignorant of, including politicians. This very ignorance was a contributing factor to the process in several ways.
3. The practices that were to be regulated concerned vital issues that were considered to be beyond the ordinary realm of politics. They reflected fundamental ethical questions.
4. Because of the nature of the issues involved, all the political parties let their representatives in Parliament vote according to their conscience.

The field of assisted conception had not been regulated earlier (despite attempts in the 1950s) and the active involvement of members of the social committee as well as ministers has to do with this fact. Not only did they feel that they had a special responsibility, but also that they had a real possibility to influence its formulation. In fact, when questioned about their impact on the law, many were very explicit, saying that they had had a direct influence. This influence had different channels: through discussions in the committee itself and through discussions with their respective party fractions, winning co-members over to your point of view.

Not surprisingly, members of the Labour Party were particularly candid. The Labour Party was in government and actually responsible for putting the law proposal forward. Indeed, there was intense contact between the minister of social affairs, the members of the social committee and even the prime minister (I was told) in formulating and finding support for this law. In this work, the Labour Party's women's group played an especially important role.

The degree of influence held also had to do with the amount of knowledge each representative felt they had. Several expressed frustration at not knowing enough – and yet realising that the little they knew was more than their co-members of their respective parties knew. Thus, some members established a permanent reference group with necessary expertise; others had ad hoc experts called upon when necessary. All felt the need to be fed information, although opinions varied as to whether the information received (for example from the ministry) was sufficient. My overall impression is that there was a perceived lack of knowledge and that this was enhanced by the rapid developments in the field of biotechnology.

The combination of this being a new law, the lack of specific or sufficient knowledge of the field (a kind of shared ignorance), the fear that matters might get out of hand, a recognition of the ethical nature of the issues to be treated, all combine and converge in a vote that is based on personal convictions, reflecting the individual world-view or belief (*'livssyn'*). All the people that I have spoken to were unanimous in proclaiming that this situation was very special and that they had never experienced anything like it before (this is also confirmed by the official records).[14]

BETTER SAFE THAN SORRY

When considering the perceived need to legislate, different factors have to be taken into account. Regulating assisted conception is not just about controlling biotechnological developments or about possible ways to have children; other politically contentious issues are also raised. Thus, questions pertaining to the public health system, questions related to the medical classification of infertility as well as the role of research and government funding of research are raised. Some are matters of principle (e.g. equal access to health care) others are more policy related, but positions on these issues reflect overall political differences. These differences are expressed in the deliberations and tie into the legislative process giving it its specific drift and political flavour, as well as contributing to the effect of the law.

Significantly, the alternative – not to legislate – was not considered an option. The fact that AID had been practised since 1939 without regulation was never an argument for maintaining status quo. On the contrary, with increasing public awareness (not least fuelled by the sensational headlines surrounding IVF) the political climate was conducive to legislation. Government intervention was deemed appropriate by medical practitioners as well. Hence, there is no doubt that the technological developments within the field itself represented the primary incentive to move. The fact that *in vitro fertilisation* had become a reality and that Norwegian doctors also had succeeded in producing an IVF baby made it evident that new reproductive technologies were developing at a pace which demanded some form of legislation – lest matters get out of hand.

Most of the politicians I spoke to reflected this attitude: a fear concerning the implications of the technologies; the uncertainties involved and hence the need to control. The general feeling (that I could glean from the interviews) was that the potentiality of these technologies was awesome, for some, even frightening. Not only did they concern basic notions about human beings and practices which involved fundamental life processes, but they also evoked a sense of the inevitable and irreversible: that once processes (of this nature) were set in motion, they are almost impossible to reverse. As one politician stated: 'Biotechnology concerns central ethical issues ... once you start you cannot change the course. It is this quality of being irremediable ... we cannot afford to make a mistake.' Another person stressed the importance of creating a public awareness about where to draw the line. As he said: 'Research moves the limits, politicians have to set them. It is the duty of Parliament to generate [public] debates.' In fact, the attitude that Parliament and government have an obligation to act on behalf of society on these matters is a salient feature of the reflections of all the politicians, no matter what their position on each specific issue. It is almost as if applying a precautionary principle in these matters is self-evident.

In addition, there was also a real concern (among members of Parliament and especially the Labour Party) that some medical doctors in Norway were pushing to establish private clinics offering IVF treatment. In 1986, a private medical centre (Ring medisinske senter) had initiated IVF treatment at their clinic, thereby openly challenging the public health system (and its potential monopoly) on practices of assisted conception. Moreover, it was said that there were other doctors based at public hospitals who wished to do the same. The matter of private medical clinics (which at the time was a much-debated issue in Norway) was not just an issue about who was to be allowed to practise IVF treatment, but, more importantly, whether the competence and expertise involved in developing these techniques should primarily be based in public hospitals and hence form part of the public health sector.

One of the initiators in proposing the law was Kåre Molne (then head doctor at the women's clinic at the Regional Hospital in Trondheim). He was adamant: he wanted infertility treatment to be part of the public health service and funded by the national budget (through Rikstrygdeverket). He therefore urged the government (which at the time was run by Labour) to legislate and found a willing partner. The minister of health at the time, Tove Strand Gerhardsen, issued a court injunction ('*midlertidig forføyning*') in 1986 which specified that only clinics authorised by the government were permitted to carry out IVF treatment. (The Ring centre was allowed to continue treatment of those already on their waiting lists.) This decision, however, was later overturned in Parliament by a deal made between the Right Party and the Christian Democratic Party.[15] The minister also authorised extraordinary allocations to university clinics in order that they might develop IVF methods, and she initiated the process of legislation.Thus, already at its inception, legislation of infertility treatment reflected political positions in Norway on major health-systems-related questions, that is, whether or not to permit the extension of private hospitals/clinics. However, in order to understand the need to apply a precautionary principle, the questions related to competence-building and research are perhaps of greater significance (see below). A central argument for regulating practices of assisted conception was to ensure a continued evolution of the techniques-cum-knowledge in Norway as part of the public health sector.

Two issues of subsequent importance are involved here: one has to do with the classification of infertility – whether it is to be considered an illness or not (see Gunbjørud 1990). This in turn has to do with the priority given to this treatment in the public health system. The other has to do with what kind of knowledge and competence Norwegian authorities deem it necessary that the Norwegian nation should possess. The classification of infertility as an illness or not is no longer a major issue, but its priority within the health system is. There have been moves to give infertility a low priority and by implication reduce or even withdraw public spending on such treatments.[16] There have also been suggestions to impose full fees for such treatment (within the public system). However, until now these moves have been unsuccessful, not least due to the lobby of the involuntary childless themselves.[17]

Although I will not pursue this issue further, it is important to note that reasons for wanting to impose fees do not necessarily have to do with the classification of infertility as an illness or not; nor does it necessarily have to do with another parallel debate concerning whether to have a child is to be considered a right. Some politicians openly expressed that they prefer adoption to IVF treatment as a solution to involuntary childlessness.[18] They, therefore, would like to align these two forms of having children. Imposing costs on IVF treatment can then be seen as an incentive to push people toward opting for adoption (which has no public coverage, but part of the expenses are tax deductible) rather than IVF. In this way, the state can practise its morality through economic (dis)incentives. What is evident is that the legislative process with regard to new reproductive technologies and assisted conception mobilises a political agenda which goes beyond – but nevertheless feeds into and thereby constitutes – this particular socio-political field.

SCIENCE AND THE PROBLEM OF ETHICS

I mentioned that a major concern in the debates, which was subsequently reiterated by the politicians I spoke to, was the question of knowledge and competence-building. Granted that there was a general feeling of ignorance about the whole field of biotechnology, the following comment by one of the politicians is intriguing: 'The law is not based on expert knowledge – that is what makes it so special.' This statement highlights a tension between expert knowledge and lay knowledge, not least the fact that this law is seen as grounded in other values than those represented by the so-called experts. The comment underscores the significance of common sense (which is a value Norwegians appreciate) in vital matters; it also draws attention to the moral underpinnings of this legislative process, and perhaps government more generally.

The issues concerning knowledge and competence-building are interesting because they gloss different themes that somehow converge to speak to the same thing: ethics. Overall, there is the (perceived) problem of the rapid developments in science and technology. The perception is that it is impossible to keep pace with these new developments. This perception, however, leads to two opposed 'solutions'. These solutions are in turn grounded in very different attitudes towards science and technologies – and, not least, towards scientists. The problem of competence-building also broaches the question of whether Norway should be part of an international community of researchers and partake in an international development of science and technology within the field of biotechnology, including assisted conception. As the law forbids research on embryos, this possibility is in part precluded.

Norwegian researchers in this field have to travel abroad in order to gain knowledge of and practice in new methods and developments.

Those who are characterised as pro-technology will support arguments by medical doctors and researchers who say that it is hypocritical and parasitical for Norway to uphold a restrictive law while at the same time making use of knowledge and technologies being produced elsewhere (see e.g. Hazekamp and Hamberger 1999). The counter-argument is that Norway has the right and the obligation to practise what Norway – or Norwegians – deem ethically correct. The problem, of course, is that there is no general agreement about what is ethically correct. Nevertheless, when it comes to the matter of ethics it is as if those who are more restrictive perceive themselves as 'more ethical' than those who are not. So much so that in the parliamentary debates, those supporting the most liberal aspects of the law (representatives from the Right Party and the Labour Party) found it necessary to explicitly state that their positions are also ethically grounded.[19]

A prevailing attitude towards the practice of biotechnology is that one cannot leave it to the individual practitioner (or patient) to decide what should or could be done. It is in the nature of science and researchers that, if left to their own devices, they will always push to supersede existing limits. Opinions on these matters reflect a view of the relationship between 'research' (the term referring specifically to research in the natural sciences) and government. There were those who stated that it is the job of politicians to be ahead of research – in the sense that government can – and should – stop questionable or unethical developments before they are reality. 'We must not go faster ahead than what we are able to control ... The way it is now legislation is adapting to research.' Or, as another person said: 'Things happen that you have never heard about until Dolly is born, so you have to try to be a horse's length ahead and it may seem then that we are restrictive.' Others scorned this view saying that you cannot hinder – or regulate for – something if you do not know what it is. Moreover, for those who are more positive as to the uses of biotechnology, the attitude is that 'it is not desirable nor possible that law makers can be ahead of the technological developments; one has to regulate in the wake of developments'. Thus, the best one can do is to regulate *ex post facto*. In this draw, it seems that those who wish to be ahead of research are winning – by enforcing restrictions.[20]

At the heart of these controversies lie not only attitudes to science (and not least scientists) but also to ethics. There is a fundamental scepticism about the role of scientists and their ability to attend to major ethical concerns. To put it bluntly (and in my own words): science runs rampant and is in need of control; scientists are only interested in their research and therefore incapable of making sound ethical judgements. In order to control science and impose reasonable limits, ethical judgement and decisions are necessary. As ethics is not considered a field for experts (alone) ethical judgements can just as well be made by non-experts, that is. ordinary people. Politicians also feared that without legislation people might take matters into their own hands and arrange systems of private donation or develop a commercial black market in eggs and sperm.[21] Thus, 'private enterprise' was to be discouraged through strict regulation. Not only do these attitudes reflect a lack of confidence in scientists, they also reflect a lack of confidence in people.

Returning again to the question of ignorance, one possible conclusion is that ignorance in conjunction with scepticism towards science and a lack of confidence in scientists' ethical judgement contributed to the making of a restrictive law. Somehow these two strands (of ignorance and expertise) converge, and the point of convergence is articulated in a concern for ethics. 'Better safe than sorry' was the option that won.

Nevertheless, it was (and still is) the potential that these technologies represent to meddle with vital processes that made the issues so significant and hence sensitive. The possibility of selective breeding was (and is) one major concern. Taken together with the fact that the use of these technologies was (and is) perceived as upsetting the natural order, the practices related to assisted conception were placed on a plane above and beyond the ordinary field of politics. The very recognition that these questions had to do with ethical issues rooted in personal convictions came to dominate the debates and the consensus achieved.

QUESTION OF RIGHTS AND THE PROBLEMS OF NATURE

Although it is not possible to pinpoint an overarching rights discourse in relation to assisted conception, the question of rights is one that crops up in many different contexts: not only the right to treatment – but also whether it is a right to have children. None of the politicians I spoke to supported such a position. On the contrary, most agree that it is not. As one person put it: 'Treatment should not be a right but the public health service should have the necessary skill and competence.' In other words, assisted conception should be on offer within the public health system to those deserving of it.

A more profound view, however, is that pertaining to the best interest of the child and child rights. Over the past decade or so, a children's rights discourse has gained a prominent place in the public consciousness. Although the question of children's rights was mentioned in the debates about artificial insemination in the 1950s, it was not central. Other issues were more important – such as marriage, the question of lying (in the case of anonymous sperm donation) and whether the practice of AID breaks with Norwegian law (adultery, quackery). However, in today's rhetoric children's rights are in part the nexus around which the arguments gravitate. As one politician from the far right answered to a question about the limits of the state (and the liberal dilemma of interference with individual choice): 'Children's rights take priority over parents' wishes. We feel that this is something society has to be involved in.' With regard to forms of assisted conception, and especially in relation to gamete donation, children's rights are invariably invoked.

How the rights of children – to parents, home, security, knowing their identity, etc. – are perceived influences the various positions held. Thus, for example, those who say that children have the right to both a father and a mother would be against lesbians and gays having access to infertility treatment and adoption. Those who claim that knowledge of one's biological origin is a right would be against anonymous sperm donation. Those who insist on the unity of mother and child and that a child can only have one true mother are against egg donation. In fact, the use of children's rights discourse to ground arguments for and against is an interesting finding in itself. Moreover, I believe that the very framing of these issues in terms of children's rights makes it easier to defend (and accept) the intervention of government. It is as if the notion of the child and their rights evokes an implicit yet shared understanding that comes close to an idea of the sacred. Things done in the name of children's rights are by definition good (and right). Hence, I suggest that it is the evocation of a children's rights discourse that permits the restrictive provisions of the law, in at least two senses: (1) defending the embryo in terms of rights and human worth ('*menneskeverdet*') and (2) tying identity to biology.

The ontological status of the embryo is a fundamental aspect of this discourse (cf. Mulkay 1997; Sirnes 1997). Insofar as the embryo has been successfully removed from a scientific domain and placed in a 'humanistic' one, it is extremely difficult to reverse the process. Once the embryo is perceived and recognised as a (potential) human life, it is hard to reduce it to a bunch of cells (and thus the object of research). Hence valid counter-arguments are almost impossible to make. The same mechanism seems to be at work with the biology–identity link: once it is an accepted fact that to deny a child knowledge of its biological origin is tantamount to denying it the right to know who she is, then knowledge of biogenetic origin becomes paramount.

Indeed, framing the question of anonymous donor sperm in terms of children's rights might have been constitutive for the general change in opinion on this matter. When I asked the politicians if they had in the course of time changed their opinion on any of these issues, anonymous sperm donation was invariably mentioned. If they were to vote today, they said, they would vote for the rescinding of donor anonymity. References were made to the adoption law and to international conventions, stating that a child has the right to know its biological origin. In their view, donor children and adopted children are 'the same', and hence have the same rights. The fact that these are two very different ways of coming into being is irrelevant. Moreover, arguments put forth by medical expertise about the problem of recruiting donors and that AID would most likely be suspended in Norway have little or no weight, and are more or less ignored.[22]

In view of the above, it is perhaps not surprising that with respect to egg donation positions have been more constant.[23] Significantly, these are tied almost exclusively to ideas of nature and not rights. When confronted with the question of why permit sperm donation and not egg donation, there were a few who could see that this seemed unfair from the point of view of gender equality (male and female infertility should be treated the same, hence sperm and eggs should be treated the same). Yet, this was not the fundamental issue. As one person put it: 'Egg and sperm is not a question of gender equality, it has to do with biology.' The issue of egg donation touches deeper emotional strings that have to do with notions of motherhood. Egg donation (in addition to being a much more complicated technique than sperm donation) violates fundamental ideas about the natural unity of mother and egg (read child). 'I can accept an unknown donor ... one or the other father, it does not make a difference [however] ... mother and egg belong together,' as one female politician stated. Put succinctly: eggs belong where they come from. The unity of the woman/uterus/egg was – and is – considered to be inviolable; conception, pregnancy, birth is seen as a unified process, and the notion of 'mother belonging' was used to underscore the uniqueness of this natural relation (between a woman and her eggs). (See Alonso this volume for a very different yet tangential argument about gender, motherhood and the body.) Sperm donation is accepted because there is an intrinsic uncertainty about paternity as sperm 'comes from the outside' (in contrast to eggs which are on the inside) and does not create a situation different from natural reproduction (see Melhuus 2003 for a detailed elaboration of the arguments). The prohibition of IVF with donor sperm was also based on ideas of unnaturalness: adding donor sperm to an already unnatural conception is just too much.[24]

What we have, then, is a law that is basically premised on ideas of nature and notions of rights, collapsing the two within a discourse of ethics. This law privileges heterosexual couples over homosexual ones; couples over single persons, and, on a different plane, sperm over eggs. It privileges biological bonds over social ones; and it privileges the interest of the unborn child over those of the intending parents.

THE LAW: ON BEHALF OF WHOM?

One of the questions I asked the politicians was who they represented in the questions regarding assisted conception and the law that was put in place. Considering the powerful lobby from the involuntary childless themselves and parts of the medical/clinical milieus, the answers are perhaps somewhat surprising. No one stated that they represented their constituency; and no one said they represented the interests either of the involuntary childless or of the medical profession. On the contrary, many answered that in these questions they represent themselves. In these matters it is not possible to represent certain interest groups or 'the people' in any way. As one person said: 'Party politics cannot be applied to such matters,' or in the words of another: 'As leaders, we have to think ahead and not just be trendy.' One politician even evoked the idea of '*folkeopplyser*', that is, an enlightened leadership, adding 'I do not represent the people – but must lead.' Regulation is seen as a public social obligation. An extreme comment to my question was the following: the politician interviewed compared his situation as a politician (who must decide about assisted conception) to being a witness to someone committing suicide: 'You have the right and the obligation to intervene.'

There was a recognition that there was something special about regulating as restrictively as was done. (Even in Parliament several of the spokespersons made it clear that although the law proposal may seem liberal to some Norwegians, in an international context it was very restrictive.) Several of those interviewed alluded to Norway being a 'different kind of country' – '*et annerledes land*'. Some meant it ironically, while others gave it a positive value. 'We do what we think is best (for us) – in spite of what others may think' was the impression conveyed. When I drew attention to the argument put forward by some medical doctors that Norway 'exports its ethical dilemmas', letting others do our dirty work, the response was that it is our right and our privilege to do what is best for Norway and not necessarily take into account what other countries do. As a person from the left said: 'We are a bit special in Norway in the sense that it is very regulated and [we have] very strict provisions' – the point being that to be special is all right.

Tied in with this notion of otherness is the specific skew towards ethics. However, what makes the situation particular – if not peculiar – is the understanding of what ethics is or implies. Obviously, there are different positions, but a salient feature of this material is that ethics is related to personal conviction and a sense of public duty. Biotechnology and assisted conception pertain to the realm of conscience and belief ('*livssyn*') and were (and are) considered sensitive, emotional, personal and hence ethical. As such they are classified as being beyond ordinary politics. It is this extraordinary quality that also evokes the sense of responsibility on the part of government to legislate and legislate restrictively.

The fact that it was not deemed correct to use the party whip for the vote in Parliament is indicative. All the political parties let their members vote according to their own conscience, which is unusual. Thus it is not primarily party policies but personal convictions that directed the outcome of the vote. Moreover, and in retrospect, all concurred that the debates in the committee and even in Parliament were characterised by mutual respect. Those who were for the restrictions also agreed that these were difficult decisions to make: to act on the basis of principle when confronted with individual and tragic fates. Almost all of those interviewed also referred to private reasons for being emotionally engaged. They had personal experience among family and friends and thereby first-hand knowledge of the pain of childlessness, IVF treatments or adoption. Whatever the reasons for casting their vote, the result is that Norway has one of the most restrictive laws in Europe.

Although it might be correct to say that individual beliefs and personal convictions were significant for the outcome of this law, it is also correct to say that the law was made on behalf of society. The obligation to act in the face of potentially negative developments was an underlying motive, as was the wish to ensure an all-inclusive society without discrimination. The law was passed on the basis of a precautionary principle, 'better safe than sorry'. This is a position which, in the Norwegian context, is easy to defend, congruent with public opinion and thus generally accepted, despite disagreements on some of the provisions. The intent of the law is to figure as a corrective to and brake on 'experts' while at the same time representing a kind of moral guide for the people. The effect of the law, however, is to create – if not a morally responsible state – at least an image of a moral state. It remains an open question whether this image also embraces that of a certain moral supremacy[25] but there is no doubt that Norwegian politicians are well aware that the Norwegian position in questions related to biotechnology is exceptional, and it was possible to discern – if not pride – at least satisfaction with the ethical standards that the law projects.[26]

The link to ethics derives from the quality of the issues at hand. They have to do with vital processes, fundamentally associated with nature. In this concrete sociocultural universe of procreation an essentialising discourse grounded in biology has gained prominence. Tying these issues into a rights discourse only serves to underline this specific quality. Through the legislative process, rights are aligned with nature. Together they produce a 'natural unit', a heterosexual family constituted on the basis of (the right to) certain knowledge of biological relatedness. This unit, moreover, does not break in any fundamental way with notions of Norwegian kinship. It is a reflection of dominant values of relatedness which at the same time hides alternative views, practices and meanings. What we have is a law that is basically premised on ideas of nature and notions of rights, collapsing the two within a discourse of ethics. This discourse has an impressive persuasive power. It emanates from the state in such a way that the state becomes coextensive with it. Perhaps even more significantly the result has the semblance of being self-evident.

NOTES

The research upon which this article is based has been funded by the Norwegian Research Council (NFR) and EU. Funding has been granted for the following successive and overlapping projects: 'Kinship *quo vadis?* The meanings of kinship in Norway and beyond' (NFR; a joint project with Signe Howell); 'The transnational flow of concepts and substances' (NFR; a collaborative programme at the Department of Social Anthropology, University of Oslo; funded by NFR); 'The public understanding of genetics' (an interdisciplinary and transnational programme with seven collaborating partner countries, funded by the EU). A first version of this paper was presented at the workshop 'Explorations of the State' organised by Christian Krohn-Hansen and Knut Nustad at the Department of Social Anthropology, University of Oslo. I want to thank them both for pushing me into this and not least for very suggestive comments on early drafts. I also want to thank Kari Anne Ulfsness who has been a research assistant on two of these projects, and whose continued help while I was Dean, made this research possible.

1. The first law regulating assisted conception in Norway was passed in 1987 (Act No. 68 of 12 June 1987; Law on Artificial Procreation). In 1994 this Act was replaced by

Act No. 56 of 5 August 1994: the Act Relating to the Application of Biotechnology in Medicine. This was in turn based on Report No. 25 (1992–93) to Parliament entitled 'Biotechnology Related to Human Beings'. My focus in this article is by and large on the processes leading up to the first law and its revision in 1994.

2. I ask the reader to keep in mind that this article was written in 2003. One main trait of the field of biotechnology is its continual flux; since this article was written a new law on biotechnology has been passed: Lov 2003.12.05 nr 100. Lov om humanmedisinsk bruk av bioteknologi m.m. (bioteknolologiloven).

3. In this work I have had the continued assistance of Kari Anne Ulfness; she has been present at most interviews; she has also carried out interviews of medical doctors on her own.

4. Within anthropology, issues tied to NRT, assisted conception and adoption, have rekindled debates about kinship, bringing to the fore such crucial notions as belonging, relatedness and identities (see e.g. Strathern 1992a, 1992b; Edwards et al. 1993; Ragoné 1994; Carsten 2000; Faubion 2001; Franklin and McKinnon 2001).

5. The Norwegian version is more explicit: 'Formålet med denne loven er å sikre at medisinsk bruk av bioteknologi utnyttes til beste for mennesker *i et samfunn der hvor det er plass til alle*' (my stress) where the literal translation is: 'in a society where there is room for everyone' (Act No. 56 of 5 August 1994; The Act Relating to the Application of Biotechnology in Medicine). This was repeated in the revision of 2003.

6. Pre-implantation diagnosis is defined as 'the genetic examination of an embryo before it is implanted in the uterus' (Act No. 56 of 1994, chapter 4, section 4–1). Prenatal diagnosis is defined as 'a) the examination of the foetus or pregnant woman to detect genetic disease or development anomalies, b) ultrasound examination of a pregnant woman' (chapter 5, section 5–1).

7. NOU (Norske Offentlige Utredninger) 1991: 6, *Om mennesker og bioteknologi*. The committee was led by Julie Skjæråsen, MD.

8. St.meld. nr 25 1992–93. Om mennesker og bioteknologi (Sosialdepartementet); English version 'Biotechnology Related to Human Beings', Report No. 25 (1992–93); Ministry of Health and Social Affairs.

9. These historical facts are rarely – if ever – mentioned by those people whom I have interviewed unless I specifically bring the matter to their attention. See also Sirnes (1999), who points out that eugenic practices (sterilisation) continued into the 1950s and 1960s.

10. For more detail of the nuances in the debates of the 1950s see Løvset (1951), Rønne-Petersen (1951), Sandemose (1952), Molne (1976) and Melhuus (2001, 2003). See also 'Innstilling fra Insemninasjonslovkomitéen', March 1953, Ministry of Justice.

11. Norway's abortion law grants the woman self-determination within the first 12 weeks of pregnancy; this provision was included in 1978 (Act of 16 June 1978 No. 66). The right to self-determination is tied to notions of the female body and its relation to the foetus; that is, the foetus is seen as part of the woman's body and not an entity in itself with independent legal status.

12. See Brekke (1995) for a discussion (and classification) of the views that came forth through the hearing documents.

13. In Parliament (Odelstinget) each proposal was voted on separately; the whole law was voted on in the end. Principle of anonymity: 53 for, 41 against; freezing of embryos for 12 months: 62 for, 31 against; research on embryos: 46 for, 48 against; treatment only to be offered to married couples: 49 for, 45 for opening it to cohabiting couples. The vote on the whole law: 67 for, 27 against. (See *O.tidene* 25.5.1987: sak nr 2. Innstilling fra sosialkomiteen om lov om kunstig befruktning, Stortingsforhandlinger sesjon 1986–87, pp. 340–45.)

14. *O.tidene* 25.5.1987 (forhandlinger i Odelstinget): Sak nr 2 'Innstilling fra sosialko-mitéen om lov om kunstig befruktning', Stortingsforhandlinger sesjon 1986–87, pp. 308–45.

15. The Christian Democrats agreed to vote to allow private clinics if the Right Party would vote for only permitting married couples to be granted treatment.

16. See NOU (Norske Offentlige Utredninger) 1987: 23 (p. 96), *Retninglinjer for prioriteringer innen norske helsetjenester* (Guidelines for Priorities within the Norwegian Health Services); this was followed up with NOU 1997: 18, *Prioriteringer på ny* (Priorities Once Again; also called *Lønning Utvalget I and II*). If infertility treatment is removed from the public health care system, this will have implications for the continued practice of such treatments in Norway.

17. Another important argument against imposing full fees is that this would break with the fundamental ideology that health services should be equally available to all, irrespective of the ability to pay.

18. This idea is not new; it was suggested by a committee appointed to evaluate health priorities, the so-called Lønning utvalget (see Tranøy 1990).

19. The most contentious issues in the debates in Parliament were anonymity of the donor; research on embryos; and, perhaps somewhat surprisingly, the freezing of embryos. Representatives of the Church find it 'unethical to freeze life that way' as one person told me.

20. The alliance between government and medical expertise is tenuous and this is partly due to the fact that the experts themselves are not agreed. The Norwegian Christian Doctors Association is actively involved in ethical questions, both with regard to abortion and biotechnology. It seems that in the matter of ethics, there is a stronger alliance (although this is not always explicit) between the opinions of the Church (which are variously expressed) and government.

21. Such private initiatives already exist. Some lesbian couples who wish to have a child draw on private networks to find potential sperm donors (see Riksaasen 2001).

22. Norway imports donor sperm from Cryos, a Danish sperm bank, which operates on the principle of anonymity. With the rescinding of the anonymity clause, Norway will have to develop its own sperm bank based on known donors; those wanting anonymous sperm will travel abroad. However, new methods such as ICSI (which is permitted in Norway) might reduce the need for donor sperm.

23. The proposal put before Parliament in 1994 included a provision for egg donation. However, the Labour Party was split in its own ranks and the proposal was voted down.

24. This provision has since been revised, and is now permitted.

25. Cf. Hemingsen (1997) who argues that an idea of moral supremacy is characteristic of Scandinavian identity. He states:

> ... [almost] all constructions of a Nordic identity right down to the 'model' debates of today on the Scandinavian welfare state are permeated by the structural element of political and moral superiority ... the claim of the North to moral superiority is part of both the auto-stereotype and the hetero-stereotype. (1997: 93)

26. That fertility experts from other Nordic countries find the Norwegian position strange, if not incomprehensible is another matter entirely.

REFERENCES

Aasen, H.S., 1990. 'Noen historiske perspektiver knyttet til dagens utvikling innen prenatal diagnostikk', in A. Hellum, A. Syse, H.S. Aasen, eds, *Mennekse, natur og fødselsteknologi*. Oslo: Ad Notam.

Brekke, O.A., 1995. *Differensiering og integrasjon. Debatten om bioteknologi og etikk i Norge*. Rapport 9509. LOS senteret. Bergen: University of Bergen.

Carsten, J., ed., 2000. *Cultures of Relatedness: New Approaches to the Study of Kinship*. Cambridge: Cambridge University Press.

Edwards, J., S. Franklin, E. Hirsch, F. Prices and M. Strathern, eds, 1993. *Technologies of Procreation: Kinship in the Age of Assisted Conception*. Manchester: Manchester University Press.

Faubion, J., ed., 2001. *The Ethics of Kinship: Ethnographic Enquiries*. Lanham, MD: Rowman & Littlefield.

Fox, R., [1993] 1997. *Reproduction and Succession: Studies in Anthropology, Law and Society*. New Brunswick: Transaction Publishers.

Franklin, S., 1997. *Embodied Progress: A Cultural Account of Assisted Conception*. London: Routledge.

Franklin, S. and S. McKinnon, eds, 2001. *Relative Values: Reconfiguring Kinship Studies*. Durham, NC: Duke University Press.

Gunbjørud, A.B., 1990. 'Kunstig befruktning, profesjonsperspektiv og samfunnsperspektiv', in A. Hellum, A. Syse, H.S. Aasen, eds, *Menneske, nature og fødselsteknologi. Verdivalg og rettslig regulering*. Oslo: Ad Notam.

Halvorsen, M., 1998. 'Norway: The Act Relating to the Application of Biotechnology in Medicine with Particular Regard to Questions in Family Law', in A. Bainham, ed., *The International Survey of Family Law 1996*. The Netherlands: The International Society of Family Law.

Hansen, T.B. and F. Stepputat, 2001. 'Introduction', in T.B. Hansen and F. Stepputat, eds, *States of Imagination: Ethnographic Explorations of the Postcolonial State*. Durham, NC: Duke University Press.

Hazekamp, J. and L. Hamberger, 1999. 'The Nordic Experience', in P. Brindsen, ed., *A Textbook of In Vitro Fertilization and Assisted Reproduction: The Bourn Hall Guide to Clinical and Laboratory Practice*. New York: Parthenon Publishing Group.

Hellum, A., A. Syse, H.S. Aasen, eds, 1990. *Menneske, natur og fødselsteknologi. Verdivalg og rettslig regulering*. Oslo: Ad Notam.

Hemingsen, B., 1997. 'The Swedish Construction of Nordic Identity', in Ø. Sørensen and B. Stråth, eds, *The Cultural Construction of Norden*. Oslo: Scandinavian University Press.

Howell, S., 2003. 'Kinning: The Creation of Life Trajectories in Transnational Adoptive Families', *Journal of the Royal Anthropological Institute*, 9(3): 465–84.

Kirkerådet, 1989. *Mer en gener. Utredning om bioteknologi og menneskeverd*. Oslo: Kirkerådet.

Løvset, J., 1951. 'Artificial Insemination: The Attitude of Patients in Norway', *Fertility and Sterility*, 2(5): 414–29.

Melhuus, M., 2001. 'Kan skinnet bedra? Noen meninger om assistert befruktning', in S. Howell and M. Melhuus, eds, *Blod – tykkere enn vann? Betdyninger av slektskap i Norge*. Bergen: Fagbokforlaget.

Melhuus, M., 2003. 'Exchange Matters: Issues of Law and the Flow of Human Substances', in T.H. Eriksen, ed., *Globalisation: Studies in Anthropology*. London: Pluto.

Mitchell, T., 1999. 'Society, Economy and the State Effect', in G. Steinmetz, ed., *State/Culture: State Formation after the Cultural Turn*. Ithaca, NY: Cornell University Press.

Molne, K., 1976. 'Donorinseminasjon. En oversikt og et materiale', *Tidsskrift for Den norske legeforening*, 17–18: 982–86.

Mulkay, M., 1997. *The Embryo Research Debate: Science and the Politics of Reproduction*. Cambridge: Cambridge University Press.

Nielsen, T.H., 2000. *Livets tre og kodenes kode. Fra genetikk til bioteknologi. Norge 1900–2000*. Oslo: Gyldendal Akademisk.

Nielsen, T.H., 2003. 'Bioteknologi – et dilemma for det liberale samfunn', *Aftenposten*, 13 June: 11.

NOU (Norske Offentlige Utredninger). 1987. *Retningslinjer for prioriteringer innen norske helsetjenester*, 1987: 23. Oslo.

NOU (Norske Offentlige Utredninger). 1991. *Om mennesker of bioteknologi*, 1991: 6. Oslo.

NOU (Norske Offentlige Utredninger). 1997. *Prioriteringer på ny*, 1997: 18. Oslo.

Rådet for medisinsk forskning (RMF; utvalg for forskningsetikk), 1983. *Etiske retningslinjer ved kunstig befruktning (AID) og in vitro fertilisering (IVF)*. Oslo: NAVF/RMF.

Ragoné, H., 1994. *Surrogate Motherhood: Conception in the Heart*. Boulder, CO: Westview Press.

Riksaasen. G., 2001. 'To mammaer, går det an? En annerledes familieplanlegning', in S. Howell and M. Melhuus, eds, *Blod – tykkere enn vann? Betydninger av slkektskap i Norge*. Bergen: Fagbokforlaget.

Roll-Hansen, N., 1980. 'Den norske debatten om rasehygiene', *Historisk Tidsskrift*, 3: 259–83.

Rønne-Petersen, E., 1951. *Prøvrørsmäniskan. En studie i moderne magi*. Stockholm: Bokforlaget biopsykologi.

Sandemose, A., 1952. 'Unnfanget i løgn', *Årstidene*.

Seip, A.-L., 1994. *Veiene til velferdsstaten. Norsk sosialpolitikk 1920 –75*. Oslo: Gyldendal Norsk Forlag.

Sirnes, T., 1997. *Risiko og meining*. Rapport nr. 53. Bergen: University of Bergen, Institutt for administrasjon og organisasjonsvitenskap.

Sirnes, T., 1999. '"Alt som er fast, fordamper?" Normalitet og identitet i endring', in S. Meyer and T. Sirnes, eds, *Normalitet og identitetsmakt i Norge*. Oslo: Ad Notam Gyldendal.

Strathern, M., 1992a. *After Nature: English Kinship in the Late Twentieth Century*. Cambridge: Cambridge University Press.

Strathern, M., 1992b. *Reproducing the Future: Anthropology, Kinship and the New Reproductive Technologies*. Manchester: Manchester University Press.

Syse, A., 1993. *Abortloven. Juss og verdier*. Oslo: ad Notam Gyldendal.

Tranøy, K.E., 1990. 'Feminisme, kvinnerett og kjønnsnøytralitet – kommentar til Brita M. Gulli og Marianne Fastvold', in A. Hellum, A. Syse, H.S. Aasen, eds, *Menneske, nature og fødselsteknologi. Verdivalg og rettslig regulering*. Oslo: Ad Notam.

Warnock Committee, 1985. *A Question of Life: The Warnock Report on Human Fertilisation and Embryology*. Oxford: Blackwell.

11 THE STATE OF THE STATE IN EUROPE, OR, 'WHAT IS THE EUROPEAN UNION THAT ANTHROPOLOGISTS SHOULD BE MINDFUL OF IT'?

Cris Shore

INTRODUCTION: EUROPEAN UNION AND THE PARADOX OF THE MODERN STATE

A few years ago Daniel Hannan, a British Member of the European Parliament (or 'MEP' in the acronymic language of contemporary Euro-speak), made a surprising discovery about his employer.[1] Writing in a reflexive and empirical vein many anthropologists would be proud of, he gives a vivid personal account of an official European parliamentary delegation visit to Uzbekistan which, for the purposes of my analysis, is worth considering in some detail. 'We had spent half an hour ticking off our Uzbek hosts about the autocratic nature of their country, where the president has almost untrammelled powers and where the parliament is a rubber-stamping chamber', so begins Hannan's account.

We were feeling pretty pleased with ourselves until one of the Uzbeks asked how we did things in Brussels. With much clearing of throats and shuffling of bottoms, we admitted that the European Parliament didn't have any legislative powers either. Euro-MPs, our chairman explained, could only debate proposals that came down from the European Commission. It was, we had to concede, a system rather similar to that in Uzbekistan – with the difference that at least their executive had some kind of direct mandate ... They had elected their president, Islam Karimov, with a fishy-looking 91 percent of the vote. We, on the other hand, dispensed with elections altogether, and simply appointed our president, Romano Prodi. Their Uzbek judges struck us as dangerously close to the regime. But our Euro-judges were, in practice *part* of the regime, making rather than interpreting the law. The Uzbeks were struggling to de-collectivise their farms. We in Europe, on the other hand, continued to operate the CAP on essentially Marxist lines. And so on, *mutatis mutandis*, through virtually every sphere of government activity. (Hannan 2001)

Notwithstanding its ironic and sceptical tone, Hannan's article raises some key issues in the vexed debate about the European Union's (EU's) evolving political system and how we should theorise it. At the heart of the debate is arguably the most contentious question of all: is the EU an embryonic state?

234

To give this a slightly different twist, is the integration process leading to a United States of Europe? If not, then (to echo Mark Twain) what exactly *is* the EU that anthropology should be mindful of it? As I hope to show, these questions provide an optic for examining problems of a more theoretical nature concerning the analysis of modern states in our increasingly transnational world. I also hope to show why the enigma of the European Union opens up for critical analysis wider issues of fundamental importance to current debates about the nation-state, European democracy and the analysis of contemporary systems of supranational governance.

This chapter is therefore a contribution to political anthropology, to EU Studies, and more specifically, to recent attempts to rethink the state from an anthropological perspective (Mitchell 1991; Scott 1998; Steinmetz 1999). In part, and as Neumann (this volume) observes, this requires us to take 'culture' more seriously in our attempts to understand state formation and to look more closely at the role of narrative in the construction of modern states. Such an approach is necessarily concerned with issues of meaning, representation and everyday practice as well as with governance and power. As Akhil Gupta puts it:

... to think of states as cultural artefacts whose distinctiveness is embodied not only in culturally-embedded imaginaries, but in culturally marked practices, is an essential corrective to strongly institutionalist perspectives that would unproblematically compare states to one another along variables from rates of economic growth to degrees of urbanisation. (2005: 175–76)

Like nations, states are also distinguished largely by the *style* in which they are imagined (cf. Anderson 1983). This focus on representation and cultural imaginaries brings us to a key problem in the ethnography of states in the age of globalisation. As Michel-Rolph Trouillot (2001) has noted, a curious paradox has emerged in the world today. On the one hand, the transnational imperatives of globalisation seem to have rendered the modern state increasingly obsolete and irrelevant 'not only as an economic actor but also as a social and cultural container' (2001: 125). Yet at the same time, the state, particularly the disciplinary and regulatory state, has everywhere augmented its presence in people's lives. Despite the fact that deregulation and the freedom of the individual have become the hallmarks of contemporary Western culture, the hand of government now extends into virtually every aspect of our existence, monitoring, regulating and ordering what we do as citizens, parents, taxpayers and consumers.[2] In the words of Ralph Miliband, writing over three decades ago, 'more than ever before men now live in the shadow of the state' (1969: 1).

Part of the challenge for an ethnography of the state, I believe, is to explain this contradiction, and to try to understand how globalisation is transforming not only the relationship between state and society, but also the very definition of these concepts. In the case of Europe (as I argue below), the 'hollowing out' of the nation-state by the European Union and other supranational bodies is another factor that is blurring these distinctions[3] (cf. Dyson 1994; Jessop 1999: 388; Mitchell 1999), rendering the boundaries between the bureaucracies of the EU and those of national governments increasingly permeable and indistinct. An anthropology of the state in Europe needs to explore these processes and ask what exactly does 'living under the shadow of the state' mean in a world of ever-more integrated, overlapping and confused transnational regimes of governance of the kind epitomised by the EU or the World Trade Organisation (WTO)? To do this I suggest we must first ask what *constitutes* the state? If the modern state is (*pace* Bourdieu 1999) a seemingly 'autonomous field', how can we recognise states-in-the making or state-like entities that deny their autonomy and disguise their power, or that, like the EU, fall outside our conventional categories? This is more than simply a problem of semantics. To paraphrase Renan, the key question for EU scholars is not 'What is a state?' so much as '*When* is a state?'

The suggestion that the EU might be transforming itself into a state is typically rejected or ignored in most official EU narratives that deal with the history and evolution of the integration process. The primary objective behind the creation of the European Community, as we are often told, was to ensure that 'never again' would Germany and France go to war, and beyond this, to promote economic stability and growth in Europe – thereby providing a bulwark against Soviet Communism. However, the dominant vision underlying Monnet and Schuman's plan for a European Coal and Steel Community was to control the excesses of the nation-state, with its assumed propensity for violence. By removing its power over the coal and steel production, and later atomic energy (the sinews of war), and by imposing a system of 'supranational' institutional constraints, the European Community would supposedly provide an antidote to the negative features of the state and statist discourse. But behind this lay a more ambitious project of political and social engineering. As the founding treaties proclaim, the aim was to establish 'an ever closer union among the European peoples' (CEC 1983: 113), and beyond this:

... to substitute for age-old rivalries the merging of their essential interests ... and to lay the foundations for institutions which will give direction to a destiny henceforth shared.

This is the narrative that the European Union tells *to* itself *about* itself. However, while EU analysts may agree about its origins and formative conceptions and concur that integration is a 'process' with its own dynamic, there is a striking lack of consensus on where that process is leading, or what that 'shared destiny' might be. EU leaders say that their goal is to create a new European order that will 'go beyond' the logic of nation-states and nationalism by creating a pan-national and supranational political architecture. But what these construction metaphors mean in practice, and how this new federal 'architecture' will impact upon the political landscape of state, nationhood and democracy in Europe are unclear. Significantly, most

Europeans themselves have little understanding of what the EU is, or how to define it. As Perry Anderson observes:

The Union remains a more or less unfathomable mystery to all but a handful of those who, to their bemusement, have recently become its citizens. It is well-nigh entirely arcane to ordinary voters; a film of mist covers it even in the mirror of scholars. (Anderson 1997: 51)

Part of the difficulty is that the EU has no parallel in history and cannot be compared to other recognisable federal polities (such as the USA, Switzerland or Canada) as it is not a sovereign state in the conventional sense. As Jacques Delors once famously remarked, the EU is a 'UPO' – an Unidentified Political Object – whose complex institutional structure defies categorisation. In short, the EU is a constitutional anomaly; an 'enigma wrapped in a mystery', to use Churchill's description of that other unique, post-national high-modernist political union of the twentieth century. However, anomalies, as Mary Douglas observed long ago, are typically associated with disorder and pollution. If the EU is an anomaly and '*sui generis*', as its protagonists claim, what sort of anomaly is it, and to what extent can it be compared to, or analysed against, our understanding of modern states? Defining the EU has not only become a problem for academics, but equally for citizens in the member states and applicant countries whose governments have signed up for membership: as Clifford Geertz might have put it, 'What the devil do they think they are joining?'

In probing these questions, I also want to explore how anthropological approaches to the state might clarify our understanding the EU and, conversely, how analysing the EU can shed light on the way European nation-states are themselves being transformed. My argument is that to understand modern states and state formation we must look not only at formal institutions of government, but equally, at the more diffuse and informal processes of moral regulation and social engineering (cf. Rose 1989; Burchell et al. 1991; Foucault 1991). As Corrigan and Sayer (1985) put it, state formation is 'cultural revolution' – an ongoing process of social as well as structural change.[4] Finally, I wish to reflect critically on the concept of 'multi-level governance' and the claim that the EU has created a new form of 'government without statehood' that, far from undermining Europe's nation-states has actually strengthened them.[5] My conclusion rejects as spurious the second argument and reverses the first: the EU is indeed an embryonic state, but the novel political system it is creating is best characterised as 'statehood without government'.

ANTHROPOLOGICAL PERSPECTIVES ON THE STATE

Let me begin with the problem of the modern state and how we might study it anthropologically. Carole Nagengast (1994) argues that despite its presence in virtually every society studied, anthropologists have generally avoided studying the modern state per se, preferring to treat it as an 'unanalysed given' or at best as a 'hostile and intrusive presence in local social life' (Herzfeld 1997: 1). There are numerous reasons for this, including the colonial roots of the discipline and the fact that trying to study states using participant-observation poses considerable methodological and conceptual problems. As Foucault once remarked, one should refrain from theorising the state 'in the sense that one abstains from an indigestible meal' (cited in Gordon 1991: 4).

Much of the difficulty with analysing the modern state lies in the fact that it is not easy to observe, nor is it the cohesive, tangible entity that traditional writing on the subject often assumes.[6] Indeed, the variety of institutions that comprise the state today imply that it does not always act as a unified or homogeneous entity. What is striking today, as Gupta (1995: 375) observes, 'is the degree to which the state has become implicated in the minute texture of everyday life', through its myriad links with schooling, policing, taxation and local administration. It is precisely this ubiquity of the state that renders it difficult to perceive. The classical definition of Max Weber – that the state is the body that exercises a monopoly over the legitimate use of violence within a given territory – is therefore no longer adequate for understanding modern state systems.[7] Or rather, if we are to think of the state in these terms, we need to adopt broader concepts of 'legitimacy' and 'coercion' and ask, how are these functions achieved? In other words, it is not reducible to 'bodies of armed men' or formal governmental structures: it is also a type of abstraction and, more importantly, an exercise in legitimation.[8] This is not to suggest that the state has withered away or lost its grip over its citizens. Rather, as Mitchell (1999) and Trouillot (2001) argue, 'state-like effects' previously produced by the institutions of the state have to an increasing extent been relocated to other institutions such as NGOs, educational systems, the social sciences and global corporations – which have no obvious geographical or spatial fixity and which very often bypass the power of nation-states.[9]

I raise these points not to argue against tackling complex subjects such as the state and modern systems of government – but on the contrary, to propose that we *can* study these subjects, and from several distinctly anthropological perspectives.[10] However, our starting point must be the recognition that we need a broader conception of the state: one that focuses on the exercise of power and the practices of government, rather than deducing the modern activities of government from the state's assumed essential properties.[11] The idea that the state has a substantive 'essence' also needs to be questioned. As Nagengast says:

… the state is not just a set of institutions staffed by bureaucrats who serve the public interest. It also incorporates cultural and political forms, representations, discourse, practices and activities, and specific technologies and organisations of power that, taken together, help to define public interest, establish meaning, and define and naturalise available social identities. (Nagengast 1994: 116)

The problem is that scholars have all too often objectified and personified the state, thereby endowing it with a 'misplaced concreteness' (Alonso 1994: 380). This has resulted in a conception of the state as a unified, coherent entity with a clear hegemonic project, rather than a complex and messy set of agents and processes that do not necessary share a common purpose at all.[12] Against this, as Corrigan and Sayer argue, the state should be seen more as a 'message of domination' – 'an ideological artefact attributing unity, morality and independence to the disunited, amoral and dependent workings of the practice of government' (1985: 77). This shifts the focus of analysis to the cultural forms and practices that constitute the state: those everyday state routines, rituals, activities and policies that 'regulate the social making of meaning and of subjects' (Alonso 1994: 380).

My point here is simply that political anthropologists increasingly recognise that the power of the state lies in its *cultural* forms: above all, in its capacity to engender moral regulation and, as Marx pointed out long ago, the illusion of its own coherence. To understand modern states, we therefore need to explore the more diffuse ways that power and governance work – including the everyday rules and normalising technologies that govern conduct and render populations governable in the first place. This is what Abrams (1988) terms 'politically organised subjection', and what Foucault (1991) calls 'governmentality'; the myriad techniques used by the modern state to individualise and objectify its subjects. To analyse these techniques requires a focus on the taxonomies states use to classify and order their populations: that is, the way modern relations of rule and forms of discipline are constructed, and the way people – as 'citizens, voters, taxpayers, ratepayers, jurors, parents, consumers, homeowners – individuals' (Corrigan and Sayer 1985: 5) – are classified within the state community.[13]

Yet another way of studying states ethnographically is to look at their symbolic and cultural manifestations: how they represent themselves, how they create and recreate the illusion of their own coherence – and how they construct our political realities. The political scientist, Michael Walzer, put it succinctly when he wrote; 'the state is invisible; it must be personified before it can be seen, symbolised before it can be loved, imagined before it can be conceived' (1967, cited in Kertzer 1988: 6). To study the state anthropologically, as Donald Carter (1994: 73) says, we therefore need to explore the way it is 'envisioned through official documents' and elsewhere. In short, we must look behind the façade of its formal structures (although these too are important) and explore the more diffuse ways that governance and power work.

NARRATING THE NEW EUROPE: EU 'CULTURAL ACTION'

These arguments provide a useful context for understanding the European Union. Since 1992 the main focus of my research has been the 'cultural politics of European integration' and the 'organisational cultures' of the

EU institutions themselves. One aim of that research was to examine the various ways EU policy elites were using cultural policy and 'cultural action' to promote a sense of belonging and identity among the peoples of Europe. That strategy, which was developed after 1984 under the heading of 'The People's Europe Campaign', led to a host of EU-sponsored symbolic initiatives designed to capture the loyalties and affections of European citizens and, beyond this, to forge a European public as a self-recognising body politic (or *demos*). As officials in Brussels informed me, the aim was not simply to stimulate greater consciousness of 'Europe' among member-state nationals, but rather to create a European consciousness that would mobilise the peoples of Europe towards a new conception of themselves as 'Europeans' rather than exclusive nationals.

To these ends, the Commission set about introducing a series of measures to rectify the perceived lack of awareness among Europeans of their 'shared cultural heritage', from EU-funded European sports competitions, artistic awards and literary prizes, to town-twinning initiatives, student exchange programmes and the invention of a whole new repertoire of symbols for 'Europeanness' (cf. Shore 1993). Foremost among these was the new EC emblem and flag – a circle of twelve yellow stars set against an azure background – hoisted for the first time outside the Commission headquarters in Brussels at a formal ceremony on 29 May 1986. It is now seen emblazoned on umbrellas, sweatshirts, bags, and in every kind of tourist-shop artefact.

Other symbolic vehicles for communicating the 'Europe idea' included the creation of the standardised European passport, driving licence and car number-plates, and a European anthem, taken from the fourth movement of Beethoven's ninth symphony – the 'Ode to Joy'. To these were added various high-profile cultural initiatives including the formation of a European Community 'Youth Orchestra', 'Opera Centre', and a series of projects to promote Europe's architectural heritage – beginning with a major scheme for 'the conservation and restoration of the Parthenon' (CEC 1992: 3). The Commission also proposed creating a European Academy of Science, Technology and Art, 'voluntary work camps for young people', a Euro-lottery and pan-European postage stamps bearing portraits of EC pioneers such as Robert Schuman and Jean Monnet (Adonnino 1985: 22–24). That the mundane postage stamp should be appropriated as an agent for promoting the 'European idea' is of secondary significance: more important is the fact that it also becomes instrumental in creating the new category of 'Community history'. This idea was later developed in several EC-funded projects to rewrite history textbooks from a European perspective (cf. Duroselle 1990) in order to bolster the 'European dimension in education' (Adonnino 1985: 24).

Similarly, the EU's Eurostat Office – with its six-monthly 'Eurobarometer' surveys of public opinion across the Union – is another potent way in which the category of a 'European public' has been invented. As Hacking (1991) notes 'statistics' are powerful shapers of consciousness – or political technologies. They create new ways of seeing, inculcate new norms of conduct and generate new typologies of persons. And as he also reminds us, statistics are, by definition, part of the armoury of the state and the way it renders its population knowable (and hence, governable).

Finally, the Adonnino Committee also proposed the creation of a host of new celebratory markers in the ritual calendar, including European Years dedicated to particular EU themes, special 'European Weeks' (to accompany the European City of Culture initiative), and a new pan-European public holiday on 9 May – official 'Europe Day' – to mark the anniversary of the Schuman Plan – the proposal for Germany and France to pool coal and steel production.

Interestingly, most officials were quite unapologetic about this instrumental use of culture. Typically, they would justify it with the comment that: 'People are ignorant about their shared cultural heritage as Europeans ... we merely want to educate them about their common identity', or 'We are simply carrying out the decisions of the EU member states: this is what their governments signed up to ... it's not the Commission imposing its own agenda.'

What is striking about these and other EU-funded cultural initiatives (which include the creation of the 'euro' and the invention of the category of European Citizenship), is their similarity to the techniques of nation-building and state formation pursued by nineteenth-century nationalist elites. Flags, anthems, passports, national currencies and historiography were all strategies used by nation-states to instil national consciousness among their subjects.[14] As Tom Nairn wrote, '[t]he new middle class intelligentsia of nationalism had to invite the masses into history; and the invitation-card had to be written in a language they understood' (Nairn 1977: 340). State formation in Europe historically involved both the penetration of a given territory by a set of governing institutions, and an orchestrated process of identity-construction from above – the classic model being Jacobinist France after 1789. But these parallels raise interesting questions: is the EU seeking to create a sense of European *nationhood*? And how useful is it to compare European integration with nineteenth-century state formation – the very model against which the EU typically defines itself?

Beyond exploring these attempts to forge European subjects, my fieldwork also explored the extent to which EU civil servants might themselves embody the kind of European identity and subjectivity implied in the EU's project for forging ever closer union. To adapt a phrase from Benedict Anderson (1983), are EU officials the 'Creole pioneers' of Europeanism – an ideology that might one day challenge the hegemonic grip that nationalism continues to hold over the modern imagination? My conclusion was that this was, in fact, the way many see themselves and that a very distinctive 'consciousness of kind' or 'European identity' is developing among those who occupy the bureaucratic habitus of the EU's institutions in Brussels. In this respect, the EU's supranational organisations are engendering a new type of European subjectivity – much as Jean Monnet, the EU's foremost visionary and architect, had predicted. Whether this process is creating the cadres for a new European state remains a matter of debate. But like Crais (this volume), I believe the study of administrators and bureaucrats provides a particularly useful lens for exploring patterns of state formation. What I want to do in the remainder of this chapter is develop these themes further by analysing the way European political elites and scholars in other disciplines have tackled these issues, particularly the question of the emergence of a European state.

WHAT IS THE EU? CRITIQUING THE CRITIQUE OF STATIST PERSPECTIVES

In Britain, the public debate about European integration is particularly fraught. The increasing transfer of powers from the national capitals to EU institutions in Brussels, the creation of the European Central Bank, the new euro currency zone ('Euroland'), and growing calls for the Commission to represent member states at international fora such as the WTO and G7 meetings, have led many analysts to suggest that European integration is leading inexorably towards the formation of a European 'superstate'. This, however, is emphatically denied by government officials and ministers who accuse their critics of 'scaremongering' or fanaticism. As Commissioner Chris Patten declared, the idea of Europe becoming a superstate is 'as likely as discovering the moon is made of cheese', and those who suggest otherwise 'are barking'.[15] Similarly, the British Prime Minister Tony Blair, setting out proposals for closer European military cooperation – including the creation of a European Rapid Reaction Force – declared that he wanted to see the EU become a 'superpower' but not a 'superstate'. However, the distinction between a superpower and a superstate is not at all clear. Indeed, the only superpowers in living memory have invariably been states characterised by all the usual trappings of statehood such as courts, armies, citizenship, currencies, foreign policies and well-defined borders. Moreover, many European political leaders, including Romano Prodi, have stated publicly that a European army and a European foreign and security policy are logical and necessary steps forward in the evolution of the EU.

For EU supporters, this is something to be welcomed. The steady transfer of national sovereignty to supranational institutions in Brussels is seen as something both inevitable and desirable – part of Europe's historical mission to build a new post-national order that will deliver Europe from the evils of nationalism. For some, European integration is perceived as a continuation of the Enlightenment project – even its apotheosis – with the EU institutions as the epitome of mankind's march towards reason, progress and civilisation.[16] Interestingly, European policy elites now typically refer to the EU project of 'European construction' and 'Europeanisation' as the 'domestication' of the nation-state.[17] This is a curious choice of metaphor given how reminiscent of nineteenth-century colonial discourses is the idea of 'domesticating' a people or territory.

Alan Milward's 1992 book *The European Rescue of the Nation-State* provides the clearest argument against this view. Milward's thesis, briefly, is that there never was any significant antithesis between the European Community and the nation-state. 'The evolution of the European Community since 1945', he says, 'has been an integral part of the reassertion of the nation-state' (1992: 2–3). Far from epitomising the federalist vision of the EU's 'founding fathers', the EU was a rational, pragmatic and self-interested response to the loss of national sovereignty. According to Milward (1992: 17), the EU is primarily an 'aspect of national diplomacy'. Indeed, 'to supersede the nation-state would be to destroy the Community' (1992: 3). However, Milward was writing *before the 1992 Maastricht Treaty*, which, by its own reckoning, marked a 'new phase' in the history of European integration. What he ignores is the incremental and processual nature of integration and the fact that it has its own dynamism and autonomy. As Borneman and Fowler (1997: 489) put it, the EU is 'both cause and effect of itself': it is a self-reinforcing system of institutions that work to enlarge each other's power.[18]

Since the Maastricht Treaty there have been too the further major constitutional treaties at Amsterdam and Nice (1997 and 2001). The result is that national politics and European politics have become ever more institutionally entwined such that the whole context of national politics and policy-making has been radically transformed.[19] This Europeanisation of the nation-state is not a matter of dispute: what is, though, is whether the dynamics of integration have created something beyond this.

EU scholars generally concede that it has, but the interpretations of what that 'something' entails are characteristically opaque. Typically, the EU's nexus of institutions is seen as the embryo of a fundamentally new type of polity, one that is simultaneously national, transnational, supranational and possibly 'post-national'. From a legal perspective this analysis is correct: the EU is a hybrid without parallel. Never before have a group of old nation-states 'pooled' their sovereignty to create such a complex political system. As Sbragia (1993: 24) says, the EU 'does not fit into any accepted category of governance'.[20] John Ruggie (1993: 140) calls it, 'the first truly postmodern international form' adding that we lack an adequate vocabulary to describe its evolving architecture.[21]

The typical argument is that comparisons between the European Union and the nation-states are meaningless because the EU is both *sui generis* and an 'unfinished project' whose 'ultimate trajectory is unknowable'. Many legal scholars have joined the argument, proclaiming that the EU's hybrid form of 'postnational constitutionalism' cannot be meaningfully translated into old-fashioned 'state-centric' categories (Walker 2003). Others sidestep the question altogether by dismissing it as a sterile debate over semantics. Taking their cue from contemporary academic discourses, many EU leaders and analysts have abandoned the old language of states and territories and speak instead of 'overlapping layers' of European economic and political 'spaces' tied together, as Jacques Delors put it, by the 'Community's spiderlike strategy to organise the architecture of a Greater Europe' (cited in Ruggie 1993: 140). This has inspired some writers to new heights of creativity in their attempt to capture in words the indescribable uniqueness of the EU. For Mark Leonard (1999), the EU is a 'network or networks' or transnational 'matrix'. For Peter Gowan (1997: 91), it is an 'historically peculiar ensemble of institutions [that] cannot easily be framed within any one of the conventional frameworks for understanding political and economic phenomena'. It cannot be a state, he says, because 'it lacks that most elementary attribute of a state – an enforcement apparatus of its own'. However, since this was written, the EU has acquired new powers, including the embryo of a common foreign and security policy, and its own military capability – the so-called 'Rapid Reaction Force' – a 60,000-strong force to be deployed for what are officially termed 'peace enforcement tasks'.

In their celebrated textbook on policy-making in the EC, Wallace et al. (1983) concluded that the EC was 'less than a federation [but] more than a regime' – a formula that subsequently became the new 'common sense' for students of European Union Studies.[22] William Wallace has subsequently revised this proposition. Taking up arguments developed in the recent literature on 'multi-level governance' (see Marks and Hooghe 1996; Börzel and Risse 2000), he suggests the EU has evolved into a novel form of 'government without statehood' (Wallace 1996: 439). For anthropologists 'government without statehood' invariably invites comparisons with the extensive literature on acephalous societies, or what used to be termed 'tribes without rulers'. To apply this notion to the EU is an interesting thesis, but is it accurate? Certainly, governance has become more complex and diffuse than the old nineteenth-century state model would suggest. But does the novelty of the EU's multi-level structure dissolve the question of statehood?

My contention is that it does not. There are two fundamental problems with Wallace's argument. First, it rests on a comparison not with the modern, broader conception of the state (understood as a series of diffuse institutions and effects), but with the static, outdated Weberian model that most analysts (including Wallace himself) would agree no longer exists. Since the EU invariably fails to measure up to that model, he concludes that the EU cannot be a state in the 'conventional sense'. But if we define the state in terms of regulatory power and governance in the widest sense, a very different picture emerges. Second, if the EU's emerging system of institutionalised, interstate cooperation is 'government without statehood', we should recall the anthropological critique of supposedly 'stateless societies'. As Talal Asad (1972) and Akbar Ahmed (1976) demonstrated in their critique of Barth's study of the political system of the Swat Pathans, what appears to be a political system based on loose, segmentary and shifting alliances, when viewed over the longer term turns out to be ever less fluid structures of political rule and class domination.

POLITICAL HYBRID OR EMERGENT SUPERSTATE?

To most critics it seems the European Community has acquired most of the characteristics of a state, even in the 'conventional' sense.[23] Although they may be novel and unusual, the EU's institutional structures are nonetheless recognisable approximations of those of a nation-state in a least five major ways:

First, it has an 'executive arm', in the shape of the European Commission. Although its 20,000-odd bureaucracy is smaller than the average city municipality, its budget is less than 1.4 per cent of area GDP, and it has no direct powers of taxation (although this is now being seriously proposed),[24] it has an immense influence over policy. A study by France's Conseil d'État in the early 1990s estimated that 55 per cent of new French domestic laws were being drafted in Brussels – a percentage that has undoubtedly increased in the intervening years.[25] Among its many functions, the Commission administers that budget, issues regulatory directives, acts as the 'Guardian of the Treaties' and, most important, holds the exclusive right to initiate European legislation.

Second, it has a Council of Ministers, a series of parallel intergovernmental meetings in Brussels that now cover virtually all areas of policy. This provides the legislative function – which it shares with the Commission. As Anderson (1997: 67) describes it, the Council, is a 'hydra-headed entity in virtually constant session at Brussels, whose deliberations are secret, most of whose decisions are sewn up at a bureaucratic level below the assembled ministers themselves, and whose outcomes are binding on national parliaments'. But the Council is also much more than this. It is the buckle that fastens the EU to its member states and that brings together the purposes and resources of the Commission with the much larger resources of the nation-states wherever there are agreed decisions. In short, it clamps the powers of the nation-state to the will of the Community, thereby amplifying its decisions.

Third, it has the European Court of Justice (ECJ) in Luxembourg, whose judges adjudicate in any conflict between national and community law, and who have come to regard the European Treaties as something approximating a European constitution. As Daniel Hannan's (2001) remarks made clear at the outset of this chapter, ECJ judges are dangerously close to the regime. Furthermore, the ECJ's interpretations of European law are constantly expanding the scope of European law and the EU's powers (or 'competences') through a process that critics, including Lord Patrick Neill (1995), have termed 'judicial activism'.

Fourth, the EU now has a Constitution. While British government spokesmen were busy belittling its significance and describing it as simply a 'tidying up exercise', other European leaders showed no such caution. Valéry Giscard d'Estaing, who chaired the European Convention that produced the Draft Constitutional Treaty, compared the Convention's deliberations to those of the drafters of the United States' Constitution at the historical Philadelphia

Convention of 1789. If this comparison is correct, the signing of the EU Constitution in October 2004 marks the symbolic birth of the United States of Europe.

Finally, it has the European Parliament, the EU's only 'popular' and elective body, but which possesses no common electoral system; no permanent home; no powers of taxation; no control over the exchequer (being confined to simple yes/no votes on the Community budget as a whole); virtually no say over executive appointments;[26] and no rights to initiate legislation, simply the ability to amend or veto it. The institutional upshot of all this, as Perry Anderson (writing in 1997) put it:

... is thus a customs union with a quasi-executive of supranational cast ... a quasi-legislature of inter-governmental ministerial sessions, shielded from any national oversight ... a quasi-supreme court that acts as if it were the guardian of a constitution which does not exist; and a pseudo-legislative lower chamber, in the form of a largely impotent parliament that is nevertheless the only elective body, theoretically accountable to the peoples of Europe. All of this superimposed on a dozen nation-states determining their own fiscal, social, military and foreign policies. (Anderson 1997: 68)

Although a little out of date, this is nonetheless a fairly accurate description of the EU's evolving institutional complex: and to all intents and purposes the EU *is* an embryonic state. What Anderson might have added is that the European Community[27] is also an internationally recognised body which, like a state, has the power to negotiate and make international treaties; that its laws and Court take precedence over national laws; that within large policy areas it exercises a monopoly on decision-making and jurisdiction over a defined territory and its population; and that it now has its own single currency, the euro, an independent Central Bank empowered to set interest and exchange rates for the entire EU, and the legal authority to fine member states who fail to comply with its public spending and borrowing targets.[28] As Joschka Fischer, the German Foreign Secretary, recently declared: 'In Maastricht one of the three essential sovereign rights of the modern nation-state – currency, internal security and external security – was for the first time transferred to the sole responsibility of a European institution.'[29]

The 1992 Maastricht Treaty also created the legal category of 'Citizenship of the Union'. However ambiguous that concept seems, 'citizenship' is generally a marker of nationality and the state to which one belongs. This begs the question, is European citizenship a form of nationality? If the EU is not a state, how can one be a citizen of a 'non-state'? And what are the duties of European citizenship?

Another key feature of modern states is the ability to control one's external frontiers and the movement of people across national borders. The EU claims these powers for itself as part of the precondition for creating the single market and a 'Europe without frontiers'. There is also increasing pressure on EU member states to bring immigration, law and order – the third 'pillar' of the

Union – under the jurisdiction of supranational organisations rather than, as at present, intergovernmental ones. Indeed, the '9/11' terrorist attacks on the US generated the political will to push through the idea to create a European arrest warrant – 'which had hitherto been too controversial, since it expands the EU's remit into criminal law'.[30] The EU also possesses its own embryonic equivalent of the FBI (called 'Europol') whose jurisdiction has quietly expanded to cover all crimes involving money-laundering. As Ambrose Evans-Pritchard (2001: 19) observes, '[t]he foundations of an EU federal judiciary and an EU police and security system are now largely in place'.

What the EU does not yet have is a monopoly over the legitimate use of violence, a key criterion in Max Weber's traditional definition of statehood. However, neither did many pre-modern states, as Anthony Giddens points out (1985).[31] It is only in times of war that military might becomes the defining feature of a state; in peace-time what matters is ultimate legal authority, and this now resides with the European Court of Justice. But the development of a common European army, as Romano Prodi declared recently, is the 'logical next step' after merging national defence industries.[32] Moreover, with the incremental spillover (or 'Treaty-creep' as critics describe it) towards a common foreign and security policy it is becoming increasingly difficult to separate issues of diplomacy from those of defence and military matters.

Those who reject claims that the EU is transforming itself into a state often adopt the legalistic arguments that it cannot be a state because it does not define itself as a state, nor is it recognised as a state in international law. That said, the European Constitution agreed by EU heads of state in June 2004 bestows 'legal personality' on the Union, enabling it to act as a state under international law. Others make two kinds of argument. First, they argue that an entity that commands a mere 1.4 per cent of the EU's GNP cannot be regarded as a superstate. However, when the Commission can get its member states to commit their resources according to EU policy objectives using qualified majority voting in the Council of Ministers, then it has control over a much larger budget. As Laura Cram (1993) put it, the EU is 'playing the tune without paying the piper'. Second, they argue that the power of the Council of Ministers over decision-making at the European level is proof that sovereignty still resides with national governments. But this power no longer exists where there is qualified majority voting (QMV) or in areas where EU jurisdiction is specified. Under the terms of the European Constitution, the list of EU competences includes transport, energy, trade, competition, agriculture, fisheries, space exploration, social policy, public health, employment policy, consumer protection, asylum, immigration, criminal justice and foreign affairs.[33]

More importantly, though, it has become increasingly difficult to distinguish between those laws and regulations that come from Brussels and those that emanate from the member states. As I have argued elsewhere (Shore 2000), the process of *engrenage* (or the progressive enmeshing of national officials and civil servants within the EU's institutional world) has created an almost continuous administrative hierarchy in which it is difficult to fathom where Europe ends and the nation-state begins. The Council of Ministers – the most secretive and bureaucratic of EU institutions – has effectively *become part of the machinery of EU governance* and of the EU's 'spiderlike webs' of power. Just as the Single European Act created the conditions for the Single European Market, so the close integration between national and European officials and politicians is creating the conditions for the rise of a 'single bureaucratic apparatus' – which is yet another characteristic of the state.[34]

All this should come as little surprise. The process of cumulative integration through functional 'spillover' that was so clearly described by the early theorists of European integration is necessarily laying the foundations of a centralised European state. That is what EU leaders have long aspired to create, and that is what the 'Monnet method' was designed to achieve. In Brussels these facts are readily acknowledged and accepted by political leaders. The goal of European integration, as Monnet consistently argued, is a United States of Europe.[35] According to Helmut Kohl, this is precisely what the Maastricht Treaty would lead to – and why he signed up to it.[36]

CONCLUSION: WHAT KIND OF 'STATE' IS THE EU?

'It would be more than ironic', wrote the constitutional expert J.H. Weiler, 'if a polity set up as a means to counter the excesses of statism ended up coming round full circle and transforming itself into a (super) state' (1995: 13). What Weiler does not ask is under what conditions might this occur? The evidence clearly points to the conclusion that the EU is developing into a 'superstate', federal or otherwise. With its citizenship, central bank, single currency, diplomatic machinery, military arm, treaty controls over the money supply and ultimate legal authority, the EU is acquiring the powers of a sovereign state. The result, to paraphrase Ken Dyson (1994), is that existing nation-states are being 'hollowed out' as their powers are progressively transferred to Brussels. This is not the 'rescue' of the nation-state or its 'retreat', but rather its incorporation and subordination into the EU's growing web of regulatory power: it is the Brusselsisation of the nation-state. Terms like 'multi-level governance', 'post-national constitutionalism' and 'subsidiarity' disguise the fundamental inequality between tiers of government within the EU's evolving federal model.

A good illustration of this is the *acquis communautaire* – or 'patrimony of Community law' – to which new member states must sign up before being granted accession. This is the sum total of the past 46 or so years of Community legislation, including all EC Treaties, laws, regulations, policies, practices, obligations and objectives. In 1998 it was reported that Lithuania, after an entire year's work, had succeeded in translating 4,000 pages of the *acquis*. That left another 36,000 pages to go.[37] As officials in Brussels frequently told me, the European Community is 'a community of law'. Yet none of these thousands of legislative acts – which take supremacy over national law – will have been scrutinised or publicly debated within the applicant states of Eastern Europe. If the modern state is to be understood (*pace* Foucault), as a totalising web of regulatory and normative power, then the EU, with its *acquis communautaire*, falls squarely into that definition.

Perhaps the key question to end with is 'Does it matter if the EU is developing into a superstate?' Is this something to be welcomed and assisted, or lamented and opposed? This question opens up a vast and serious debate that is only just beginning in the public domain. Among EU elites, by contrast, the debate has moved way beyond this to the discussion of what Joschka Fischer (2000) has called the *finalité politique* of European integration[38] and the creation of an EU constitution and fully fledged European government.

The problem, however, is that the European Union is an embryonic state without a corresponding nation: it has created the political roof for a new system of European governance, but it has yet to create 'Europeans' beyond the elite enclaves of its own institutions.[39] This absence of a transnational public is a fundamental obstacle to the success of the EU project. As Anthony Smith (1997: 325) points out, 'today no state possesses legitimacy which does not also claim to represent the will of the "nation", even where there is as yet patently no nation for it to represent'. In short, the legitimacy of modern states is founded upon aspirations of political community and popular sovereignty.

For all the talk about 'supranationalism' and 'multi-level governance', without a European people ('demos'), a transnational public culture and a truly pan-national European media and political parties, the EU can never be a liberal democracy. And without democratic foundations, the notion of 'the European interest' becomes meaningless or, worse, a mask to disguise what are in effect the *raisons d'état* of a self-styled 'non-state'. 'Pooled sovereignty' in practice tends to mean divided accountability – which only reinforces the EU's democratic deficit.[40] The danger is not that the EU is developing into a system of 'government without statehood' but rather the obverse: that it is developing into a form of statehood without democratic government. For some EU enthusiasts – like Jean Monnet himself – the absence of democracy in the Community system is of secondary importance. The 'passive consent' of the masses was deemed sufficient to enable European elites to carry on with their project for 'European construction', without bothering too much about consulting the people. That may have been acceptable during the early nineteenth century when nation-states were being created, but it is unacceptable for Europe in the twenty-first century. To return to Daniel Hannan, the EU is unlikely to evolve into a totalitarian system, but, as he points out, 'the requisite mentality may be in place' for something like that to happen.

As I hope to have demonstrated, an anthropology of the EU is, de facto, an anthropology of the state and state formation. Rather than taking the EU's proclamations about itself at face value and treating as an 'unanalysed given' the way it represents itself, we should look to our own disciplinary traditions and to wider social science theories of the modern state to make sense of what the European Union is and, more importantly, where its project of Europeanisation is leading.

NOTES

1. Earlier versions of this paper were presented as the Annual Distinguished Lecture in the Anthropology of Europe, at the University of Massachusetts (Amherst) in October 2003 and at the 7th International Conference of the Societé Internationale d'Ethnologie et de Folklore in Budapest in 2001. I would like to thank the organisers and participants of both those meetings for their helpful and constructive comments. I would also like to thank the Economic and Social Research Council of the United Kingdom for its financial support, which made it possible for me to carry out the fieldwork in Brussels upon which these research findings are based.

2. As Christopher Pearson (1996) among others has noted, nowhere is this dualism more apparent in Anglo-American culture than in the symbolism and constraints that govern the use of the private car.

3. The term 'hollowing out' applies not only to the internationalisation of policy regimes and to supranational bodies operating above the level of the nation-state (such as the EU, the World Bank and WTO), but equally to sub-national entities, the growth of regional government and the trend towards increasing translocal linkages (see Jessop 1999 for a more detailed analysis).

4. As Steinmetz (1999: 8) writes:

    But states are never 'formed' once and for all. It is more fruitful to view state-formation as an ongoing process of structural change and not as a one-time event. Structural features of states involve the entire set of rules and institutions that are involved in making and implementing polices: the arrangement of ministries or departments, the set of rules for the allocation of individual positions within these departments, systems for generating revenues, legal codes and constitutions, electoral rules, forms of control over lower bodies of government, that nature and location of boundaries between state and society, and so forth.

5. For analyses of this debate, see in particular Milward (1992), Hoffman (1995), Wallace (1996).

6. For a good review of conceptions of the state, see Vincent (1992).

7. Charles Tilly (1990) defines states in a more qualified yet subtle way as 'coercion wielding organisations that are distinct from households and kinship groups and exercise clear priority in some respects over all other organisations within substantial territories' (cited in Steinmetz 1999: 9).

8. Cf. Abrams (1988). This argument also derives from Weber's definition of the state – the emphasis being precisely on the 'legitimacy' of its monopoly over the means of coercion.

9. A good example of this, as George Monbiot (2000) shows, is the increasing use by governments of private–public finance initiatives ('PFIs') to fund major public building programmes, and the transfer of responsibility from the public to the private sector for the running of prisons, hospitals, schools and other social services.

10. There is a growing body of literature on the modern state that highlights the different ways in which anthropologists have risen to this challenge. In some cases this has entailed a focus on functionary–client relationships (Grillo 1980) and on popular resistance to state hegemony (Joseph and Nugent 1994); elsewhere anthropologists have explored the state ethnographically through a focus on everyday forms of corruption (Gupta 1995) and the activities of local bureaucrats (Herzfeld 1992).

11. For an elaboration of this argument, see Gordon (1991).
12. As James C. Scott has noted (1994: xi), 'we cannot simply take it for granted that state elites have a "hegemonic project at all". This must be an empirical question, not a supposition.'
13. See also Nikolas Rose (1989) and Andrew Barry et al. (1996) for examples of how Foucault's ideas have been applied to the study of neoliberal governance.
14. As Smith (1990: 184) observes:

    ... [t]o create the nation it is not enough simply to mobilise compatriots. They must be taught who they are, where they come from and whither they are going. They must be turned into co-nationals through a process of mobilisation into the vernacular culture, albeit one adapted to modern social and political conditions.

15. Chris Patten, interviewed on BBC Radio 4's *Today* programme, 7 December 2000.
16. See Weiler (1995). See also Riff (1987: 86), who makes a similar argument for the concept of 'European integration', which he defines as a clearly articulated, albeit ambiguous, political ideology.
17. For Lord Cockfield, former European Commissioner and a major architect of the European single market, '[t]he gradual limitation of national sovereignty is part of a slow and painful forward march of humanity' (cited in Milward 1992: 2).
18. The result, they say, is that integration is 'fundamentally reorganizing territoriality and peoplehood, the two principles that have shaped modern European order' (Borneman and Fowler 1997: 489).
19. Here I agree with the argument in David McKay's book (1999). Maastricht radically shifted the terms of reference and has laid the groundwork for a European state.
20. Trouillot also calls the EU unique. He concludes that while national states are likely to hold on to their power to define political boundaries, the European Union is a 'spectacular exception ... [a] truly innovative and changing formation of which we cannot even guess the long-term political consequences' (2001: 132).
21. Comparisons are sometimes made between the EU and the United States of America, but these only work by playing down fundamental differences of history and culture that characterise their formation. While the EU represents an amalgam of established national states, the USA is essentially a large nation-state.
22. This definition echoes that of Keohane and Hoffman (1991: 10) who proposed that the EU 'is best characterised as neither an institutional regime nor an emerging state but a network involving pooling sovereignty'.
23. As the 1933 Inter-American Convention on Rights and Duties of States defines it: 'The state as a person of International Law should possess the following qualifications: (a) a permanent population; (b) a defined territory; (c) government; and (d) the capacity to enter into relations with other states' (Osmańczyk 1990: 871).
24. Ian Black, 'Belgian PM Wants Euro-Tax which would Bypass Governments', *Guardian*, 10 Feb. 2001.
25. *The Economist*, 10 May 2003: 46.
26. The European Parliament's rejection in October 2004 of Italy's choice of Commissioner, Rocco Buttigliani, may herald a shift, albeit small and belated, in this respect.
27. It is one of those complex anomalies of the EU that under Article 210 of the Treaty of Rome, the European Community has 'legal personality', whereas the European Union – of which the European Community is one pillar – does not. However, the EU increasingly acts as though it possesses de facto legal personality – particularly in the area of common foreign and security policy – and as Bainbridge (1998: 331) notes, sooner or later this will be reflected in an amendment to the Treaty on European Union.
28. 'Unless they happen to big states like France and Germany', as one wry EU official put it, reflecting on the way that both these large member states have violated the terms of the Stability and Growth Pact.

29. Source: http://www.germanembassy.org.au/eu-fisch.html. David McKay (1999) draws the same conclusion regarding the constitutional significance of economic and monetary union.
30. *The Economist*, 10 May 2003: 46.
31. As Gledhill (1994: 17) observes, the Weberian definition of the state is appropriate only to the modern European nation-state. As Foucault (1991) notes, what distinguishes the modern state from its predecessors is the degree of 'penetration' of everyday life and the extent of surveillance over the population.
32. Prodi's statement was made in an interview to the BBC programme *On the Record*; see also *Financial Times*, 10 May 1999: 2. Calls for the formation of a European army are not new. As Monnet (1978: 382) reminds us, the Italian Christian Democrat leader, de Gasperi, never tired of repeating: 'The European Army is not an end in itself: it is the instrument of a patriotic foreign policy. But European patriotism can develop only in a federal Europe.'
33. For assessments of the provisions of the European Constitution, see Parker and Dombey writing in the *Financial Times* (19 June 2004), Hannan in *The Spectator* (26 June 2004: 12–14) and Jack Straw in *The Economist* (10 July 2004: 40).
34. Furthermore, as decision-making in the Council of Ministers moves from the rule of unanimity to that of qualified majority voting this process is set to continue.
35. On this point Jean Monnet (1978: 401–02) was also adamant:

> Our countries have become too small for the present-day world ... The union of European peoples in the United States of Europe is the way to raise their standard of living and preserve peace. It is the great hope and opportunity of our time.

36. Helmut Kohl, speech delivered at the Bertelsman Forum, Petersburg Hotel, 3 April 1992.
37. *The Economist*, 29 August 1998: 38.
38. The final 'Declaration on the Future of the Union' in the draft Nice Treaty calls for a further summit in 2004 to agree upon 'how to establish and monitor a more precise delimitation of competencies between the European Union and the Member-States, reflecting the principle of subsidiarity' (Annex IV, point 5).
39. See Shore (2000) for further discussion of this.
40. This was clearly demonstrated by the Committee of Independent Experts whose damning report into fraud, nepotism and corruption precipitated the mass resignation of the Commission in March 1999 (CIE 1999).

REFERENCES

Abrams, P., 1988. 'Notes on the Difficulty of Studying the State', *Journal of Historical Sociology*, 1(1): 58–89.
Adonnino, P., 1985. 'A People's Europe: Reports from the Ad Hoc Committee', *Bulletin of the European Communities*, Supplement 7/85. Luxembourg: Office of Official Publications of the European Community.
Ahmed, A., 1976. *Millennium and Charisma among Pathans*. London: Routledge & Kegan Paul.
Alonso, A.M., 1994. 'The Politics of Space, Time and Substance: State Formation, Nationalism, and Ethnicity', *Annual Review of Anthropology*, 23: 379–405.
Anderson, B., 1983. *Imagined Communities*. London: Verso.
Anderson, P., 1997. 'Under the Sign of the Interim', in P. Gowan and P. Anderson, eds, *The Question of Europe*. London: Verso.
Asad, T., 1972. 'Market Model, Class Structure and Consent: A Reconsideration of Swat Political Organisation', *Man* (NS), 7: 74–94.
Bainbridge, T., 1998. *The Penguin Companion to European Union*. Harmondsworth: Penguin.

Barry, A., A.T. Osborne and N. Rose, eds, 1996. *Foucault and Political Reason: Liberalism, Neo-Liberalism and Rationalities*. Chicago: University of Chicago Press.

Borneman, J. and N. Fowler, 1997. 'Europeanization', *Annual Review of Anthropology*, 26: 487–514.

Börzel, T. and T. Risse, 2000. 'Who is Afraid of a European Federation? How to Constitutionalise a Multi-Level Governance System', *Harvard Law School – Jean Monnet Working Paper*, No.7/00 (Symposium: 'Responses to Joschka Fischer'), Cambridge, MA.

Bourdieu, P., 1999. 'Rethinking the State: Genesis and Structure of the Bureaucratic Field', in G. Steinmetz, ed., *State/Culture*. Ithaca, NY: Cornell University Press.

Burchell, G., C. Gordon and P. Miller, eds, 1991. *The Foucault Effect: Studies in Governmentality*. London: Harvester Wheatsheaf.

Carter, D., 1994. 'The Art of the State: Difference and Other Abstractions', *Journal of Historical Sociology*, 7(1): 73–102.

CEC, 1983. *Treaties Establishing the European Communities*, abridged edition. Luxembourg: Office of Official Publications of the European Community.

CEC, 1992. *New Prospects for Community Cultural Action*, COM92 149 final. Brussels 29 April: Office of Official Publications of the European Community.

CIE (Committee of Independent Experts), 1999. *First Report on Allegations regarding Fraud, Mismanagement and Nepotism in the European Commission*. Brussels: European Parliament and Commission of the European Communities.

Corrigan, P. and D. Sayer, 1985. *The Great Arch: English State Formation as Cultural Revolution*. Oxford: Blackwell.

Cram, L., 1993. 'Calling the Tune Without Paying the Piper? Social Policy Regulation: The Role of the Commission in European Union Social Policy', *Policy and Politics*, 21: 135–46.

Duroselle, J.-B., 1990. *Europe: A History of Its Peoples*. London: Viking.

Dyson, K., 1994. *Elusive Union: The Process of Economic and Monetary Union in Europe*. Harlow: Longman.

Evans-Pritchard, A., 2001. 'Police State', *The Spectator*, 6 October: 18–19.

Fischer, J., 2000. 'From Confederacy to Federation – Thoughts on the Finality of European Integration', Speech at Humboldt University, Berlin, 12 May 2000 (http://www.germanembassy.org.au/eu-fisch.htm).

Foucault, M., 1991. 'Governmentality', in G. Burchell, C. Gordon and P. Miller, eds, *The Foucault Effect: Studies in Governmentality*. London: Harvester Wheatsheaf.

Giddens, A., 1985. *The Nation-State and Violence*. Berkeley: University of California Press.

Gledhill, J., 1994. *Power and Its Disguises: Anthropological Perspectives on Politics*. London: Pluto Press.

Gordon, C., 1991. 'Government Rationality: An Introduction', in G. Burchell, C. Gordon and P. Miller, eds, *The Foucault Effect: Studies in Governmentality*. London: Harvester Wheatsheaf.

Gowan, P., 1997. 'British Euro-Solipsism', in P. Gowan and P. Anderson, eds, *The Question of Europe*. London: Verso.

Grillo, R., ed., 1980. *'Nation' and 'State' in Europe: Anthropological Perspectives*. London: Academic Press.

Gupta, A., 1995. 'Blurred Boundaries: The Discourse of Corruption, the Culture of Politics, and the Imagined State', *Current Anthropology*, 22(2): 375–402.

Gupta, A., 2005. 'The State of Corruption: Official Fictions, Anthropological Accounts', in D. Haller and C. Shore, eds, *Corruption: Anthropological Perspectives*. London: Pluto Press.

Hacking, I., 1991. 'How Should We Do the History of Statistics?', in G. Burchell, C. Gordon and P. Miller, eds, *The Foucault Effect: Studies in Governmentality*. London: Harvester Wheatsheaf.

Hannan, D., 2001. 'How I Explained the EU to the King of Brobdingnag', *Daily Telegraph*, 20 July: 26.

Herzfeld, M., 1992. *The Social Production of Indifference: Exploring the Symbolic Roots of Western Bureaucracy*. Oxford: Berg.

Herzfeld, M., 1997. *Cultural Intimacy: Social Poetics in the Nation-State*. New York and London: Routledge.

Hoffman, S., 1995. *The European Sisyphus: Essays on Europe, 1964–1994*. Boulder, CO: Westview Press.

Jessop, B., 1999. 'Narrating the Future of the National Economy and the National State: Remarks on Remapping Regulation and Reinventing Governance', in G. Steinmetz, ed., *State/Culture: State-Formation after the Cultural Turn*. Ithaca, NY and London: Cornell University Press.

Joseph, G. and D. Nugent, eds, 1994. *Everyday Forms of State Formation: Revolution and the Negotiation of Rule in Modern Mexico*. Durham, NC and London: Duke University Press.

Keohane, R. and S. Hoffman, 1991. 'Institutional Change in Europe in the 1980s', in R. Keohane and S. Hoffman, eds, *The New European Community: Decision-Making and Institutional Change*. Oxford: Westview Press.

Kertzer, D., 1988. *Ritual, Politics and Power*. New Haven, CT and London: Yale University Press.

Leonard, M., 1999. *Network Europe: The New Case for Europe*. London: Foreign Policy Centre.

McKay, D., 1999. *Federalism and European Union*. Oxford: Oxford University Press.

Marks, G. and E. Hooghe, 1996. 'European Integration from the 1980s: State-Centric v. Multi-Level Governance', *Journal of Common Market Studies*, 34(3): 341–78.

Miliband, R., 1969. *The State in Capitalist Society*. London: Quartet Books.

Milward, A., 1992. *The European Rescue of the Nation-State*. London: Routledge.

Mitchell, T., 1991. 'The Limits of the State: Beyond Statist Approaches and Their Critics', *American Political Science Review*, 85(1): 77–96.

Mitchell, T., 1999. 'Society, Economy, and the State Effect', pp. 76–97 in G. Steinmetz, ed., *State/Culture: State-Formation after the Cultural Turn*. Ithaca, NY and London: Cornell University Press.

Monbiot, G., 2000. *Captive State: The Corporate Takeover of Britain*. London: Macmillan.

Monnet, J., 1978. *Memoirs*, trans. R. Mayne. London: Collins.

Nagengast, C., 1994. 'Violence, Terror and the Crisis of the State', *Annual Review of Anthropology*, 23: 109–36.

Nairn, T., 1977. *The Break-Up of Britain*. London: New Left Books.

Neill, P., 1995. The European Court of Justice: A Case Study in Judicial Activism (unpublished manuscript, 13 January).

Osmañczyk, E., 1990. *Encyclopedia of the United Nations and International Relations*. New York: Taylor & Francis.

Pearson, C., 1996. *The Modern State*. London and New York: Routledge.

Riff, M.A., ed., 1987. *Dictionary of Modern Political Ideologies*. Manchester: Manchester University Press.

Rose, N., 1989. *Governing the Soul: The Shaping of the Private Self*, 2nd edn. London and New York: Free Association Books.

Ruggie, J., 1993. 'Territoriality and Beyond: Problematizing Modernity in International Relations', *International Organisations*, 47(1): 137–74.

Sbragia, A., 1993. 'The European Community: A Balancing Act', *Publius*, 23(summer): 23–38.

Scott, J.C., 1994. 'Foreword', in G. Joseph and F. Nugent, eds, *Everyday Forms of State Formation: Revolution and the Negotiation of Rule in Modern Mexico*. Durham, NC and London: Duke University Press.

Scott, J.C., 1998. *Seeing Like a State: How Certain Schemes to Improve the Human Condition Have Failed*. New Haven, CT and London: Yale University Press.

Shore, C., 1993. 'Inventing the "People's Europe": Critical Perspectives on EC Cultural Policy', *Man*, 28(4): 779–800.

Shore, C., 2000. *Building Europe: The Cultural Politics of European Integration*. London and New York: Routledge.

Smith, A.D., 1990. 'Towards a Global Culture?', in M. Featherstone, ed., *Global Culture: Nationalism, Globalization and Modernity*. London: Sage.

Smith, A.D., 1997. 'National Identity and the Idea of European Unity', in P. Gowan and P. Anderson, eds, *The Question of Europe*. London: Verso.

Steinmetz, G., ed., 1999. *State/Culture: State-Formation after the Cultural Turn*. Ithaca, NY and London: Cornell University Press.

Trouillot, M.-R., 2001. 'The Anthropology of the State in the Age of Globalization: Close Encounters of the Deceptive Kind', *Current Anthropology*, 42(1): 125–38.

Vincent, A., 1992. 'Conceptions of the State', in M. Hawkesworth and M. Kogan, eds, *Encyclopaedia of Government and Politics*, vol. 1. London: Routledge.

Walker, N., 2003. 'Postnational Constitutionalism and the Problem of Translation', in J.H. Weiler and M. Wind, eds, *European Constitutionalism Beyond the State*. Cambridge: Cambridge University Press.

Wallace, H., W. Wallace and C. Webb, eds, 1983. *Policy-making in the European Community*. Chichester, UK and New York: Wiley.

Wallace, W., 1996. 'Government without Statehood: The Unstable Equilibrium', in H. Wallace and W. Wallace, eds, *Policy-Making in the European Union*. Oxford: Oxford University Press.

Weiler, J.H.H., 1995. 'Europe after Maastricht – Do the New Clothes Have an Emperor?', *Harvard Law School – Jean Monnet Working Paper* 12/95, Cambridge, MA.

CONTRIBUTORS

Ana M. Alonso is Associate Professor of Anthropology, University of Arizona

Helga Baitenmann is Associate Fellow at the Institute for the Study of the Americas, University of London

Clifton Crais is Professor of History, Emory University

Penelope Harvey is Professor of Social Anthropology, University of Manchester

Bruce Kapferer is Professor of Social Anthropology, University of Bergen

Christian Krohn-Hansen is Senior Lecturer in Social Anthropology, University of Oslo

Marit Melhuus is Professor of Social Anthropology, University of Oslo

Iver B. Neumann is Director of Research at the Norwegian Institute of International Affairs

Knut G. Nustad is Senior Lecturer in Social Anthropology, University of Oslo

Cris Shore is Professor of Anthropology, University of Auckland

Kristi Anne Stølen is Professor at the Centre for Development and the Environment, University of Oslo

INDEX

Compiled by Sue Carlton